DEVELOPMENTAL SYSTEMS: INSECTS

Volume 1

This book is dedicated with deep respect and affection
to
PROFESSOR FRIEDRICH SEIDEL
who pioneered in the causal analysis of insect development.

DEVELOPMENTAL SYSTEMS: INSECTS

Edited by

S. J. COUNCE

Departments of Anatomy and Zoology
Duke University, Durham, North Carolina, U.S.A.

and

C. H. WADDINGTON

Institute of Animal Genetics, Edinburgh, Scotland

Volume 1

1972

ACADEMIC PRESS
London and New York

ACADEMIC PRESS INC. (LONDON) LTD.
24/28 Oval Road
London NW1

United States Edition published by
ACADEMIC PRESS INC.
111 Fifth Avenue
New York, New York 10003

Library of Congress Catalog Card Number: 76-185202
ISBN: 0-12-193301-6

Text set in 11/12pt. Monotype Ehrhardt, printed by letterpress,
and bound in Great Britain at The Pitman Press, Bath

CONTRIBUTORS

D. T. ANDERSON, *School of Biological Sciences, University of Sydney, Australia.*

O. M. IVANOVA-KASAS, *Department of Embryology, Leningrad State University, U.S.S.R.*

CZESLAW JURA, *Zoology Department, Jagellonian University, Krakow, Poland*

ANTHONY P. MAHOWALD, *Biology Department, Marquette University, Milwaukee, Wisconsin, U.S.A.**

* Present address: Department of Zoology, Indiana University, Bloomington, Indiana, U.S.A.

CONTRIBUTORS TO VOLUME 2

S. J. COUNCE, *Departments of Anatomy and Zoology, Duke University, Durham, North Carolina, U.S.A.*

WINIFRED W. DOANE, *Department of Biology, Yale University, New Haven, Connecticut, U.S.A.*

W. J. GEHRING, *Department of Anatomy, Yale University, New Haven, Connecticut, U.S.A.*

PETER A. LAWRENCE, *Department of Genetics, University of Cambridge, Cambridge, England* and *Medical Research Council Laboratory of Molecular Biology, Hills Road, Cambridge, England.**

R. NÖTHIGER, *Zoological Institute, University of Zurich, Zurich, Switzerland.*

C. H. WADDINGTON, *Institute of Animal Genetics, West Mains Road, Edinburgh, Scotland.*

* Present address.

PREFACE

Insects have been utilized for experimental studies of development for more than seventy years. Yet much significant work of general interest remains virtually unknown to biologists outside the field itself. The aim of these volumes is to provide, for both specialist and neophyte, detailed and critical analyses of several aspects of the developmental biology of insects. Because an understanding of normal development is essential to the appreciation of experimental studies, and, more importantly, to the identification of those species uniquely or especially well suited as material for further investigation of particular problems of interest to developmentalists, Volume 1 deals with oogenesis and normal embryogenesis in the major insect groups, followed by a chapter on development in polyembryonic species. Chapter 1 in Volume 2 reviews causal analyses of the developmental mechanics of insect embryos and serves as a bridge to chapters dealing with two special systems, the hypodermis and imaginal discs, which are being utilized to study such general topics as the origins of pattern and form, the stability of the differentiated state, and the control of gene action in development. There follows a broad consideration of hormonal action in insect development, and the volume concludes with a general discussion and historical appreciation of studies on gene action and pattern formation.

To keep the volumes within a manageable size and yet provide each contributor with the opportunity to examine in breadth and depth the subjects chosen for inclusion, some areas of interest such as regeneration, metamorphosis as a developmental phenomenon, developmental cytology and genetics, and the biochemistry of development are not dealt with separately, although each is considered in several chapters. It has not been possible to provide detailed technical information, desirable as it would be in a volume with the aims of this one, but appropriate literature citations in each chapter will enable the interested reader quickly to find such information.

This book has been made possible by the generosity and good will of those who have contributed to it at the expense of their own research efforts, and by the larger body of colleagues who have provided suggestions, illustrative material, and access to much unpublished data. My own long-standing intellectual debt to three friends and teachers—Professors Edwin R. Helwig, C. H. Waddington, and D. F. Poulson—is a pleasure to acknowledge. Finally,

grateful acknowledgement is made of the patient support provided during
the long gestational period of this volume by my departmental chairman,
Professor J. David Robertson, and my husband, Professor R. Bruce Nicklas.

S. J. COUNCE

July, 1972
Duke University
Durham, North Carolina

CONTENTS

1. OOGENESIS
Anthony P. Mahowald

2. DEVELOPMENT OF APTERYGOTE INSECTS
Czeslaw Jura

3. THE DEVELOPMENT OF HEMIMETABOLOUS INSECTS
D. T. Anderson

CONTENTS TO VOLUME 2

INTRODUCTION

The scientific study of animal development has enjoyed two great times of blossoming in the last half-century. The first began with Spemann's discovery of "the organiser" around 1920, the second with the acceptance of the "DNA makes RNA makes protein" doctrine in the 1950's. The character of the science, and the special skills of its leading workers, have been rather different in the two periods. In the earlier, the advances were mainly in the analysis of causal processes affecting cells or tissues; the traditions were those of anatomy combined with skill in manual manipulation. Although chemical analysis played a secondary role at that time, in the later period it has, of course, come to occupy the centre of the stage, and analysis is most frequently in terms of molecules or at least sub-cellular particles. But even though binocular microscopes, hair loops and glass needles have given way to ultra-centrifuges, counters and fraction collectors, and the level of analysis pushed down from the cellular to the molecular, the basic problem remains: what causal processes bring about the changes which we can see or otherwise detect as an egg develops into an adult? The new methods of study have still to be applied to embryos if they are to provide answers to embryological problems.

These volumes survey various types of embryos or other developing systems in an attempt to bring out the types of developmental problems for which they seem to offer specially favourable approaches. Biological research, even in its most abstract phases, has usually depended critically on the exploitation of a few particularly appropriate experimental materials; witness the roles played, in various aspects of genetics, by *Drosophila*, *Neurospora*, *Chlamydomonas* and *E. coli*. The older tradition of embryology explored many developmental systems, and went far to determine their particular merits and demerits for the types of experimentation then possible, and to define the essential problems arising from the facts which could be observed. The volumes discuss how the old problems can be restated in terms of the newer insights, what progress has been made towards their solution, and the opportunities the different experimental materials offer to the more recent analytical tools.

Institute of Animal Genetics   C. H. WADDINGTON
Edinburgh, Scotland

1 | Oogenesis[1]

ANTHONY P. MAHOWALD[2]

Biology Department, Marquette University, Milwaukee, Wisconsin, U.S.A.

I. INTRODUCTION

Today we are rightly proud of and enthusiastic over the great advances that have been made in molecular biology. We know the chemical characteristics of the genetic code and we feel confident that the basics of information transcription and translation are understood. This just enthusiasm for modern molecular approaches bears with it unfortunately a sense of frustration for the complexities of the actual living cell. We do not know how the genetic material is actually structured with proteins, phosphoproteins, phospholipids, RNA, etc. to form the complex organelle, the eukaryotic chromosome. We do not, in fact, have clear ideas about the structure in molecular terms of any of the organelles of higher organisms.

Probably the most complex cell is the oocyte. It is not only the largest cell type, but it also has the potential to develop into the larval or nymph stages,

[1] The author wishes to acknowledge the support of the National Science Foundation Grants GB-5155 GB-5780 and GB-7980.
[2] Present address Department of Zoology, Indiana University, Bloomington, Indiana, 47401, U.S.A.

1

for example in insects, without exterior influence except gaseous and sometimes fluid exchange. We have only the bare outlines of some of the key facts
in this amazing potential. The egg has completed meiosis and thus has a
haploid set of genes. It contains sufficient nitrogen and energy reserves to
form all of the cells of the embryo. During the initial hours of embryonic life
ribosomes and probably mitochondria and other cellular organelles are
already present in sufficient numbers so that multiplication of nuclei is the
first chief event. But many experiments in both amphibians and echinoderms
have made it clear that informational RNA is also present, and recently
Lockshin (1966) and Hansen-Delkeskamp (1969) have shown that insects
probably have the same reserve. Moreover, experimental embryology has
abundantly indicated the presence of organization in the egg which is necessary for normal development (Krause and Sanders, 1962; Counce, 1972).
Studies on female sterility factors (e.g. Beatty, 1949; King, 1970; Wright,
1970) have indicated the role of some genes in the process of oogenesis and it
is assumed that the cytoplasmic information present in the egg and necessary
for the total development of the embryo is also produced by nuclear genes.
Thus it is evident that the process of oogenesis is the central preparatory
event for embryogenesis.

Many aspects of the total story on oogenesis will not be treated here,
although some of them will be covered in other chapters. For example, the
process of egg production is dependent upon various hormonal controls, but
the various hormonal relationships existing in insects are treated separately
(Doane, 1972). There have been many female sterility genes studied especially in *Drosophila*, but since many of these have been studied principally
because of the changed developmental potentialities of the egg, they will
be considered in other chapters (Wright, 1970; Counce, 1972). Those
that have clear effects on the process of oogenesis have been reviewed
recently (King, 1964, 1970) and will be introduced here to illuminate
certain areas.

Because of the importance of understanding oogenesis for any investigation of development of the early embryo, it is not surprising that the area had
been reviewed frequently. Raven (1961) has surveyed the whole field of
oogenesis and discussed it in the context of a process of storage of developmental information for the embryo. Oogenesis in insects is considered in
some detail in Engelmann's (1970) treatise on the physiology of reproduction
in insects while Bonhag (1958) has thoroughly reviewed the cytological data
in insects obtained with the light microscope, and Telfer (1965) has analyzed
comprehensively the data on vitellogenesis including the ultrastructural data
that had accumulated to that date. Recently, Bier (1967) has discussed the
process of insect oogenesis from the viewpoint of the variety of methods used
by insects to produce eggs with their characteristically low DNA/cytoplasmic

ratios. In a more general review, Nørrelung (1968) has surveyed the ultra-structure of oogenesis in which brief mention of certain features of insect oogenesis have been included. And finally, King (1970) has reviewed oogenesis in *Drosophila melanogaster*, emphasizing genetic studies. The central focus of this chapter is a comparative analysis of the process of oogenesis in the different orders of insects, depending primarily on autoradiographic and electron microscopic data. Insofar as necessary, histochemical and cyto-logical studies with the light microscope will be used as they have added to our basic understanding of the events described with the aid of the elec-tron microscope, or where these results have gone beyond those previously reviewed.

The point of view taken in this chapter is that oogenesis is the necessary first step for development of the animal embryo since only in this unique cell does the nucleus exhibit its totipotent properties required for supporting normal embryogenesis. Hence the process of oogenesis can be considered to be a series of biological functions whereby the egg cell is endowed both with the nutritional prerequisites for normal development and with the necessary informational content so that in interactions with the zygote nucleus proper differentiation occurs.

The cytological mechanisms involved in each of these steps appear to be sufficiently discrete to allow independent treatment. However, within the class Insecta there are very distinct modes of solving the biological problem of oogenesis, and consequently careful distinctions will be made in the ways in which different orders of insects proceed in oogenesis.

II. TYPES OF OOGENESIS IN INSECTS

The developmental process leading to the production of a mature egg varies greatly from one group of organisms to another. Within the class Insecta there are two major types of oogenesis, the distinction being based primarily on the cellular mechanisms used for the synthesis of the reserves of RNA-containing organelles, although trophic tissues contribute more than just RNA to the egg. The first type, the panoistic ovary, resembles the com-mon form of oogenesis found throughout most of the animal kingdom in which the oocyte nucleus is the source of all of the RNA contained within the mature egg. The second type, the meroistic ovary, is characterized by the presence of a cluster of cells, the nurse cells or trophocytes, which have their origin from germinal tissue but do not form part of the mature egg. They pro-duce all or nearly all of the RNA of both the growing oocyte and the mature egg. There are many variations of this type of ovary, but for the most part meroistic ovaries fall into two further classes: the telotrophic ovary, in which the trophocytes are located at the anterior-most portion of the ovary and are connected to the growing oocytes by cytoplasmic connections called nutritive cords or tubes through which RNA and other substances move to the growing oocyte; and the polytrophic ovary, in which a cluster of nurse cells are derived from the germ line and form a part of the growing egg chamber. These nurse cells produce all or nearly all of the RNA of the egg and ultimately most of the ooplasm through fusion of the nurse cell cytoplasm with the egg. Only their nuclei are excluded from the mature egg. This mode of egg formation appears especially adapted to the mechanism of rapid and continuous egg production found in dipterans, hymenopterans, lepidopterans, etc. The source of much of the protein yolk in all of these types of oogenesis has been clearly shown to be the hemolymph and ultimately the fat body (Telfer, 1965; Pan et al., 1969).

First, I will give a brief review of the structure of these major classes of ovaries, their histological differentiation from embryonic and larval tissue, and then proceed to analyze in detail the process of oogenesis in each. Because of the many differences in the histology of the ovarioles in each type, it is difficult to find consistent terminology in the literature. However, for consistency in the subsequent description, I will use the following divisions of the insect ovary. The ovary is usually composed of linear arrays of growing oocytes called ovarioles. The ovariole can be divided into five regions: Region 1, the terminal filament; Region 2, the germarium; Region 3, the previtellogenic stages of the vitellarium; Region 4, the vitellogenic stages; and Region 5, the mature egg. In more detailed studies, further subdivisions of specific regions into zones or stages have been made to facilitate description, and these subdivisions will be indicated in their appropriate place.

A. The Panoistic Ovary

The panoistic ovary consists of several ovarioles, the number of which varies among species; for example, there are eight in *Periplaneta americana* and 40 to 50 in *Tachycines asynamorus* (von Kraft, 1960*b*). Each ovariole (Fig. 1) consists of a linear array of oocytes in different stages of development. At the anterior end of the ovariole (region 1) is the terminal filament, composed of flattened cells, surrounded by basement lamina and an ovarian sheath. These two latter structures are found in every ovarian type and surround the entire ovariole. The second region[1] is the germarium and can be

---

[1] The most detailed studies of the histology of the panoistic ovary have been made by Bonhag (1959) and Anderson (1964) and they divide the ovariole into six zones. I have included their zones two and three within the germarium in order to obtain some consistency in terminology among the three types of insects ovarioles. In the two types of merioistic ovarioles, the germarium includes all the oogonia, oocytes in meiotic prophase, and the early stages of oocyte growth prior to the formation of the layer of follicle cells surrounding individual oocytes. By including zones two and three of Bonhag within region 2, the terminology for all of the ovarioles can be made consistent. Furthermore, the germarium demands further subdivision in each type, so that the clarity of Bonhag's description is not lost.

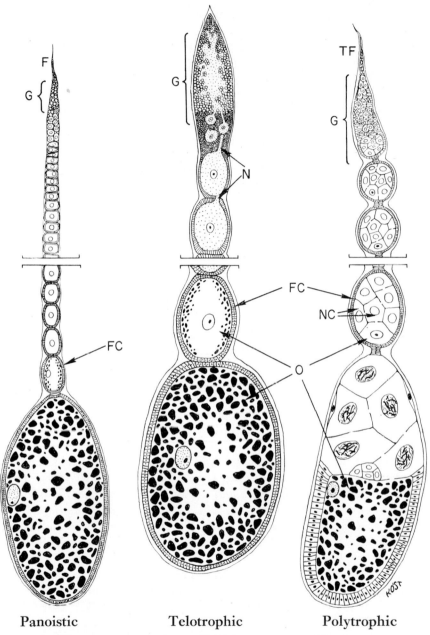

Panoistic   Telotrophic   Polytrophic

Fig. 1. Diagrams of panoistic, telotrophic and polytrophic ovarioles. The upper portion of the figure shows the germarium and the early growth stages while the lower portion has the pre-vitellogenic and vitellogenic stages. No attempt has been made to draw the different ovarioles to scale. The upper portion of the figure is enlarged to a greater extent than the lower in order to make details of germarial structure clear. Labels: FC, follicle cell; G, germarium; N, nutritive cord; NC, nurse cell; O, oocyte; and TF, terminal filament. (Drawings made by Mrs. Kathleen T. O'Sullivan.)

subdivided into the anterior and posterior portions or zones. The anterior portion of the germarium is composed of oogonia adjacent to the terminal filament and separated from it by the transverse septum. The oogonia are followed by oocytes in the early stages of meiosis. In the posterior portion, the meiotic chromosomes pass from a compact diplotene to a diffuse stage, both the nucleus and the cytoplasm become very basophilic and rich in RNA, and multiple nucleoli appear. At this time the individual oocytes are still incompletely surrounded by follicle cells. In *Acheta domesticus*, where no further oogonial divisions occur and all the oocytes are in meiotic prophase, this region has been called the end chamber rather than the germarium (Netzel, 1968). Oocytes are considered to be in region 3 when the cytoplasmic volume has increased until the oocyte extends across the whole width of the ovariole and has been surrounded by a complete follicular epithelium. The growth in this region is mostly in cytoplasmic components and the nuclear morphology remains similar to that in the posterior portion of region 2. Region 4 is characterized by vitellogenesis. Initially the yolk appears along the follicular border but it soon fills the ooplasm. The large yolky oocytes have a decreased basophilia in the ooplasm, presumably due to a dilution effect as the yolky elements are produced (Bonhag, 1959). The germinal vesicle becomes located along the mid-dorsal or concave surface of the oocyte throughout the yolk deposition stages and this location may be responsible for the production of the bilateral symmetry of the egg (Netzel, 1968). The final region is filled with mature eggs. The ovariole is joined to the oviduct through a special structure, the pedicel. The ontogeny of the ovary in *Tachycines* and *Acheta domesticus* has been described by von Kraft (1960a) and by Echard (1962) respectively.

The fine structure of the panoistic ovary has been investigated in a number of organisms: *Periplaneta americana* (Anderson, 1964); *Gryllus bimaculatus* (Favard-Séréno, 1964); *Gryllus capitatus* (Favard-Séréno, 1968, 1969); *Blatta orientalis* (Gresson and Threadgold, 1961, 1962); *Locusta migratoria, Blatella germanica, Acheta domesticus* (Bier *et al.*, 1967); *Aeschna* (Beams and Kessel, 1969); *Tibellula pulchella* (Kessel and Beams, 1969); *Leucophaea maderae*, (Scheurer, 1969); *Leptinotarsa decemlineata* (de Loof and Lagasse, 1970). The emphasis has been either on vitellogenesis or nucleolar changes especially at the time of vitellogenesis and the results will be presented in the appropriate section. The most complete description has been given by Anderson (1964). Mitochondria, Golgi elements and ribosomes are present in great abundance but there is very little endoplasmic reticulum. Lamellar bodies are randomly distributed in the cytoplasm but their function is not known. Prior to vitellogenesis the oocyte plasma membrane is tightly applied to that of the follicle cells and they frequently interlock, but during vitellogenesis an intercellular space appears and pinocytosis is common. Anderson (1964) and Scheurer

(1969) have shown that the symbiotic bacteria common in orthopterans (*cf.* Richards and Brooks, 1958) are extracellular in *Periplaneta* and *Leucophaea* respectively, located between the follicle cells and the oocyte, while Gresson and Threadgold (1961) propose that they are intracellular in *Blatta*.

B. The Telotrophic Meroistic Ovary

The telotrophic ovary consists of a number of ovarioles (four in *Gerris remigis* and seven in *Oncopeltus fasciatus*). The ovariole can be divided into five regions (Fig. 1). The unusual structure in this ovary is the germarium and it can be best described by following the stages in its ontogeny in *Gerris remigis* (Wick and Bonhag, 1955). At the end of embryonic development, the ovary has already differentiated into four ovarioles. During the first four nymphal instars, the number of oogonia continues to increase by mitosis within each spindle-shaped ovariole. The oogonia form a ball of cells surrounded by an epithelial sheath of mesodermal origin. At the time of the transition from the fourth to the last nymphal instar, the oogonia (it is not clear whether all or only a portion of the oogonia) go through a division in which one daughter cell becomes a trophocyte and the other daughter cell becomes an oocyte. The trophocytes become located anteriorly and proceed to differentiate into the trophocytes of the mature germarium. Moreover, the acellular trophic core appears and subsequently becomes connected to each oocyte by a distinct nutritive tube. Below the trophocytes and separated from them by an incomplete and inconspicuous cellular septum (Eschenberg and Dunlap, 1966) are clustered the mass of oocytes and below them the pre-follicular cells. As an oocyte begins its process of growth, it acquires a connection with the trophic core by means of the nutritive tube, and as it passes into the pre-follicular mass of cells it becomes surrounded by a follicular epithelium. One unusual feature of the ontogeny of this type of ovary is that a mass of oocytes are eliminated prior to the formation of clearly distinguishable oocytes (Wick and Bonhag, 1955). There is no indication of the function of this elimination. Possibly it is analogous to the fate of the pole cells of higher dipterans in which only a fraction of them take part in the formation of the embryonic ovary (Sonnenblick, 1950).

Subsequent regions of the ovariole are similar to those of panoistic ovaries. There is a period of oocyte growth by addition of cytoplasmic elements, then a period of vitellogenesis, and finally the formation of the protective envelopes of the egg.

Cytochemical and autoradiographic investigations (see below) have identified the trophocytes as the origin of the RNA of the growing oocyte. With the electron microscope Anderson and Beams (1956) have shown nucleolar fragments passing through the nuclear membrane of trophocytes in *Rhodnius prolixus*. The trophic core and nutritive tubes are intensely basophilic and show a fibrillar structure with the light microscope. Macgregor and Stebbings (1970) have shown with the polarized light and electron microscopes that the tubes contain a massive array of microtubules, approximately 30,000 in a tube 15 μ wide. Interspersed between the microtubules are abundant ribosomes. The microtubules are lost following exposure to cold treatment, colchicine (Macgregor and Stebbings, 1970) or vinblastine sulfate (Huebner and Anderson, 1970; Stebbings, 1971). Inasmuch as dissolution of the microtubules with colchicine results in the trophic core being invaded by nuclei and cells, it appears that the microtubules are essential for the maintenance of structure within the telotrophic ovary. It is also possible that the microtubules are important in the movement of RNA-containing organelles through the nutritive tubes to the oocytes. The processes of RNA synthesis and vitellogenesis will be treated in their proper sections.

C. The Polytrophic Meroistic Ovary

The polytrophic ovariole can readily be divided into five regions on the basis of general morphology (Fig. 1). At the anterior end the terminal filament, composed of flattened cells, attaches the ovariole to the thoracic wall. The germarium comprises the second region and can be subdivided into the anterior portion containing one or more stem line oogonia and various daughter cells (cystoblasts) of the oogonia in the process of dividing synchronously to produce a cluster of cells interconnected by fusomes (Meyer, 1961). These cells subsequently differentiate into an oocyte and the rest into nurse cells. The number of these nurse cells typically is constant within each species but varies from one species to another, from one in *Anisolabis maritima* (Anopleura) (Bonhag, 1956) to 31 in *Pimpla turionellae* (Hymenoptera) (Meng, 1968).[2] In the central region of the germarium, pre-follicular cells grow between the clusters of cells, and finally in the posterior region the typical egg chamber is formed, with the oocyte located posterior to the nurse

---

[2] Although it is almost a universal rule that the trophic tissue of meroistic ovaries is derived from the same cell lineage as the oocyte, in certain dipterans exceptions are found both in regard to the origin of the nurse cells and in regard to the number. In *Miastor* and *Heteropeza* there is common agreement that most of the nuclei in the syncytial nurse chamber are mesodermal in origin. Matuszewski (1968) has shown in two different species of gall midges that, although the number of nurse chamber nuclei differs from chamber to chamber, the volume of the nurse chamber is constant, due to a lower degree of polyploidy in chambers with few nuclei. Many investigators have claimed that all of the nurse chamber nuclei are mesodermal in origin, most recently Panelius (1968). Frequently, however, one of the nurse nuclei is distinctly larger and it has been proposed to originate from the germ line (Camenzind, 1966; Counce, 1968). Recent ultrastructural evidence supports this germinal origin (Mahowald and Stoiber, 1971). During the formation of the egg chamber and prior to the presence of multiple nuclei in the nurse chamber, two germ line cells are found joined by a fusome or cytoplasmic bridge, presumably resulting from incomplete cytokinesis. Both nuclei have the identical fine structure. Later, one nucleus begins meiosis and the other nucleus becomes associated in a syncytium with many small nuclei. Thus, it appears clear that in *Miastor* one of the nurse nuclei is germinal in origin. The fusome remains throughout oogenesis.

cells and the nurse cell-oocyte complex surrounded by a follicular epithelium. The process of formation of an egg chamber and the ultrastructural changes that occur have been thoroughly analyzed by King and coworkers and by Mahowald and Strassheim (1970) in *Drosophila melanogaster*. The four divisions of the original daughter cell of the stem line oogonium result in 16 interconnected cells which always have the same pattern of ring canals or fusomes: two cells with four canals, two with three canals, four with two canals and eight with one canal. The oocyte is always one of the two with four canals (Brown and King, 1964; Koch and King, 1966). Because of the restrictions placed upon the plane of cytokinesis necessary to obtain such a rigid pattern of fusomes, King (1964) postulated that the critical material determining which of the two cells with four fusomes will become the oocyte is a specific cortical region of the original cystoblast retained by one of the cluster of cells. More recently Koch and King (1968) have shown that the oocyte has more of its surface contacting the follicular epithelium. Recently another possibility has become evident. Mahowald (1962) had noticed an accumulation of centrioles in a growing oocyte (stage 3 according to stages of King *et al.*, 1956). In an electron microscopic study Mahowald and Strassheim (1970) observed in the clusters of cells forming in the anterior region of the germarium, that single centrioles are found at the margin of the ring canals prior to the separation of the clusters by the pre-follicular cells. After the pre-follicular epithelium has migrated between the 16-cell clusters, most of the centrioles are found in one of the two cells having synaptonemal complexes, and the cell with the accumulation of centrioles retains the complexes and becomes the oocyte. Thus the process of determining the oocyte may also involve a selective migration of centrioles into one cell. Centriolar migration is common in cells producing cilia or flagellae (e.g., Heist and Mulvaney, 1968) but this is the first indication of a migration of centrioles from one cell to another. Hsu (1952) has probably described the resulting cluster of centrioles in the oocyte earlier as the idiosome-like granule.

The third region follows the germarium. It is composed of egg chambers (stages 2 to 7 of King *et al.*, 1956) in which the follicle cells at first increase in number and then become polyploid, the nurse cells do not divide but immediately become polyploid, and the oocyte grows by addition of nurse cell cytoplasm which flows through the fusomes. The fourth and final region is composed of the stages of vitellogenesis (stages 8 to 13) in which at first the nurse cells continue to increase in size and polyploidy. When the oocyte is approximately one-half the size of the mature egg, the nurse cells break down and their cytoplasm pours into the oocyte. The vitelline membrane and chorion are formed around the oocyte by the follicle cells, resulting in the mature egg. The total increase in oocyte volume is approximately 100,000-fold (King *et al.*, 1956).

The ovarioles differentiate from the ovarian mass of cells during late larval and early pupal life in *Drosophila melanogaster* (Bucher, 1957; King *et al.*, 1968). The terminal filaments have already formed in the late larval ovary and by 24 hours after puparium formation the germaria have become separated from the intervening mesodermal cells by the newly-formed tunica propria. By 30 hours, the first 16-cell cysts have formed.

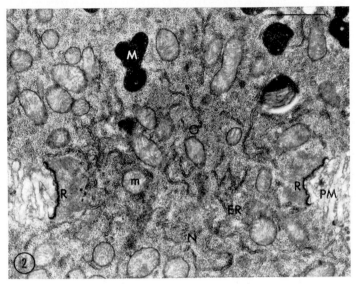

Fɪɢ. 2. Fusome or ring canal between a nurse cell (N) and oocyte (O) in *Drosophila immigrans*. The plasma membranes (PM) of the two cells are extensively folded at the edges of the ring canal. The ring canal itself (R) consists of an electron-dense ring adjacent to the plasma membrane and an amorphous region, approximately 0.5μ in thickness, within this dense region. These features of ring canals characterize their structure at all stages of oogenesis.

The cytoplasm is clearly continuous between the two cell types. Granular endoplasmic reticulum (ER) is common in *Drosophila* oocytes, but most ribosomes are free and show very little polysome formation. This is characteristic of oocytes in general until after fertilization when polysomes form. The dense multivesicular bodies (M) are one of the many types of unusual membranous structures found in oocytes. Mitochondria (m) are very common within ring canals and presumably are in transit from the nurse cells to the oocyte.

Glutaraldehyde-osmium fixation and uranyl-lead staining are used in Figs 2, 3, 4, 9, 10 and 12. The line in all figures in the upper right corner equals one micron except for the insert of Fig. 9, where it equals one-tenth micron.

Considerable electron microscopy has been done on polytrophic ovaries concerning nearly every aspect of oogenesis. Some aspects of the ultrastructure of polytrophic ovaries will be treated along with other types of evidence which allow a functional interpretation of the structures. Certain other structures will be described here.

The fusome (Fig. 2) has a clearly recognizable ultrastructure wherever it has been examined. Adjacent to the pore there is a relatively thick layer of amorphous material of moderate electron density. Cytochemical observations indicate that this material is probably a mucoprotein (King, 1960). In contact with the plasmalemma of the two cells joined by the fusome there is a 300–500 Å thick electron-dense layer that forms a complete ring around the intercellular canal. This layer is found only within the confines of the canal. The plasma membranes are typically convoluted where they join to a fusome. It would seem that the role of the two characteristic layers of the fusome is to

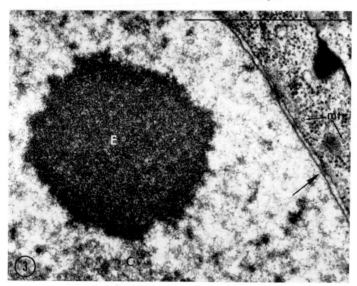

FIG. 3. Endobody (E) of the oocyte nucleus in *Drosophila melanogaster*. It is attached to chromatin (C) at one corner and is composed of 70 Å fibrils. Nuclear annuli (arrow) are present in the nuclear envelope but not as abundantly as in nurse cells (*cf.* Fig. 4). Microtubules (mt) are found both adjacent to the nuclear envelope and at the periphery of the oocyte throughout oogenesis.

maintain the intracellular connection. It is doubtful that they could also function in regulating flow by changing the diameter of the aperture, although this has been postulated by Meyer (1961). This type of regulation would require further specializations that should be evident in the ultrastructure. Recently a modification of the canal in ovaries of *Habrobracon juglandis* has been found (Cassidy and King, 1969) which might play a role in regulating the size of the canal. In this species the ring canal joining cystocytes is composed of eight overlapping leaves which compose the walls of the canal. This type of ring canal may be dilatable. In any case, it seems certain that a prominent role in governing the amount and duration of the cytoplasmic flow through the canals is played by the bands of musculature located in the connective tissue sheath of the ovariole.

The special differentiations of the fusome appear very early in *Drosophila*. After glutaraldehyde fixation, which usually preserves microtubules (e.g. Figs 3, 9, 10), microtubules are found in great abundance within the fusome (Mahowald and Strassheim, 1970). This strongly supports the suggestion that fusomes are the result of an incomplete cytokinesis of a dividing cystocyte (Brown and King, 1964; Mahowald, 1971*d*). Microtubules are found in the early stages of oocyte formation in the germarium but no special orientations are visible adjacent to the ring canals (Mahowald and Strassheim, 1970). During subsequent stages of oogenesis they are present adjacent to the nuclear envelope (Fig. 3) and near the oocyte borders (Figs 9, 10). No special orientations of the microtubules have been found in these later stages.

The Golgi region is not a prominent feature of the ultrastructure of ovaries, except possibly in relationship to vitellogenesis (see below). But many other unusual structures have been described by various workers although their function remains unknown. Some of these may be of special interest because of their subsequent localizations in the egg. For example, very dense multivesicular bodies are found in *Drosophila* nurse cells (Fig. 2) which become preferentially located in the periplasm of the developing embryo and break down at the time the cleavage nuclei first reach this region of the embryo (Mahowald, unpublished observations).

III. ANALYSIS OF OOGENESIS

There are certain key biological processes that must be treated in some detail in a functional consideration of oogenesis. First, we should know when premeiotic DNA synthesis occurs and at what stage meiosis is arrested in the mature egg. Second, what is the source of the RNA of the egg, not only ribosomal and transfer RNA but also mRNA. Third, what are the processes involved in vitellogenesis. Fourth, how is the organization of the mature egg accomplished, and for this the localization of the oosome or polar granules provides a good clue to some of the processes involved. Finally, what are the distinctive ultrastructural features of insect eggs that deserve attention in each of these processes. While recognizing that differences exist between the various types of insect oogenesis, it is helpful to treat these events in the various types at one time thus clarifying both their similarities and differences.

A. Replication and Structure of Chromosomes in Insect Ovaries

(1) Oocyte Nucleus (Germinal Vesicle)
   (a) *Synaptonemal Complexes.* In every species studied pre-meiotic DNA synthesis occurs shortly after the primary oocytes have been formed by division of an oogonium, and in a number of instances, synaptonemal complexes characteristic of early meiotic prophase have been identified with the

electron microscope (Sotelo and Wettstein, 1964, in *Gryllus argentinus*; Koch *et al.*, 1967, in *Drosophila melanogaster*; Roth, 1966, in *Aedes aegypti*; Mahowald and Stoiber, 1971, in *Miastor*). The most detailed work has been accomplished in dipterans. In *Aedes*, synaptonemal complexes are present at zygonema and pachynema when the homologous chromosomes have paired. The complex "consists of three dense parallel ribbon-like units" (Roth, 1966). Each of the dense elements is about 35 to 40 mμ thick, 100 mμ wide and extends the length of the chromosome. Only the two outer ribbons appear to be attached to the chromosomes and have a similar fibrillar organization, while the median element consists of many parallel units each 400 Å long and 60–70 Å thick. These are separated from each other by a less dense space of 70–80 Å. As the meiotic chromosomes go into diplonema, the synaptonemal complexes are no longer found with the chromosomes but appear to aggregate into series of synaptonemal complexes which Roth (1966) has termed polycomplexes. The fate of these is not known, but because of this finding it appears that the distinctive structures of synapsed chromosomes are probably non-chromosomal in nature (Moses, 1968). Polycomplexes have occasionally been found in some nurse cells which suggests that some attempt at meiosis has occurred in these sister cells of the oocyte. Koch *et al.* (1967) have also noticed the appearance of synaptonemal complexes in *Drosophila* in both of the cells with four fusomes but only one of these becomes the oocyte. Since polycomplexes do not form in *Drosophila*, it is impossible to confirm that only one nurse cell has these polycomplexes, but this should be checked in *Aedes*.

(b) *Meroistic Ovaries.* In polytrophic ovaries after the 16 cell cyst has become surrounded by follicle cells, all of the chromatin (Chandley, 1966) becomes clumped in one region, the karyosome, which is about 3 μ in diameter in *Drosophila* and other dipterans. At first, synaptonemal complexes are still evident but they disappear before vitellogenesis (Koch *et al.*, 1967). The dimensions of the karyosome gradually increase during subsequent growth stages of the oocyte until the stages of vitellogenesis when the karyosome becomes spread out to about 7 μ at which time some RNA synthesis occurs (see below). And finally as the egg reaches maturity, the karyosome disappears, diplonema occurs followed by metaphase I of meiosis, at which time the cell is arrested until ovulation.

Very little work has been done on the chromosomes of the telotrophic ovary although they seem to follow the same pattern as in polytrophic ovaries. During the growth stages, however, the chromosomes enter a diffuse stage but their availability for RNA synthesis is still restricted (Vanderberg, 1963; Bier, 1964; Macgregor and Stebbings, 1970).

(c) *Panoistic Ovaries.* The early stages of meiosis appear similar to that in dipterans, but subsequent to pachynema the chromosomes enter a diffuse stage in which they are active in RNA synthesis. Recent pictures have indicated that they form lampbrush chromosomes similar to those of amphibian oocytes (Kunz, 1967b). After vitellogenesis has begun, the chromosomes again condense into diplotene stage and proceed to metaphase I at which time they are arrested.

(2) Auxiliary Cells

(a) *Follicle Cells*. The follicle cells originate from mesodermal tissue and have a similar life history in all forms of oogenesis. They surround the growing oocyte during the early cytoplasmic growth phase and continue to divide until shortly before vitellogenesis occurs. At this time the nuclei become polyploid and the cells increase greatly in size as they become active, possibly in vitellogenesis, but primarily in the secretion of the protective coverings of the egg (King and Koch, 1963; Quattropani and Anderson, 1969; Beams and Kessel, 1969; Telfer and Smith, 1970). In telotrophic ovaries the follicle cells become binucleate, probably through a process of amitosis (Bonhag, 1955; Eschenberg and Dunlap, 1966) while in panoistic ovaries the nuclei become very irregular in shape and often give the appearance in sections of having divided, although squash preparations of *Carausius morosus* Br. indicate that they have not split into two nuclei (Pijnacker, 1966). In *Drosophila* the follicle cells reach a DNA content of 16 n (Schultz, 1956), and presumably similar levels of polyploidy exist in other organisms. After the formation of the chorion, the follicle cells degenerate and are sluffed off as the egg leaves the ovariole.

(b) *Nurse Cells*. The nurse cells of dipterans are the most thoroughly studied example of this cell type. DNA replication begins after the nurse cell–oocyte complex is surrounded by follicle cells. The early series of endopolyploid DNA replications are synchronous in all nuclei, but subsequently, as the DNA content reaches 64C and 128C, the nuclei of the more posterior nurse cells increase their DNA content more rapidly. A final wave of DNA synthesis occurs at the time the nurse cells pour their cytoplasm into the egg. Simultaneous with this last synchronous replication, both the mitochondrial DNA and probably the adenine-thymidine (AT-DNA) polymer recently identified in *Drosophila* eggs (Travaglini *et al.*, 1968) undergo a wave of synchronous DNA replication (Muckenthaler and Mahowald, 1966). Only the oocyte nucleus does not take part in this wave of synthesis. Neither the cause of this synchronous DNA synthesis nor the function of the AT-DNA polymer have yet been determined. At the time the nurse cells degenerate, large gaps appear in their nuclear membranes (Okada and Waddington, 1959; King and Divine, 1959) (Fig. 4). It is not known how much of the contents of these nuclei is released to the oocyte, but probably most of the karyoplasm and possibly a small amount of chromatin (Jacob and Sirlin, 1959) become part of the ooplasm.

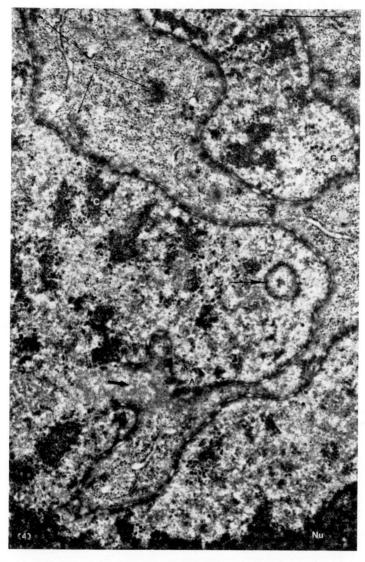

FIG. 4. Nurse cell nucleus of *Drosophila immigrans* prior to the breakdown of the nurse chamber. The nuclear outline is very irregular with deep indentations of cytoplasm. Occasionally these are seen in cross-section (thin arrow). The nuclear envelope possesses a dense accumulation of annuli (A), and occasional discontinuities (heavy arrow) of the envelope are present which are filled with a fine fibrillar material. The nucleolus (Nu) shows nucleolonema-like strands composed of 200 Å granules. Along the chromatin (C) irregularly shaped 500 Å particles are common and occasionally spherical granules (G) are present in the nucleoplasm at this time. The cytoplasmic side of the nuclear membrane has accumulations of fibrous material (F) throughout the period of nurse cell growth.

The total DNA content of the nurse cells reaches about 512C to 1024C amounts in *Drosophila melanogaster* (Schultz, 1956; Jacob and Sirlin, 1959) and even higher amounts in *Calliphora erythrocephala* (Bier, 1957). In *Calliphora* the nurse cell chromosomes are at first banded in typically polytenic fashion, but as the degree of ploidy increases, they become dispersed throughout the nucleoplasm (Bier, 1960). Puffing of polytenic chromosomes has usually been interpreted as due to the unwinding of the chromatin in order to free it for transcription. In the nurse cells it would appear that most of the chromatin is active in making RNA so that the polytenic chromosomes have lost their organized structure (King, 1964). This would also explain why the nucleolus forms, not as one structure typical of the salivary gland or follicle cells, but as many structures distributed throughout the nucleus. Occasionally, in *Calliphora* the chromosomes are in giant polytenic form and then the nucleolus remains as one large structure attached to a chromosome (Bier, 1960). Nucleolar blebs are seen to form from this one nucleolus. Recently, these secondary nucleoli have been shown to possess DNA and to be active in RNA synthesis (Ribbert and Bier, 1969). These authors suggest that differential replication of the nucleolar organizer region has occurred in these cells in a manner similar to that demonstrated in amphibian oocytes and in some insects (see below). In the female sterility mutant of *D. melanogaster*, *fes*, polytenic chromosomes are occasionally found in the nurse cells and in these instances one large nucleolus is formed (Koch and King, 1964). The complete dispersal of chromatin in nurse cell nuclei correlates well with the dispersal of chromatin in oocyte nuclei that are active in RNA synthesis. These oocyte nuclei (germinal vesicles) are usually Feulgen-negative and frequently possess lampbrush chromosomes which are synthesizing RNA along most of the chromatin of the chromosomes. Similarly, the nurse cells produce most of the RNA of the polytrophic oocyte (see below). The development of the nucleolus in nurse cells of *D. melanogaster* has recently been described by Dapples and King (1970).

(c) *Trophocytes.* The pattern of DNA synthesis in telotrophic ovaries has not been followed in nearly as much detail as in polytrophic ovaries (Schrader and Leuchtenberger, 1952; Vanderberg, 1963; Bier, 1964). In *Rhodnius* it is apparent that the large trophocytes of the germarium, besides originating by nuclear fusion (Schrader and Leuchtenberger, 1952), must also increase in size by endopolyploidization since all the trophic cells are seen to incorporate ^{3}H-thymidine (Vanderberg, 1963). Radioactivity appears in the oocyte after some time and DNA has recently been detected cytochemically with the Feulgen reaction (Eschenberg and Dunlap, 1966). It is not certain in what form this DNA has passed into the oocyte, but it is probably in a depolymerized form. Since mitochondria are known to have DNA, the Feulgen positive ooplasm may be due to these or to a similar AT-DNA as found in *Drosophila*.

(3) DNA Body of Oocyte Nuclei

Experiments within the last few years have begun to clarify a classical problem in insect oogenesis. In widely divergent groups of insects a form of "metabolic" or extra DNA is present in the oocyte nucleus. This was first

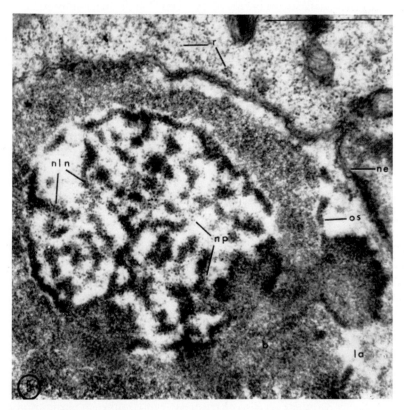

Fig. 5. Oocyte of *Tipula* at early prophase of meiosis, showing the DNA body (b) within which a nucleolus has formed with nucleolonema (nln) and typical 200 Å nucleolar particles (np). The DNA body has an outer shell, portions of which are seen in this picture (os), which separate it from the more diffuse regions of the nucleus (la). The nuclear envelope (ne) possesses many annuli and the cytoplasm is filled with ribosomes (r). Buffered OsO_4 fixation. (From Lima-de-Faria and Moses, 1966.)

noticed by Giardini in 1901 in *Dytiscus*, a coleopteran, and subsequently it has been described in various species of the *Tipulidae* (Bayreuther, 1956) and more recently in various orthopterans (e.g. *Acheta*: Nilsson, 1966; Kunz, 1969) and possibly in *Simulium vittatum*, a lower dipteran (Zalokar, 1965). In *Tipula oberacea*, the DNA-body accumulates up to 56% of the DNA in the oocyte nucleus and the synthesis of DNA is asynchronous with respect to the chromosomal DNA (Lima-de-Faria, 1962). The first indications of the function of this extra DNA were discovered in this species. Lima-de-Faria and Moses (1966) showed that the structure is composed of interwoven fibrils of DNA-histone. Along one surface it is attached to the nuclear membrane while the other surfaces are bordered by a 500–700 Å shell composed of 150–250 Å particles (Fig. 5). Within the DNA body are DNA-negative regions which appear as vacuoles after the Feulgen technique, but are actually composed of nucleolonema strands consisting of 150–250 Å particles. These particles have the same dimensions as the cytoplasmic ribosomes, so that from these initial studies it appeared that the DNA may actually be replicated regions of the nucleolar organizer region of the genome. The location of the nucleolus within the DNA-body was also found in *Dytiscus marginalis* (Urbani and Russo-Caio, 1964). Gall *et al.* (1969) have recently shown by means of DNA-RNA hybridization with ribosomal RNA, that the DNA body in these dytiscid water beetles is enriched with the genes for RNA. Their evidence indicates that other regions of the chromosomes are also differentially replicated, so that Giardina's body represents, cytologically, all of this extra DNA.

In orthopterans, the total functioning of the oocyte nucleus has been found to be very similar to that of the amphibian germinal vesicle. Many workers have proposed that the fuzzy outlines of the chromosomes in insect germinal vesicles might be similar to lampbrush chromosomes, but a detailed structural analysis of these chromosomes has only been accomplished recently by Kunz (1967*a*, *b*, 1969). First in *Locusta migratoria* (1967*a*) and then more clearly in a variety of grasshopper and cricket species (1967*b*), he has shown that the pachytene chromosomes of the germinal vesicle during the growth stages of the egg have loops similar to those found in amphibians (Figs 6, 7). Not only are loops present but the chromosomes can be stretched to about ten times their original length and they are fragmented by DNase. Both of these properties are also characteristic of lampbrush chromosomes of amphibians (Callan, 1956). A further similarity between these insect germinal vesicles and those of amphibians is in the presence of many small granules, from 2–7 μ in diameter which are formed in connection with the chromosomes or in a special "necklace-like" chromosome. In *Acheta* (Kunz, 1969) they can be isolated from the nucleus at the stage when these strings of granules become free of the chromosomes. They are then seen to be actually composed of six to ten small granules, 0·5 μ in size, attached to each other in a circle by a strand below the resolution of the light microscope (Fig. 8). Because of the amazing similarity between this structure and the multiple nucleoli of amphibian oocytes (Lane, 1967), it is likely that these ring nucleoli are connected by a strand of DNA. Recent ultrastructural studies (Allen and Cave, 1968; Kunz, 1969) have supported the nucleolar nature of these nuclear

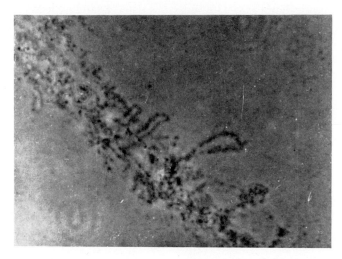

FIG. 6. Lampbrush chromosome from *Decticus albifrons*, clearly showing loops. (From Kunz, 1967*b*.)

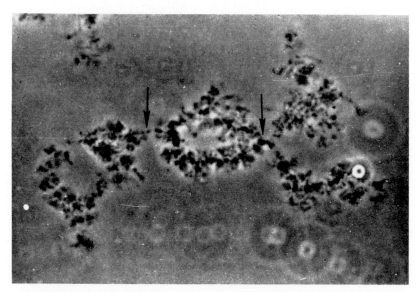

FIG. 7. Isolated lampbrush chromosomes of *Decticus albifrons* at the diplotene stage. The location of the chiasmata are indicated by the arrows. (From Kunz, 1967*b*.)

bodies. Lima-de-Faria *et al.* (1969) have isolated a satellite heavy DNA from the ovary and find that there is an 18-fold increase in DNA which hybridizes with rRNA in the ovary compared to that found in the testis. Thus it appears clear that there is a differential replication of ribosomal RNA genes in certain insect species.

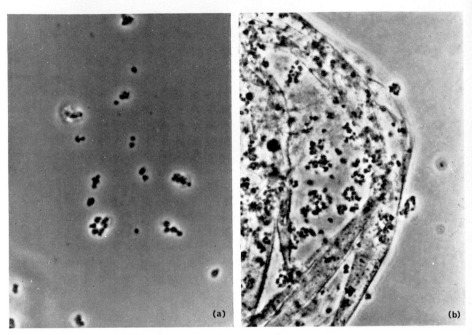

FIG. (8a) and (b). Ring-nucleoli of *Acheta*. (From Kunz, 1967*b*.)

(4) *Nucleoli and Endobodies*

Nucleoli differ in shape in each of the cell types within the ovary but the fine structural components are typical. In follicle cells the nucleoli are typically large, round bodies located centrally in the nuclei (King and Koch, 1963) (Fig. 10 see p. 35). The central region is composed of fine fibrils of about 50 Å and surrounding this region are 150–250 Å granules. Usually no distinct nucleolonema is seen. In the nurse cells the nucleolus is most frequently multiple as already discussed. Occasionally nucleolonema are found, but for the most part granules are released in clusters and move to the nuclear membrane where they are released to the cytoplasm. Many 500 Å granules are found in the karyoplasm (Fig. 10); their function is unknown. All nuclei of the ovary show typical annuli in the nuclear membrane (Figs 3, 4, 10).

Many large nuclear inclusions have been described in insect oocytes, and prior to the clarification of the function of nucleoli as the site of ribosomal

RNA synthesis and ribosomal assembly (*cf.* Vincent and Miller, 1966), these inclusions were usually termed "nucleoli". Because of the clarification of nucleolar function, the identification of nucleoli must be done more carefully. Recently, Bier *et al.* (1967) have described a new nuclear structure in insect oocytes. It contains RNA but shows no incorporation of labeled RNA precursors even after many hours. With the electron microscope, the structure is seen to consist of fine fibrils (70 Å in *Drosophila*, Fig. 3) (Mahowald and Tiefert, 1970) and to contain no ribosome-like granules typical of nucleoli. Thus, both on the basis of RNA metabolism and on structure, these nuclear inclusions differ from nucleoli, and these authors suggest the name "endobody" (*Binnenkörper*). Endobodies vary in size from one micron in *Drosophila* (Fig. 3) to 10 μ in *Carabus nemoralis* (Bier *et al.*, 1967). Bier *et al.* (1967) have shown that endobodies accumulate radioactivity rapidly after the injection of radioactive amino acids, and they postulate that they may be the sites for the accumulation of cytonucleoproteins.

Probably not all nuclear inclusions that are non-nucleolar are identical to the endobodies. For example, in *Gerris* an RNA-deficient nuclear structure is present which produces small buds that move to the cytoplasm (Bonhag, 1955; Eschenberg and Dunlap, 1966). Halkka and Halkka (1968) have described a structure in the oocyte nucleus of the dragonfly, *Cordulia aenia*, which, in contrast to the endobody, accumulates ³H-uridine into some soluble form of RNA and consequently may be involved in the metabolism of this RNA. Thus it is doubtful whether all of these nuclear structures are strictly homologous. Until the morphological identification can be related to a function, this will have to remain open. But it is clear that these nuclear structures should not be called nucleoli unless they can be related to ribosome synthesis.

B. RNA Synthesis During Insect Oogenesis

Besides the accumulation of mature ribosomes in the egg during oogenesis, other RNA species such as transfer RNA and messenger RNA are also produced. Very little information is available about the time of synthesis of these RNA species or whether they have discrete localizations in the egg, but it is important to be aware of the fact that the RNA seen with either cytochemical or autoradiographic techniques will not distinguish these types. Because of the short lifetime of some types of mRNA this species may be identified occasionally (Bier, 1963b), but it is also clear that other forms of mRNA are produced during oogenesis which are stable (Lockshin, 1966; Hansen-Delkeskamp, 1969).

(1) RNA Synthesis in Panoistic Ovaries

The basic outline of RNA synthesis in panoistic ovaries has already been given in clarifying the nature of the DNA body (Section III, A, *3*) and autoradiographic studies have confirmed this (Bier, 1967). The oocyte nucleus through its multiple nucleoli produces the ribosomes of the mature egg. The synthesis of other forms of RNA is presumably carried out on the lampbrush chromosomes. Hansen-Delkeskamp (1969) has recently investigated the times during oogenesis when the various molecular species of RNA found in the mature egg are synthesized. Eggs were collected 3–17 days after a single injection of labeled uridine and the RNA analyzed by means of sucrose density centrifugation. Ribosomal RNA is made in appreciable amounts throughout this period while soluble or transfer RNA is made in only limited amounts. There is also some indication of the synthesis of RNA with sedimentation constants intermediate between 4S and 18S and this RNA may be mRNA. If this interpretation is correct, some of the maternal mRNA found in mature eggs (Lockshin, 1966) may be produced as much as 17 days prior to fertilization.

(2) RNA Synthesis in Meroistic Ovaries

In telotrophic ovaries the trophocytes become polyploid and are the source of nearly all the RNA found within the oocyte while the oocyte nucleus fails to show any RNA synthesis (Vanderburg, 1963; Bier, 1964; Macgregor and Stebbings, 1970). The massive array of microtubules within the trophic core and nutritive tubes are obviously important in the movement of RNA-containing organelles to the oocyte which is hundreds of microns and even millimeters away (Macgregor and Stebbings, 1970). Similar transport of RNA for use in another site is known in nerve cells and in certain plants (cf. Bier, 1967). No attempt has been made to distinguish types of RNAs in these studies.

In polytrophic meroistic ovaries the situation is more complex although this complexity may be only a reflection of the more intensive studies that have been made on this type of ovary. Intensive RNA synthesis occurs in the nurse cells throughout oogenesis. After very short pulses of ^{3}H-uridine the incorporation of the isotope is restricted to the nuclei (Zalokar, 1960), but after 60 minutes the cytoplasm is equally labeled. Some of this RNA is transferred through the fusomes to the oocyte (Bier, 1963b). This passage of RNA-containing structures can be seen both from the gradient of incorporated isotope about two hours after the injection of the radioactive precursor, being heavier near the oocyte and lightest in the anterior-most nurse cells, but especially by the concentration of labeled RNA that extends from the ring canals of the oocyte into the oocyte proper. The passage of nurse cell cytoplasm into the oocyte becomes especially intense after the nurse cells have reached their maximum size and have begun to break down. Bier (1963b) has noted that prior to the mass transfer of cytoplasm at this latter time, there is no notable accumulation of radioactivity in the oocyte. He interprets this to mean that in the early stages most of the RNA is unstable and thus resembles messenger RNA, while at the time of nurse cell breakdown, most of the ribosomal reserves of the egg are transferred from the nurse cells. However, it is possible that the amount of RNA transferred to the oocyte prior to nurse cell breakdown (stages 7–10) is relatively small so that the labeled RNA is immediately dispersed in a large volume. In *Drosophila*, yolk synthesis takes place primarily before nurse cell breakdown, so that the great increase in ooplasmic volume between stages 7 and 10 is primarily of non-cytoplasmic structures, while the final rapid increase in oocyte volume occurs because of the addition of the nurse cell cytoplasm, a volume nearly equal to that of the stage 10 oocyte (stages of *Drosophila* according to King *et al.*, 1956). Quantitative autoradiography would be necessary to determine whether there is a separation in time as to when mRNA and ribosomal RNA are added to the *Drosophila* or *Musca* oocyte.

Recent studies of nucleolar function in *Drosophila* nurse cells have utilized genetic mutants. From an analysis of *suppressor*[2] of *Hairy-wing* mutant, Klug *et al.* (1968, 1970) have found that the nucleolar morphology and physiology is changed in the mutant. From an analysis of rates of RNA and protein synthesis in the mutant, they speculate that the suppressor mutation may affect the structure of the ribosome. Another approach has utilized the *bobbed* mutation which has been shown to affect the genes for ribosomal RNA (Ritossa *et al.*, 1966). Mohan and Ritossa (1970) found a decreased rate of egg maturation in *bobbed* flies, but each mature egg produced had the same amount of RNA per egg as in the wild-type (Mohan, 1971). Thus it is evident that feedback controls are present which provide for the proper amount of RNA. Recently, Barr and Markowitz (1970) have shown that sufficient ribosomes are present in the mature egg to complete embryogenesis in the absence of new ribosome synthesis, but that the first instar larvae die soon after hatching. This finding is similar to that found in the anucleolate mutant of *Xenopus laevis* in which extensive analyses have been made (Brown, 1967).

The oocyte nucleus in higher dipterans carries on little or no RNA synthesis. No ^{3}H-uridine incorporation into RNase extractable material has been found from the earliest identifiable stages until late in oogenesis. During vitellogenesis there is some indication of incorporation of isotope (Zalokar, 1965; Bier *et al.*, 1967) that is limited in time to a very brief period of stage 10 (Mahowald and Tiefert, 1970). The failure of the oocyte nucleus to incorporate RNA precursors has been correlated with the fact that all of the DNA of the egg nucleus (Chandley, 1966) is condensed into one region, the karyosome. Electron microscopy has indicated that at the time the small amount of RNA is made in the karyosome, 500 Å granules appear around the chromosomes which are beginning to separate from the karyosome (Mahowald and Tiefert, 1970). There is no indication of nucleolus formation so that it would appear that the RNA made by the oocyte nucleus is of a non-ribosomal type.

These chromosomally associated granules are the same size as the Balbiani ring granules which were suggested to be carriers of mRNA to the cytoplasm (Stevens and Swift, 1966). Similar electron-dense granules are found in the mosquito oocyte nuclei (Roth, 1966) in association with the chromosomes, but no autoradiographic studies have yet been done on this species to confirm the presence of RNA in these granules.

Not all polytrophic meroistic ovaries follow the pattern of RNA synthesis seen in higher dipterans such as *Musca* and *Drosophila*. In *Simulium vittatum*, a black fly, Zalokar (1965) has found that the oocyte nucleus rapidly incorporates RNA and that this RNA is transferred to the ooplasm. A DNA-body is also found in this organism so that this exception may be similar to that already discussed for Tipulidae where it appears that the nucleolar DNA is replicated as a type of metabolic DNA similar to that found in amphibian eggs. In these dipterans the nurse cells also contribute RNA to the oocyte as in other polytrophic ovaries. Roth (1966) has described the large nucleolus of *Aedes* oocyte nuclei. In early oocytes it is 3 μ in diameter and composed of whorls of laminar sheets consisting of 150 Å particles. By the pre-vitellogenesis stage the nucleolus attains 7 μ in diameter and consists of a dense reticulate nucleolonema that spreads throughout the nucleoplasm and a granular portion. During vitellogenesis the nucleolus breaks down. Thus the ultrastructural evidence indicates that in *Aedes* the oocyte nucleus is active at least in ribosomal RNA synthesis.

In adephagous coleopterans, the oocyte nucleus participates in RNA synthesis to the same extent as the nurse cells during the earliest stages of egg growth but as vitellogenesis starts, synthesis of RNA by the egg nucleus ceases (Bier, 1965). There is no evidence yet for a nucleolus in these coleopterans (*Carabus cancellatus* and *C. granulatus*), but in *Dysticus*, where the DNA body is found, a true nucleolus occurs (Bier *et al.*, 1967). There is also no clear evidence for contributions of RNA by the nurse cells (Urbani and Russo-Caio, 1964) in these species. However, it would be difficult to detect the transfer of labeled RNA into an oocyte that is already heavily labeled.

The oocyte nuclei of lepidopterans and hymenopterans make a small amount of RNA during the early, pre-vitellogenesis stages of oocyte growth, but none during vitellogenesis (Bier, 1965; Pollack and Telfer, 1969). In Hymenoptera, accessory nuclei are formed prior to the beginning of yolk deposition, but there is no indication of the presence of DNA (Cruikshank, 1964) or RNA synthesis (Bier, 1965). However, it should be remembered that the oocyte nucleus is frequently Feulgen-negative even though DNA is known to be present. On the basis of histochemical and electron microscopic studies, Hopkins (1964) believes that there is RNA metabolism in these accessory nuclei. Many granules 3 μ in diameter and containing RNA, are found and they increase in number during vitellogenesis. These structures resemble similar granules found in the oocyte nucleus at the time that the accessory nuclei are formed. The accessory nuclei first appear adjacent to the oocyte nucleus during the pre-vitellogenesis growth phase. When viewed with the light microscope they appear to form as blebs from the nucleus (Hopkins, 1964; Meng, 1968) but this has not been seen with the electron microscope. They increase in number by dividing amitotically and then spread along the periphery of the oocyte during vitellogenesis.

Many studies have attempted to clarify the origin and function of these accessory nuclei but so far much doubt remains. Electron microscopy has indicated the presence of a typical nuclear membrane and has shown that annulate lamellae (reviewed by Kessel, 1968) form at the periphery, possibly from small vesicles that bleb off from the outer nuclear membrane (King and Richards, 1968). Although annulate lamellae have frequently been presumed to be associated with transfer of nuclear information to the cytoplasm, this is questionable since these accessory nuclei have undetectable amounts of DNA and fail to show uridine incorporation. A comparable situation is present in *Drosophila* where annulate lamellae form adjacent to the oocyte nucleus throughout oogenesis (Okada and Waddington, 1959; King, 1960; Mahowald and Tiefert, 1970) and yet no appreciable amounts of RNA are made except during one short period and this small amount of RNA synthesis is probably localized in the 500 Å granules. Accessory nuclei are thought to have a role in vitellogenesis (Hopkins, 1964), in the formation of the vitelline membrane (Cruikshank, 1964) and in lipid metabolism (King and Richards, 1968).

Kessel and Beams (1969) have described a distinctive RNA-rich structure in the oocyte of the dragonfly, *Libellula puchella*. It is a homogeneous, amorphous mass of slightly greater electron density than the ribosomes. It contains RNA in a non-granular form, i.e. non-ribosomal. Within these amorphous masses annulate lamellae form during the early stages of vitellogenesis. These structures may be identical to the "yolk nucleus" and Balbiani bodies frequently described in insect oogenesis (Bonhag, 1958; Raven, 1961), but instead of being important in yolk synthesis, they are the source of annulate lamellae and possibly other organelles.

(3) Summary Remarks on RNA Synthesis in Oogenesis

Two distinct manners of oogenesis, with a variety of intermediate forms, have developed within insects for producing the immense stores of RNA present within the individual egg. In panoistic ovaries RNA is synthesized for the oocyte by the germinal vesicle and possibly some by the follicle cells. These egg types are slow growing as might be expected because of the limited amount of DNA available (4C amount) for transcription. However, they appear to have selectively replicated the DNA for ribosomal RNA synthesis in a manner similar to that found in amphibian oogenesis. Thus, the chromosomes of the egg which must give rise to the embryo and consequently cannot become polyploid have solved the problem of synthesis of sufficient ribosomes in this manner (cf. Bier, 1967, for discussion).

In meroistic ovaries the oocyte nucleus is nearly inactive although it shows detectable amount of RNA synthesis either prior to vitellogenesis (Hymenoptera, Lepidoptera) or during vitellogenesis (higher dipterans). This RNA, at least in *Drosophila* and *Musca*, is not associated with a true nucleolus and consequently is probably not ribosomal RNA. In both telotrophic and polytrophic meroistic ovaries nearly all of the RNA synthesis occurs in the trophocytes and nurse cells respectively. These cells originate from the germ line (except in a few dipterans) and become highly polyploid either through nuclear fusion and polyploidization (trophocytes) or through polyploidization (nurse cells). The nurse cell and trophocyte cytoplasm is contributed to the egg while chromatin is not or at least is only contributed after breakdown into acid-soluble form (Vanderberg, 1963; Bier, 1964). These ovaries, probably because of the high amounts of nuclear DNA present in the trophic cells of the ovary for each growing oocyte, can achieve rapid egg production.

C. Oosome or Polar Granules

Eggs are not amorphous, disorganized masses of cytoplasm and yolk reserves, but display a high degree of organization that results in normal embryogenesis. The initial interaction between the cleavage nuclei and the cortex, particularly in eggs showing mosaic development, results in distinct differences in the developmental fate of the cells (cf. Counce, 1972). The manner in which specific localization of information in the cortex is effected in oogenesis is one of the central unanswered problems in oogenesis. Both the nature of this organization and its source remain unknown except for the oosome or polar granule region of some egg types (cf. Mahowald, 1971c). The oosome is associated with the formation of the cells that become the primordial germ cells (cf. Anderson, 1972). Because of their relation to germ cell origin, these organelles have been frequently thought of as germ cell determinants. The presence of RNA and protein in these organelles has been demonstrated cytochemically in a large group of organisms (Bier, 1954; Counce, 1963; Gill, 1963; Jazdowska-Zagrodzińska, 1966; Meng, 1968; Nicklas, 1959; Poulson and Waterhouse, 1960; Wolf, 1967; Mahowald, 1971b). They have been found in Hymenoptera, Megaloptera, Diptera and Coleoptera. An analysis of their structure and composition can give us some indication of how developmentally significant information becomes localized in the egg.

Some of the most complete data on these organelles comes from the work on *Drosophila*. Polar granules are first clearly seen at stage 9 to 10 (Mahowald, 1962; Gill, 1963) as small fibrous organelles, not bounded by a membrane and lying free in the cytoplasm. They rapidly increase in size and become attached to mitochondria in most species of *Drosophila* (Mahowald, 1968*b*). The polar granules are restricted to the posterior tip throughout these stages and in the mature egg form a very localized region of the periplasm only 5–10 μ deep (Fig. 12 see p. 42).

The structure of the granules varies in some of the dipteran species examined. In *Drosophila* polar granules are present as discrete organelles whose size and morphology are species specific (Counce, 1963; Mahowald, 1968*b*). The granules adhere to each other, however, in clusters of three or four and these are usually attached to mitochrondria. In *Miastor* (Mahowald, 1968*a*; Mahowald and Stoiber, 1971) the fibrous material of the polar granules is interconnected throughout most of the posterior tip during late oogenesis. In both *Drosophila* and *Miastor*, during cleavage of the early embryo, the oosome fragments into granules that are indistinguishable from each other. Similar fragmentation also occurs in the hymenopteran *Pimpla* (Meng, 1968).

In *Pimpla turionellae* (Hymenoptera) the oosome forms at approximately an equivalent stage as that in *Drosophila* (Meng, 1968). However, it appears more anteriorly as a thin strand that reaches to the middle of the growing egg. Later as the mass of the oosome increases, it rounds into a spherical organelle. It is not known whether the clearly demarcated oosome in *Pimpla* is actually bounded by a membrane or whether mitochondria are associated with this region as in the dipterans. Meng (1970) has found that proteins are synthesized within the oosome region during oogenesis, but that there is no detectable RNA synthesis within the oosome.

There is some indication in *Pimpla* of a stream of oosome material coming from the nurse cells at an earlier stage (Meng, 1968). In *Drosophila* detailed studies of the origin of polar granules have been made (Mahowald, 1962, 1971*a*, *b*) and occasionally polar granules can be found in pre-vitellogenic stages of oocytes, but there is no accumulation of polar granule material until shortly before nurse cell breakdown. When the fate of polar granules was studied in primordial germ cells of the embryo, the granules were found to fragment and become attached to the nuclear envelope (Counce, 1963; Mahowald, 1968*b*, 1971*a*) and to change their fibrous structure from a fibril of 150 Å to one of about 50 Å. These fibrous bodies remain attached to the nuclear membranes or to annulate lamellae until oogenesis begins in the pupal ovary when they disappear from the oocyte nucleus. However, structures that are indistinguishable from these organelles remain on the nurse cell nuclear membrane throughout oogenesis until the nurse cells degenerate and add their cytoplasm to the egg. At this time they disappear (Mahowald, 1971*a*). However, in *Miastor* the fibrous bodies from the nurse cell nuclei are seen to become attached to mitochondria and move into the ooplasm. They remain attached in this way until the egg starts development when they are no longer detectable either on the nuclear membrane or elsewhere. These latter structures appear to be different from polar granules because they become attached to mitochondria after the polar granules or oosome has appeared at the posterior tip, because they are not localized at the posterior tip but are found throughout the egg, and because they are no longer cytologically detectable after development starts (Mahowald and Stoiber, 1971). Similar structures have also been found in mature eggs of *Drosophila* and they also disappear at fertilization (Mahowald, 1971*a*). It seems possible that these fibrous bodies which originate at the nuclear membrane may be a different type of developmentally significant information which also becomes localized specifically in the egg.

Much more work remains to be done. Some method of labeling the polar granule material is needed so that more definitive studies on its origin can be done. This is paramount from the point of view of localization of information in the egg during oogenesis. In *Drosophila* polar granules have been shown to have RNA in the mature egg, but that during the period of pole cell formation they lose their basophilia (Mahowald, 1971*b*). Inasmuch as polysomes become associated with the polar granules at the time their RNA content is decreasing, the hypothesis has been proposed that polar granules contain messenger RNA (Mahowald, 1968*b*). Since these organelles first become visible at significant distances from the nuclei which must be their source of RNA (100 μ from the germinal vesicle and more than 200 μ from the nurse cells in *Drosophila*), there must be mechanisms present in the oocyte for localizing these structures in specific places so that normal development can follow. Similar mechanisms must exist for structuring the remaining regions of the cortex as well. There is no indication by any technique that the follicle cells are related to this process.

D. Vitellogenesis

(1) Introduction

During recent years two reviews have appeared on the process of vitellogenesis in insects. The first, by Bonhag in 1958, considered the information provided by cytological and histological techniques. This has been followed by Telfer (1965) in which the information provided by immunological, autoradiographic and electron microscopic procedures has been analyzed. The reader is referred to these reviews for an extensive analysis of the kinds of evidence available on the process of yolk formation.

On the grounds of purely quantitative amounts of material in an insect egg, the various yolky components comprise most of the volume of the egg.

Although yolk serves principally as a source of nutriment during embryonic development, many lines of evidence implicate it in morphogenetic processes (Counce, 1972). An important facet of the mechanism for this morphogenetic role of yolk may be related to the constituents of the yolk reserves themselves. Recent work on explants of chick embryos (Klein, 1968) have clearly shown that not every type of yolk from the avian egg is equivalent in supporting the growth of explanted chick embryos. In fact, there is evidence that certain classes of yolk are important in the normal differentiation of specific regions of the chick embryo. Thus there may be constituents of yolk present in low concentrations and thus difficult to analyze and yet which are critically important for normal embryogenesis.

There is a certain amount of evidence that the protein yolk constituents of the insect egg arise in two different modes: firstly and primarily, synthesis outside the egg and transport to the oocyte, and secondly, by synthesis within the egg itself. The evidence for the first is clear-cut but for the second, it is somewhat equivocal. I will discuss first the evidence for the origin of yolk protein outside of the egg and then treat of the type of data which indicates that some yolk may arise from within the egg.

(2) Protein Uptake from the Hemolymph

Although many experiments have indicated the absorption by the egg of materials from the hemolymph, three types of experiments have unequivocally demonstrated this phenomenon: (1) immunological studies of Telfer and his associates; (2) electron microscopy of the oocyte-follicle cell border with or without tracer molecules such as ferritin; and (3) autoradiographic studies.

(a) *Immunological Studies.* Wigglesworth (1943) was the first to prove conclusively that proteins were concentrated from the hemolymph into the eggs of *Rhodnius prolixus*. By using absorption spectra of proteins in the blood meal, the hemolymph, and the oocytes, he demonstrated that the denatured protein of hemoglobin was selectively taken up by the egg. Telfer, in a series of immunological studies, has been able to show clearly that blood proteins are accumulated in the *Hyalophora cecropia* egg (reviewed in Telfer and Melius, 1963). Every antigen detectable in the serum has been found in the yolk. Moreover, from this work it has also become clear that there is a selective uptake of protein from the hemolymph. In *Hyalophora* there is a sex-limited protein found in the blood of females. This protein decreases in concentration in the blood at the same time that yolk accumulation occurs. Telfer has shown that the egg accumulates this protein 20- to 30-fold above the concentration found in the hemolymph. Because every blood protein becomes included in the oocyte, it has been possible to follow this process with the electron microscope. Ferritin was injected into the abdomen and at various times after the injection, ovaries were prepared for observation with the electron microscope (Stay, 1965). Ferritin was found between the follicle cells, in the micropinocytotic vesicles (see below) and finally within the forming yolk particles themselves. Similar observations have been made on *Drosophila melanogaster*, the only difference being that the time sequence is much shorter (Mahowald, 1972). In *Hyalophora* the process takes one hour before ferritin is seen in yolk granules while in *Drosophila* this occurs in less than 30 minutes.

(b) *Electron Microscopy*. The ability of proteins in the hemolymph to transverse both the epithelial sheath cells and the basement lamina has been confirmed by immunological studies and by the observations with the electron microscope of ferritin disposition. Internal to the basement lamina the columnar layer of follicle cells surround the oocyte and also must be penetrated by these blood proteins. Observations with the light microscope had already suggested that there were intercellular spaces between the cells and this has been substantiated many times with the electron microscope (Telfer and Smith, 1970). Within this space blood proteins are concentrated 2·5 to 4·5 times that found in the blood (Anderson and Telfer, 1970). More significantly, in every species of insects investigated, there are invaginations of the oocyte border forming structures that have been called micropinocytotic invaginations or pitted vesicles. Roth and Porter (1964) have given the first and most extensive description of these invaginations of the oocyte border. In *Aedes aegypti* during the time of most intense vitellogenesis following a blood meal, the surface of the egg is surrounded with about 300,000 pits, 140 μ in overall diameter. These have a characteristic ultrastructure with three morphologically distinct layers (Fig. 9). The middle and most dense layer possesses the typical "unit membrane" structure of cellular membranes and is continuous with the plasmalemma of the oocyte. Internal to the membrane there is a layer of material 250–400 A thick which has the same appearance as the external surface of the oocyte membrane. External to the middle layer (the cytoplasmic side) there is a layer about 200 Å thick which appears to be made up of "bristles" or "hairs" radiating outward from the dense line. Within the peripheral cytoplasm of the oocyte tubules are found (Fig. 9) which connect to forming yolk spheres (Favard-Séréno, 1964; Anderson, 1969; Telfer and Smith, 1970; Mahowald, 1972). These tubules have a unique structure which closely resembles pinosomes: the unit membrane has the same thickness as the pinosome membrane and the internal surface bears the 250 Å thick border of "fuzz" material characteristic of pinosomes, but they lack the bristles on their cytoplasmic surface. The origin of these tubules is unknown, but presumably they are derived from pinosomes and form a mode of transit for protein ingested and moving to forming yolk spheres. Thus, the conclusion based on these and similar observations in other organisms (Anderson, 1964, 1969; Beams and Kessel, 1969; Bier and

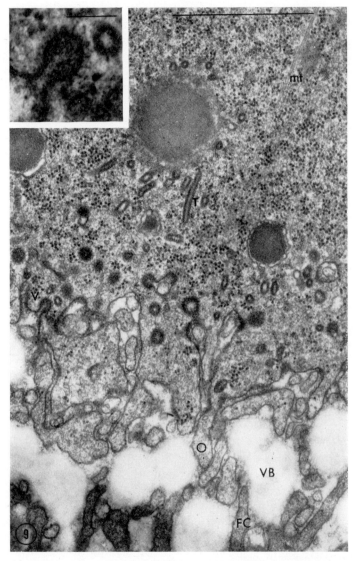

FIG. 9. Oocyte (O)-follicle cell (FC) border of *Drosophila melanogaster* showing presence of many micropinocytotic invaginations (V). The insert shows one of these pitted vesicles at high magnification. Tubules (T) are found running from the oocyte border to the yolk granules. These tubules also possess a 200 Å fibrillar interior similar to that found in pitted vesicles. Ribosomes are scattered throughout the ooplasm and there is a dense fibrillar background. Microtubules (mt) are also common along the oocyte border. The follicle cell has numerous microvilli extending between the vitelline bodies (VB). Those bodies will subsequently fuse to form the vitelline membrane.

Ramamurty, 1964; Cummings and King, 1970; de Loof and Lagasse, 1970; Favard-Séréno, 1969; Hopkins and King, 1966; Kessel and Beams, 1963; Mahowald, 1972; Roth and Porter, 1964; Scheurer, 1969; Stay, 1965; Telfer and Smith, 1970) is that the coated pits are important in the uptake of protein from the space between the oocyte and the follicle cells and in their segregation into vesicles which subsequently fuse and increase in size until they become the large yolk granules of the egg. This interpretation of the electron microscopic pictures corresponds with the experimental data by means of immunological and autoradiographic techniques.

The structural relationships between the follicle cells and the oocyte in *Gryllus* appear to be different (Favard-Séréno, 1964). The oocyte has deep invaginations formed by evaginations of the follicle cells which fit into the oocyte depressions as fingers in a glove. Pitted vesicles form in these deep invaginations and the concentrated protein is then moved along 30 mμ tubules to the forming yolk granules. Thus instead of the large intracellular space that forms in the other organisms examined with the electron microscope, in *Gryllus* there is only an intercellular space of 13 mμ. However, the deep invaginations greatly increase the surface area available for micropinocytosis. Because of the high rate of protein synthesis in follicle cells (Bier, 1963a), it is possible that these cells secrete protein into this space. Similar interdigitations occur to some extent in *Bombus terrestris* (Hopkins and King, 1966).

(c) *Autoradiographic Studies.* Radioactive amino acids are incorporated into all cellular proteins made and hence cannot be used as a selective marker for protein synthesis of yolk. However, it has been possible to distinguish two periods of incorporation of isotope into the oocytes of dipterans (Bier, 1962, 1963a). Immediately after injection of the isotope into *Musca domesticus*, all cellular types are seen to synthesize protein with the highest rate of incorporation being in the follicle cells, then the nurse cells, and the lowest rate in the oocyte. However, after 30–60 minutes, the follicle cells show less label than the nurse cells, indicating a rapid turnover of protein. In the oocyte, dense accumulations of label appear at the follicle cell-oocyte border, representing newly-formed yolk granules. These become rapidly dispersed throughout the oocyte. In order to determine the origin of this yolk protein, Bier (1963a) transplanted ovaries into flies that had been previously injected with radioactive amino acids so that the hemolymph proteins were labeled but no appreciable free radioactive amino acids were present in the hemolymph. He then found only the second wave of protein incorporation into the oocyte, namely, yolk formation at the follicle cell-oocyte border.

No labeled protein was seen to move from the nurse cells to the oocyte (Bier, 1963a) even though movement of RNA is detectable (see above). However, the failure to detect such a protein movement may be due to the high levels of protein label already present in the oocyte. When the nurse cells break down, labeled protein is seen to move into the oocyte from the nurse cells.

Bier's original observation has been confirmed in cecropia moths (Melius and Telfer, 1969), in *Pimpla turionellae* (Meng, 1970), in *Anagasta kühniella* (Cruickshank, 1971), and in *Acheta domesticus* (Kunz and Petzelt, 1970). In all of these instances, radioactive proteins have accumulated in the peripheral yolk spheres at a time interval adequate to account for transport through the hemolymph to the ovary. The site of synthesis of these proteins has been shown to be the fat body (Pan *et al.*, 1969).

The role of the follicular epithelium in vitellogenesis has been obscure until the recent work of Telfer, Anderson and co-workers on cecropia moths. The rapid turnover of proteins synthesized by follicle cells (Bier, 1963*a*) indicated that these cells might transfer protein to the oocyte. However, because of the known role of these cells in forming the protective coats of the oocyte (see below), it was difficult to determine the role of these proteins. The use of vital dyes such as trypan blue (Ramamurty, 1964; Telfer and Anderson, 1968; Mahowald, 1972) and ferritin showed that the hemolymph proteins did not pass through the follicle cells but between them. Recently, a series of experiments have clearly shown that the follicle cells add a protein product to yolk. By autoradiography the follicle cells were shown to synthesize protein, probably a mucoprotein (Anderson and Telfer, 1969); this protein, or proteins, is accumulated in the peripheral yolk spheres independently of the uptake of vitellogenins from the hemolymph. Hausman *et al.* (1971) showed that the presence of vitellogenin, the female specific protein, enhances the protein uptake potential of isolated follicles. Anderson (1971) has succeeded in dissociating the oocyte from the follicular epithelium, and has demonstrated that the follicle cell makes a non-dialysable product, presumably protein, which is accumulated in peripheral yolk spheres by the isolated oocyte.

There have been previous indications of such a follicle cell product. Telfer (1960) had shown that there were certain antigens present in yolk which were absent in the hemolymph. Scheurer (1969) has also found by electrophoresis many more proteins in yolk of *Leucophaea* than in the hemolymph. Bell (1970) has found in yolk, besides the two principal vitellogenins of the hemolymph of *Periplaneta americana*, a third protein which is more concentrated in the hemolymph than in yolk, and a fourth protein that is absent from the hemolymph. This latter protein may be the follicle cell contribution. Petzelt and Bier (1970*a, b*) found that inhibition of RNA synthesis with actinomycin D also inhibited protein synthesis in the follicle cells as well as pinocytosis of blood proteins. Thus, their experiments suggested that a protein produced by the follicle cells is needed for vitellogenesis.

A clear demonstration of the function of this follicle cell product has been elusive. It appears to play a role in concentrating hemolymph proteins in the intercellular space (Anderson and Telfer, 1970). However, in experiments with isolated oocytes (Anderson, 1971), the presence of the follicle cell product did not stimulate uptake of vitellogenin even though the product itself was incorporated into yolk. An important area of investigation concerns the control of synthesis of this product (cf. Bell, 1969) and its role in pinocytosis.

Studies on the metabolism of the follicle cell are complex because of the clear role these cells play in the synthesis of the protective coverings (vitelline membrane and chorion) of the egg. King and Koch (1963) have shown in a number of female sterility mutants that the follicle cells are primarily responsible for the secretion of material for the vitelline membrane in *Drosophila*. The fine structure of the follicle cells confirms that these cells are very active in protein synthesis: in *Aeschna*: Beams and Kessel (1969); in *Drosophila*: King and Koch (1963), Quattropani and Anderson (1969), Mahowald (1972); in *Hyalophora*: King and Aggarwal (1965), Stay (1965), Telfer and Smith (1970); in *Leptinotarsa*: de Loof and Lagasse (1970). During the time the precursors to the vitelline membrane are forming, the follicle cells have an elaborate endoplasmic reticulum (ER), often approaching in extent and complexity the ER found in exocrine secretory cells (Fig. 10). Electron-dense material accumulates in the ends of ER cisternae and is subsequently transferred to Golgi regions (Beams and Kessel, 1969; Telfer and Smith, 1970). Much of this material also accumulates at the base of the follicle cell adjacent to the oocyte and is probably released by fusion with the plasma membrane. At the completion of vitelline membrane formation, the follicle cells immediately begin the secretion of the material for the chorion which forms adjacent to the follicle cell plasmalemma (King, 1960; King and Koch, 1963; Quattropani and Anderson, 1969; Beams and Kessel, 1969; Telfer and Smith, 1970). The chorion is a complex structure composed of the endochorion which forms a thin layer adjacent to the vitelline membrane and a complex exochorion composed of struts and a covering. The outside surface of the chorion bears imprints of the follicle cells which formed it. Recent studies with the scanning electron microscope have indicated the complexity of the chorion surface in *Culex pipiens* (Hinton, 1968).

The follicle cell is interesting from a cellular point of view in that it changes its function very quickly from producing the macromolecules which presumably self-assemble to form the vitelline membrane to producing a new set of molecules which will form the chorion. At this transition, the cisternal form of endoplasmic reticulum is transformed into a tubular meshwork of granular ER (Mahowald, 1972). The Golgi has become less evident, probably because the precursors for the chorion are not accumulated in the Golgi prior to their transfer through the plasma membrane to form the intricate structure of the chorion. The nucleus shows no major transformations during these events.

In *Drosophila* gap junctions (cf. Revel and Karnovsky, 1967), thought to

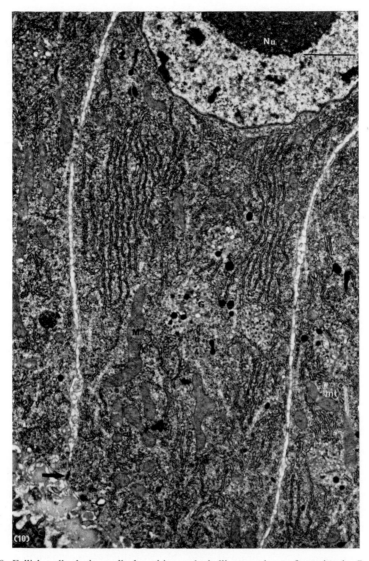

FIG. 10. Follicle cells during yolk deposition and vitelline membrane formation in *Drosophila immigrans*. Typically, intercellular spaces occur between follicle cells except at the oocyte border where a desmosome-like structure (arrow) is visible. The nucleus is spherical and contains a centrally located nucleolus (Nu) and scattered clumps of chromatin. The outer nuclear membrane is covered with ribosomes and the cytoplasm is filled with regularly arranged ER as well as with many free ribosomes. Golgi regions (G) are found with electron-dense inclusions. These inclusions are released at the oocyte-follicle cell border. Occasional microtubules (mt) are found parallel to the long axis of the follicle cell. Mitochondria (M) are typical in structure.

be the sites of free ionic communication between cells, are found between adjacent follicle cells throughout oogenesis (Mahowald, 1972). A *zonula adhaerens* (*cf.* Farquhar and Palade, 1963) is also present at the base of each follicle cell. After the completion of vitelline membrane formation, septate junctions appear between adjacent follicle cells adjacent to the *zonula adhaerens*. These specialized cellular junctions have not yet been described in the follicular layer of other insect species. They are probably important in the integration of the follicular epithelium into a functioning unit.

(3) Protein Synthesis within the Oocyte

The evidence for the synthesis of some of the constituents of the protein yolk by the insect oocyte during early phases of vitellogenesis is tenuous. In crustacean oogenesis, large quantities of yolk are formed by the endoplasmic reticulum of the oocyte (Beams and Kessel, 1963) and amphibians show yolk formation within mitochondria (Ward, 1962) but neither of these processes has been observed in insects. There are certain indications that some yolk proteins may be made by the oocyte. In *Leucophaea maderae* many minor yolk proteins are present during the early stages of vitellogenesis (Dejmal and Brookes, 1968; Scheurer, 1969). In *Drosophila* the first appearance of protein yolk is seen prior to the time micropinocytosis begins at the follicle cell-oocyte border (Mahowald, 1972). The yolk forms within multivesicular bodies which seem to originate from Golgi regions (Fig. 11). Small vesicles appear to fuse with these structures and it is reasonable to suggest that these structures could form from the ER that is relatively plentiful in the *Drosophila* oocyte. These same multivesicular organelles are present throughout oogenesis so that intraovarian yolk synthesis may also be important in subsequent stages of oogenesis. During the period of active pinocytosis of hemolymph proteins, it is difficult to show yolk synthesis within the oocyte due to the rapid synthesis of ooplasmic proteins (Bier, 1963*a*).

There is some evidence that the oocytes also contribute to protein yolk synthesis in the terminal stages of vitellogenesis. Telfer and Anderson (1968) have investigated the processes involved in the final maturation of the *Hyalophora* egg. From the time that uptake of protein from the hemolymph has stopped to the time that the egg reaches its mature size with its chorion, there is an increase in volume of 50%. Most of the volume change is due to hydration since the dry weight of the egg increases only about 10%. Using ^{3}H-histidine they showed that most of this increase in dry weight is due to an endogenous protein synthesis by the oocyte, and that this synthesis is restricted to the peripheral $30\,\mu$ of the egg. This protein forms a more refractile type of protein granule of smaller size than the previously produced protein yolk. The significance of this endogenous protein synthesis is not known. Possibly these proteins made by the oocyte itself may have specific roles in

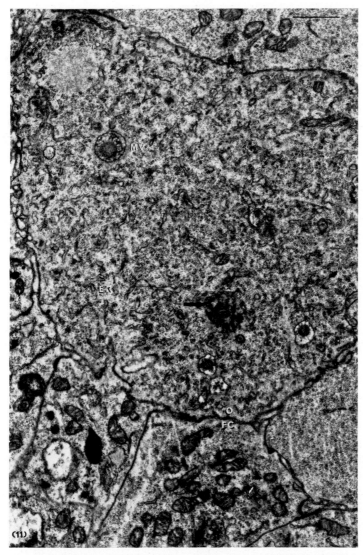

Fig. 11. *Drosophila immigrans* oocyte (O) prior to the time of protein uptake at the oocyte–follicle cell (FC) border. Granular ER (ER) is found that is tubular in form as indicated by the round and oblong profiles in thin section. Multivesicular bodies (MV) are common and show an accumulation of dense material which appears identical to the yolk formed at later stages. The cluster of small vesicles (arrow) is thought to be a stage in the origin of the multivesicular organelles.

future development, while the rather unspecific process of pinocytosis is more concerned in obtaining sufficient nutritional reserves for development.

Many workers (*cf.* Bonhag, 1958; King, 1960) have shown the presence of non-glycogen polysaccharide in protein yolk spheres with cytochemical techniques. In some species the major vitellogenin is a mucoprotein (Kunz and Petzelt, 1970; Ramamurty, 1968; Favard-Séréno, 1969), but in other instances (e.g. dipterans) the presence of polysaccharide in protein yolk spheres could be the result of pinocytosis. There have been frequent demonstrations of the presence of a mucopolysaccharide on cell surfaces, especially those surfaces active in pinocytosis (Revel and Ito, 1967). As a consequence of the fusion of pinocytotic vesicles with developing yolk spheres, an accumulation of polysaccharides in yolk would be expected. Besides the polysaccharide component of the yolk spheres, there have also been cytochemical indications for various lipid components in yolk (e.g. King, 1960) and evidence from electrophoresis that the major yolk protein of *Leucophaea* has a lipid moiety associated with it (Dejmal and Brookes, 1968). The biological significance of these components is not known.

(4) Glycogen Synthesis

The utilization of available carbon sources for glycogen synthesis at the end of oogenesis has been studied with radioactive ^{3}H-glucose (Engels and Drescher, 1964; Engels, 1966, 1968; Engels and Bier, 1967; Ramamurty, 1968). In three different insects, *Musca*, *Apis* and *Panorpa*, ^{3}H-glucose is incorporated into diastase-sensitive, PAS-positive material (i.e., glycogen) throughout the oocyte even after periods as short as one minute. There is no evidence for incorporation by the nurse cells or follicle cells. Moreover, the newly-formed glycogen is present throughout the cytoplasmic regions of the oocyte. Thus it seems clear that at least in these species and probably in all insects glycogen is made in the oocyte and not transported to it from other sources.

Glycogen synthesis occurs at the termination of vitellogenesis, after both RNA and protein synthesis have ceased or diminished. In *Musca*, at least, the enzymes necessary for glycogen synthesis (or at least the mRNA for the formation of the enzymes) must have been present before this time. When actinomycin D is injected into adult *Musca* females (Engels and Bier, 1967) or when flies are placed at 4°C for extended periods of time (Engels, 1970), glycogen synthesis occurs earlier than in untreated flies, even before vitellogenesis. Glycogen deposits can also be detected in the cytoplasm of nurse cells but not in follicle cells. These results indicate that the enzymes for glycogen synthesis are present prior to the time of ordinary synthesis. They have also been interpreted to indicate that glycogen synthesis occurs only when the energy being used for RNA synthesis and protein accumulation has stopped. Normally this energy surplus occurs as the egg nears completion and the nurse cells have broken down, but this can be experimentally induced by stopping RNA synthesis. Similar close interrelationships between the storage of carbohydrates in polysaccharides and the presence of excess levels of ATP have been postulated by Atkinson (1965) to be due to allosteric controls of the enzymes of glycolysis and gluconeogenesis. Whether similar mechanisms are actually operative in polytrophic oocytes is yet to be determined.

In *Anisolabis* (Bonhag, 1956), *Hyalophora* (King and Aggarwal, 1965) and *Bombus* (Hopkins and King, 1966) there is cytochemical evidence that the first phase of glycogen synthesis occurs in the nurse cells but that the main increase in glycogen yolk occurs simultaneously with protein yolk formation. These results indicate that the enzymes for glycogen synthesis are also present in the nurse cells in these species.

(5) *Fat Storage in the Oocyte*

A distinction must be made between those lipids which are complexed with other macromolecules in membranes and other cellular structures and those that are specifically produced as energy reserves for future development. Lipids in the first category are present as structural elements of cell organelles. Since there is no reason to believe that anything unique occurs with regard to these "functional" lipids, they will not be treated here. However, some aspects of the formation of storage lipids of insect eggs have interest. The lipids appearing early in oogenesis are primarily phospholipid while those appearing later are triglycerides (Nath *et al.*, 1958). Possibly this sequence is actually a reflection of the biological needs of the system. While the egg is still growing phospholipids are continually needed for structural roles in membranes, etc. Only as egg growth is nearing completion do the triglycerides appear for energy storage. These fats are probably represented in electron micrographs, after the ordinary preparatory procedures, as clear vacuoles with no limiting membrane, and usually about $0.5\,\mu$ in diameter (King, 1960; Mahowald, 1962). Many workers using the light microscope (e.g. Nath *et al.*, 1958) have presumed that these droplets of fat originate from Golgi vesicles or from modified mitochondria. Probably only electron microscopy joined with autoradiography will be able to clarify our knowledge on this point.

E. Determination of the Oocyte Axis

A more recent concern in studies of insect oogenesis has been to discover how the mature egg acquires its final organization. The amount of information available is limited, even though this must be considered one of the cardinal events in oogenesis. Most of our current information available on egg organization is derived from studies of embryogenesis and consequently is more aptly treated in other chapters (Anderson, 1972; Counce, 1972). Studies on oogenesis have given us some knowledge on the manner in which some of the axes of the egg are produced. The anterior-posterior axis always conforms to the same axis in the mother. In meroistic ovaries the anterior end of the oocyte is adjacent to the trophic tissue which may play a role in establishing this axis. More significant information on the nature of this axis will probably come from some recent experiments in dipterans. Yajima (1960) has shown that by the proper type of centrifugation of the early *Chironomus* embryo the anterior end produces abdominal segments and the posterior portion produces anterior regions of the larvae. Ultraviolet irradiation of the anterior third of the early embryo resulted in 20% of the treated eggs developing as double abdomens and uv irradiation of the posterior third resulted in 20% developing as double cephalon embryos (Yajima, 1964). Kalthoff and Sander (1968) have obtained similar results in *Smittia parthenogenetica*. The sensitivity shown to uv light of 254 mμ suggests that nucleic acid is important in the development of the anterior portion of the embryo, and because of the poor penetrating power of uv, that this material is located at the surface. The cleavage nuclei are probably not affected. Bull (1966) has found a genetic mutant of *Drosophila melanogaster*, *bicaudal*, which produces double-abdomen embryos. These experimental approaches to the investigation of the factors determining embryonic axes give hope for a further understanding of the basis for determining the anterior-posterior axis.

The germinal vesicle assumes a mid-dorsal location in *Acheta* (Netzel, 1965, 1968) and may be responsible for the formation of the final egg shape in this species. Netzel's work indicates that the reduced vitellogenesis in the vicinity of the germinal vesicle coupled with the heightened vitellogenesis of the mid-ventral region could result in the concave dorsal and convex ventral shape of the mature egg. Gill (1964) has studied the formation of the egg axes in *Drosophila*. Prior to vitellogenesis, the oocyte nucleus shows no distinctive localization relative to the future axes of the egg. As vitellogenesis begins, the nucleus assumes an anterior location adjacent to the nurse cell border, and by stage 9 (stages according to King *et al.*, 1956) it becomes localized below the anterior dorsal follicle cells which become more columnar. Throughout the remainder of oogenesis the oocyte nucleus retains this anterior dorsal position. The mechanisms involved in determining these nuclear positions or whether this position is critical in the formation of the axes is unknown.

Some attempts have been made to identify ultrastructural differentiations of the cortex of the egg. The distinctive features of the posterior polar plasm have been mentioned, and this region remains as the only clear example of cortical differences. Okada and Waddington (1959) showed the presence of annulate lamellae and folds of the plasma membrane in the cortex of the

Drosophila egg, but indicated no regional differentiations. Mahowald (1963*a*, *b*; unpublished observations) has made extensive investigations of the cortical regions of *Drosophila* eggs and pre-blastoderm embryos, and, except for the posterior tip, has found no regional differentiations. The periplasm of the mature egg contains the usual organelles, e.g. mitochondria, ribosomes, ER, annulate lamellae, multivesicular bodies, (Fig. 12), but these organelles are also found in the yolky regions of the egg. Moreover, Overton and Raab (1967) have shown that all of these cortical organelles can be moved from the cortex by centrifugation so that the cortex does not appear to be firmly structured. However, since yolky elements are excluded from the periplasm of the egg, some structure must exist. Further studies must be made to determine more fully the distinctive features of the cortex of the insect egg.

IV. CONCLUDING REMARKS

Studies on insect oogenesis have had remarkable success in distinguishing phases of growth and in delineating with amazing clarity the specific roles of each of the cell types composing the ovariole. Moreover, within the one class of the Arthropoda, three diverse forms of oogenesis have evolved which succeed in producing the RNA requisite for the mature egg in diverse manners. The recent discoveries that specific replication of the nucleolar organizer region of the genome not only occurs in panoistic ovarian types but has been developed independently (or retained?) in evolution in a number of lower dipteran species are of special interest. They underline again the realization that has come from studies on oogenesis in amphibians that some type of polyploidy for the ribosomal-RNA genes is a frequent if not universal necessity in oogenesis. Furthermore, within the Insecta this polyploidy has been achieved in different manners. Besides the method just mentioned for the panoistic type, the meroistic form of oogenesis has polyploid sister cells of the oocyte which are responsible for most of the RNA synthesized for the oocyte. Recent work even suggests that there is differential replication of the ribosomal cistrons in their nurse cells. Because of the polyploidy found for the whole genome, these forms, especially the polytrophic variety, are also able to achieve a very rapid production of eggs.

Probably the greatest lacuna in our knowledge of oogenesis whether in insects or elsewhere is both in the nature of the organization of the egg which produces normal development (principally a property of the cortex or periplasm) and the mechanisms by which this information becomes localized. Investigations on the oosome found in some insect orders is one approach that has been used to start investigations on this key problem of oogenesis, but further studies of other systems are needed. The use of genetic mutations such as the female sterility factors in *Drosophila* is one important approach to

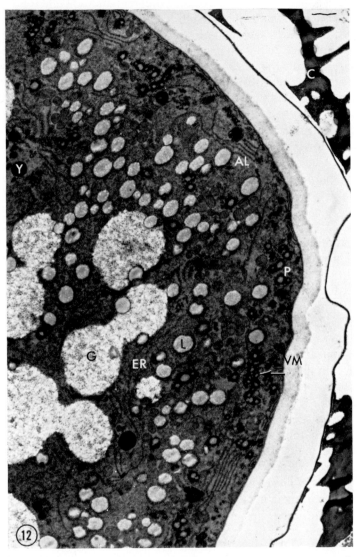

FIG. 12. Posterior tip of a mature *Drosophila hydei* egg. Polar granules (P) are common in the peripheral 5 to 10 μ of the egg and are typically hollow and joined in strings (arrow). Lamellar ER, annulate lamellae (AL), background of free ribosomes, mitochondria, lipid droplets (L), protein yolk (Y) and glycogen (G) are all evident in this picture. The vitelline membrane (VM) and chorion (C) form the protective coverings of the egg.

studying these processes. Ultimately, the purpose of oogenesis is to produce the ordered arrangement of reserves and cytoplasm which will interact with the cleavage nuclei to produce the proper differentiation of the embryo. These studies are just beginning.

REFERENCES

Allen, E. R. and Cave, M. D. (1968). *Z. Zellforsch. mikrosk. Anat.*, **92**, 477–486.
Anderson, D. T. (1972). In *Developmental Systems: Insects* (S. J. Counce and C. H. Waddington, eds), Vol. 1, p. 95 and p. 165. Academic Press, London and New York.
Anderson, E. (1964). *J. cell Biol.*, **20**, 131–155.
Anderson, E. (1969). *J. Microsc. (Paris)*, **8**, 721–738.
Anderson, E. and Beams, H. W. (1956). *J. biophys. biochem. Cytol.*, Suppl. **2**, 439–443.
Anderson, L. M. (1971). *J. cell Sci.*, **8**, 735–750.
Anderson, L. M. and Telfer, W. H. (1969). *Tissue Cell*, **1**, 633–644.
Anderson, L. M. and Telfer, W. H. (1970). *J. cell Physiol.*, **76**, 37–54.
Atkinson, D. E. (1965). *Science, N.Y.*, **150**, 851–857.
Barr, H. J. and Markowitz, E. H. (1970). *J. cell Biol.*, **47**, 13a.
Bayreuther, K. (1956). *Chromosoma*, **7**, 508–557.
Beams, H. W. and Kessel, R. G. (1963). *J. cell Biol.*, **18**, 621–649.
Beams, H. W. and Kessel, R. G. (1969). *J. cell Sci.*, **4**, 241–264.
Beatty, R. A. (1949). *Proc. R. Soc. Edinb.*, Sect. B, **63**, 249–270.
Bell, W. J. (1969). *J. Insect Physiol.*, **15**, 1279–1290.
Bell, W. J. (1970). *J. Insect Physiol.*, **16**, 291–299.
Bier, K. (1954). *Biol. Zbl.*, **73**, 170–190.
Bier, K. (1957). *Chromosoma*, **8**, 493–522.
Bier, K. (1960). *Chromosoma*, **11**, 335–364.
Bier, K. (1962). *Naturwissenschaften*, **49**, 332–333.
Bier, K. (1963a). *Wilhelm Roux Arch. EntwMech. Org.*, **154**, 552–575.
Bier, K. (1963b). *J. cell Biol.*, **16**, 436–440.
Bier, K. (1964). *Zool. Anz. Suppl.*, **27**, 84–91.
Bier, K. (1965). *Zool. Jb., Physiol.*, **71**, 371–384.
Bier, K. (1967). *Naturwissenschaften*, **54**, 189–195.
Bier, K. and Ramamurty, P. S. (1964). *Naturwissenschaften*, **51**, 223–224.
Bier, K., Kunz, W. and Ribbert, D. (1967). *Chromosoma*, **23**, 214–254.
Bonhag, P. F. (1955). *J. Morph.*, **96**, 381–438.
Bonhag, P. F. (1956). *J. Morph.*, **99**, 433–463.
Bonhag, P. F. (1958). *A. Rev. Ent.*, **3**, 137–160.
Bonhag, P. F. (1959). *Univ. Calif. Publs Ent.*, **16**, 81–124.
Brown, D. D. (1967). In *Current Topics in Developmental Biology* (A. A. Moscona and A. Monroy, eds), pp. 47–73. Academic Press, New York and London.
Brown, E. H. and King, R. C. (1964). *Growth*, **28**, 41–81.
Bucher, N. (1957). *Revue suisse Zool.*, **64**, 91–187.
Bull, A. L. (1966). *J. exp. Zool.*, **161**, 221–242.
Callan, H. G. (1956). In *Symposium on the Fine Structure of Cells* (*Leiden*), Intern. Union Biol. Sci. Publ., **B21**, 89–109.
Camenzind, R. (1966). *Chromosoma*, **18**, 123–152.
Cassidy, J. D. and King, R. C. (1969). *Biol. Bull.*, **137**, 429–437.
Chandley, A. C. (1966). *Expl. Cell Res.*, **44**, 201–215.

Counce, S. J. (1963). *J. Morph.*, **112**, 129–145.

Counce, S. J. (1968). *Nature, Lond.*, **218**, 781–782.

Counce, S. J. (1972). In *Developmental Systems: Insects* (S. J. Counce and C. H. Waddington, eds), Vol. 2, p. 1. Academic Press, London and New York.

Cruickshank, W. J. (1964). *Nature, Lond.*, **201**, 734–735.

Cruickshank, W. J. (1971). *J. Insect Physiol.*, **17**, 217–232.

Cummings, M. R. and King, R. C. (1970). *J. Morph.*, **130**, 467–478.

Dapples, C. C. and King, R. C. (1970). *Z. Zellforsch. mikrosk. Anat.*, **103**, 34–47.

Dejmal, R. K. and Brookes, V. J. (1968). *J. Insect Physiol.*, **14**, 371–381.

de Loof, A. and Lagasse, A. (1970). *J. Insect Physiol.*, **16**, 211–220.

Doane, W. W. (1972). In *Developmental Systems: Insects* (S. J. Counce and C. H. Waddington, eds), Vol. 2, p. 291. Academic Press, London and New York.

Echard, G. (1962). *Bull. Soc. zool. Fr.*, **87**, 52–70.

Engelmann, F. (1970). In *The Physiology of Insect Reproduction*. Pergamon Press, New York.

Engels, W. (1966). *Zool. Anz.*, Suppl. **29**, 243–251.

Engels, W. (1968). *J. Insect Physiol.*, **14**, 869–879.

Engels, W. (1970). *Wilhelm Roux Arch. EntwMech. Org.*, **166**, 89–104.

Engels, W. and Bier, K. (1967). *Wilhelm Roux Arch. EntwMech. Org.*, **158**, 64–88.

Engels, W. and Drescher, W. (1964). *Experientia*, **20**, 445–447.

Eschenberg, K. M. and Dunlap, H. L. (1966). *J. Morph.*, **118**, 297–316.

Farquhar, M. G. and Palade, G. E. (1963). *J. cell Biol.*, **17**, 375–412.

Favard-Séréno, C. (1964). *J. Microsc. (Paris)*, **3**, 323–338.

Favard-Séréno, C. (1968). *J. Microsc. (Paris)*, **7**, 205–230.

Favard-Séréno, C. (1969). *J. Microsc. (Paris)*, **8**, 401–414.

Gall, J. C., Macgregor, H. C. and Kidston, M. E. (1969). *Chromosoma*, **26**, 169–187.

Gill, K. S. (1963). *J. exp. Zool.*, **152**, 251–278.

Gill, K. S. (1964). *J. exp. Zool.*, **155**, 91–104.

Gresson, R. A. R. and Threadgold, L. T. (1961). *Q . Jl. microsc. Sci.*, **101**, 295–297.

Gresson, R. A. R. and Threadgold, L. T. (1962). *Q . Jl. microsc. Sci.*, **103**, 141–145.

Halkka, L. and Halkka, O. (1968). *Science, N.Y.*, **162**, 803–805.

Hansen-Delkeskamp, E. (1969). *Wilhelm Roux Arch. EntwMech. Org.*, **162**, 114–120.

Hausman, S. J., Anderson, L. M. and Telfer, W. H. (1971). *J. cell Biol.*, **48**, 303–313.

Heist, H. E. and Mulvaney, B. D. (1968). *J. Ultrastruct. Res.*, **24**, 86–101.

Hinton, H. E. (1968). *J. Insect Physiol.*, **14**, 145–161.

Hopkins, C. R. (1964). *Q . Jl. microsc. Sci.*, **105**, 475–480.

Hopkins, C. R. and King, P. E. (1966). *J. cell Sci.*, **1**, 201–216.

Hsu, W. S. (1952). *Q . Jl. microsc. Sci.*, **93**, 191–206.

Huebner, E. and Anderson, E. (1970). *J. cell Biol.*, **46**, 191–198.

Jacob, J. and Sirlin, J. L. (1959). *Chromosoma*, **10**, 210–228.

Jazdowska-Zagrodzińska, B. (1966). *J. Embryol. exp. Morph.*, **16**, 391–401.

Kalthoff, K. and Sander, K. (1968). *Wilhelm Roux Arch. EntwMech. Org.*, **161**, 129–146.

Kessel, R. G. (1968). *J. Ultrastruct. Res.*, Suppl. **10**, 1–82.

Kessel, R. G. and Beams, H. W. (1963). *Expl Cell Res.*, **30**, 440–443.

Kessel, R. G. and Beams, H. W. (1969). *J. cell Biol.*, **42**, 185–201.

King, P. F. and Richards, J. G. (1968). *Nature, Lond.*, **218**, 488.

King, R. C. (1960). *Growth*, **24**, 265–323.

King, R. C. (1964). In *Insect Reproduction* (H. C. Highnam, ed.), pp. 12–25. Royal Entomological Society, London.

King, R. C. (1970). In *Ovarian Development in* Drosophila melanogaster. Academic Press, New York and London.

King, R. C. and Aggarwal, S. K. (1965). *Growth*, **29**, 17–83.

King, R. C. and Divine, R. L. (1959). *Growth*, **22**, 299–326.

King, R. C. and Koch, E. A. (1963). *Q . Jl. microsc. Sci.*, **104**, 297–320.

King, R. C., Rubinson, A. C. and Smith, R. F. (1956). *Growth*, **20**, 121–157.

King, R. C., Aggarwal, S. K. and Aggarwal, V. (1968). *J. Morph.*, **124**, 143–166.

Klein, N. W. (1968). *J. exp. Zool.*, **168**, 239–256.

Klug, W. S., Bodenstein, D. and King, R. C. (1968). *J. exp. Zool.*, **167**, 151–156.

Klug, W. S., King, R. C. and Wattiaux, J. M. (1970). *J. exp. Zool.*, **174**, 125–140.

Koch, E. A. and King, R. C. (1964). *Growth*, **28**, 325–369.

Koch, E. A. and King, R. C. (1966). *J. Morph.*, **119**, 283–304.

Koch, E. A. and King, R. C. (1968). *J. cell Biol.*, **39**, 74a.

Koch, E. A., Smith, P. A. and King, R. C. (1967). *J. Morph.*, **121**, 55–70.

Krause, G. and Sanders, K. (1962). In *Advances in Morphogenesis*, 2 (M. Abercrombie and J. Brachet, eds), pp. 259–303. Academic Press, New York and London.

Kunz, W. (1967a). *Chromosoma*, **20**, 332–370.

Kunz, W. (1967b). *Chromosoma*, **21**, 446–462.

Kunz, W. (1969). *Chromosoma*, **26**, 41–75.

Kunz, W. and Petzelt, C. (1970). *J. Insect Physiol.*, **16**, 945–947.

Lane, N. S. (1967). *J. cell Biol.*, **35**, 421–434.

Lima-de-Faria, A. (1962). *Chromosoma*, **13**, 47–59.

Lima-de-Faria, A. and Moses, M. J. (1966). *J. cell Biol.*, **30**, 177–192.

Lima-de-Faria, A., Birnstiel, M. and Jaworska, H. (1969). *Genetics, Princeton*, Suppl. 61, 145–159.

Lockshin, R. A. (1966). *Science, N.Y.*, **154**, 775–776.

Macgregor, H. C. and Stebbings, H. (1970). *J. cell Sci.*, **6**, 431–449.

Mahowald, A. P. (1962). *J. exp. Zool.*, **151**, 201–216.

Mahowald, A. P. (1963a). *Expl Cell Res.*, **32**, 457–468.

Mahowald, A. P. (1963b). *Devl. Biol.*, **8**, 186–204.

Mahowald, A. P. (1968a). *J. cell Biol.*, **39**, 84a.

Mahowald, A. P. (1968b). *J. exp. Zool.*, **167**, 237–262.

Mahowald, A. P. (1971a). *J. exp. Zool.*, **176**, 329–344.

Mahowald, A. P. (1971b). *J. exp. Zool.*, **176**, 345–352.

Mahowald, A. P. (1971c). In *Origin and Continuity of Cell Organelles* (J. Reinert and H. Ursprung, eds), pp. 158–169. Springer-Verlag, New York and Heidelberg.

Mahowald, A. P. (1971d). *Z. Zellforsch. mikrosk. Anat.*, **118**, 162–167.

Mahowald, A. P. (1972). *J. Morph.*, (in press).

Mahowald, A. P. and Strassheim, J. M. (1970). *J. cell Biol.*, **45**, 306–320.

Mahowald, A. P. and Tiefert, M. (1970). *Wilhelm Roux Arch. EntwMech. Org.*, **165**, 8–25.

Mahowald, A. P. and Stoiber, D. L. (1971). (In preparation).

Matuszewski, B. (1968). *Chromosoma*, **25**, 429–469.

Melius, M. E., Jr. and Telfer, W. H. (1969). *J. Morph.*, **129**, 1–16.

Meng, C. (1968). *Wilhelm Roux Arch. EntwMech. Org.*, **161**, 162–208.

Meng, C. (1970). *Wilhelm Roux Arch. EntwMech. Org.*, **165**, 35–52.

Meyer, G. (1961). *Z. Zellforsch. mikrosk. Anat.*, **54**, 238–251.

Mohan, J. (1971). *J. Embryol. exp. Morph.*, **25**, 237–246.

Mohan, J. and Ritossa, F. M. (1970). *Devl. Biol.*, **22**, 495–512.

Moses, M. (1968). *A. Rev. Genet.*, **2**, 363–412.

Muckenthaler, F. A. and Mahowald, A. P. (1966). *J. cell Biol.*, **28**, 199–208.

Nath, V., Gupta, B. L. and Lal, B. (1958). *Q . Jl. microsc. Sci.*, **99**, 315–332.
Netzel, H. (1965). *Wilhelm Roux Arch. EntwMech. Org.*, **156**, 88–95.
Netzel, H. (1968). *Wilhelm Roux Arch. EntwMech. Org.*, **160**, 119–166.
Nicklas, R. B. (1959). *Chromosoma*, **10**, 301–336.
Nilsson, B. (1966). *Hereditas*, **56**, 396–398.
Nørrelung, A. (1968). *Int. Rev. Cytol.*, **23**, 113–186.
Okada, E. and Waddington, C. H. (1959). *J. Embryol. exp. Morph.*, **7**, 583–597.
Overton, J. and Raab, M. (1967). *Devl. Biol.*, **15**, 271–287.
Pan, M. L., Bell, W. J. and Telfer, W. H. (1969). *Science, N.Y.*, **165**, 393–394.
Panelius, S. (1968). *Chromosoma*, **23**, 333–345.
Petzelt, C. and Bier, K. (1970a). *Wilhelm Roux Arch. EntwMech. Org.*, **164**, 359–366.
Petzelt, C. and Bier, K. (1970b). *Wilhelm Roux Arch. EntwMech. Org.*, **164**, 341–358.
Pijnacker, L. P. (1966). *Experientia*, **22**, 158–159.
Pollack, S. B. and Telfer, W. H. (1969). *J. exp. Zool.*, **170**, 1–24.
Poulson, D. F. and Waterhouse, D. F. (1960). *Aust. J. biol. Sci.*, **13**, 541–567.
Quattropani, S. L. and Anderson, E. (1969). *Z. Zellforsch. mikrosk. Anat.*, **95**, 495–510.
Ramamurty, P. S. (1964). *Expl Cell Res.*, **33**, 601–605.
Ramamurty, P. S. (1968). *J. Insect Physiol.*, **14**, 1325–1330.
Raven, C. P. (1961). In *Oogenesis: the Storage of Developmental Information*. Pergamon Press, New York.
Revel, J. and Ito, S. (1967). In *Specificity of Cell Surfaces* (B. D. Davis and L. Warren, eds), pp. 211–234. Prentice-Hall, Englewood Cliffs, New Jersey, U.S.A.
Revel, J. P. and Karnovsky, M. J. (1967). *J. cell Biol.*, **33**, C7–C12.
Ribbert, D. and Bier, K. (1969). *Chromosoma*, **27**, 178–197.
Richards, A. G. and Brooks, M. A. (1958). *A. Rev. Ent.*, **3**, 37–56.
Ritossa, F. M., Atwood, K. C. and Spiegelman, S. (1966). *Genetics, N.Y.*, **54**, 819–834.
Roth, T. F. (1966). *Protoplasma*, **61**, 346–386.
Roth, T. F. and Porter, K. R. (1964). *J. cell Biol.*, **20**, 313–332.
Scheurer, R. (1969). *J. Insect Physiol.*, **15**, 1673–1682.
Schrader, F. and Leuchtenberger, C. (1952). *Expl Cell Res.*, **3**, 136–146.
Schultz, J. (1956). *Cold Spring Harb. Symp. quant. Biol.*, **21**, 307–328.
Sonnenblick, B. P. (1950). In *Biology of Drosophila* (M. Demerec, ed.), pp. 62–167. John Wiley, New York.
Sotelo, J. R. and Wettstein, R. (1964). *Chromosoma*, **15**, 389–415.
Stay, B. (1965). *J. cell Biol.*, **26**, 49–62.
Stebbings, H. (1971). *J. cell Sci.*, **8**, 111–125.
Stevens, B. J. and Swift, H. (1966). *J. cell Biol.*, **31**, 55–77.
Telfer, W. H. (1960). *Biol. Bull.*, **118**, 338–351.
Telfer, W. H. (1965). *A. Rev. Ent.*, **10**, 161–184.
Telfer, W. H. and Anderson, L. M. (1968). *Devl. Biol.*, **17**, 512–535.
Telfer, W. H. and Melius, M. E. (1963). *Am. Zool.*, **3**, 185–191.
Telfer, W. H. and Smith, D. S. (1970). In "Insect Ultrastructure", *Symp. R. ent. Soc. Lond. No. 5* (C. Neville, ed.), pp. 117–134. Blackwell Scientific Publications, Oxford, England.
Travaglini, E. C., Petrovic, J. and Schultz, J. (1968). *J. cell Biol.*, **39**, 136a.
Urbani, E. and Russo-Caio, S. (1964). *Rc. Ist. Sci. Camerino*, **5**, 19–50.
Vanderberg, J. P. (1963). *Biol. Bull.*, **125**, 556–575.
Vincent, W. S. and Miller, O. (eds) (1966). *The Nucleolus, its Structure and Function*. National Cancer Institute Monograph 23, Bethesda, Maryland, U.S.A.
von Kraft, A. (1960a). *Zool. Jb., Abt. Anat.*, **78**, 458–484.
von Kraft, A. (1960b). *Zool. Jb., Abt. Anat.*, **78**, 485–558.

Ward, R. T. (1962). *J. cell Biol.*, **14**, 309–341.
Wick, J. R. and Bonhag, P. F. (1955). *J. Morph.*, **96**, 31–60.
Wigglesworth, V. B. (1943). *Proc. R. Soc., Lond.*, **131**, 313–339.
Wolf, R. (1967). *Wilhelm Roux Arch. EntwMech. Org.*, **158**, 459–462.
Wright, T. R. F. (1970). *Adv. Genet.*, **15**, 261–395.
Yajima, H. (1960). *J. Embryol. exp. Morph.*, **8**, 198–215.
Yajima, H. (1964). *J. Embryol. exp. Morph.*, **12**, 89–100.
Zalokar, M. (1960). *Expl Cell Res.*, **19**, 184–186.
Zalokar, M. (1965). *Revue suisse Zool.*, **72**, 241–261.

2 | Development of Apterygote Insects

CZESLAW JURA

Zoology Department, Jagellonian University, Kraków, Poland

I. INTRODUCTION

The subclass Apterygota comprises about 3500 species of rather inconspicuous insects, to which much significance has been attached in phylogenetic speculation, particularly concerning the origin of Pterygota. Recently Apterygota have formed the focus of revived theoretical discussions by entomologists. More and more voices have been raised in support of a separation of entognathous apterygotes—Collembola, Protura, Diplura—from ectognathous ones—Thysanura, and even of removing the Entognatha from the class Insecta (compare Handschin, 1952; Remington, 1954; Paclt, 1954, 1956; Tuxen, 1959; Manton, 1964).

For embryologists it may be rather a secondary problem whether or not to call entognathous apterygotes Insecta. From the embryological point of view, the Apterygota as a group are extremely interesting, with many characteristics of a general interest. For example, within this group all modes of transition from total to purely superficial type of cleavage, a most striking feature of Pterygota embryogenesis, may be found.

The most fruitful period of apterygote embryology, initiated by Nicolet (1842), was the end of the nineteenth century. Since that time the Apterygota have almost been neglected. As a consequence, apterygote embryology remains essentially descriptive in nature. No studies have been made utilizing those biochemical, physiological or developmental genetic techniques which

49

have been successfully applied to pterygote embryology. Moreover, when reading published papers, one is struck by the fact that many are too poorly documented to be accepted without further study. Many statements should be verified. Moreover the four orders of Apterygota have been unevenly treated: studies have mainly concentrated on Collembola, while the embryology of the Protura is unknown.

In this survey, perforce limited to the descriptive aspects, we will emphasize the main points of existing controversies and offer suggestions for future investigations.

II. EMBRYOGENESIS OF ENTOGNATHOUS APTERYGOTA

A. Collembola

(1) Egg Organization

The eggs of Collembola are generally described as spherical, but flattened eggs have also been observed. They are minute, measuring 0·03–0·15 mm in diameter, pale yellow in colour, and the colour may change as the embryo develops. During the course of development, eggs increase in size and change

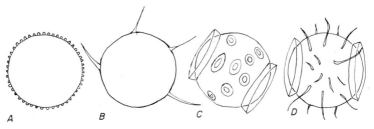

FIG. 1. Collembola eggs. A, *Isotoma grisea*; B, *Hypogastrura armata*; C, *Onychiurus armatus*; D, *Orchesella cinta*. (After Prowazek, 1900a; Tiegs, 1940; Handschin, 1952.)

their shapes from spherical to oval. At optimal temperatures collembolan eggs require days (*Folsomia candida*), or months (*Tetrodontophora bielanensis*) to hatch.

The egg, when laid, is covered by a chorion, the surface of which may be smooth, granular, conspicuously sculptured, or even furnished with long delicate spines (Fig. 1). With the exception of flattened eggs, the chorion ruptures at about the middle period of embryonic development. As a rule, micropyles are not present. A thin vitelline membrane has been noted in most species studied although Philiptschenko (1912a) failed to observe one in *Isotoma cinera*. During the course of embryonic life, embryos of Collembola produce under the vitelline membrane one to four additional noncellular membranes Subsection 4 p. (60). The eggs are deposited at the different seasons or throughout the year. The existence of regular diapause has not been established for Collembola eggs. Parthenogenesis occurs but is rare (Christiansen, 1964). Maturation and fertilization have not been studied.

(a) *Inner Egg Structure*. The eggs are centrolecital, rich in yolk, and do not evidence bilateral symmetry, a characteristic feature of Pterygota.

The cytoplasm of the egg presents the usual internal reticulum for the support of the yolk. At the periphery of the egg the yolk globules are much smaller and the cytoplasm more abundant. There is, however, no distinct

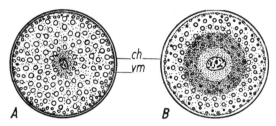

FIG. 2. Collembola eggs, inner structures. A, *Tetrodontophora bielanensis*, B, *Isotoma cinerea*. ch, chorion; vm, vitelline membrane. (After Jura, 1965; Philiptschenko, 1912*a*.)

layer of yolk free periplasm; such egg structure is also common among primitive pterygotes (*cf.* Anderson, 1972).

The egg nucleus lies in the centre of the egg and usually is surrounded by a small amount of cytoplasm; however in *Anurida maritima* (Claypole, 1898), and in *Isotoma cinerea* (Philiptschenko, 1912*a*), a large central mass of protoplasm surrounds the nucleus (Fig. 2).

(2) Cleavage

Early cleavage is total. Formerly the only exceptions to this were reported in *Anurophorus laricis* (Lemoine, 1883) and *Tetrodontophora bielanensis* (=*T. gigas*) (Heymons, 1896). More recent investigations, however, have shown beyond doubt that early cleavage of *Tetrodontophora* is in fact total (Jura, 1965), and only later becomes superficial. Moreover, as Lemoine did not study sectioned material, cleavage in *Anurophorus* should be reinvestigated.

In *T. bielanensis*, the species most recently studied (Jura, 1965), prior to cytoplasmic cleavage the zygotic nucleus undergoes two successive divisions, giving rise to four daughter nuclei. These four nuclei then migrate from the centre into opposite quarters of the egg. The egg flattens at one pole and subsequently at this pole two cleavage furrows appear (Fig. 3A–C). The furrows deepen, extend to the sides towards the opposite pole, and increasingly engirdle the egg. Thus four blastomeres of equal size become separated (Figs 3D, 4A). Later a third series of furrows appears at the level of the equator of the egg. After the four-cell stage, the synchrony of divisions is lost, and irregularity of form and inequality in size of the blastomeres increases during the next cleavage divisions. No cleavage cavity forms and the basal parts of adjacent blastomeres are adherent to one another (Fig. 4A).

The cleavage phenomena described above are similar to those of other Collembola studied. Early unequal holoblastic cleavage has been recorded in *Degeeria pruni*, *Achorutes tuberculatus* and *Anurophorus fimetarius* (Uljanin, 1875); *Sminthurus fuscus* (Lemoine, 1883); *Achorutes armatus* and *Tomocerus vulgaris* (Uzel, 1898a, b); *Anurida maritima* (Claypole, 1898, 1899; Folsom,

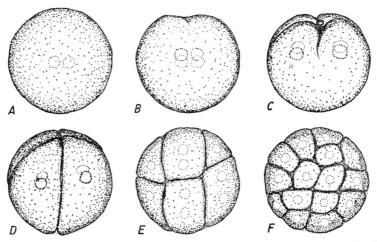

FIG. 3. *Tetrodontophora bielanensis*. Early developmental stages, surface view. A, freshly laid egg; B, four-daughter nuclei stage; C, beginning of cytoplasmic cleavage; D, four-cell stage; E, eight-cell stage; F, thirty-two-cell stage. (After Jura, 1965.)

1900); *Isotoma grisea* (Prowazek, 1900a, b); and in *I. cinerea* (Philiptschenko, 1912a, b).

In *Achorutes armatus*, according to Uzel (1898a), pronounced unequal cleavage occurs with the formation of micro- and macromeres. The presence of a cleavage cavity (Fig. 5A) has been noted by Uzel (1898a), Prowazek (1900a), and Philiptschenko (1912a).

(a) *Transition from Total to Superficial Cleavage and Blastoderm Formation.* In *Tetrodontophora bielanensis*, total cleavage of the egg lasts only until the eight-blastomere stage is reached (Jura, 1965). Subsequent cleavages do not involve the division of the whole yolk material; rather, new boundaries form at the inner ends of the blastomeres above the previous blastomere walls and some yolk, free of nuclei, becomes isolated in the centre of the egg (Fig. 4B). Thus the periblastula is formed and superficial cleavage is initiated. In sectioned material of the early periblastula stage, the blastomeres appear as irregular yolky pyramids surrounding the central undivided yolk mass (Fig. 4B).

In the transition from 16- to 32-, and then from 32- to 64-cell embryo, the blastomeres further diminish in size and again separate off at their bases, additional yolk thus increasing the central yolk mass. Meantime, the nucleus shifts from the centre of each blastomere towards its outer end. In this respect the movement of the nuclei toward the egg surface resembles the movement of the nuclei of Pterygota towards the egg periplasm at the time of

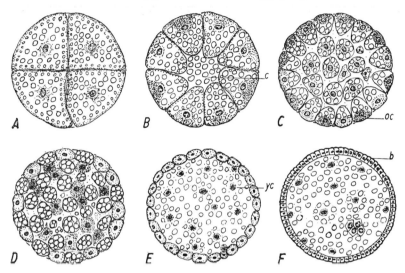

FIG. 4. *Tetrodontophora bielanensis*. Cleavage and blastoderm formation. A, four-cell stage; B, sixteen-cell stage (beginning of superficial cleavage); C–F, successive stages of blastoderm formation. b, mature blastoderm; c, central yolk mass; oc, outer-layer cell; yc, yolk cell. (After Jura, 1965.)

blastoderm formation, only the migration in Collembola takes place within the blastomeres.

At about the 64-cell stage, in *T. bielanensis*, new events occur, altering its morphological organization. Within the blastomeres, occasional radially directed mitoses may be encountered, and large polygonal, yolk filled cells begin to appear beneath the layer of pyramidal blastomeres. During the next developmental stages, both the cells of the outer layer as well as the cells occupying the egg interior undergo further cell divisions, and finally the whole uncleaved central yolk mass becomes divided into large polygonal cells (Fig. 4C).

Shortly after their formation, the inner large polygonal cells divide and become replaced by smaller ones, irregularly spherical, roughly of the same size as the cells of the outer layer. The condition of the blastomeres forming the outer layer also changes. The blastomeres lose the character of yolk pyramids, and become more spherical. Their nuclei, together with cytoplasm surrounding them, move from the centre to the periphery of the blastomeres. The embryo enters into early blastoderm stage.

Formation of the definitive blastoderm is preceded by the isolation of the superficial blastomeres from yolk globules. The yolk contained within the cells is released. This occurs simultaneously in all surface blastomeres. Subsequently, the egg is temporarily covered by loose cells devoid of yolk, separated by ball-like yolky structures (Fig. 4D), i.e. yolk globules isolated from

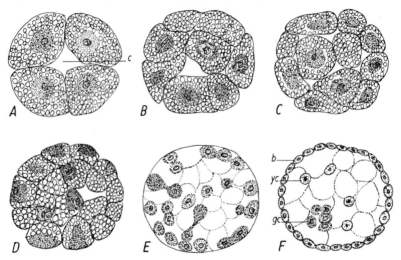

FIG. 5. *Isotoma cinerea*. Cleavage and blastoderm formation. A, eight-cell stage; B, sixteen-cell stage; C, thirty-two-cell stage; D, sixty-four-cell stage; E, peripheral migration of cleavage nuclei; F, early blastoderm stage. b, blastoderm; c, cleavage cavity; gc, germ cells; yc, yolk cell. (After Philiptschenko, 1912*a*.)

blastomeres and held within the plasmatic reticulum. As development progresses, those blastomeres devoid of yolk continue to multiply. Previously oval in shape, the blastomeres becomes columnar, and finally a superficial epithelium (=blastoderm) with the appearance of regularity is formed (Fig. 4): the embryo reaches a blastoderm stage, which in every respect is comparable to that of Pterygota.

The isolation of yolk globules from blastomeres forming the outer layer is accomplished by the same process going on in the egg interior. But there the process goes on asynchronally and takes more time. The inner cells, free of yolk, disperse loosely and unevenly between the yolk globules (Fig. 4F).

The transition from total to superficial cleavage and blastoderm formation, as described by Uljanin (1875) for podurids, Claypole (1898) for *Anurida maritima*, and Philiptschenko (1912*a*) for *Isotoma cinerea* (Fig. 5), does not essentially differ from that of *Tetrodontophora bielanensis*, described above. In *Tomocerus vulgaris*, however, certain temporal relationships are much altered.

According to Uzel (1898a) cleavage in *T. vulgaris* occurs much as in Crustacea and some Myriapoda. Cleavage starts with division of the nucleus, but it is not until the third or fourth division that the yolk also begins to divide. At the 32-cell stage, the walls of the large yolky cells disappear, and some of the nuclei pass to the periphery of the egg, where through the tangential divisions of the nuclei, the blastoderm is completed. Nevertheless, in *T. vulgaris*, as in other Collembola, the cleavage period leads to the formation of an embryo composed of two kinds of cells: the so-called "blastodermal cells" forming the superficial epithelium, and so-called "yolk cells" singly dispersed within the yolk material. The cells of the outer layer, during the whole period of blastoderm formation, may contribute to the increase in yolk cell number (Philiptschenko, 1912a; Jura, 1965). On the other hand, the yolk cells may contribute to the formation of blastoderm (Philiptschenko, 1912a). But neither process is a frequent or regular phenomenon. The question of interpretation of the processes leading to this end result now arises.

Claypole (1898), and Jura (1966), both assuming that the yolk cells contribute to the formation of the midgut epithelium of the collembolan embryo, interpret the processes leading to the blastoderm stage as gastrulation. But Philiptschenko (1912a) reserves the term "gastrulation" for the stage when inner layer formation occurs. Philiptschenko homologizes the blastoderm stage of Collembola with the blastula of other animals. According to Philiptschenko the cells left behind in the yolk during blastoderm formation function in Collembola exclusively as vitellophages. The question will be raised again in the section dealing with midgut formation.

(3) *Blastoderm Differentiation*

The mature blastoderm of the Collembola embryo is of uniform thickness and fairly sharply delimited from the underlying yolk. The blastoderm stage is of short duration. Further changes lead to the differentiation of the original blastoderm into two different portions. At one pole of the egg the blastodermal cells become taller. In consequence, within the blastoderm two regions become distinguishable: a region built of larger cells, representing material for the future so-called "dorsal organ" (Fig. 6A), and a region of smaller cells, destined to give rise to the future embryonic rudiment (germ band) and the embryonic membrane.

(a) *Dorsal Organ*. Formation of a dorsal organ has been observed in all Collembola studied to date, but the time of its appearance may vary somewhat. In *Tetrodontophora bielanensis*, according to Jura (1965, 1967a), its formation really represents the first step of blastoderm differentiation (Fig. 6). The same seems to be true for *Hypogastrura armata* (Tiegs, 1941). But in *Sminthurus fuscus* (Lemoine, 1883), *Anurida maritima* (Claypole, 1898), and *Isotoma cinerea* (Philiptschenko, 1912a), differentiation of the dorsal organ is delayed until the formation of the inner layer.

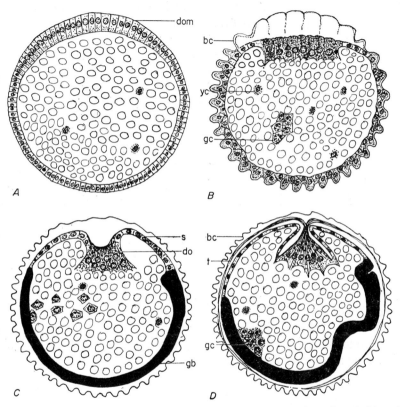

FIG. 6. *Tetrodontophora bielanensis*. Successive stages of dorsal organ formation. A, blastoderm differentiation; B, formation of blastodermic cuticle and anlage of the dorsal organ; C, sinking of the dorsal organ into the yolk; D, mature dorsal organ stage. bc, blastodermic cuticle; do, dorsal organ; dom, dorsal organ material; gb, germ band; gc, germ cells; s, serosa; t, tendrils; yc, yolk cell. (After Jura, 1967b.)

Owing to the minute size of the embryos of Collembola, difficulty has been experienced in making accurate observations on the origin of the dorsal organ. In three works only (Claypole, 1898; Philiptschenko, 1912a; Jura, 1967b) have actual sections been employed for the purpose, and these authors are in agreement as to the main points of dorsal organ differentiation.

The dorsal organ arises from a large group of blastodermal cells occupying an antero-dorsal position in relation to the future larva (Figs 6, 7, 8, 9, 12).

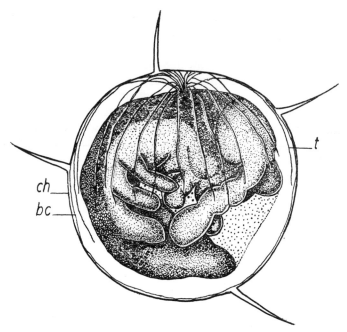

FIG. 7. *Hypogastrura armata*. Mature dorsal organ stage. bc, blastodermic cuticle; ch, chorion; t, tendril. (After Tiegs, 1941.)

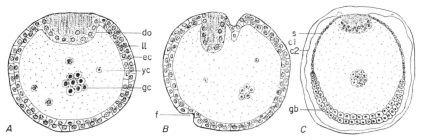

FIG. 8. *Isotoma cinerea*. A, two-layered stage; B, development of meridional furrow, longitudinal section; C, germ band formation stage, cross section of posterior end. c1, blastodermic cuticle; c2, second cuticle; do, dorsal organ; ec, ectoderm; f, meridional furrow; gb, germ band; gc, germ cells; ll, lower (inner) layer; s, serosa; yc, yolk cell. (After Philiptschenko, 1912a.)

At this pole the blastodermal cells become taller (Fig. 6A). As the cells destined for the dorsal organ enlarge, their nuclei also enlarge. These cells, unlike the rest of the blastodermal cells, undergo no further divisions. During the next step of development the whole material progressively invaginates into the underlying yolk (Figs 6B, 8).

The external surface area of the dorsal organ, invaginating into the yolk, becomes much reduced as a result of contraction of the outer portions of its cells. The neighbouring cells of the blastoderm fold and close around the dorsal organ, leaving only a narrow opening above its centre, and the dorsal organ assumes the shape of a mushroom (Fig. 6C, D).

At the time when the stomodaeal invagination is appearing, remarkable delicate tendrils begin to grow out from the external surface of the dorsal organ, and start to penetrate through the opening within the already differentiated embryonic membrane (Figs 6D, 7). Soon the tendrils invest the embryo.

The mature dorsal organ has a typical glandular appearance. The tendrils, described above, are the visible product of the dorsal organ secretory function (Tiegs, 1941; Jura, 1967*b*). In *Tetrodontophora bielanensis* (Jura, 1967*b*), in addition to tendrils, the dorsal organ produces large quantities of fluid which accumulates around the embryo. In *Anurida maritima* (Claypole, 1898) and in *Isotoma cinera* (Philiptschenko, 1912*a*), only short tendrils grow out from the dorsal organ. Philiptschenko postulated that the tendrils represent the outer ends of cells, drawn out and elongated, and not secretory products of the dorsal organ. The dorsal organ is a transitory structure in Collembola, and degenerates at the end of embryonic life. During blastokinesis it assumes its comparatively largest size and highest activity. After blastokinesis it ceases to produce both tendrils and fluid. In *T. bielanensis* (Jura, 1967*b*) the tendrils may persist until the end of development, but the fluid diminishes in quantity as the embryo enlarges. In *Hypogastrura armata* (Tiegs, 1941) the tendrils are no longer to be seen after degeneration of the dorsal organ.

The function of the dorsal organ is not clear. Jura (1967*b*) has tested experimentally the function of the dorsal organ in *T. bielanensis*. If the material destined for the dorsal organ, or the mature dorsal organ itself, are damaged by thermocautery, blastokinesis does not occur. The rigidity of yolk material appears to be much reduced, the embryo does not change its volume and shape, and the chorion does not rupture. As a consequence, morphogenetic processes become disturbed and a kind of monster develops which does not hatch. Philiptschenko (1912*a*) proposed that the tendrils of the dorsal organ are a means whereby the embryo attaches itself to the investing cuticle. Slifer (1938) suggested that it may be a water-absorbing organ, and this was supported by Tiegs (1941). Jura's experimental work strongly suggests that this organ is engaged in yolk utilization, which produces tendrils and the fluid surrounding the embryo.

(b) *Formation of Germ Anlagen.* As the dorsal organ forms, the rest of the blastoderm differentiates into a germ anlage (embryonic rudiment) and an embryonic membrane.

The germ anlage arises by a ventral thickening of blastoderm. The blastodermal cells destined to give rise to the embryo proper gradually become columnar, and the germ anlage appears in form of a belt at the pole opposite to the dorsal organ (Figs 6C, 9A). During further development, mitotic activity becomes restricted to this area.

Formation of the germ anlage by the ventral thickening of the blastoderm is a familiar process in the development of all Insecta. It is noteworthy that in Collembola the germ anlage when formed is relatively large, its head and tail ends nearly meeting the dorsal organ.

(c) *Embryonic Membrane.* The cells of the blastoderm which occupy the area between the dorsal organ and embryonic primordium become flattened

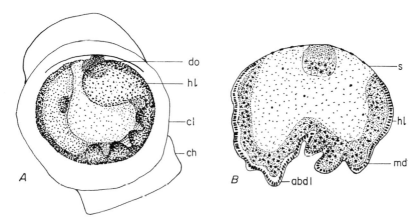

Fig. 9. *Isotoma cinerea.* A, advanced germ band stage, surface view; B, beginning of blastokinesis, longitudinal section. abd 1, first abdominal segment; c 1, blastodermic cuticle; ch, chorion; do, dorsal organ; hl, head lobes; md, mandible; s, serosa. (After Philiptschenko, 1912*a*.)

and thinner and remain one-layered (Figs 6A, C, D; 8C; 9B). This blastoderm region will form a provisional dorso-lateral body wall (embryonic membrane) for the developing embryo. Since the embryonic membrane in Collembola is exclusively derived from original blastoderm it should be called the serosa.

During the invagination of the germ band into the yolk, the serosa spreads well down over the anterior and posterior poles, but the ventral surface of the embryo is never covered by this cellular layer. During the final stage of development the cells of serosa are gradually replaced by ectodermal cells (Fig. 15E–F) proliferating from the edges of the embryonic rudiment (Philiptschenko, 1912*a*; Jura, 1965). But Wheeler (1893), based on his studies on *Anurida maritima,* postulated transformation of "serosa cells" into definitive epithelium, assuming that these represent ectoderm. Wheeler's conclusion may be the inevitable consequence of his exclusively external observations.

(4) Protective Layers Produced by the Embryo

During the course of embryonic development, in all Collembola hitherto studied there are formed one to four cuticular envelopes. These noncellular membranes may be secreted by the embryo before blastoderm differentiation, or later.

Lemoine (1883) was the first to describe the production, by the collembolan embryo, of protective layers in addition to the chorion and vitelline membrane. According to Lemoine the first membrane appears shortly after formation of the blastoderm. He considered it to be cellular, formed of many cells identical in origin with blastodermal cells, and called it the "amniotic membrane". The membrane is connected with the dorsal organ by an "amniotic ampula", and is peculiar in its behaviour. It possesses great power of expansion and contraction, increasing the size of the egg. The second sheet appears later, and is noncellular. As no sections were made, Lemoine's observations concerning the origin of the first membrane seem somewhat vague and unsatisfactory. The secretion of the cuticle on the outer surface of the blastoderm (blastodermic cuticle) has recently been studied in detail by Jura (1965, 1967*b*).

According to Jura, in *Tetrodontophora bielanensis*, every blastodermal cell contributes to the formation of the cuticle, including those cells giving rise to the dorsal organ. The processes are as follows. Shortly after reaching the mature blastoderm stage, the outer regions of the blastodermal cells become transparent and homogeneous and coagulate into a layer closely adhering to the blastodermal cells. Loosening of this homogeneous layer is initiated at the pole occupied by the cells destined for the future dorsal organ (Fig. 6B). Before that occurs, the blastoderm, together with cuticle adhering to it, becomes regularly wrinkled into the folds, then the blastomeres smooth out, while the newly formed cuticle remains wrinkled for a long period of time (until the chorion ruptures). The separated cuticle becomes loosely situated between vitelline membrane and blastoderm (Fig. 6C). It is within the space enclosed by this cuticle and the embryo that the tendrils and fluid products of the dorsal organ are later found.

Secretion of the blastodermic cuticle has been noted in *Degeeria pruni*, *Achorutes tuberculatus*, and *Anurophorus fimetarius* (Uljanin, 1875); *Macrotoma plumbea* (Sommer, 1885); *Anurida maritima* (Ryder, 1886; Wheeler, 1893; Claypole, 1898); *M. vulgaris* (Uzel, 1898*a*); *Isotoma grisea* (Prowazek, 1900*a*); *Isotoma cinerea* (Philiptschenko, 1912*a*); *Hypogastrura armata*, *Pseudosinella alba*, *Sminthurus viridis* (Tiegs, 1941); *Orchesella cinta* (Sedlag, 1951/1952); *Neanura muscorum*, *O. cinta*, *I. cinerea* (Bretfeld, 1963).

Secretion of a second, additional cuticular membrane, appearing at germ band stage or later, has been observed in *A. maritima* (Claypole, 1898); *I. cinerea* (Philiptschenko, 1912a); *H. armata, P. alba, Sminthurus viridis* (Tiegs, 1941). Bretfeld (1963) has observed two additional successively appearing cuticles in *I. cinerea* and *O. cinta*, and three in *N. muscorum*.

Coagulated fluid appearing between the first and second cuticular membranes has been noted by Tiegs (1941) in *H. armata*. The connection of the dorsal organ, by means of tendrils, with the second cuticle was assumed by Claypole (1898) for *A. maritima*, and Philiptschenko (1912a) for *I. cinerea* (Fig. 8D). The connection is not present in *H. armata, P. alba*, nor *S. viridis*, the species studied by Tiegs (1941).

It is generally accepted that the cuticles, formed after the rupture of the chorion, function as an egg shell, but nothing is actually known as to their permeability to water or air.

(5) *Inner Layer Formation*

The origin of the inner layer in Collembola embryos has not been studied in detail. Its formation occurs at blastoderm stage, or later, when the germ anlage is already formed.

In the first instance, dipolar (*Degeeria pruni*, Uljanin, 1875) or multipolar (*Anurida maritima*, Claypole, 1898; *Isotoma cinerea*, Philiptschenko, 1912a)

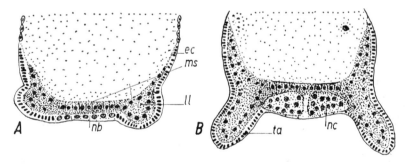

FIG. 10. *Isotoma cinerea.* Cross section through thoracic part of germ band. A, at early and B, at middle period of appendages differentiation stage. ec, ectoderm; ll, lower (inner) layer; ms, middle strand of lower layer; nb, neuroblasts; nc, nerve cord; ta, thoracic appendage. (After Philiptschenko, 1912a.)

division of blastodermal cells gives rise to a complete second layer of cells interior to the first (Fig. 8A, B). Later the inner layer becomes limited to the germ band only (Fig. 8C) by migration of cells (Philiptschenko, 1912a), or by a combination of migration and disintegration (Claypole, 1898).

In the second instance (*Tetrodontophora bielanensis*, Jura, 1965) the inner layer appears at the early germ anlage stage and is restricted to the germ band. The germ anlage, initially one-layered, becomes two-layered as the result of division and migration of the cells of its outer layer.

There is disagreement as to the interpretation of the morphogenetic value of the inner layer in Collembola. According to Claypole (1898) and Jura (1965, 1966) the inner layer in Collembola gives rise exclusively to the organs which are usually regarded as mesodermal. However Uljanin (1875) derived endoderm cells in *Degeeria pruni* out of the inner layer while Philiptschenko (1912*a*, *b*) contended that in *I. cinerea* the median part of the lower layer (Fig. 10A) gives rise to both endoderm and mesoderm (see also: Midgut Formation).

(6) Meridional Furrow

In the egg of *Isotoma cinerea* (Philiptschenko, 1912*a*), after the blastodermic cuticle and lower layer have formed, a deep meridional furrow (Fig. 8B) develops around the embryo, passing behind the dorsal organ. As this furrow deepens, the dorsal organ is somewhat swung out of position, the chorion then ruptures, and the embryo expands, causing the furrow to smooth out. The role of the furrow in embryogenesis is not clear.

(7) Yolk System

As we have already mentioned, the yolk system in Collembola is much like that in the Pterygota. It is not known whether yolk material in Collembola serves exclusively as a source of nutrient for the developing embryo, or constitutes also a significant morphogenetic agent comparable to that of most Pterygota (*cf.* Counce, 1961, 1972).

Jura (1967*b*) has noted in *Tetrodontophora bielanensis* some influence of the dorsal organ on the yolk behaviour. When this organ is absent, the yolk material at the second half of development does not change its shape, while in control insects the yolk material becomes croissant-like at this stage. Moreover, as we have described in Subsection 3(a) p. 58, the rigidity of yolk material in embryos lacking the dorsal organ appears to be much reduced.

Secondary yolk cleavage, a well known phenomenon in Pterygote embryogenesis, has been noted in *Macrotoma vulgaris* by Uzel (1898*a*), and in *T. bielanensis* by Jura (1965), and figured by Uljanin (1875) in *Degeeria pruni*.

In *T. bielanensis* secondary yolk cleavage is very obvious at the time the dorsal organ is being formed. The yolk material, previously syncytial in character, divides into subspherical blocks. But later, at the period when the germ anlage first becomes apparent, the yolky blocks again disintegrate.

(a) *Yolk Cells.* The yolk cells of Collembola differ somewhat in mode of origin from those of Pterygota (see Anderson, 1972), as they are derived from superficial blastomeres at an early cleavage stage (see above). They are, however, thought to be primary yolk cells because their differentiation takes place before the blastoderm forms. They are polynuclear in origin, and when formed do not differ from blastomeres of the outer layer. Located in the egg interior, before the blastoderm stage, the yolk cells increase considerably in number by mitotic divisions.

For a discussion concerning the morphogenetic role of yolk cells in collembolan embryogenesis, see Section IIA and Subsection (13), p. 72, below.

(8) Germ Band Segmentation and Development of External Form of the Embryo

Segmentation of germ band begins early. The first indication of germ band differentiation in Collembola is the appearance of the head lobes (cephalic lobes): the region bearing the eyes, labrum, mouth, and antennae (Figs 9, 12). Then the gnathal segments and the first thoracic segment are laid down in succession. The remainder of the body, especially that part destined for the abdomen, does not become segmented until later (Fig. 9A).

The metamerism of the body first becomes apparent in the transversely divided mesoderm, then in the developing appendages, and finally in transverse grooves formed in ectoderm.

The appendage rudiments may appear almost at once at the level of different segments, as in *Anurida maritima* (Claypole, 1898), or successively from the head backwards, as more frequently occurs.

(a) *The Head.* According to most authors (Uljanin, 1875; Lemoine, 1883; Ryder, 1886; Wheeler, 1893; Claypole, 1898; Prowazek, 1900a; Philiptschenko, 1912a, b; Hoffmann, 1911) six segments make up the collembolan head. These are:

(1) The preantennal segment (optic, ocular or labral) devoid of appendages.
(2) The antennary segment.
(3) The intercalary segment with vestigial appendages, or devoid of appendages.
(4) Mandibular segment.
(5) Maxillary I.
(6) Maxillary II.

Folsom (1900) alone proposes the presence of an additional head segment in the gnathal region of *Anurida maritima*. He maintains that a nerve ganglion exists (Fig. 11) between the mandibular and the maxillary ganglion together with the corresponding head segment, having a pair of appendages. Later authors disagree with Folsom and consider that the appendages observed by him represent solely the lateral processes of the developing hypopharynx (e.g. Philiptschenko, 1912a).

The preantennal region presents the usual difficulties in interpretation (compare Anderson, 1972). Pairs of coelomic sacs, pairs of appendages, together with triple division of a brain into proto-, deuto- and tritocerebral lobes (corresponding to the first three cephalic segments) are usually taken as evidence of a corresponding metamerism of the protocephalic portion of the arthropod head. In Collembola the brain develops out of three successive portions (Subsection 10, p. 69). But, as in all other insects, the head lobes (protocephalon) do not show any external sign of segmentation. Preantennal appendages have never been noted. Coelomic sacs are totally lacking in

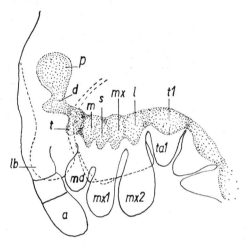

Fig. 11. *Anurida maritima*. Paramedian section through cephalic nervous system, advanced embryo. a, antenna; d, deutocerebrum; l, ganglion of second maxilla; lb, labrum; m, ganglion of mandible; md, mandible; mx, ganglion of first maxilla; mx1, maxilla I; mx2, maxilla II; p, protocerebrum; s, ganglion of superlingua; t, tritocerebrum; t1, ganglion of first thoracic segment; ta1, first thoracic appendage. (After Folsom, 1900.)

collembolan embryos; even lateral mesodermic somites are absent in the preantennal portions of the head (Subsection 11, p. 70). At present it is impossible to define clearly what lies in front of the antennal segment in Collembola.

On the other hand, the composition of the gnathocephalic region of the head is quite clear. The intercalary segment is early incorporated in the head lobes, the two forming the protocephalon. Later the gnathal segments, bearing three pairs of appendages, are incorporated with the protocephalon to form the definitive head.

As generally accepted, the labrum arises as an evagination anterior to and distant from the bases of the antennae (Fig. 12). At no period does it give evidence of a paired origin (Wheeler, 1893; Claypole, 1898; Folsom, 1900; Philiptschenko, 1912a; Haget and Garaudy, 1964). The exception was made by Lemoine (1883) who postulated that in *Sminthurus fuscus* and *Anurophorus laricis* paired rudiments give rise to the labrum. Nevertheless in his figures they appear to be merely lobes of a single large labral rudiment.

At the same time as the labral anlage appears, but behind it, invagination of the stomodaeum occurs, assuming the form of a crescent-like groove (Fig. 12).

The lingua of the hypopharynx originates as a median unpaired outgrowth from the sternum between the first maxillae, and the superlinguae, from

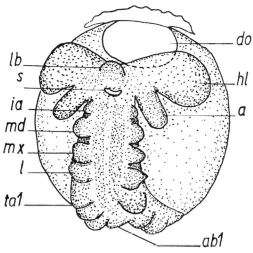

Fig. 12. *Anurida maritima*. Embryo shortly before blastokinesis, surface view. a, antenna; ab1, first abdominal appendage; do, dorsal organ; hl, head lobe; ia, intercalary appendage; l, labium; lb, labrum; md, mandible; mx, maxilla; s, stomodaeum; ta1, first thoracic appendage. (After Haget and Garaudy, 1964.)

paired anlagen appearing between mandibles (Uzel, 1898*a*; Folsom, 1900; Hoffmann, 1911; Philiptschenko, 1912*a*).

The principal mouth parts, the mandibles and maxillae, in adults of Collembola, are hidden in a cavity and covered by the labrum (entognathy). The embryonic basis of entognathy have been studied by Claypole (1898), Folsom (1900), and Garaudy (1967), for *Anurida maritima*, and by Philiptschenko (1912*a*) for *Isotoma cinerea*. Folsom, Garaudy, and Philiptschenko are in agreement that entognathy comes about through the formation of two independent folds (*plicae orales*) appearing on each side of the head in the region of the mandibles, and proceeding forward and backward to the fundaments of the labrum and labium (Fig. 14B). In this way, the folds become united and enclose a single common cavity. According to Claypole, however, *plicae orales* develop from intercalary appendages, but this view has not been generally accepted.

(b) *The Abdomen.* In Collembola six abdominal segments are present, the terminal anus-bearing segment being the sixth. Segmentation of the abdominal part of germ band starts much later than in the head and thorax. The four anterior segments appear first, and then the posterior portion of abdomen also becomes segmented.

(c) *The Appendages.* The appendages appear as lateroventral lobe- or papilla-like evaginations of the germ band (Figs 9, 10, 12, 13). During the

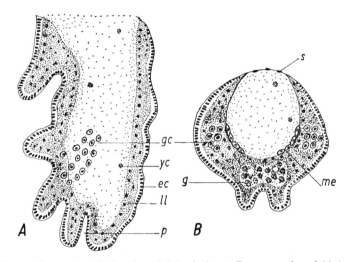

FIG. 13. *Isotoma cinerea.* A, sagittal section of abdominal part; B, cross section of third abdominal segment. Advanced embryos. ec, ectoderm, g, ganglion, gc, germ cell; ll, lower (inner) layer; me, midgut epithelium; p, proctodaeum; s, serosa; yc, yolk cell. (After Philiptschenko, 1912a.)

early period of their formation the most conspicuous appendages are the antennae, but later, thoracic appendages become more distinct (Fig. 14).

The antennae develop from the posterior boundaries of the procephalic lobes, more lateral than the other paired appendage fundaments, and post-orally. Before hatching of the larva they assume a preoral position. Such migration of the antennae is characteristic for all insects. The intercalary appendages and three pairs of mouth appendages are next in succession.

The formation of transient, vestigial premandibular appendages (Fig. 12) in embryonic development of Collembola has been noted by several authors (Wheeler, 1893; Claypole, 1898; Folsom, 1900; Hoffmann, 1911; Philip-tschenko, 1912a; Bretfeld, 1963; Haget and Garaudy, 1964).

The rudiments of the mandibles appear nearer to the median plane of the head part of the germ band than the antennae, and show no trace of lobation (Fig. 12).

The rudiments of maxillae I appear next after those of the mandibles. Early bifurcation of the maxillae I into the anlagen of *lobus externus* and *lobus internus* was noted by Folsom (1900), Hoffmann (1911), and Philiptschenko (1912*a*).

The maxillae II are the last of the gnathal appendages to differentiate. They show a median fusion to form a lower lip, as in all insects.

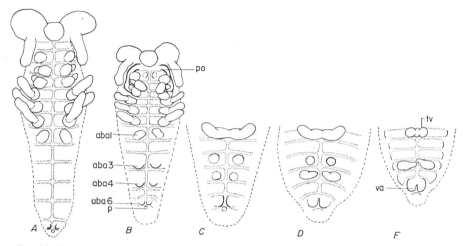

FIG. 14. *Anurida maritima*. Diagrams of relation of somites to the appendages at successive developmental stages. abahe 1, 3, 4, 6, anlagen of appendages of the equivalent abdominal segments; p, proctodaeum; po, plica oralis; tv, tubus ventralis; va, valvules anales. (After Garaudy, 1967.)

Much attention has been paid to the appendages appearing on the abdominal part of the embryo. The data are controversial. Ryder (1886) postulated six pairs of abdominal appendages in *Anurida maritima*; however, according to Wheeler (1893) and Claypole (1898), in this species only the first four abdominal segments bear paired appendages, and the same is claimed for *Anurophorus laricis* and *Sminthurus fuscus* by Lemoine (1883). But Uzel (1898*a*) in *Macrotoma vulgaris*, Philiptschenko (1912*a*) in *Isotoma cinerea*, and Bretfeld (1963) in *Orchesella cinta* and *Neanura muscorum*, have observed only three pairs of abdominal appendages. According to the latter authors, a pair of buds develop on the first abdominal segment which later are modified into the *tubus ventralis* (Fig. 14). The second segment is devoid of appendages while the third bears the *tenaculum*, and the fourth the *furcula*. Recently Garaudy (1967) has reinvestigated embryonic development of *Anurida maritima*. She has generally accepted the point of view of Uzel, Philiptschenko, and of Bretfeld, but has interpreted the anal valves (Fig. 14) as developing from paired appendage-like anlagen of the sixth abdominal segment.

The development of the tenaculum and furcula from paired anlagen in Collembola was noted as early as 1872 by Packard and in 1875 by Uljanin.

(9) Blastokinesis

Blastokinesis is a regular process in development of Collembola, and was noted by pioneers in Collembola embryology (Nicolet, 1842; Uljanin, 1875; Barrois, 1879). Blastokinesis may occur early at the beginning of germ band segmentation, or later when appendages are already well differentiated. In both cases it is a comparatively simple process, involving neither rotation nor revolution. [Anderson (1972) has proposed that the term *blastokinesis* be limited to active movements of the embryo relative to the yolk. However, the term has been widely used to cover a variety of changes in position of the embryo with regard to the yolk, and we retain it here in this more general sense.)]

During the early period of blastokinesis, the ventral surface of the embryo between the first maxillary segment and first abdominal segment becomes somewhat flattened and then begins to push into the yolk (Figs 6D, 9B). Prior to this, the germ band lies on the surface of the yolk material with its ventral part turned outwards. As a result of blastokinesis the embryo reverses its position, bringing the dorsal side to the surface (Fig. 15). The anterior and posterior parts of germ band come to lie nearly parallel, and the embryo becomes restricted to less than one half of the circumference of the egg. The embryo retains this position until emergence.

Blastokinesis apparently brings the dorsal surface of the embryo into a spatially and mechanically more favourable position. As we have already mentioned, if there is no blastokinesis the normal course of morphogenesis is distorted and the embryo is incapable of hatching.

(10) Ectodermal Derivates

The differentiation of the outer layer in Collembola is much the same as in other insects.

(a) *Nervous System.* In its fundamental features the development of the nervous system in Collembola, including origin of ganglia from neuroblasts, formation of brain, formation of suboesophageal ganglion, and development of ventral nerve cord, is identical with that of Pterygota.

The neuroblasts differentiate within the ectoderm at a comparatively early stage of embryonic life, shortly after the inner layer is formed (Fig. 10A). When differentiated, as in all insects, they form a pair of median thickenings (Figs 10B, 13B). The neural groove was noted by Uzel (1898a) in *Macrotoma vulgaris*, Prowazek (1900a) in *Isotoma grisea*, and figured by Philiptschenko (1912a) for *I. cinerea*.

The brain anlage may be readily seen to have three successive portions: proto-, deuto- and tritocerebrum. Of the brain segments, the tritocerebrum is the smallest and is postoral in position. In *Anurida maritima* (Claypole, 1898) the optic lobes form a large part of the young protocerebrum. The brain is fully formed during the second half of the developmental period, when the ganglia of three gnathal segments also fuse into the definitive suboesophageal ganglion.

Folsom (1900) postulated four pairs of ganglia (Fig. 11) in the gnathal region of *A. maritima*. This statement, however, as we have already mentioned (Subsection 8(a), p. 63), has not been accepted.

Claypole (1898) observed distinct pairs of ganglia in each abdominal segment of the early embryo of *A. maritima*, none however were found by Philiptschenko (1912*a*) in the sixth abdominal segment of *I. cinerea*. Moreover, according to Philiptschenko, in the fifth abdominal segment, ganglia are indicated only by presence of ephemeral neuroblasts. The abdominal ganglia in both species fuse early with thoracic ganglia to form a compound mass.

An anlage of a sympathetic system was reported by Claypole (1898) in *Anurida maritima*.

(b) *Fore and Hind Gut*. These two parts of the alimentary system arise, as in all insects, by invagination of ectoderm at early germ band differentiation stage (Fig. 15).

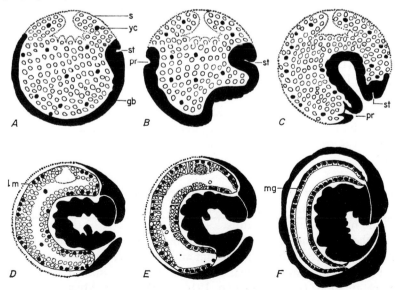

FIG. 15. *Tetrodontophora bielanensis*. Successive stages of alimentary system formation, sagittal sections. gb, germ band; lm, limiting membrane; mg, midgut; pr, proctodaeum; s, serosa; st, stomodaeum; yc, yolk cell. (After Jura, 1966.)

Both the stomo- and proctodaeum may have an inductive influence on development of midgut: at the tips of the stomo- and proctodaeum the formation of the definite wall of mesenteron proceeds more rapidly (Jura, 1966).

(c) *The Tracheae*. Tracheae are lacking in most members of this group (small forms respire through the body walls); when present nothing is known about their embryogenesis. It is noteworthy that in *Anurida maritima*, Claypole (1898) reported no invaginations that represent even the rudiments of a tracheal system. However, she did note at the bases of the legs and at different levels of the abdomen, large unicellular glands that, according to her, may have some relation to tracheal openings. This statement needs further investigation.

(11) Mesodermal Derivatives

The inner germ layer, from its first appearance, consists of several cell layers over much of its length. Later, it undergoes differentiation into a pair of thick irregular cords, which lie along the ventro-lateral margins of the germ band, and a thin median irregular sheath, situated between the cords on the floor of the germ band (Fig. 10A) and broadened and thickened at both ends. During the subsequent developmental stages the lateral cords undergo segmentation, and somites form. In *Isotoma cinerea* (Philiptschenko, 1912*a*, *b*), the species most closely studied in this respect, only 13 pairs of somites appear. Lateral mesodermic somites are apparently lacking in the first head and in the sixth abdominal segments. The premandibular (intercalary) somites are vestigial but clearly visible. Coelomic cavities are totally lacking in *I. cinerea* (Philiptschenko, 1912*a*), and in *Tetrodontophora bielanensis* (Jura, 1965, 1966, 1967*a*). Hoffmann (1911), however, observed coelomic cavities in the intercalary somites of *Tomocerus vulgaris* embryos, and Claypole (1898) postulated the presence of coelomic cavities in *Anurida maritima*, although they were not clearly marked in all segments. She also noted the curious fact that there was greater reduction in the coelomic space in the male than in the female.

(a) *Differentiation of Somites*. The somites of Collembola embryos differentiate in a similar way as in Pterygota (see Anderson, 1972).

(i) The musculature. The muscles of the main body of the embryo, and those of the appendages, arise from the somatic portion of the mesoderm.

The musculature of the stomodaeum and proctodaeum develops from the preoral and postoral mesodermal cells, situated in the immediate vicinity of these invaginations (Philiptschenko, 1912*a*; Jura, 1966). Musculature of the midgut arises from the splanchnic part of corresponding somites. The formation of the muscular coat of midgut proceeds more slowly on the dorsal side of the midgut than on the ventral one. At first splanchnic mesodermal cells are largely concentrated along the ventral half of the midgut, thereafter these cells begin to spread more evenly over the midgut wall (Jura, 1966).

(ii) Fat body. The fat body is derived from the median somatic wall of somites (Philiptschenko, 1912a).

(iii) Circulatory system. Little is known concerning development of the circulatory system. According to Philiptschenko (1912a) the cardioblasts develop in *Isotoma cinerea* at a comparatively late embryonic period. They appear shortly before dorsal closure, laterodorsally, on both sides of the embryo where splanchnic and somatic mesodermal cells meet.

(iv) Body cavity. Formation of the definitive body cavity in Collembola remains an open question. In Pterygota the epineural sinus becomes enlarged and forms the definitive body cavity. With the conversion of the walls of coelomic sacs into musculature, the coelomic cavities also integrate with the epineural sinus.

Philiptschenko (1912a) failed to find an epineural sinus in *Isotoma cinerea*. Whether the absence of an epineural sinus is characteristic for Collembola is not known. Coelomic cavities, as we have already mentioned (Section 11), are absent.

(v) Tubular head glands. The tubular head glands of Collembola develop exclusively from the labial mesoderm except for a portion of the ducts which are ectodermal (Philiptschenko, 1912a). They appear in the labial segment at the level of the nerve ganglia as little glandular vesicles; later an ectodermal connection with them is established. According to Philiptschenko these glandular structures appear to be homologous with nephridial head glands in certain other Arthropoda.

(12) Germ Cells and Gonad Formation

(a) *Germ Cells.* In collembolan eggs, no visible germ cell determinants have been detected. Nothing is known as to the factors operative in determining whether a given cell becomes a germ cell or remains as a part of soma. Nevertheless, early differentiation of germ cell primordia in Collembola seems to be a general phenomenon.

In *Isotoma cinerea* (Philiptschenko, 1912a) germ cells appear at the 16- or 32-cell stage. In *Tetrodontophora bielanesis* (Jura, 1967a), and *Anurida maritima* (Garaudy-Tamarelle, 1969), the germ cells originate at about the 64-cell stage from 2–5 superficial blastomeres, which are the first ones to begin dividing tangentially.

After their differentiation, the germ cells shift into the yolk, and multiply mitotically. Until the blastoderm stage the germ cells superficially do not differ from other cells (yolk cells) localized within the yolk. When the mature blastoderm stage is reached, germ cells accumulate at the centre of the yolk and form a cluster (Figs 5F, 6B, 8). Now they appear as large polygonal cells, differing from yolk cells in having clearly visible cell boundaries, large oval nuclei, and large amounts of homogeneous transparent cytoplasm (Jura, 1967a).

At the time the stomodaeal invagination starts to appear, the cluster of germ cells collapses into groups of 2–5 cells which start to migrate through the yolk towards the abdominal part of the germ band (Fig. 6C). One half migrates to the right side, the other to the left. At the level of the middle of the abdominal part of the germ band (Fig. 8D), the germ cells attach to the lateral cells of the inner layer (mesodermal cords) on both sides of the embryo, and finally they sink into the developing cords. After the invagination of the germ band into the yolk, the germ cells become enclosed by the developing gonad sheath (Fig. 13B).

(b) *Gonad Formation.* The gonads develop in a comparatively simple manner. Cells of the developing mesodermal cords, in the immediate vicinity of the germ cells, arrange themselves to form an encasing epithelium. Well defined mesodermal genital ridges, appearing in most Pterygota, never form in Apterygota.

The gonads extend ventro-laterally in relation to the midgut (in Pterygota dorso-laterally), through the first to third abdominal segments (Philiptschenko, 1912a; Jura, 1967a). The mesoderm contributes only to the envelope of the gonads, internal supporting and accessory cells are absent (Jura, 1967a). During their development, the gonads in Collembola are devoid of any segmentation.

According to Claypole (1898) in *Anurida maritima* considerable amounts of yolk are included within the reproductive organs at their formation stage.

(13) Midgut Formation

Uljanin (1875) was the first to consider the origin of midgut epithelium in Collembola. In his opinion, the epithelium of midgut in *Degeeria pruni* originates from cells of the inner layer which migrate around the yolk material and progressively arrange themselves into a regular epithelium.

Uzel (1898a) described midgut formation in *Macrotoma vulgaris* and *Achorutes armatus*. In both species, cleavage cells migrating back from the periphery, both before and after the formation of the blastoderm, and gathering into a ball of cells in the interior of the egg, were considered by him to be endodermal rudiments but his observations are vague and unsatisfactory: he seems in fact to have mistaken the germ cells for the midgut rudiments.

Formation of midgut epithelium by yolk cells was postulated by Claypole (1898) for *Anurida maritima*, and by Prowazek (1900a) for *Isotoma grisea*. According to Philiptschenko (1912a) however, the epithelium of the midgut in *I. cinerea* arises much as in pterygote insects, from anterior and posterior rudiments and a middle strand (Fig. 10A), components of the inner layer. The anterior and posterior rudiments each give rise to a pair of endodermal ribbons, while cells liberated from the middle strand migrate to the yolk surface where they later unite with the ribbons, which have lengthened and widened and finally cover the yolk. Thus according to Philiptschenko, the lower layer contributes toward building of midgut epithelium as well as its musculature (of lateral cords).

More recently the question has been raised again by Jura (1966). Based on his study on *Tetrodontophora bielanensis* he concluded that in Collembola the yolk cells actually represent endoderm, and during the course of embryonic

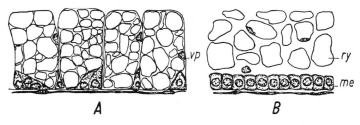

A   *B*

Fig. 16. *Tetrodontophora bielanensis*. Midgut cells of the advanced embryo. A, at early and B, at end of midgut epithelium formation stage. me, midgut epithelium; ry, remnant of yolk material; vp, vitellophage. (After Jura, 1966.)

life differentiate into two types of cells of different morphogenetic value: (1) the vitellophages functioning only during embryonic life, (2) and true endodermal cells giving rise to the midgut epithelium. Both accomplish digestive functions, the first ones during embryonic life, the second, during the postembryonic life. The midgut epithelium forms in *T. bielanensis* during the final stages of development. At the time the body segments are well defined, the yolk shrinks and becomes invested by a non-cellular limiting membrane. At the same time some of the yolk cells destined for the future midgut epithelium tend to move peripherally and locate under the forming membrane. Only a few of the yolk cells remain between the yolk globules in the more central part of the nutritive material. During further development, the nuclei of the yolk cells located under the limiting membrane assume more spherical shapes, the cytoplasm surrounding them appears more abundant and sends fine processes towards the inside of the nutritive material, dividing it into large compartments, which progressively assume the shapes of columns (Fig. 16A). At the same time the first indication of the midgut lumen appears by shrinkage of the yolky columns from the middle (Fig. 15). During the last days of development, the yolk within the columns diminishes in quantity, the nuclei at the bases of the columns multiply and form small clusters, while the cytoplasm under the limiting membrane begins to accumulate (Fig. 16A). Further proliferation of the cells of the clusters gives rise to the epithelial lining of the midgut (Fig. 15), while the rest of the yolk material separated from the epithelium becomes loosely dispersed (Fig. 16B).

In the light of the data presented above, any general conclusion concerning endoderm problem in Collembola seems to be premature. For a general discussion of this topic, see Anderson (1972).

(14) Dorsal Closure

As we have already mentioned, the serosa, after blastokinesis, forms the temporary lateral and dorsal walls of the embryo. But soon the edges of the ectoderm of germ band gradually start to replace the serosal cells (Fig. 13B). Later, the midgut also closes, and splanchnic mesoderm grows around and separates the midgut epithelium from ectoderm. Thus dorsal closure of both hypoderm and gut is completed.

B. Diplura

Amongst Diplura only four species have been studied: *Japyx solifugus* (Grassi, 1885), *Campodea staphylinus* (Uzel, 1897b, 1898a), *Protojapyx maior* (Silvestri, 1933), and *C. fragilis* (Tiegs, 1944), and observations have been limited almost solely to external embryonic features. Uzel's research is the only investigation to utilize fixed and sectioned materials.

(1) Egg Organization

The eggs are spherical, measuring from 0·4 (*Campodea*) to 1·5 mm (*Protojapyx*) in diameter, and covered by a thick granulated chorion. Micropyles are absent. The precocious rupturing of the chorion, so commonly seen in Collembola, does not occur in Diplura (Tiegs, 1944).

The eggs are centrolecital, the periplasm is at first exceedingly thin, but becomes more abundant during early cleavage stages (Uzel, 1898a).

The eggs are laid during warmer months of the year; embryogenesis requires about two weeks (*Campodea*).

(2) Cleavage and Blastoderm Formation

According to Uzel (1898a), cleavage in Diplura is superficial (Fig. 17). Each cleavage nucleus is surrounded by a scanty asteroidal cytoplasm, but cleavage nuclei are not connected with each other by cytoplasmic strands.

At the sixth division, 64 blastomeres are formed, and now all begin to migrate to the periphery (Fig. 17) and reach the periplasm where the nuclei continue to divide to form a unilayered blastoderm. At this stage no nuclei remain behind in the yolk.

(3) Secondary Yolk Cleavage

The yolk in Diplura, though devoid of yolk cells, undergoes secondary cleavage shortly after the blastoderm stage is reached (Grassi, 1885; Uzel, 1898a).

(4) Blastoderm Differentiation and Embryo Rudiment Formation

Early differentiation of the blastoderm in Diplura, as described by Uzel (1898a), is peculiar in having no analogy in any other group of Insecta.

(a) *Origin of Endoderm and Mesoderm.* As development progresses, the blastoderm at one pole of the egg designated by Uzel as the vegetative pole becomes thicker. A small circular area forms provided with two irregular

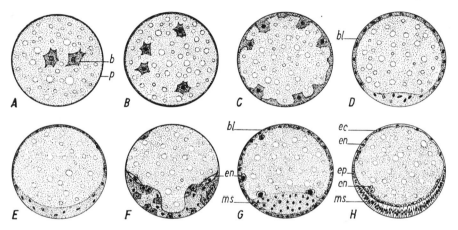

Fig. 17. *Campodea staphylinus.* Early developmental stages. For details see text. b, blastomere; bl, bastoderm; ec, ectoderm; en, endoderm; ep, germ band (ectoderm); ms, mesoderm; p, periplasm. (After Uzel, 1898a.)

layers of nuclei (Fig. 17D). Subsequently, from all parts of the surface, nuclei migrate toward the margin of the circular area, with the result that the upper two-thirds of the blastoderm loses most of its nuclei and the lower third gains them (Fig. 17D, E). In this manner, a thick ring of cells forms (Fig. 17D).

During the further developmental stages, some of the nuclei of the circular area accumulate at the sides, leaving but a single layer in the centre. Occasional cells come to lie above on the inner side of the thickened ring of cells: these are the future endoderm cells (Fig. 17F).

Another migration of nuclei then takes place, reducing the thickness of the cellular ring and restoring the nuclei to the upper part of the egg as well as to the centre of the ring. The cells in the centre of the ring increase in number and later give rise to the mesoderm (Fig. 17G).

Meantime, the endoderm cells multiply, and become scattered on the inside of the thin blastoderm wall as well as on the inside of the mesoderm (Fig. 17H). Later the endoderm cells migrate into the yolk.

Uzel's interpretation of cells differentiating out of the primary blastoderm as mesodermal or endodermal is arbitrary, since Uzel has given no information on their further history. His interpretation is generally considered to be erroneous.

(b) *Germ Band Formation*. Immediately after endoderm and mesoderm formation, blastodermal cells at the vegetative pole become columnar (Fig. 17H), while at the opposite pole, cells become thin. Thus the blastoderm differentiates into a nonembryonic part (serosa) and germ rudiment (ectoderm). The early rudiment in *Campodea staphylinus* is large, similar in this respect to that of Collembola, extending nearly around the egg periphery (Fig. 18A). The mature germ band is broadest at the head end where the head lobes are prominent, narrower in the middle section, and somewhat wider again at the posterior end.

(5) *Blastokinesis*

Blastokinesis occurs when body segments and appendage rudiments are clearly visible (Uzel, 1898a). This is a simple process, showing a close correspondence to that occurring in Collembola (Fig. 18). After blastokinesis the embryo acquires a somewhat spiral position in the egg.

(6) *Dorsal Organ Formation*

The dorsal organ is a common feature of dipluran embryogenesis (Fig. 18B). It appears when embryonic rudiment is already fully segmented (Grassi, 1885; Uzel, 1898a; Tiegs, 1944). In this respect the dorsal organ in Diplura differs notably from that of Collembola, where dorsal organ arises before there is any trace of the germ band.

The dorsal organ in Diplura is formed by a dorsal migration of cells from the serosa (Uzel, 1898a). When completed, it is a highly differentiated and specific embryonic organ comparable in structure to that of Collembola (Tiegs, 1944); as in Collembola it sends fine tendrils into the space between the embryo and cuticular envelope secreted by the embryo (Tiegs, 1944).

After the completion of blastokinesis, the dorsal organ, despite its relatively late appearance, begins to degenerate. According to Tiegs (1944), the degenerating dorsal organ does not lie within the lumen of the developing midgut, as in Collembola, but disintegrates within the haemocoele.

(7) *Cuticular Envelope Produced by the Embryo*

A non-cellular cuticular envelope is produced by the embryo before dorsal organ formation (Uzel, 1898a; Tiegs, 1944). The details of its formation are

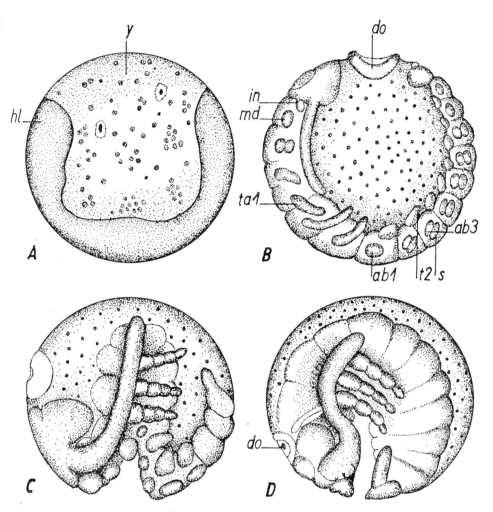

FIG. 18. *Campodea staphylinus*. Middle developmental stages. A–B, germ band segmentation and appendage rudiment formation; C, germ band invagination; D, advanced embryo. ab1, first abdominal appendage; ab3, third abdominal appendage; do, dorsal organ; hl, head lobes; in, intercalary appendage; md, mandible; s, stylus, t2, tergum of second abdominal segment; ta1, first thoracic appendage; y, yolk material. (After Uzel, 1898a.)

unknown. When shed, the cuticle is extremely thin, and forms a closed sac within which the embryo is contained.

(8) Segmentation and Development of Appendages

The processes leading to the formation of head and head appendages seem to parallel strictly those in Collembola. According to Silvestri's (1933) and

Uzel's (1898a) observations, (limited *solely* to external embryonic features) the head in Diplura is composed of six segments. Since sections have not been made, at present it is impossible to discuss the presence or absence of a preantennal segment in dipluran head (compare also Subsection 8a, p. 63 and Anderson, 1972).

The antennae, as in all insects, develop from the posterior boundaries of the procephalic lobes, and postorally. The labrum arises as a single evagination (Fig. 19). The intercalary segment and intercalary appendages may be

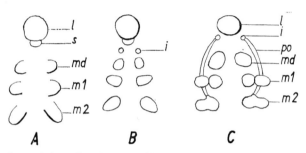

Fig. 19. *Campodea staphylinus*. Development of head appendages, successive stages. i, intercalary appendage; 1, labrum; md, mandible; m1, first maxilla; m2, second maxilla; po, plica oralis; s, stomodaeum. (After Uzel, 1898a.)

readily noted (Uzel, 1898a). The hypopharynx represents the fused paired anlagen appearing between the mandibles, and a median unpaired outgrowth appearing between the first maxillae. Entognathy results, as in Collembola, from formation of two folds (*plicae orales*) appearing on each side of the head at the level of the mandibles (Fig. 19B).

The abdomen in *Campodea staphylinus* consists of ten segments (Uzel, 1898a). Embryonic appendages occur on the first to ninth segments while the tenth bears the furca (Fig. 18B–D). The anlagen of appendages of the second to seventh abdominal segments divide early in development into dorsal and ventral halves, the dorsal halves differentiating into styli.

III. EMBRYOGENESIS OF ECTOGNATHOUS APTERYGOTA

A. Thysanura

(1) Egg Organization

The eggs of Thysanura are elongate, oval (*Lepisma saccharina, Thermobia domestica, Ctenolepisma lineata*; Brandt, 1878; Heymons, 1896, 1897; Uzel, 1897a, 1898a; Sahrhage, 1953; Sharov, 1953; Wellhouse, 1954; Woodland, 1957), or laterally compressed (*Machilis alternata*; Heymons and Heymons, 1905). When laid, the eggs are pale yellow in colour, and this changes as development progresses, into light-brownish. The eggs are polarized: in *Lepisma saccharina* the anterior narrowed pole may be easily distinguished from the broader posterior one (Heymons, 1897). In some thysanuran species, ovoviviparity has been noted (Bourhier, 1957).

The eggs are covered by two membranes: an outer chitinous membrane, the so-called "exochorion", and an inner nonchitinous one, the so-called "endochorion". Micropyles are present at the anterior pole of the egg.

The periplasm is very thin, and adheres to the endochorion. The inner cytoplasmic reticulum enclosing the yolk globules is rather scanty. The oocyte nucleus lies at the centre of the egg, and is surrounded by a small amount of yolk free cytoplasm. In general the inner structure of Thysanura eggs resembles that of Pterygota, but polar plasm is not present. Details of fertilization and maturation are unknown. The larvae emerge 14–16 (*Lepisma*) or 53–69 (*Thermobia*) days after laying of the eggs.

(2) Cleavage and Blastoderm Formation

Cleavage is superficial, closely resembling that of Pterygota.

In *Thermobia domestica* (Woodland, 1957) the spindle axis of the first cleavage division is usually oblique to the longitudinal axis of the egg, and the first two cleavage nuclei divide synchronously. Synchrony is lost during fourth division. In *Ctenolepisma lineata* (Woodland, 1957) the first five divisions are synchronous, and spindle axes are arranged parallel to the surface of the egg. During subsequent cleavage divisions, the cells of the posterior half of the egg begin to divide faster than those in the anterior half.

Each cleavage nucleus in Thysanura is surrounded by a scanty asteroidal cytoplasm, but the nuclei are not connected by cytoplasmic strands, as found in most Pterygota.

The cleavage nuclei eventually migrate to the periphery of the egg, except for those which remain behind and function as yolk nuclei. The migrating nuclei reach the surface almost simultaneously, although here and there a few nuclei may arrive at the surface a little before the others.

The cleavage nuclei, with their investing cytoplasm, after reaching the surface, become distributed over the egg quite isolated from each other, but then undergo repeated mitotic divisions and finally cover the whole egg surface to form the blastoderm. The completed blastoderm in Thysanura shows conspicuous unevenness: its cells are flattened, and the cells borders are difficult to distinguish.

(3) Blastoderm Differentiation

(a) *Germ Anlage Formation.* After the blastoderm forms, numerous mitotic figures appear at the posterior end of the egg. The blastodermal cells occupying this area become smaller in diameter, but taller than those in the other parts of the egg, and gradually form the germ anlage, which is minute, and disc shaped.

The germ disc of *Lepisma saccharina* (Fig. 20) forms posterioventrally (Heymons, 1897; Uzel, 1897a, 1898a; Sharov, 1953), while in *Machilis alternata* (Heymons and Heymons, 1905), *Thermobia domestica* and *Ctenolepisma lineata* (Woodland, 1957), it arises at the extreme posterior end of the egg.

The early germ anlage in Thysanura is composed of a single layer of closely packed cells, forming a cuboidal, rather irregular, epithelium. The

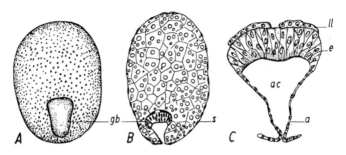

Fig. 20. *Lepisma saccharina*. A, early germ anlage stage; B, first blastokinesis stage, longitudinal section; C, germ band after first blastokinesis stage, cross section. a, amnion, ac, amniotic cavity; e, ectoderm; gb, germ band; ll, lower (inner) layer; s, serosa. (After Sharov, 1953.)

density of the cells increases slightly from the periphery to the centre of the disc.

(b) *Embryonic Membranes.* Thysanura greatly differ from previously described Apterygota (Collembola, Diplura) with respect to the formation of the embryonic membranes. In this group two modes of formation are found, which are transitional to those occurring in Pterygota. *Machilis alternata* represents the first mode. In this species, according to Heymons and Heymons (1905), within the extra-embryonic portion of the blastoderm two zones may be distinguished: a zone having small nuclei immediately surrounding the germ band, and a second much larger zone with large nuclei (Fig. 21A). The smaller zone the authors designated as the "proamnion", and the larger as "proserosa". During the course of development the germ band sinks into the yolk and is carried towards the centre of the egg. Simultaneously the proamnion is stretched and occupies the posterior half of the egg with a corresponding reduction of the area of the proserosa (Fig. 21B–D). The sinking inward of the germ band, according to Heymons and Heymons, is not in the nature of an invagination, comparable to that occurring in embryogenesis of Pterygota; their interpretation however is open to serious question. Because of lateral compression of the egg of *Machilis alternata*, the furrow that carries the embryo inwards remains open at the sides, exposing the lateral margins of the embryo. Also the furrow is not comparable to an amniotic cavity of Pterygota, for its walls are made up of a part of both proserosa and proamnion, for which reason Heymons and Heymons chose the terms "proamnion" and "proserosa" rather than "amnion" and "serosa".

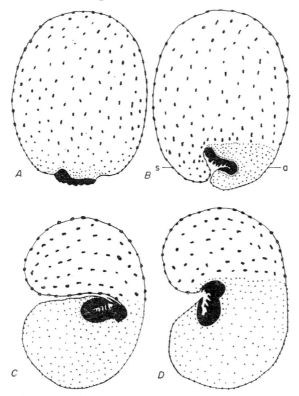

FIG. 21. *Machilis alternata*. Blastokinesis and embryonic membrane formation, successive stages. a, amnion; s, serosa. (After Heymons and Heymons, 1905.)

In *Lepisma saccharina* (Heymons, 1897; Sharov, 1953), *Thermobia domestica*, and *Ctenolepisma lineata* (Woodland, 1957), a further advance towards the development of the embryonic membranes may be observed, and a true amnion and serosa form. In all the above species, during germ anlagen formation, the cells of the extra-embryonic part of the blastoderm remain large and flat. These cells contribute to the serosa, while the amnion arises later during the invagination of the germ band into the yolk (Fig. 20A, B). As the embryonic rudiment sinks and spreads under the serosa, cells proliferating from its margins produce the amnion. The cells of the amnion resemble those of the serosa but are much smaller.

In *Lepisma saccharina*, the amniotic cavity produced as a result of the sinking of the embryo rudiment into the yolk, unlike that of most Pterygota, is relatively large (Fig. 20B, C) and remains open to the exterior at the amniotic pore (point of germ band invagination). According to Woodland (1957), fusion of the amnio-serosal folds, resembling the event characteristic for Pterygota, occurs in *Ctenolepisma lineata*.

(4) Primary Dorsal Organ

During the early blastoderm stage, at the extreme anterior end of the egg of *Thermobia domestica*, Woodland (1957) observed a group of six to ten closely packed cells, clearly different from the other serosa cells. These represent, according to him, the primary dorsal organ, comparable to those of Collembola and Diplura. The fate and significance of this very small dorsal organ have not been determined.

If true, Woodland's observations are extremely interesting in view of the phylogenetic significance which has been attached to this embryonic structure. A primary dorsal organ, so commonly seen in lower apterygotes as a conspicuous and specialized structure, has previously not been noted in Thysanura. (In Pterygota, a dorsal organ is rare, and when it occurs it is vestigial and transient.)

(5) Blastokinesis and Formation of the Secondary Dorsal Organ

(a) *Blastokinesis.* Blastokinesis in *Lepisma saccharina*, *Thermobia domestica*, and *Ctenolepisma lineata* (Heymons, 1897; Sharov, 1953; Woodland, 1957), consists of two phases: an ascending phase (anatrepsis), and a descending phase (katatrepsis). The first phase, already described (Subsection 3(b). p. 80), involves invagination and growth in length of the germ band. When completed, the germ band with its flexed head and caudal parts, forms the bottom of a sac whose sides constitute the amnion (Fig. 20B, C). The second phase occurs at about the middle period of development, when segmentation of germ band is fully advanced.

During the descending phase, the serosa contracts anterodorsally, and amnion everts, the embryo thereby being drawn head first towards the periphery. Following this, the amniotic pore expands and the two membranes with the embryo cover the yolk. (This is blastokinesis in the restricted sense used by Anderson, 1972, associated with membrane withdrawal and probably contractile activity on the part of the embryo.) The embryo now lies at the surface except for the ventrally flexed part of the abdomen (flexion of the abdomen is maintained until the end of development).

(b) *Secondary Dorsal Organ.* As the second phase of blastokinesis proceeds and the serosa contracts, the margins of the embryo proliferate more amnion cells, so that the amnion gradually replaces the serosa as more and more of the latter become contracted (Fig. 22A, B). The contracted serosa at the anterior end of the egg sinks into the yolk, forming the so-called "secondary dorsal organ". During the final stages of development the secondary dorsal organ undergoes degeneration (Heymons, 1897).

(6) Yolk System

Little is known of the behaviour of the nutritive material in Thysanura. Secondary yolk cleavage has been noted by Heymons (1897) and Sharov (1953) in *Lepisma saccharina*, and by Woodland (1957) in *Thermobia domestica* and *Ctenolepisma lineata*, and occurs simultaneously with the formation of the inner layer. At the completion of secondary yolk cleavage, large yolk spheres, each consisting of numerous yolk globules and a central nucleus, are readily apparent in living dissected embryos. In *L. saccharina* the subdivision of the yolk is retained until the end of development (Fig. 26), while in *T. domestica* the walls between the yolk spheres break down during midgut formation (Woodland, 1957).

(a) *Yolk Cells*. As noted above, at the time of the migration phase, an intravitelline separation of the yolk cells occurs. Since these cells differentiate before blastoderm formation, they represent primary yolk cells. Secondary yolk cells, derived from the blastoderm and reinforcing primary yolk cells, have been observed in *Lepisma saccharina* by Sharov (1953).

Yolk cells in Thysanura are double in function. Some are true vitellophages, digesting the yolk and disintegrating towards the close of embryonic life. The others contribute in whole or part to the formation of definitive midgut epithelium (see also: Midgut Formation).

(7) Protecting Sheath Produced by the Embryo

During early blastokinesis, the serosa in Thysanura secretes a chitinous cuticle lining the endochorion (Heymons, 1897; Sharov, 1953; Woodland, 1957). The serosal cuticle is homogeneous and thin, except for a chitinous plug forming within it at the level of the amniotic pore.

Secretion during blastokinesis by the embryo of a periembryonic fluid, filling the amniotic cavity and subcuticular space, has been observed in *Lepisma saccharina* (Sharov, 1953) and in *Thermobia domestica* (Woodland, 1957).

(8) Inner Layer

The inner layer develops early in Thysanura prior to blastokinesis. In *Lepisma saccharina* (Heymons, 1897; Sharov, 1953) it develops by proliferation of cells of the central part of the germ band. It is composed of a single layer of cells, interrupted in the median longitudinal line of the germ band, except at the cephalic end (Fig. 20C).

Wellhouse (1954) described inner layer formation in *Thermobia domestica* as following no regular pattern, with seemingly random inward migration of cells from any part of the germ band, but according to Woodland (1957), the inner layer in both *T. domestica* and *Ctenolepisma lineata* begins with the appearance of a conical group of cells produced by unipolar migration from the centre of germ band. Cells of the cone spread out and inner layer production continues in such a way that a single layer of cells forms under the ectoderm, which has meantime become several cell layers thick. The authors are in agreement that in Thysanura this layer represents mesoderm.

(9) Segmentation and Development of External Form of the Embryo

The first indication of germ band differentiation is appearance of head lobes. Subsequently, antennae and clypeo-labral rudiments appear. In *Lepisma saccharina* (Heymons, 1897; Sharov, 1953) the gnathal and first thoracic segments, and in *Thermobia domestica* (Woodland, 1957) the gnathal, thoracic and first two abdominal segments, appear almost simultaneously, then the other segments become visible. According to Heymons and Sharov, segmentation of mesoderm in *L. saccharina* precedes ectodermal segmentation. However, according to Woodland, formation of intersegmental clefts of ectoderm in *Thermobia domestica* causes separation of the mesoderm into somites, an exceptional mode of mesodermal segmentation in insects.

(a) *The Head.* The definitive head in Thysanura, as in other apterygotes, develops from head lobes, the region bearing the labrum, mouth, eyes and antennae, and from four post antennal elements: an intercalary and three gnathal segments. In Thysanura, as in all insects, the head lobes (protocephalon) never show any external sign of segmentation. For a general discussion concerning the head composition see Subsection 8(a), p. 63, and Anderson (1972).

The antennae grow out rapidly from the posterior boundaries of the procephalic lobes (Fig. 22), lateral and posterior to the stomodaeal invagination. During blastokinesis the antennae migrate to a preoral position. The labral rudiment arises as a single median projection of the prognathal region of the head part of the germ band (Fig. 22). A pair of tiny intercalary appendages was observed in *Lepisma saccharina* by Sharov (1953), and in *Thermobia domestica* by Woodland (1957). They are ephemeral appendages that disappear soon after formation. The development of the appendages of the gnathal region offers nothing unusual.

(b) *The Abdomen.* The abdominal part of the germ band in Thysanura undergoes segmentation into 11 segments.

According to Woodland (1957), the first abdominal segments of *Thermobia domestica* and *Ctenolepisma lineata* develop glandular embryonic structures comparable to the pleuropodia of Pterygota. They develop as paired hemispherical protuberances, enclosing a mass of mesoderm in which a coelomic cavity is starting to form. Later the pleuropodia shorten and become withdrawn into the body. During blastokinesis they assume a glandular appearance. Woodland postulates that the pleuropodia in *T. domestica* produce enzymes that, by the end of blastokinesis, dissolve the cuticle secreted by the

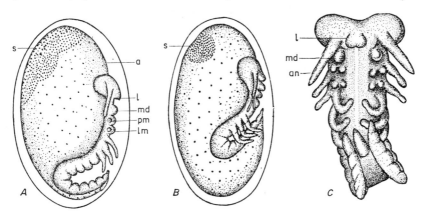

FIG. 22. *Lepisma saccharina*. A, B, successive stages of secondary dorsal organ formation (second blastokinesis stage); C, advanced embryo. a, amnion; an, antenna; l, labrum; lm, maxillary lobe; md, mandible; pm, maxillary palpus; s, serosa. (After Heymons, 1897.)

serosa. Subsequently the pleuropodia show signs of degeneration. On the remaining abdominal segments of *T. domestica* and *Lepisma saccharina* (Heymons, 1897), from the second to tenth, small knob-like appendage primordia appear, and on the last abdominal segment (11th) the caudal filament and cerci differentiate (Fig. 22). The median caudal filament arises dorsal to the proctodaeal invagination, the cerci ventral to it. In later development the cerci migrate laterad. The rudimentary appendages of the second to tenth segments are obliterated during the final stage of development.

(10) Ectodermal Derivates

The outer layer in Thysanura, as in other insects, differentiates at a comparatively early stage of embryonic life. The development of ectodermal organs show close correspondence to those of Pterygota (Heymons, 1897; Woodland, 1957).

(a) *Nervous System*. The beginning of the differentiation of the nervous system is marked by the appearance of the neural groove (Heymons, 1897;

Woodland, 1957). The neuroblasts, differentiating within the outer layer, form a pair of medial thickenings which undergo segmentation and form paired ganglia. In *Thermobia domestica* (Woodland, 1957) the median cord differentiates from the roof of the neural groove. It appears to become a part of the ganglia, possibly it contributes to fibres of the commissures.

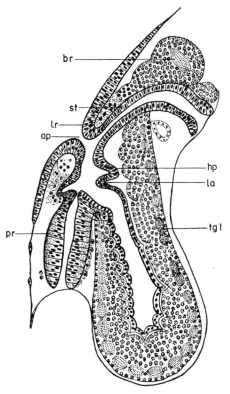

FIG. 23. *Lepisma saccharina*. Middle developmental stage, descending phase of the embryo. ap, amnion pore; br, brain; hp, hypopharynx; la, labium; lr, labrum; st, stomodaeum; tg1, first thoracic ganglion; pr, proctodaeum. (After Heymons, 1897.)

As in insects in general, the brain of Thysanura develops three pairs of ganglia which correspond to the first three cephalic segments: the optic, the antennary, and the intercalary segment, respectively. The primordium of the protocerebrum is relatively extensive because of the large lateral optic lobes.

The suboesophageal ganglion is derived from fused gnathal ganglia. Paired ganglia appear in the thoracic as well as in each of the abdominal segments (Fig. 23). The fused ninth, tenth and eleventh ganglia of the abdomen move forward and become incorporated with the eighth abdominal ganglion (Woodland, 1957).

(b) *Fore and Hindgut.* The stomodaeal invagination may appear before segmentation of germ band (*Thermobia domestica*; Woodland, 1957), or later when somites are already differentiated (*Lepisma saccharina*; Sharov, 1953). The proctodaeal invagination appears when all thoracic segments are well visible. From it, two pairs of small evaginations arise which form the Malpighian tubules (Heymons, 1897; Woodland, 1957).

(c) *Tracheal System.* The primordia of spiracles appear at the stage when dorsal closure occurs. They appear as small clusters of ectodermal cells at the body surface. Most of the cells of the clusters soon invaginate, leaving on the surface a unilayered ring of closely packed cells.

In *Lepisma saccharina*, Heymons (1897) observed two thoracic pairs (localized on meso- and metathorax), and nine, and probably a rudimentary tenth, embryonic abdominal spiracle anlagen. Only eight pairs of abdominal spiracles have been found in the embryos of *Thermobia domestica* and *Ctenolepisma lineata* (Woodland, 1957).

(11) Mesodermal Derivates

In Thysanura a total of at least 17 pairs of coelomic sacs arise out of the inner layer (Heymons, 1897; Wellhouse, 1954; Woodland, 1957). Four pairs of large coelomic sacs develop in the head portion of the germ band: an

Fig. 24. *Thermobia domestica*. Cross sections through germ band at successive stages of coelomic sac formation. a, amnion; c, coelom; e, ectoderm; ll, lower layer. (After Woodland, 1957.)

antennal pair, and three gnathal. The labral mesoderm appears solid, and coelomic sacs have also not been identified in the intercalary head segment. A pair of coelomic sacs has been found in each of three thoracic segments, as well as in each first ten abdominal ones.

The coelomic sacs form by the growing and folding over (Fig. 24) dorsally and medially of the lateral margins of the mesoderm layer (Woodland, 1957). Some of the coelomic sacs, especially those of the abdomen, remain open dorsally for some time (Heymons, 1897; Woodland, 1957), but close when the dorsal ectoderm wall closes. In Thysanura, the coelomic sacs are not connected by a median sheet of mesodermal cells (compare in this respect Collembola), as we have already mentioned, the inner layer after formation becomes interrupted along the median longitudinal line. The development of musculature, circulatory system, and haemocoele in Thysanura has not been studied in detail. In general the coelomic sacs differentiate much as in Orthoptera.

The appendicular musculature develops from the somatic mesoderm of the ventral lobes of the coelomic sacs. The trunk musculature develops from the layer of somatic mesoderm that is in contact with ectoderm. Mesoderm of the labral region gives to the stomodaeal mesoderm and thence to the foregut musculature. The muscles of the hindgut arise from the unsegmented mesoderm near the posterior end of the body.

The fat body develops from the somatic mesoderm at the late dorsal closure stage (Woodland, 1957).

Formation of the heart occurs from posterior to anterior. The cardioblasts differentiate at the junction of the splanchnic and somatic mesoderm as these layers grow around the yolk dorsally. The aorta arises from the antennary mesoderm. The dorsal diaphragm develops from somatic mesoderm just lateral to the cardioblasts.

(12) Germ Cells and Gonad Formation

(a) *Germ Cells*. The data concerning germ cell differentiation in Thysanura is scanty and fragmentary. In *Lepisma saccharina* (Heymons, 1897), germ cells are first visible as a knob-like protuberance at the extreme posterior end of germ band at about the time it sinks into the yolk. Later the germ cells migrate to the segmentally arranged genital ridges (see below). They may be distinguished from the mesoderm cells by their somewhat larger nuclei. However Sharov (1953) has claimed that the germ cells in *L. saccharina* are segregated earlier, at the beginning of the germ anlagen stage. Early segregation of germ cells has not been observed in *Thermobia domestica* (Wellhouse, 1954; Woodland, 1957) or *Ctenolepisma lineata* (Woodland, 1957). In these species, germ cells can be identified only when they appear in association with the splanchnic portion of some abdominal coelomic sacs.

(b) *Gonad Formation*. Definitive gonads in Thysanura differentiate after emergence of the larva, during early postembryonic life. Mesodermal gonad rudiments develop out of segmentally arranged genital ridges (ventral lamellae of coelomic sacs), in the second to sixth abdominal segments of females, and in the fourth to sixth abdominal segments of males. The cells of genital ridges invest the germ cells and then the rudiments unite on each side into a single group (Heymons, 1897; Sharov, 1954; Woodland, 1957).

(13) Midgut Formation

The definitive midgut epithelium also forms in Thysanura during post-embryonic life. In the final stages of embryonic life the splanchnic mesoderm forms a temporary midgut epithelium (Fig. 25).

Data concerning the origin of midgut epithelium in Thysanura are extremely controversial, even in the same species studied by different authors.

Heymons (1897) postulated formation of midgut epithelium in *Lepisma saccharina* out of yolk cells, which he regarded as representing endoderm. But according to Sharov (1953), in this species the anterior and posterior extremities of the midgut are directly derived from the ectoderm cells, the cells proliferating from the tips of stomo- and proctodaeum respectively, and only the middle section develops from yolk cells.

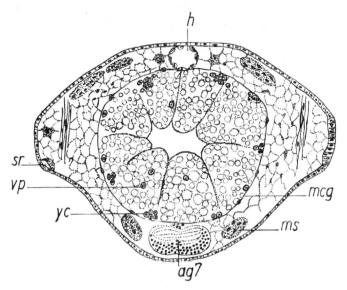

FIG. 25. *Lepisma saccharina*. Advanced embryo. Cross section through seventh abdominal segment. ag7, ganglion of seventh abdominal segment; h, heart; mcg, muscular coat of midgut; ms, muscles; sr, spiracle; vp, vitellophage; yc, yolk cell (endoderm). (After Heymons, 1897.)

Midgut development in *Thermobia domestica* has been described by three authors. Sahrhage (1953) believed the ectoderm (tips of stomo- and proctodaeum) to be the sole source of midgut epithelium. Wellhouse (1954) suggested that midgut epithelium originated from two sources: proliferation of cells from the stomo- and proctodaeum, and yolk cells migrating peripherally from the yolk. Woodland (1957) agrees with Heymons, and states that the midgut epithelium in *T. domestica* is derived exclusively out of yolk cells (endoderm). According to Woodland, the septa between the large yolk spheres, which were formed earlier by the secondary yolk cleavage, break down shortly after blastokinesis is completed and some of the yolk cells migrate to the periphery of the yolk. In newly hatched larvae, the peripheral yolk cells multiply and give rise to formation of a regular midgut epithelium.

In *Lepisma saccharina*, as figured and described by Heymons (1897), the walls of large yolk compartments (Fig. 25) later dissolve, after the young larva leaves the egg.

The disappearance of the last of the yolk occurs in the second or third instar larvae. At this time those yolk cells, which do not contribute to the midgut epithelium formation but function as true vitellophages, degenerate.

(*14*) Dorsal Closure

After blastokinesis is completed, the lateral margins of the embryo proper start to grow up around the yolk. Dorsal closure in Thysanura progresses from posterior to anterior (Fig. 26). It is not known in what way the amnion cells are replaced by the ectodermal cells.

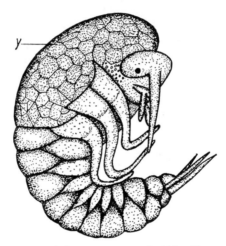

FIG. 26. *Lepisma saccharina*. Dorsal closure stage. y, yolk. (After Sharov, 1953.)

IV. GENERAL REMARKS

The foregoing survey shows that amongst Apterygota the general features of development only of two orders—Collembola and Thysanura—are known.

From the standpoint of embryological characters, the more immediate relationship of Collembola lies with myriapods on the one hand, and with Thysanura-Pterygota on the other. Collembola have in common with myriapods (Symphyla, Diplopoda), but with no other insects, the total cleavage of the egg and a gonad of the myriapod type (Metschnikoff, 1874; Lignau, 1911, 1912; Tiegs, 1940). In the manner of egg organization, precocious rupturing of chorion, development of a blastodermic cuticle and a dorsal organ, blastoderm formation and differentiation, blastokinesis, and development of embryonic envelope (Fig. 27), the Collembola closely resemble the Symphyla

(Tiegs, 1940). The dorsal organ in Collembola in its structure finds the nearest approach to that of Symphyla, also the absence of gonadal segmentation confirms the relationships of this group with Symphyla.

The resemblance of Collembola to Thysanura-Pterygota is expressed in blastoderm organization, germ band formation, general development of nervous system, and in early segregation of germ cells. On the other hand, the embryos of Collembola, when compared with thysanuran ones, are more

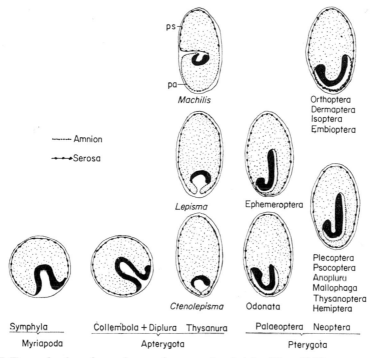

FIG. 27. Types of embryonic membranes of some myriapods (after Tiegs, 1940), apterygotes, and pterygotes (after Ando, 1962), in relation to germ bands after their invagination into the yolk. For details see text. pa, proamnion; ps, proserosa.

advanced in development: in Thysanura the definitive midgut and gonads develop during postembryonic life. However, the Collembola show a more primitive type of embryonic development expressed in reduction of the coelom and lack of gonad segmentation.

Thysanura undoubtedly show the closest relationship with Pterygota. Early developmental stages and development of internal and external organs, occurs in this last group much as in winged insects. The manner of embryonic membrane formation in the Thysanura, however, appears more primitive than the most primitive groups of Pterygota (Fig. 27).

The Protura and Diplura still await embryological investigations. The Diplura have not been completely investigated. The early development of *Campodea staphylinus*, a representative of Diplura, as described by Uzel (1898*a*) differs considerably from that of Collembola. But germ anlagen formation, germ band invagination and differentiation, development of embryonic membrane, development of head and body segments in *Campodea* show how great is the likeness of the development of this group and the Collembola, and gives rise to some doubt concerning the accuracy of Uzel's description of cleavage, endoderm and mesoderm formation. Re-investigation of Diplura is desired.

At present nothing further can be said on the affinities of the four orders of Apterygota within the myriapod-hexapod group. Also, in view of the still prevailing diverse opinions concerning formation of the midgut in Apterygota, the discussion of endoderm origin, one of the most controversial problems of insect embryology, seems to be premature and verballistic. One of the major reasons so little work has been done on Apterygota embryology is that their biology is poorly known, and for embryological studies we need more work on their life cycles.

REFERENCES

Anderson, D. T. (1972). In *Developmental Systems: Insects* (S. J. Counce and C. H. Waddington, eds), Vol. 1 p. 95–163. Academic Press, London and New York.

Ando, H. (1962). *The Comparative Embryology of Odonata with Special Reference to a Relic Dragonfly* Epiophlebia superstes *Selys*, pp. 205. Japan Society for Promotion of Science, Tokyo.

Barrois, M. J. (1879). *C. r. Ass. fr. Avanc. Sci.*, 7th session 1878, 778–779.

Bourhier, A. (1957). *C. r. Hebd. Séanc Acad. Sci. Paris*, **244D**, 506–508.

Brandt, A. (1878). *Über das Ei und seine Bildungsstatte* W. Engelmann, Leipzig.

Bretfeld, G. (1963). *Zool. Jb. (Abt. Anat. Ontog.)*, **80**, 309–384.

Claypole, A. M. (1898). *J. Morph.*, **14**, 219–300.

Claypole, A. M. (1899). *Zool. Bull. Div. Zool. Pa. Dep. Agric.*, **2**, 69–76.

Christiansen, K. (1964). *A. Rev. Ent.*, **9**, 145–178.

Counce, S. J. (1961). *A. Rev. Ent.*, **6**, 295–312.

Counce, S. J. (1972). *Developmental Systems: Insects* (S. J. Counce and C. H. Waddington, eds), Vol. 2 p. 1. Academic Press, London and New York.

Folsom, J. W. (1900). *Bull. Mus. comp. Zool. Harv.*, **36**, 87–158.

Garaudy, M. (1967). *Act. Soc. linn. Bordeaux*, **104**, 1–13.

Garaudy-Tamarelle, M. (1969). *C. r. Hebd. Séanc. Acad. Sci. Paris*, **268D**, 945–947.

Goto, H. E. (1960). *Nature, Lond.*, **188**, 958–959.

Grassi, B. (1885). *Atti Accad. gioenia Sci. Nat.*, **19**, 1–83.

Haget, M. A. and Garaudy, M. (1964). *C. r. Hebd. Séanc. Acad. Sci. Paris*, **258D**, 3364–3366.

Handschin, E. (1952). *9th Int. Congr. Ent.*, **1**, 235–240.

Heymons, R. (1896). *Sber. preuss. Akad. Wiss.*, **51**, 1385–1389.

Heymons, R. (1897). *Z. wiss. Zool.*, **62**, 583–631.

Heymons, R. and Heymons, H. (1905). *Verh. dt. zool. Ges.*, **15**, 123–135.

Hoffmann, R. W. (1911). *Zool. Anz.*, **37**, 353–377.
Jura, Cz. (1965). *Acta biol. cracov. Zool.*, **8**, 141–157.
Jura, Cz. (1966). *Acta biol. cracov. Zool.*, **9**, 93–102.
Jura, Cz. (1967a). *Acta biol. cracov. Zool.*, **10**, 97–103.
Jura, Cz. (1967b). *Acta biol. cracov. Zool.*, **10**, 301–310.
Lemoine, V. (1883). *C. r. Ass. fr. Avanc. Sci.*, **11**, 483–520.
Lignau, N. (1911). *Zool. Anz.*, **37**, 144–153.
Lignau, N. (1912). *Mem. Soc. Nat. Odessa.*, **38**, 57–305.
Manton, S. M. (1964). *Phil. Trans. R. Soc.* **B247**, 1–183.
Metschnikoff, E. (1874). *Z. wiss. Zool.*, **24**, 253–283.
Nicolet, H. (1842). *Nouv. Mém. Soc. Helv. Sci. Nat.*, **6**, 1–88.
Packard, A. S. (1871). *Mem. Peabody Acad. Sci.*, **2**, 1–24.
Packard, A. S. (1872). *Proc. Boston Soc. nat. Hist.*, **14**, 13–15.
Paclt, J. (1954). *Zool. Anz.*, **153**, 275–281.
Paclt, J. (1956). *Zool. Anz.*, **156**, 272–276.
Philiptschenko, J. (1912a). *Z. wiss. Zool.*, **103**, 519–560.
Philiptschenko, J. (1912b). *Zool. Anz.*, **39**, 43–49.
Prowazek, S. (1900a). *Arb. Zool. Inst. Univ. Wien.*, **12**, 335–363.
Prowazek, S. (1900b). *J. R. microsc. Soc.*, **1900**, 580–581.
Remington, C. L. (1954). *Proc. Calif. Acad. Sci.*, Centennial vol., 495–505.
Ryder, J. H. (1886). *Am. Nat.*, **20**, 299–302.
Sahrhage, D. (1953). *Z. wiss. Zool.*, **157**, 77–168.
Sedlag, U. (1951/2). *Wiss. Z. Martin-Luther-Univ. Halle-Wittenb. math.-nat.*, **1**, 83–127.
Sharov, A. G. (1953). *Trudy Inst. Morf. Zhivof.*, **8**, 63–124.
Silvestri, F. (1933). *5th Int. Congr. Ent.*, 329–343.
Slifer, E. H. (1938). *J. Morph.*, **63**, 181–205.
Sommer, A. (1885). *Z. wiss. Zoo.*, **41**, 683–718.
Strebel, O. (1932). *Z. Morph. Ökol. Tiere*, **25**, 30–153.
Tiegs, O. W. (1940). *Q . Jl. microsc. Sci.*, **82**, 1–225.
Tiegs, O. W. (1941). *Q . Jl. microsc. Sci.*, **83**, 153–169.
Tiegs, O. W. (1944). *Q . Jl. microsc. Sci.*, **84**, 33–47.
Tuxen, S. L. (1959). *Smithson. Misc. Collns.*, **137**, 379–416.
Uljanin, W. N. (1875). *Iz. imp. Obshch. Ljub. Estest. Antrop. Etnogr. mosk. Univ.*, **16**, 1–12.
Uzel, H. (1897a). *Zool. Anz.*, **20**, 127–132.
Uzel, H. (1897b). *Zool. Anz.*, **20**, 232–327.
Uzel, H. (1898a). *Studies über die Entwicklung der apterygoten Insecten.*, K. Fiedlander et Sohn, Berlin.
Uzel, H. (1898b). *Zool. Zentbl.*, **5**, 852–855.
Wagner, N. P. (1890). *Biol. Zbl.*, **10**, 428–429.
Wellhouse, W. T. (1954). *Iowa St. Coll. J. Sci.*, **28**, 416–417.
Wheeler, W. N. (1893). *J. Morph.*, **8**, 1–160.
Woodland, J. T. (1957). *J. Morph.*, **101**, 523–578.

ADDENDUM

The following papers on apterygote embryogenesis appeared after completion of the manuscript.

Collembola

Garaudy-Tamarelle, M. (1969). Les vésicules coelomiques du segment intercalaire (=pré-mandibulaire) chez les embryons du Collembole *Anurida maritima* (Guér.). *C. r. Acad.*

Sci. Paris D **269**, 198–200. (Coelomic sacs were found in all four gnathocephalic segments; compare in this chapter, Section A.11.)

Garaudy-Tamarelle, M. (1970). Observations sur la ségrégation de lignée germinale chez le Collembole *Anurida maritima* (Guér.). Explication de son caractére intravitellin. *C. r. Acad. Sci. (Paris)*, D270, 1149–1152.

Komorowska, B. (1970). Alkaline phosphatase in early stages of embryonal development of *Tetrodontophora bielanensis* (Waga). Histochemical analysis. *Zesz. Nauk. Uniw. Jagiellonsk. Prace Zool.*, **16**, 93–106. (No alkaline phosphatase activity was detected in the mature oocyte, but in all successive developmental stages a reaction was apparent in the peripheral layers of blastomeres, along their boundaries and in the cytoplasm surrounding the nuclei. The intensity of the enzymatic reaction varied with developmental stage.)

Zakhvatkin, Y. A. (1969). The morphology of cleavage of the Collembola egg. *Zool. Zh.*, **48**, 1029–1040. (Deals in detail with the morphology of early cleavage in *Sinella curbiseta* which is described as having a modified spiral pattern with a tendency toward superficial cleavage.)

Thysanura

Larink, O. (1969). Zur Entwicklungsgeschichte von *Pterobius brevistylus* (Thysanura, Insecta). *Helgoländer wiss. Meeresunters.*, **19**, 111–155. (A detailed analysis of development of this species. Of especial interest is the formation, by the blastoderm, of a cuticle several layers in thickness as well as the details of mesoderm formation and development of the extremities.)

Larink, O. (1970). Zur Kopfentwicklung von *Lepisma saccharina* L. (Insecta, Thysanura). *Z. Morph. Ökol. Tiere*, **67**, 1–15. (Development of head segments, in particular the procephalon, is described in detail. On the basis of formation of ectodermal and mesodermal derivatives, the head of *Lepisma* is considered to consist of an acron and six additional segments.)

3 | The Development of Hemimetabolous Insects

D. T. ANDERSON

School of Biological Sciences, University of Sydney, Australia

I. INTRODUCTION

Hemimetabolous insects present many problems to the descriptive embryologist. Unusual histological difficulties are engendered by the tough egg
membranes and intractable yolk of hemimetabolous eggs. The rate of development of the eggs is relatively slow, often occupying many weeks (Table
I). The embryonic rudiment, especially in the early stages of its development, is discouragingly small relative to the size of the yolk mass. Development is epimorphic, leading to hatching with all segments fully developed

TABLE I. Representative Durations of Embryonic Development
in Hemimetabolous Insects

Order	Species	Time	Source
Ephemeroptera	*Baetis rhodani*	45 days	Illies (1968)
	Ephemera vulgata	10–11 days	Heymons (1896a)
Odonata	*Platycnemis pennipes*	18 days	Seidel (1929)
	Plathemis lydia	11 days	Johannsen and Butt (1941)
Dictyoptera	*Heirodula crassa*	24 days	Görg (1959)
Isoptera	*Kalotermes flavicollis*	54 days	Striebel (1960)
	Zootermopsis nevadensis	28 days	Striebel (1960)
Plecoptera	*Pteronarcys proteus*	5½ months	Miller (1939)
Cheleutoptera	*Carausius morosus*	85 days	Fournier (1967)
Orthoptera	*Locusta migratoria*	13 days	{ Salzen (1960) Roonwal (1936)
	Gryllus domesticus	30 days	Kanellis (1952)
	Tachycines asynamorus	40 days	Krause (1939)
	Xiphidium ensiferum	5 months	Wheeler (1893)
Embioptera	*Embia*	about 40 days	Kershaw (1914)
Psocoptera	*Liposcelis divergens*	7 days	Goss (1952)
Homoptera	*Euscelis plebejus*	17 days	Sander (1959)
Heteroptera	*Rhodnius prolixus*	29 days	Mellanby (1936)
	Notonecta	18 days	Krause (1939)

and functional, and the later stages of development exhibit considerable
structural complexity. During development, the embryo usually performs
elaborate movements within the space enclosed by the egg membranes,

adopting a succession of different postures. Finally, development is specialized in ways which outrun the limitations of the classical germ layer theory. Perhaps it is not surprising, therefore, that the embryologists who gave their attention to hemimetabolous embryos in the classical descriptive period of the 1870's to 1890's of the last century met more with frustration than with success. Primitive histology allied with recalcitrant specimens could have had no other outcome. The many controversies of interpretation resulting from the juxtaposition of artifact and inappropriate theory during three decades were fully documented by Johannsen and Butt (1941) and need no further discussion. Suffice it to say that two outstanding workers of this period can now be seen to have laid the foundations on which modern interpretations of the structure of hemimetabolan embryos are based. One was the American entomologist Wheeler (1889a, 1893), whose descriptions of dictyopteran and orthopteran embryonic development still form an important part of our knowledge of these orders. The second was the German embryologist Heymons (1895, 1896a, b, 1897, 1899, 1912), who brilliantly augmented and extended Wheeler's work, adding fundamental contributions on the embryology of the Ephemeroptera, Odonata, Dermaptera, Cheleutoptera and Heteroptera. It is a telling testimony to the technical skill and intellectual foresight of Wheeler and Heymons that further significant work on hemimetabolan embryos began to appear only in the 1920's, when histology and microscopy had undergone marked technological advances.

The second phase in the description of hemimetabolan embryos was again initiated by an outstanding insect embryologist, Professor F. Seidel, who has since performed and inspired much of the important work in this field of endeavour. Seidel (1924) worked initially on the heteropteran *Pyrrhocoris apterus*, but later turned his attention mainly to Odonata and to experimental embryology (Seidel, 1929, 1935). His results, as we shall see below, still provide facts and ideas of crucial importance in the interpretation of hemimetabolan embryonic structure. Contemporaneously with Seidel's early work, an extensive pioneering study was carried out by Leuzinger *et al.* (1926) on the phasmid *Carausius morosus*. The stage was thus set for advances in several directions during the 1930's. The embryos of several Orthoptera, for example, were described by Slifer (1932a, b, 1937), Nelsen (1931, 1934) and especially Roonwal (1936, 1937) and Krause (1938a, b, 1939) in a series of papers which greatly clarified the basic embryonic structure, embryonic movements, segment formation and later organogeny of this order. Miller (1939, 1940) performed the same service for the plecopteran *Pteronarcys proteus*, while penetrating work was carried out by Mellanby (1936, 1937) on the heteropteran *Rhodnius prolixus* and by Schölzel (1937) on the Anoplura and Mallophaga. Together with lesser contributions from other workers, these studies resolved many of the controversies of classical hemimetabolan embryology and provided the basis for an important synthesis of the subject by Johannsen and Butt (1941).

In the last twenty years, however, hemimetabolan embryology has seen a third and most significant phase of advancement. Several orders, the Ephemeroptera (Illies, 1968), Plecoptera (Khoo, 1968), Embioptera (Stefani, 1961) and Dermaptera (Bhatnagar and Singh, 1965), remain little known, but the impact of modern techniques has expanded our knowledge of other hemimetabolan embryos in both breadth and depth. Görg (1959), Striebel (1960) and Ando (1962) have provided modern accounts of the embryonic development of the Dictyoptera, Isoptera and Odonata respectively. Several workers, starting with Moscona (1950) and Bergerard (1958) and continuing with Koch (1964), Scholl (1965, 1969), Malzacher (1968) and the French school at Bordeaux under the direction of Professor A. Haget (Louvet, 1964; Fournier, 1966, 1967; Cavallin, 1968, 1969; Vignau-Rogueda, 1969) has given further extensive attention to the Cheleutoptera. Professor G. Krause, leading an extremely productive German school, has inspired detailed new studies on the Orthoptera (Kanellis, 1952; Ibrahim, 1957; Mahr, 1960; Wada, 1966a, b). The Homoptera (Sander, 1956, 1959; Behrendt, 1963), the Heteroptera (Butt, 1949; Cobben, 1968), the Psocoptera (Goss, 1952, 1953), the Anoplura (Piotrowski, 1953) and the Thysanoptera (Bournier, 1960) have also been included in the current advance of knowledge. While it would not be true to say that our information on the morphology of hemimetabolan embryos is now sufficient, the position has changed significantly since Johannsen and Butt wrote their review thirty years ago. Perhaps the most important aspect of the change, as will emerge below, is the demonstration that hemimetabolan embryonic development is less diverse among the different orders than has previously been suspected.

II. EGGS

A. The Zygote

In all oviparous, hemimetabolous insects, the freshly oviposited egg is still undergoing maturation and the completion of fertilization. The manner in which these events take place will be discussed briefly in due course. For the present, in order to establish the basic features of the types of egg that hemimetabolous insects produce, it is advantageous to concentrate on the stage resulting from the completion of maturation and fertilization, namely, the *zygote*. A typical example of a primitive hemimetabolan zygote is illustrated in Fig. 1a. The most striking feature is a great preponderance of yolk over cytoplasm. Almost the entire substance of the egg consists of massed yolk bodies in the form of randomly intermingled lipid droplets and protein carbohydrate yolk granules. Yolk-free cytoplasm is obvious only as a small island around the zygote nucleus, which lies at or near the centre of the egg.

Eggs of this general constitution are characteristic of all the ancient and morphologically primitive orders of pterygotes and have been described in varying degrees of detail by many workers (Ephemeroptera: Heymons, 1896a, b; Illies, 1968; Odonata: Heymons, 1896a; Tschuproff, 1903; Johannsen and Butt, 1941; Ando, 1962; Dictyoptera: Wheeler, 1889a; Heymons, 1895; Giardina, 1897; Hagan, 1917; Görg, 1959; Isoptera: Strindberg, 1913; Striebel, 1960; Zoraptera: Goss, 1953, Plecoptera, Miller, 1939; Khoo, 1968; Cheleutoptera: Leuzinger et al., 1926; Thomas, 1936; Bergerard, 1958; Fournier, 1967; Bedford, 1970; Orthoptera: Wheeler, 1893; Heymons, 1895; Roonwal, 1936; Krause, 1938a, b, 1939; Brookes, 1952; Kanellis, 1952; Ibrahim, 1957; Mahr, 1960; Sauer, 1966; Embioptera: Kershaw, 1914; Stefani, 1961; Dermaptera: Heymons, 1895; Bhatnagar and Singh, 1965). The egg is always enclosed within two membranes, an inner *vitelline membrane* and an outer *chorion*. The vitelline membrane is thin, but is particularly resistant to penetration by chemical reagents and can be removed from the egg only by dissection. The chorion varies in thickness and opacity, but is subject to total or partial dissolution by the action of sodium hypochlorite. This simple treatment, applied to the living egg, has been a major factor in improving observations on pterygote embryonic development in recent years.

The vitelline membrane is generally said to be secreted by the oocyte, though the possibility remains that the follicle cells of the ovariole may contribute to its formation (Beams and Kessel, 1968; Mahowald, 1972). Little is known of the composition of this membrane in the Hemimetabola. In several species, the vitelline membrane disappears when development of the embryo begins (e.g. Slifer, 1937, 1938a, b). The chorion, in contrast, is a persistent, complex membrane secreted entirely by the follicle cells. In many species, the chorion is permeated by a system of air spaces through which respiratory exchange takes place between the developing embryo and the external environment (Wigglesworth and Beament, 1950, 1960; McFarlane, 1965; Cobben, 1968). One or more openings through the chorion act as micropyles, the route of sperm entry into the egg, but some of the openings interpreted by early workers as micropyles have since been shown to be pseudomicropyles, opening into the system of chorionic air spaces. The structure and composition of the chorion has been carefully studied in the orthopteran *Melanoplus differentialis* by Slifer (1946, 1949a, b, 1950, 1958) and in the heteropteran *Rhodnius prolixus* by Beament (1946a, b, 1947, 1948, 1949). The composition is mainly proteinaceous, but the membrane also includes some lipid and carbohydrate material.

The chorion and vitelline membrane together enclose and delimit an egg space within which embryonic development takes place. Initially, the shape of the egg is the shape of this space, the yolky cytoplasm being a fluid mass under pressure within the membranes. In later development, after a continuous layer of cells has been established at the surface of the embryo, the external membranes usually dilate as a result of fluid uptake, so that the egg space enlarges and the embryo within it has a greater freedom of movement and room to grow. The original shape of the membranes is always retained, however, and some of the movements performed by the growing embryo are movements by which it accommodates its own changing shape within the predetermined egg space. More will be said of these movements in later sections of the present chapter.

If we wish to select a basic shape for the eggs of primitive Hemimetabola, it is most probably that illustrated in Fig. 1a, namely, elongate ovoid with rounded ends. Eggs of this form are laid by the Ephemeroptera, some Odonata, the Isoptera, many Plecoptera, the gryllotalpid Orthoptera, the Embioptera and the Dermaptera. One dimension of the egg, marking the anteroposterior axis, is always close to or greater than a millimetre (Table II).

TABLE II. Representative Egg Dimensions in Hemimetabolous Insects

Order	Species	Length × Width in mm	Source
Odonata	*Platycnemis pennipes*	1·00 × 0·24	Seidel (1929)
Dictyoptera	*Heirodula crassa*	3·5–5 × 1–1·2	Görg (1959)
	Paratenodera sinensis	4·5	Hagan (1917)
Isoptera	*Kalotermes flavicollis*	1·22 × 0·42	Striebel (1960)
	Zootermopsis nevadensis	1·16 × 0·47	Striebel (1960)
Plecoptera	*Pteronarcys proteus*	0·74	Miller (1939)
Cheleutoptera	*Didymuria violescens*	4 × 2	Bedford (1970)
	Carausius morosus	5	Thomas (1936)
Orthoptera	*Acheta domesticus*	2–2·8 × 0·4–0·5	Kanellis (1952)
	Tachycines asynomorus	2·6	{ Mahr (1960) { Krause (1939)
	Xiphidium ensiferum	3–5 × 1·0	Wheeler (1893)
	Locusta migratoria	6–8	Salzen (1960)
Dermaptera	*Forficula auricularia*	1–1·5	Heymons (1895)
Psocoptera	*Liposcelis divergens*	0·34 × 0·18	Goss (1952)
Mallophaga	*Trichodectes scalaris*	0·4 × 0·18	Schölzel (1937)
Anoplura	*Haematopinus eurysternus*	0·9 × 0·4	Schölzel (1937)
Homoptera	*Euscelis plebejus*	0·9–1·2 × 0·22	Sander (1959)
	Aphis fabae (Winter egg)	0·55 × 0·24	Behrendt (1963)
	Porphyrophora polonica	0·55 × 0·25	Gerwel (1950)
Heteroptera	*Oncopeltus fasciatus*	1·41 × 0·63	Butt (1949)
	Rhodnius prolixus	1·5 × 0·8	Mellanby (1936)

Anterior and posterior poles can always be identified, together with dorsal and ventral surfaces, so that the egg has a visible bilateral symmetry. Frequently, the ventral surface is convex, and the dorsal surface concave, as in Fig. 1a, emphasizing the highly ordered spatial configuration of the egg. The same generalizations pertain to species of primitive Hemimetabola that lay eggs of a more specialized shape. Several variations are exhibited among different orders. Some Odonata, for instance, lay relatively long narrow eggs (Seidel, 1929; Fig. 3a). In the Dictyoptera, in association with the enclosure of a group of eggs in a specialized ootheca, each egg is bilaterally compressed (Wheeler, 1889a; Heymons, 1895; Giardina, 1897). The Cheleutoptera,

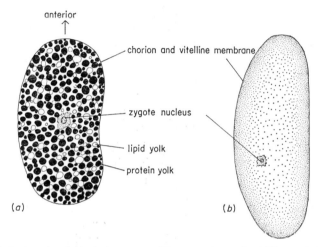

Fig. 1. (a) Sagittal section through the zygote of *Zootermopsis nevadensis* (Isoptera), based on data of Striebel (1960); (b) Zygote of *Tachycines asynomorus* (Orthoptera) in diagrammatic lateral view, after Krause (1939).

in contrast, lay large, spheroidal eggs that are only slightly bilaterally compressed, while the Orthoptera normally lay exceptionally elongated eggs, noticeably curved in the dorsoventral plane (Fig. 1b). The most aberrant modification is seen in the eggs of some Plecoptera, which are hemispherical domes with a flat ventral surface (Miller, 1939).

It is obvious from the summary given above that no precise distinction in the shape and form of the eggs can be made between the two major subdivisions of primitive Hemimetabola, the Paleoptera, comprising the Ephemeroptera and Odonata, and the Polyneoptera, comprising the Dictyoptera, Isoptera, Zoraptera, Plecoptera, Cheleutoptera, Orthoptera, Embioptera and Dermaptera. Within both groups, some species lay elongate ovoid eggs while other species lay eggs of a more specialized shape. The presence or absence of a delimiting cytoplasmic layer at the outer surface of the zygote, beneath the vitelline membrane, also varies among species of both groups. A thin *periplasm*, as this layer is called, has been described for certain odonatan, orthopteran and dermapteran eggs by Heymons (1895), Roonwal (1936), Johannsen and Butt (1941) and Bhatnagar and Singh (1965), but is reported to be absent in other species of these orders (Seidel, 1929; Mahr, 1960) and in representative Dictyoptera, Isoptera (Fig. 1*a*) and Plecoptera (Seidel, 1929; Görg, 1959; Striebel, 1960).

The hemimetabolous insects, of course, also include a group of more recently evolved orders, the Psocoptera, Mallophaga, Anoplura, Thysanoptera, Homoptera and Heteroptera, which can be categorized under the general term Paraneoptera. In many respects, the eggs of paraneopterous insects retain the features already described for the Palaeoptera and Polyneoptera. They are rich in yolk, poor in cytoplasm, elongate ovoid in shape, convex ventrally and flattened or concave dorsally, with a central nucleus in a small island of cytoplasm. The usual two membranes, chorion and vitelline membrane, enclose the egg, (Psocoptera: Goss, 1952, 1953; Mallophaga: Schölzel, 1937; Anoplura: Schölzel, 1937; Piotrowski, 1953; Thysanoptera: Bournier, 1960; Homoptera: Shinji, 1919; Böhmel and Jancke, 1942; Sander, 1959; Behrendt, 1963; Heteroptera: Seidel, 1924; Mellanby, 1936; Krause, 1939; Butt, 1949; Cobben, 1968). In many species, the dimensions of the egg also remain quite substantial (Table II), although the smaller insects of this group, such as the Psocoptera, Mallophaga and various Homoptera and Heteroptera, tend to lay eggs with dimensions of less than a millimetre. In one feature, however, the eggs of the Paraneoptera are more highly organized than those of the Palaeoptera and Polyneoptera. The yolk bodies of the egg are enmeshed within a reticulum of cytoplasm which permeates the entire egg and merges at the surface with a thin but definite periplasm. As will be seen in the next chapter, the same specialization is convergently expressed in the holometabolous insects.

B. Maturation and Fertilization

Many of the workers who have described the structure of the zygote in Hemimetabola have also provided information on the preceding events of maturation and fertilization. In general, these processes take place in the same manner in all species. When released from the ovary, the oocyte is in the metaphase of the first maturation division. The nucleus lies, at this stage, in a small island of cytoplasm at the periphery of the egg, usually in an anterodorsal location. The two maturation divisions proceed at this location after the penetration of sperm into the oocyte. Three polar nuclei and a haploid female pronucleus are formed. The polar nuclei remain grouped together beneath the surface of the oocyte, while the female pronucleus migrates back into the interior, surrounded by a small island of cytoplasm. Union with a male pronucleus is then effected. Polyspermy is usual among hemimetabolan eggs, and frequently all of the sperm nuclei which penetrate the oocyte change simultaneously into swollen, vesicular, male pronuclei, but only one becomes functional in this capacity (but *cf.* Counce, 1972). The remainder, are resorbed during early cleavage of the egg, together with the three polar nuclei.

III. CLEAVAGE AND BLASTODERM FORMATION

A. Early Cleavage

In all oviparous, hemimetabolous insects, the zygote enters into a cleavage sequence in which repeated synchronous nuclear division takes place, accompanied by the accretion and division of islands of cytoplasm around the daughter nuclei, without corresponding divisions of the egg as a whole (Heymons, 1895; Giardina, 1897; Shinji, 1919; Seidel, 1924, 1929; Roonwal, 1936; Thomas, 1936; Schölzel, 1937; Krause, 1938a, 1939; Miller, 1939; Johannsen and Butt, 1941; Böhmel and Jancke, 1942; Butt, 1949; Goss, 1952; Kanellis, 1952; Görg, 1959; Sander, 1959; Mahr, 1960; Striebel, 1960; Stefani, 1961; Behrendt, 1963). It is customary to speak of each cleavage nucleus and its associated island of cytoplasm as a *cleavage energid*. Due to technical problems in the resolution of details, there is still indecision about the source of the cytoplasm that accumulates in the cleavage energids and also some doubt as to whether the energids remain connected with one another across the yolk-filled intervals between them. Electron-microscopy will, no doubt, serve to resolve these problems in due course.

Following each synchronous nuclear division, the cleavage energids spread in all directions through the substance of the egg, which can now be termed the *yolk mass*. (Yolk-plasmodium and yolk-endoplasm system are alternative terms that have been used to describe the yolk mass after it has begun to become populated by nuclei.) Two stages in the spread of cleavage energids through the yolk mass, one with eight energids following the third synchronous cleavage, the other with 32 energids following the fifth synchronous cleavage, are illustrated for the termite *Kalotermes flavicollis* in Figs 2a and b. The manner in which the energids divide and spread during cleavage in the Hemimetabola manifests no reminiscence of any recognizable pattern of ancestral total cleavage.

The rate at which early cleavage proceeds has been measured in only a few species of Hemimetabola. The slowest rate so far described is that of the plecopteran *Pteronarcys proteus*, in which eight days are required to complete six synchronous divisions, yielding 64 nuclei (Miller, 1939). The same stage is attained in *Kalotermes* in 48 hours (Striebel, 1960; see Table IV) and in the ephemeropteran *Baetis rhodani* in 30 hours (Illies, 1968). Odonatan eggs

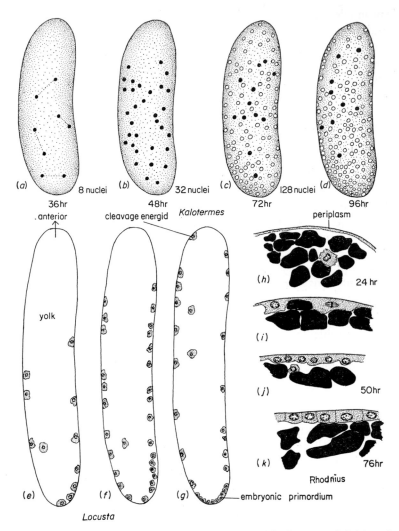

FIG. 2. (a)–(d) Cleavage stages of *Kalotermes flavicollis* (Isoptera) in diagrammatic left lateral view. Intralecithal nuclei are shown as solid circles, superficial nuclei as open circles. After Striebel (1960); (e)–(g) Diagrammatic sagittal sections of the egg of *Locusta migratoria* during cleavage, after Roonwal (1937), showing the pattern of invasion of the surface of the yolk mass by cleavage energids and onset of formation of the embryonic primordium; (h)–(k) Diagrammatic transverse sections illustrating blastoderm formation in *Rhodnius prolixus* (Heteroptera), after Mellanby (1936). The cleavage energids approach the periplasm (h), merge with it and undergo further divisions with tangential spindles (i), establishing the syncytial blastoderm (j). Cellularization of the blastoderm (k) then takes place.

complete seven divisions, yielding 128 nuclei, in 21 hours (Seidel, 1929; Fig. 3*b*), while in the Orthoptera, early cleavage may proceed as fast as one synchronous division every one and a half hours (Roonwal, 1936; Kanellis, 1952; Mahr, 1960; Sauer, 1966), giving 512 nuclei in thirteen and a half hours. The latter rate is also typical of the larger paraneopteran eggs and is increased even more in some of the smaller eggs within this group. No hemimetabolan eggs, however, exhibit cleavage rates which compare with the fastest among the Holometabola (see chapter 4).

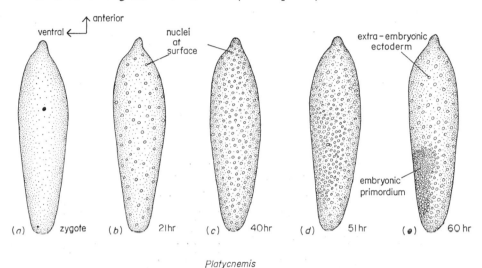

Platycnemis

FIG. 3. Development of the blastoderm and differentiation of the embryonic primordium of *Platycnemis pennipes* (Odonata) in diagrammatic lateral view, after Seidel (1929). (*a*) Zygote; (*b*) Emergence of cleavage energids at the surface of the yolk mass; (*c*) Uniform blastoderm; (*d*) Early differentiated blastoderm; (*e*) Completion of condensation of the embryonic primordium within the differentiated blastoderm.

After their initial sequence of division and spread through the yolk mass, the cleavage energids begin to move outwards and populate the surface of the yolk mass, initiating blastoderm formation. In some orders, the cleavage energids first emerge in uniform array over the entire surface of the yolk mass (Fig. 3*b*; Odonata: Seidel, 1929; Johannsen and Butt, 1941; Ephemeroptera: Illies, 1968; Plecoptera: Miller, 1939; Embioptera: Stefani, 1961; Dermaptera: Heymons, 1895; Bhatnagar and Singh, 1965; and the paraneopterous orders, Mellanby, 1936; Schölzel, 1937; Krause, 1939; Butt, 1949; Goss, 1952; Sander, 1959; Behrendt, 1963). The stage of cleavage at which the energids arrive at the surface varies among species, however, from the 64-energid stage following the sixth cleavage division in the small egg of *Liposcelis divergens* (Psocoptera), through the 128-energid stage in the

Odonata, Plecoptera and Embioptera to the 1024-energid stage following the tenth cleavage division in *Haematopinus eurysternus* (Anoplura) and *Euscelis plebejus* (Homoptera).

In complete contrast, several orders of Polyneoptera consistently exhibit a first emergence of cleavage energids at the posterior pole of the surface of the yolk mass, followed by a progressive invasion of the more anterior parts of the surface (Figs 2*e–g*; Dictyoptera: Heymons, 1895; Görg, 1959; Isoptera: Striebel, 1960; Orthoptera: Korotneff, 1885; Krause, 1939; Kanellis, 1952; Ibrahim, 1957; Mahr, 1960; Sauer, 1966; and especially Cheleutoptera: Leuzinger *et al.*, 1926; Thomas, 1936; Bergerard, 1958; Bedford, 1970). As might be expected, the tendency for the early cleavage energids to approach the surface in a localized area at the posterior pole results in a relatively precocious first emergence of energids from the yolk mass. Even in the relatively large eggs of *Kalotermes flavicollis*, *Acheta* (=*Gryllus*) *domesticus* and *Carausius morosus* (Table II), the energids are first seen at the surface at the 64-energid stage, after only six synchronous divisions have taken place.

B. Vitellophages

All hemimetabolous embryos are characterized by the formation of *vitellophages*, nuclei with encompassing islands of cytoplasm which lie within the yolk mass as agents of yolk digestion and do not participate structurally, with one possible exception—*cf*. Section XI, D, in the formation of any definitive organ of the embryo. In many cases, numerous vitellophages arise directly by the further division of cleavage energids which remain within the yolk mass as their fellow energids migrate to the surface. These *primary vitellophages*, as they may be called, are found in the Odonata (Seidel, 1929; Johannsen and Butt, 1941), the Ephemeroptera (Illies, 1968), some Dictyoptera (Görg, 1959), the Orthoptera (Ayers, 1884; Wheeler, 1893; Roonwal, 1936; Krause, 1938*a*; Kanellis, 1952; Mahr, 1960), the Embioptera (Stefani, 1961), the Dermaptera (Heymons, 1895) and the Paraneoptera (Shinji, 1919; Seidel, 1924; Mellanby, 1936; Schölzel, 1937; Böhmel and Jancke, 1942; Butt, 1949; Goss, 1952; Piotrowski, 1953; Jura, 1959; Sander, 1959). The initial number of primary vitellophages is usually small, e.g. *Kalotermes*, 12–15 (Figs 2*c, d*), *Gryllus*, about 20, *Locusta*, 36–47 (Figs 2*f, g*), but the vitellophages undergo further divisions in most species as blastoderm formation proceeds at the surface of the yolk mass. Controversies on the phylogenetic relationship between the vitellophages and the developing midgut in hemimetabolous embryos (Johannsen and Butt, 1941) can be dismissed on the grounds that almost all cleavage cells have some capacity to digest and assimilate yolk and that it is but a small step, when yolk is dense and cleavage predominantly a matter of nuclear proliferation, to confine this role to certain specialized cleavage products. There is no reason to assume that cleavage energids specialized in this way are the phylogenetic descendants of ancestral midgut cells alone

In most Dictyoptera, Plecoptera and gryllotalpid Orthoptera, as far as is known, none of the cleavage energids assume the role of primary vitellophages (Wheeler, 1889a; Giardina, 1897; Miller, 1939). All energids migrate to the surface of the yolk mass, leaving the latter temporarily devoid of nuclei. As proliferation of cleavage energids continues at the surface of the yolk mass, however, some of the division products migrate back into the interior and assume a vitellophage role. Vitellophages originating in this alternative fashion can be called *secondary vitellophages*. Like the primary vitellophages, the secondary vitellophages can be regarded as specialized cleavage products having no direct association with an ancestral midgut.

A similar invasion of secondary vitellophages into a yolk mass already populated by primary vitellophages is a common mode of augmenting the vitellophage number in other Polyneoptera and Paraneoptera (Wheeler, 1889a; Heymons, 1895; Giardina, 1897; Roonwal, 1936; Thomas, 1936; Krause, 1938a; Miller, 1939; Butt, 1949; Goss, 1952; Görg, 1959; Striebel, 1960; Stefani, 1961; Bhatnagar and Singh, 1965). Nothing is yet known of any possible functional differences between primary vitellophages and secondary vitellophages in these species.

C. Blastoderm Formation

The immediate consequence of the arrival of the cleavage energids at the surface of the yolk mass is continued proliferation leading to the formation of a superficial layer of low, cuboidal cells. The cells may be distributed uniformly over the entire surface, giving a *uniform cellular blastoderm*. Alternatively, there may already be a differential concentration of cells in a localized area at the surface, with a more attenuated distribution elsewhere. This pattern of distribution can conveniently be termed a *differentiating blastoderm*, since it represents a precocious expression of a differentiated condition later entered into by the uniform cellular blastoderm of other eggs.

Among the primitive Hemimetabola, the formation of a uniform cellular blastoderm (Fig. 3c) is characteristic of the Odonata (Seidel, 1929; Johannsen and Butt, 1941), the Ephemeroptera (Illies, 1968), the Plecoptera (Miller, 1939), some Orthoptera (Wheeler, 1893; Kanellis, 1952; Mahr, 1960; Sauer, 1966), the Embioptera (Stefani, 1961) and the Dermaptera (Heymons, 1895; Bhatnagar and Singh, 1965). It usually follows uniform emergence of the cleavage energids at the surface of the yolk mass but may, as in *Acheta domesticus*, follow polarized emergence. The energids continue to divide and move apart, populating more and more of the surface, until they meet to form a continuous layer of cells. Synchrony of division is usually maintained (*cf.* Counce, 1972). *Platycnemis pennipes*, for instance, shows two synchronous divisions after uniform emergence of the energids has taken place at the 128-energid stage (Fig. 3*b*), giving a uniform cellular blastoderm of about 500 cells (Fig. 3*c*; Seidel, 1929). *Acheta domesticus* exhibits three synchronous divisions after posterior polar emergence at the 64-energid stage, according to Sauer (1966).

Direct formation of a differentiating blastoderm (Figs 2*c*, *d* and *g*), in contrast, is observed in the Dictyoptera (Wheeler, 1889*a*; Heymons, 1895), the Isoptera (Striebel, 1960), the Cheleutoptera (Leuzinger *et al.*, 1926; Thomas, 1936; Bergerard, 1958), and a variety of orthopterans (Korotneff, 1885; Heymons, 1895; Nusbaum and Fulinski, 1909; Roonwal, 1936). Characteristically, these are species in which the cleavage energids first reach the surface of the yolk mass at the posterior pole, usually at the 64-energid stage. Unlike those species which form a uniform cellular blastoderm, the inception of a directly formed, differentiating blastoderm begins with loss of cleavage synchrony as soon as the polar group of energids emerges at the surface of the yolk mass. Divisions become random, but the division products tend to remain concentrated around the region of first emergence, spreading more thinly elsewhere. In the Isoptera and Cheleutoptera, polarization is extreme, the blastoderm being completed anteriorly only after the germ band has begun to develop at the posterior pole of the egg.

Blastoderm formation in the Paraneoptera proceeds more directly (Seidel, 1924; Mellanby, 1936; Schölzel, 1937; Böhmel and Jancke, 1942; Goss, 1952; Piotrowski, 1953; Sander, 1956; Jura, 1959). As the cleavage energids arrive uniformly at the surface of the yolk mass, they fuse with the periplasm (Figs 2*h*, *i*). A series of further synchronous, tangential mitoses now takes place and the nuclei become closely packed within a *uniform syncytial blastoderm* (Fig. 2*j*). Cell membranes then form simultaneously throughout the syncytial blastoderm, transforming it into a uniform cellular blastoderm (Fig. 2*k*).

IV. THE DIFFERENTIATED BLASTODERM

In hemimetabolous embryos, whether the cellular blastoderm is initially uniform or is precociously differentiating, a phase of development now ensues in which a part of the blastoderm, the already concentrated part in the case of a differentiating blastoderm, becomes more densely packed and columnar, while the remainder becomes attenuated over the surface of the yolk mass (Figs 3*d*, *e*). The cells which become densely packed constitute the *embryonic primordium*. The more attenuated cells form the *extra-embryonic ectoderm*. The uniform or differentiating blastoderm thus becomes a *differentiated blastoderm*. It is important to emphasize that during this phase, the embryonic primordium remains a monolayer of cells. The onset of gastrulation movements which carry some of the cells of the embryonic primordium beneath the surface as mesodermal and other internal components awaits completion of the differentiated blastoderm.

The formation of the embryonic primordium takes place more by cellular aggregation than by the proliferation of new cells (Heymons, 1895; Leuzinger et al., 1926; Seidel, 1929, 1935; Thomas, 1936; Mellanby, 1936; Roonwal, 1936; Schölzel, 1937; Miller, 1939; Krause, 1939; Butt, 1949; Goss, 1952; Kanellis, 1952; Sander, 1959; Mahr, 1960; Striebel, 1960). Contractions of the yolk mass have been shown to play a causal role in the process of aggregation of the cells of the embryonic primordium in the differentiated blastoderm in several species (*Platycnemis*, Seidel, 1929; *Acheta*, Krause, 1938a, b; Kanellis, 1952; Mahr, 1957, 1960; Sauer, 1966; *Kalotermes*, Striebel, 1960) and it seems likely that this is a universal phenomenon in the Hemimetabola.

The final location of the embryonic primordium on the surface of the yolk mass varies considerably among species (Fig. 4a–d), even though aggregation usually begins in the same way, bilaterally on the ventrolateral surfaces of the posterior half of the yolk mass, and proceeds towards the ventral midline (Heymons, 1895; Seidel, 1929; Mellanby, 1936; Roonwal, 1936; Sander, 1959; Mahr, 1960; Striebel, 1960; Stefani, 1961; Koch, 1964; Louvet, 1964; Sauer, 1966). Most frequently, the embryonic primordium is located posteroventrally, (Fig. 4a–d) as in the Odonata, Dictyoptera, Isoptera, Embioptera, some Orthoptera and all Paraneoptera, but it may be posterior, as in the Ephemeroptera, Cheleutoptera and some other Orthoptera, or midventral, as in the Plecoptera, Dermaptera and a few Orthoptera.

The shape of the embryonic primordium also varies. Most hemimetabolous orders display a precocious formation of incipient *head lobes* as paired lateral enlargements of the anterior part of the primordium. The head lobes are sometimes referred to as the *protocephalon*, in contrast to the remainder of the primordium, which is called, in this terminology, the *protocorm*. Subsequent development reveals that the head lobes comprise the rudiment of the antennal and preantennal part of the head, so that an alternative term for the protocorm is the *post-antennal* region of the embryonic primordium. The extent of direct formation of this part of the primordium differs considerably among species. The embryonic primordia of the Ephemeroptera, Odonata (Fig. 4b), blattid Dictyoptera (Fig. 4a), Embioptera, Dermaptera and the paraneopterans have a relatively long post-antennal region which develops directly into the gnathal segments, the thoracic segments and a segment-forming growth zone from which the abdomen arises (Wheeler, 1893; Heymons, 1895, 1896a, b; Kershaw, 1914; Seidel, 1924, 1929, 1935; Mellanby, 1936; Schölzel, 1937; Johannsen and Butt, 1941; Böhmel and Jancke, 1942; Butt, 1949; Goss, 1952; Sander, 1959; Behrendt, 1963; Illies, 1968). The Cheleutoptera and Orthoptera, in contrast, together with most of the

Dictyoptera, develop shorter, heart-shaped embryonic primordia in which the post-antennal region consists only of a pointed segment-forming growth zone (Wheeler, 1893; Heymons, 1895; Hagan, 1917; Leuzinger *et al.*, 1926; Nelsen, 1931, 1934; Slifer, 1932*b*; Else, 1934; Roonwal, 1936; Thomas, 1936; Krause, 1938*a, b*, 1939; Steele, 1941; Jhingran, 1947; Salt, 1949; Bodenheimer and Shulov, 1951; Matthée, 1951; Kanellis, 1952; Ibrahim,

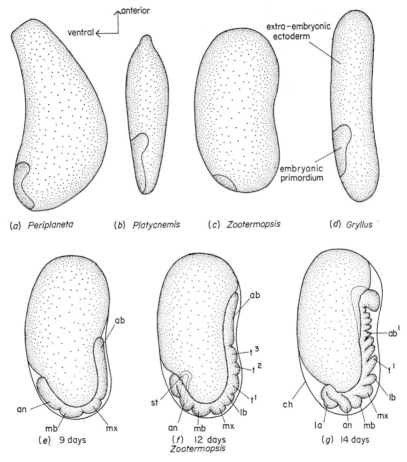

FIG. 4. (*a*)–(*d*) Diagrams showing the form and position of the embryonic primordium relative to the yolk mass in the differentiated blastoderm of a palaeopteran and various polyneopterans. (*a*) *Periplanata americana* (Dictyoptera), after Heymons (1895), (*b*) *Platycnemis pennipes* (Odonata), after Seidel (1929), (*c*) *Zootermopsis nevadensis* (Isoptera) after Striebel (1960), (*d*) *Acheta* (*Gryllus*) *domesticus* (Orthoptera), after Mahr (1960); (*e*)–(*g*) Stages in elongation and segmentation of the germ band of *Zootermopsis nevadensis*, in diagrammatic left lateral view, after Striebel (1960). The embryonic membranes are omitted in these diagrams. *ab*, abdominal rudiment; *abs*, first abdominal segment; *an*, antenna; *ch*, chorion; *la*, labrum; *lb*, labium; *mb*, mandible; *mx*, maxilla; *st*, stomo-daeum; t^{1-3}, thoracic segments.

1957; Bergerard, 1958; Görg, 1959; Shulov and Pener, 1959, 1963; Mahr, 1960; Riegert, 1961; Rakshpal, 1962; Koch, 1964; Louvet, 1964; Van Horn, 1966; Fournier, 1967; Bedford, 1970). Finally, the Isoptera (Fig. 4c) and Plecoptera develop simple, disc-shaped embryonic primordia in which not even the incipient head lobes can be distinguished (Miller, 1939; Striebel, 1960).

Krause (1939) proposed a classification of pterygote embryos based on differences in the length of the embryonic primordium relative to the size of

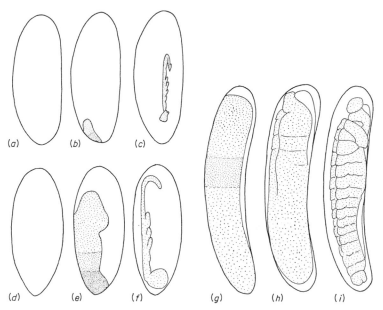

FIG. 5. The basic pterygote germ types, modified after Krause and Sander (1962). (a)–(c) *Tachycines*, (Orthoptera) a "short germ" embryo; (d)–(f) *Notonecta* (Heteroptera) a "semi-long germ" embryo; (g)–(i) *Pimpla* (Hymenoptera, Holometabola), a "long germ" embryo. All diagrams are drawn with the ventral surface on the left. The region of dense shading in the embryonic primordium in b and e is the segment-forming growth zone.

the egg, distinguishing between long, semilong and short-germ types (Fig. 5). This classification has considerable practical value, especially in discussions of the experimental analysis of causal processes in insect embryos. In terms of the hemimetabolan embryonic primordia described above, primordia with a well developed postantennal region are of the semilong type, while the remainder are of the short type. Long-germ embryos occur only in the Holometabola, which are discussed in Chapter 4.

By comparison with the Onychophora, Myriapoda and most apterygote insects, all of which tend to form the ectoderm of several segments directly in the blastoderm, the short-germ type of embryonic primordium in hemi-metabolous pterygotes can be presumed to be secondary and to have evolved convergently in several orders. The functional advantages of this modification, especially in its extreme manifestation in the Isoptera and Plecoptera, are not yet obvious.

V. ELONGATION AND SEGMENTATION OF THE GERM BAND

As soon as the embryonic primordium begins to increase in length, preliminary to the onset of external segmentation, the primordium can conveniently be called a *germ band*. In due course, when growth in length is completed and all segments of the body are delineated, the germ band becomes a *segmented germ band* (Fig. 6a–c). The first phase of growth of the germ band, prior to the onset of segment delineation, is accompanied by the formation of an inner layer of cells beneath the external layer. This process will be discussed in the next section under the heading of gastrulation. For the present, we can concentrate on changes in the external form and position of the germ band as segment delineation takes place.

A. Segment Delineation

When the post-antennal region of the embryonic primordium is relatively long and the rudiments of the first few postoral segments are already formed within it, segment delineation may begin with the third thoracic segment, immediately in front of the growth zone, and proceed forwards from this segment, then progressively backwards as the segment-forming growth zone extends the abdomen posteriorly (Ephemeroptera, Heymons, 1896a, b; Illies, 1968; Odonata, Seidel, 1929; Johannsen and Butt, 1941; *Blatella germanica*, Wheeler, 1889a). The same sequence of segment delineation (Fig. 6d–f) is retained in some embryos in which the embryonic primordium is short and all post-antennal growth stems from a growth zone (gryllid orthopterans, Krause, 1938a, 1939; Kanellis, 1952; Ibrahim, 1957; Mahr, 1960; Rakshpal, 1962; Cheleutoptera, Leuzinger *et al.*, 1926; Bergerard, 1958; Fournier, 1967; Bedford, 1970). More often, however, as is displayed for *Kalotermes flavicollis* in Figs 4e–g and 10a–c, growth of the germ band is followed by segment delineation in strict anteroposterior succession. This mode of growth occurs in the Dictyoptera, the Isoptera, the Plecoptera, the acridid and tettigoniid Orthoptera, the Embioptera, the Dermaptera and the paraneopteran, orders (Graber, 1888a, b, c, 1890; Wheeler, 1893; Heymons, 1895; Kershaw, 1914; Hagan, 1917; Nelsen, 1931, 1934; Slifer, 1932b; Else, 1934; Mellanby, 1936; Roonwal, 1936, 1937; Schölzel, 1937; Miller, 1939, 1940; Steele, 1941; Böhmel and Jancke, 1942; Jhingran, 1947; Butt, 1949; Salt, 1949; Gerwel, 1950; Bodenheimer and Shulov, 1951; Matthée, 1951; Brookes, 1952; Goss,

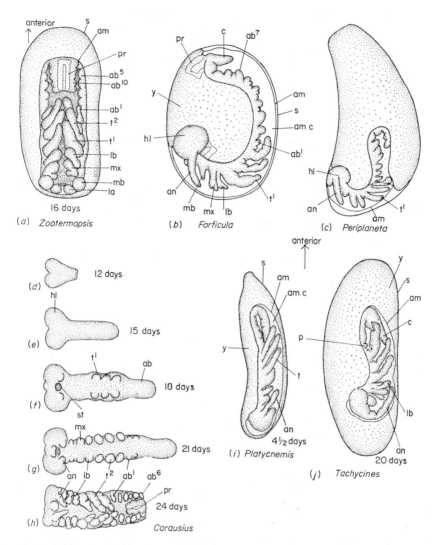

FIG. 6. (a) The segmented germ band stage of *Zootermopsis nevadensis* (Isoptera) viewed from the dorsal surface, after Striebel (1960); (b) The segmented germ band stage of *Forficula auricularia* (Dermaptera) in left lateral view, after Heymons (1895); (c) The segmented germ band stage of *Periplaneta americana* (Dictyoptera) in left lateral view, after Heymons (1895); (d)–(h) Stages in the elongation and segmentation of the germ band of *Carausius morosus* (Cheleutoptera), after Fournier (1967). The isolated germ band is shown in "ventral" view, with the anterior end on the left; (i) and (j) The segmented germ band stage of *Platycnemis pennipes* (Odonata) and *Tachycines asynomorus* (Orthoptera) in left lateral view, after Seidel (1929) and Ibrahim (1957). ab$^{1-10}$, abdominal segments; am, amnion; amc, amniotic cavity; an, antenna; c, cercus; hl, head lobe; la, labrum; lb, labium; mb, mandible; mx, maxilla; p, pleuropodium; pr, proctodeum, s, serosa; t$^{1-3}$, thoracic segments; y, yolk.

1952; Görg, 1959; Shulov and Pener, 1959, 1963; Striebel, 1960; Riegert, 1961; Stefani, 1961; Bhatnagar and Singh, 1965; Van Horn, 1966; Cobben, 1968). The small, circular embryonic primordium of Isoptera and Plecoptera precedes elongation with a phase of uniform growth by scattered cell divisions, which only gradually become confined to the posterior growth zone.

B. Superficial Growth

As the germ band increases in length and width, it extends either along the surface of the yolk mass or into the interior of the yolk mass. The Dictyoptera show the simplest pattern of growth of the segmenting germ band (Wheeler, 1889a; Hagan, 1917; Görg, 1959). Growth proceeds in a posterior direction along the ventral surface of the yolk mass, accompanied by a slight forward shift of the anterior end of the germ band and a downward flexure of the posterior end when it reaches the posterior pole of the yolk mass. Only *Periplaneta* (Figs 4a, 6c) shows some upgrowth of the elongating germ band around the posterior pole of the egg, accompanied by partial immersion of the posterior end in the yolk mass.

The Dermaptera (Fig. 6b) and the gryllotalpid Orthoptera retain the superficial pattern of growth, but in these insects the germ band extends around the posterior pole and forward along the dorsal surface to the anterior pole (Heymons, 1895; Bhatnagar and Singh, 1965). A similar mode of growth is displayed by the germ band of the Cheleutoptera, but in association with the relatively large volume of the yolk mass, the posterior end of the segmented germ band remains some distance from the anterior pole of the yolk mass (Koch, 1964; Fournier, 1967; Bedford, 1970). Further details of this process are illustrated and summarized in Figs 19 and 20 and the associated Table III. A conspicuous caudal flexure develops in the segmenting germ band of the Cheleutoptera (Fig. 6h).

The Isoptera and Embioptera display a slightly more complex pattern of growth of the germ band (Kershaw, 1914; Striebel, 1960). The details of the process are illustrated for *Nasutitermes exitiosus* in Fig. 21 and summarized for *Kalotermes flavicollis* in Table IV. Figures 4g and 6a illustrate stages in the growth of the segmenting germ band of *Zootermopsis nevadensis*. As can be seen, while the germ band grows around the posterior pole of the yolk mass and forwards along the dorsal surface, the abdomen begins to flex in the dorso-ventral plane, pressing into the yolk mass so that the germ band becomes S-shaped. Caudal flexure then takes place, bringing the last few abdominal segments close beneath the more anterior part of the abdomen (Figs 6a, 11c). In the Embioptera, the abdomen flexes more deeply into the yolk than in the Isoptera and a small amount of yolk comes to lie above the ventral surface of the abdomen on the dorsal side of the egg.

C. Immersed Growth: Anatrepsis

Immersion into the yolk mass is much more strongly expressed during the growth of the segmenting germ band of several orders of Hemimetabola, culminating in *total immersion* of the segmented germ band within the yolk mass. This phenomenon is generally regarded as the first episode in a series of embryonic movements bracketed together by Wheeler (1893) under the general term *blastokinesis*. Wheeler distinguished the preliminary, immersive phase of blastokinesis as *anatrepsis*, a term that has subsequently come into general use. The reciprocal movement, *katatrepsis*, is discussed in a later section.

Growth accompanied by anatrepsis is observed in the segmenting germ band of the Ephemeroptera, the Odonata, most Orthoptera and all para-neopterans except the heteropteran genus *Coranus*, and has been described by many workers (Ephemeroptera: Heymons, 1896a, b; Ando and Kawana, 1956; Illies, 1968; Odonata: Seidel, 1929; Johannsen and Butt, 1941; Orthoptera: Graber, 1888a, b, c, 1890; Wheeler, 1893; Nelsen, 1931, 1934; Slifer, 1932b; Else, 1934; Roonwal, 1936; Krause, 1938a, 1939; Jannone, 1939; Steele, 1941; Jhingran, 1947; Salt, 1949; Bodenheimer and Shulov, 1951; Matthée, 1951; Kanellis, 1952; Ibrahim, 1957; Shulov and Pener, 1959, 1963; Mahr, 1960; Salzen, 1960; Riegert, 1961; Rakshpal, 1962; Van Horn, 1966; Chapman and Witham, 1968; Paraneoptera: Shinji, 1919; Seidel, 1924; Mellanby, 1936; Schölzel, 1937; Krause, 1939; Böhmel and Jancke, 1942; Butt, 1949; Gerwel, 1950; Goss, 1952; Piotrowski, 1953; Jura, 1959; Sander, 1959; Bournier, 1960; Cobben, 1968). The results of the process are illustrated by Figs 6i and j, 7b and c. The growth, segmentation and anatrepsis of the germ band of *Tachycines asynamorus*, a representative and carefully studied orthopteran, are summarized in Table V.

In hemimetabolan species with an immersed germ band, the onset of activity of the growth zone is accompanied by flexure of the posterior end of the germ band forwards and upwards (Figs 7a, 16d). This bending appears to be an exaggerated and precocious onset of the curvature which carries the posterior part of the germ band of the Isoptera and Embioptera partially into the yolk mass as described above. Hemimetabolan embryos which develop an immersed germ band include species in which the embryonic primordium is located posteroventrally, or posteriorly, or ventrally, and is elongated or heart shaped, e.g. the orthopteran *Xiphidium ensiferum*, with a heart-shaped, midventral embryonic primordium and the odonatan *Platycnemis pennipes*, with an elongated, posteroventral embryonic primordium (Wheeler, 1893; Seidel, 1929). The evidence clearly suggests that anatrepsis, leading to an immersed germ band, is a secondary phenomenon in hemimetabolan development and has evolved convergently in the Palaeoptera, the Orthoptera and the Paraneoptera.

As growth continues, the posterior end of the germ band penetrates through the yolk mass towards the anterior pole (Fig. 16e). The anterior end of the germ band remains superficial during the early part of this growth, but eventually separates from the surface. Separation occurs at an early stage of growth in Orthoptera, and the germ band migrates as a whole to a position beneath the dorsal surface of the yolk mass. Krause and Sander (1962) have indicated that contractile activity of the yolk mass plays an important role in this migration. In the Odonata, the Ephemeroptera, and the Paraneoptera, in contrast, separation of the anterior end of the germ band from the surface is delayed until growth and segmentation of the germ band are more or less completed. At the end of anatrepsis, the germ band usually has the same orientation relative to the yolk mass as in the Isoptera, namely dorsal, with the head lobes directed towards the posterior pole, but is immersed rather than superficial. The similarity is further emphasized by the development of a caudal flexure, especially conspicuous in the Paraneoptera (Fig. 7b). A secondary rotation of the germ band through 180° occurs in many Heteroptera (Fig. 11f). The functional significance of anatrepsis in hemimetabolan development is not understood at the present time.

The germ band of the plecopteran *Pteronarcys proteus*, growing along the flat ventral surface of a hemispherical egg, also becomes immersed in the yolk mass, but by a different modification of the growth pattern seen in the Isoptera and Embioptera (Miller, 1939, 1940). Growth initially extends the germ band across the flat ventral face of the egg. When the posterior end of the germ band reaches the margin of this surface, however, continued growth is accompanied by a flexing of the abdomen up into the yolk mass. The germ band gradually curves more deeply into the yolk mass until, finally, the two ends are withdrawn from the surface and the germ band becomes fully immersed and rotates onto its right side, with the dorsal surface facing outwards.

D. Limb Buds, Stomodaeum, Proctodaeum and Labrum

During the growth and segmentation of the germ band, whether in a superficial or an immersed position, limb buds develop on the head and thorax (Figs 4g, 6a–j, 7b, 10c, 19, 20, 21, 22). As abdominal segment delineation nears completion, limb buds also begin to develop to the abdominal segments, but consideration of these is deferred to a later section (X, B). The sequence in which the limb buds appear on the head and thorax is a direct consequence of the order in which the segments are delineated. If this is anteroposterior, the limb buds develop in strict succession, antennal, gnathal and thoracic (Figs 4f, g, 10b, c). If, on the other hand, the segmental sequence begins in the thorax, the order of limb bud development is reversed (Figs 6f, g). The antennal limb buds always originate behind the stomodaeum, at the posterolateral corners of the head lobes (Figs 6g, 10b).

Following the onset of growth of the antennal rudiments, the labrum pouches out in the midline between the head lobes, in front of the stomodaeum (Figs 4g, 6g, 10c). The labrum almost always develops as a single lobe, a paired origin being described only in *Carausius*, *Locusta* and *Rhodnius* (Leuzinger *et al.*, 1926; Mellanby, 1937; Roonwal, 1937). Early interpretations of paired labral lobes as vestigial labral limb buds are now generally discounted (Matsuda, 1965).

As indicated above, the stomodaeum invaginates in the midline between the head lobes at an early stage of growth of the segmenting germ band (Figs 4f, 6f, 10b), just as the antennal limb buds are beginning to develop. The invagination of the proctodaeum at the posterior end of the germ band is more delayed, and does not begin until the majority of the abdominal segments have been delineated (Figs 6a, b and h, 10c).

An effective and informative way of summarizing the growth of the segmenting germ band relative to the yolk mass in hemimetabolous embryos was devised by Seidel and is presented in a modified form in Fig. 11. This figure also summarizes the various ways in which the segmented germ band later attains its final location as a result of katatrepsis (see section IX).

VI. GASTRULATION

A. Gastrulation Movements

As pointed out above, the embryonic primordium is a single layer of densely packed, columnar cells. As growth in length begins, however, some of the cells of the embryonic primordium migrate beneath the surface to form an inner layer of cells. The complex of movements through which the inner layer becomes segregated from the outer layer constitutes gastrulation. The elucidation of this process has been difficult in hemimetabolan embryos, due to the rapidity with which gastrulation takes place relative to the slow rate of general development, and to technical problems posed by the tough egg membranes and dense yolk. In some respects, our knowledge of hemimetabolan gastrulation is still unsatisfactory, but the accumulated results of recent studies have served to resolve many of the early controversies reviewed by Johannsen and Butt (1941).

It is now clear that the onset of elongation of the embryonic primordium is accompanied by formation of a groove, the *gastral groove*, extending along the ventral midline and sinking deeper in some species than in others (Odonata: Johannsen and Butt, 1941; Dictyoptera: Graber, 1878; Bruce, 1887; Cholodkowsky, 1891; Viallanes, 1891; Wheeler, 1889a, 1893; Heymons, 1895; Hagan, 1917; Görg, 1959; Isoptera: Striebel, 1960; Plecoptera: Miller, 1939; Orthoptera: Ayers, 1884; Graber, 1890, 1891; Wheeler, 1893;

Heymons, 1895; Nelsen, 1934; Roonwal, 1936; Krause, 1938b; Dermaptera: Heymons, 1895; Bhatnagar and Singh, 1965; Paraneoptera: Seidel, 1924; Mellanby, 1936; Böhmel and Jancke, 1942; Butt, 1949; Goss, 1952, 1953; Piotrowski, 1953; Jura, 1959). The beginnings of formation of the gastral groove are illustrated in Figs 7d, f and h, and the formation and closure of the groove is diagrammatically represented in Figs 9a–c.

The gastral groove results from a sinking of the midventral cells beneath the general surface of the embryonic primordium. The groove is obliterated rapidly as the superficial cells bordering it come together in the ventral midline. The invaginating cells begin to proliferate as they sink inwards, and spread out as an inner layer of cuboidal cells beneath the columnar outer layer. The inner layer spreads laterally as far as the edges of the embryonic primordium (Fig. 7e), and also migrates forwards on either side beneath the head lobes as elongation of the germ band proceeds.

In the Isoptera (Figs 7f, g) and Plecoptera, the gastral groove forms and closes precociously as a pit in the centre of the disc-shaped embryonic primordium and the disc becomes bilaminar before elongation of the germ band begins.

Early workers on several species of Hemimetabola reported an alternative mode of formation of the inner layer by random immigration of cells of the embryonic primordium (see Johannsen and Butt, 1941). In particular, this process was said to be characteristic of the Cheleutoptera (Hammerschmidt, 1910; Leuzinger et al., 1926). More careful observation, however, has tended to refute this view. Louvet (1964), for example, has recently found a typical gastral groove in the early germ band of Carausius morosus.

Around the points of closure of the two ends of the gastral groove, the cells of the outer layer subsequently invaginate and develop as the stomodaeum and proctodaeum. The remainder of the outer layer of the germ band develops as what can be conveniently called embryonic ectoderm. Adherents of the germ-layer interpretation of insect embryonic development have always insisted on calling the stomodaeum and proctodaeum ectodermal structures, and have indulged in a century of altercation over whether or not even the midgut epithelium of insects is of ectodermal origin (see Johannsen and Butt, 1941; Rempel and Church, 1969). Vertebrate embryologists, on the other hand, have abandoned such fruitless semantic discussions in favour of a more operational approach, in which the origin of each circumscribed structure is said to lie with presumptive cells of that structure formed as a result of cleavage, and each group of presumptive cells is said to make up a presumptive area of the early embryo. From the point of view both of posing the right kind of questions for the experimental analysis of causal processes in embryonic development and of making generalizations about the comparative development of different types of embryo, this approach has much to commend

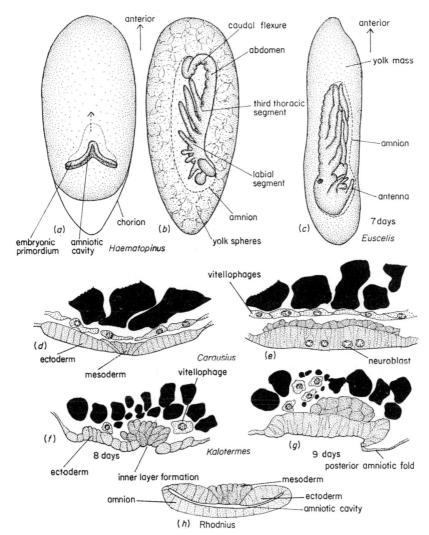

FIG. 7. (a) The embryonic primordium of *Haematopinus eurysternus* (Anoplura) shortly after the onset of elongation, seen in an egg in ventral view, after Schölzel (1937). The posterior end of the germ band has turned forwards into the yolk; (b) The segmented germ band stage of *Haematopinus eurysternus* in right lateral view, after Schölzel (1937); (c) The embryo of *Euscelis plebejus* (Homoptera) just before blastokinesis, in right ventrolateral view, after Sander (1959); (d) and (e) Transverse sections through the embryonic primordium of *Carausius morosus* (Cheleutoptera) showing formation of the inner layer, after Louvet (1964); (f) and (g) Sagittal sections through the embryonic primordium of *Kalotermes flavicollis* (Isoptera) showing formation of the inner layer, after Striebel (1960); (h) Transverse section through the embryonic primordium of *Rhodnius prolixus* (Heteroptera) during formation of the inner layer, after Mellanby (1936).

it, as will be further discussed below. For the moment we can lay the ground-work for such an interpretation by recognizing that the three products of the outer layer of the germ band in Hemimetabola are the embryonic ectoderm (as opposed to the extra-embryonic ectoderm covering the remainder of the yolk mass in the differentiated blastoderm stage), the stomodaeum and the proctodaeum. In similar vein, the cells of the inner layer develop as meso-dermal structures, except in the two locations internal to the stomodaeum and proctodaeum respectively, where they develop as *anterior* and *posterior* *midgut* rudiments (Odonata: Heymons, 1896*a*; Tschuproff, 1903; Dictyop-tera: Heymons, 1895; Rabito, 1898; Görg, 1959; Cheleutoptera: Thomas, 1936; Orthoptera: Heymons, 1895; Nelsen, 1934; Roonwal, 1936, 1937; Krause, 1938*b*; Embioptera: Stefani, 1961; Dermaptera: Heymons, 1895, 1912; Strindberg, 1915; Bhatnagar and Singh, 1965; Paraneoptera: Seidel, 1924; Ries, 1931; Mellanby, 1936, 1937; Schölzel, 1937; Butt, 1949; Goss, 1952). An exceptional subsequent development of the inner layer takes place in the Isoptera, Plecoptera and coccid Homoptera. The Plecoptera and coccids are said to have only a single, posterior, midgut rudiment (Shinji, 1919; Miller, 1939, 1940). The disc-shaped embryonic primordium of Isoptera, with its precocious formation of the inner layer, also establishes a single midgut rudiment, but in this order the rudiment occupies the entire midline of the inner layer (Strindberg, 1913; Striebel, 1960) and is not polarized to either one or both ends. It seems likely that this condition is secondary and is associated with the extreme shortening of the embryonic primordium in the Isoptera.

B. Presumptive Areas of the Blastoderm

On the basis of present information about the segregation of various com-ponents during gastrulation in the hemimetabolan embryo, it now becomes possible to trace a basic pattern of hemimetabolan presumptive areas in the embryonic primordium of the differentiated blastoderm. Each area is made up of cells which have the same general subsequent fate in normal develop-ment. The presumptive areas are (Fig. 8*b*):

   (i) Mid-ventrally, a band of presumptive mesoderm cells.
  (ii) At the ends of the presumptive mesoderm, midventral groups of presumptive anterior midgut and posterior midgut cells.
 (iii) Around the anterior edge of the presumptive anterior midgut, an arc of presumptive stomodaeal cells.
  (iv) Behind the presumptive posterior midgut, a group of presumptive proctodaeal cells.
   (v) Bilaterally on either side of the above ventral areas, paired bands of presumptive embryonic ectoderm cells, usually broadened anteriorly as presumptive head lobe ectoderm.

The fate map presented in Fig. 8*b* is that of the odonatan *Platycnemis pennipes*. Experimental evidence adduced by Seidel (1929, 1935) allows the same map to be augmented by further details in respect of the presumptive embryonic ectoderm. As shown in the figure, it is possible to localize not only the presumptive head lobe and antennal ectoderm, but also the presumptive ectoderm of the three gnathal segments and three thoracic segments and the abdominal growth zone.

Figures 8*c–e* show that essentially the same fate map, with minor variations, can be drawn for the embryonic primordium at the differentiated blastoderm stage of other hemimetabolan orders. Depending on the length of the embryonic primordium, the presumptive ectoderm may include fewer segmental units, the minimal condition of head lobes and growth zone only being exhibited when the embryonic primordium is heart-shaped (Fig. 8*c*) or discoidal (Fig. 8*d*). The Isoptera show a specialized distribution of presumptive midgut as a unitary area in the ventral midline, with presumptive mesoderm on either side. Clearly, however, all of these fate maps are variations on a theme, with a reasonable presumption that the theme is pictured in Fig. 8*b*. Furthermore, Seidel has demonstrated for *Platycnemis* that the same presumptive areas are first established in the uniform blastoderm (Fig. 8*a*). At this stage, the cells of the embryonic presumptive areas are thinly spread over a large part of the surface of the yolk mass. The presumptive areas then gain their more localized distribution by aggregation during the differentiation of the blastoderm. Figure 8*a* can thus be taken to represent a truly basic fate map for the hemimetabolan blastoderm.

The application of the presumptive area concept to comparisons between pterygote embryos and those of other terrestrial arthropods is discussed at the end of the chapter. It merely remains to point out that, in the light of this interpretation, the early controversies on the identification of the germ-layers of hemimetabolous insects become redundant. The germ layer interpretation of embryonic development was based originally on what could be seen with nineteenth century microscopes following nineteenth century histology. For insects, this was very little, as has already been pointed out. In addition, the fact that insect embryos could not be accommodated within the original germ-layer concept, e.g. in the apparent ectodermal origin of their midgut in many species, led to immediate difficulties. As better morphological and histological data have been gathered, these difficulties have increased rather than diminished, yet the germ layer terminology and associated controversy has retained its tenacious hold in paper after paper on hemimetabolan embryology. We can now see, however, that if the embryonic primordium is zoned topographically to show the subsequent normal fate of its cells, the resulting fate map identifies all the major rudiments of the embryo according to their cell locations in the blastoderm and the important experimental questions

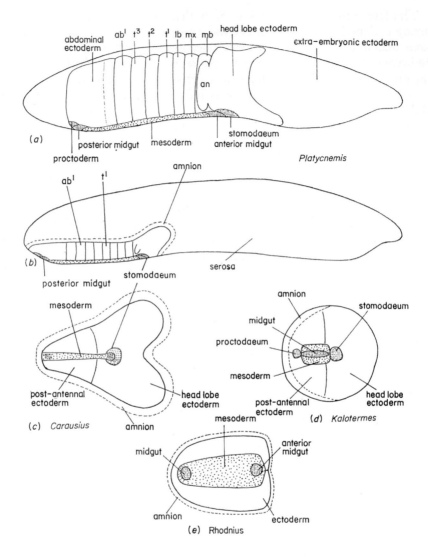

FIG. 8. Presumptive area patterns in hemimetabolous insects. All diagrams are drawn with the anterior end on the right. (*a*) Presumptive areas of the uniform blastoderm of *Platycnemis pennipes* (Odonata), seen in right lateral view at the 40-hour stage (compare Fig. 3*c*), after Seidel (1935) with modifications; (*b*) the same presumptive areas at the 60-hour, differentiated blastoderm stage, following concentration of the embryonic primordium and attenuation of the serosal rudiment (compare Fig. 3*e*); (*c*)–(*e*) presumptive areas of the embryonic primordium of *Carausius morosus* (Cheleutoptera), *Kalotermes flavicollis* (Isoptera) and *Rhodnius prolixus* (Heteroptera) in ventral view, based on data of Louvet (1964), Striebel (1960) and Mellanby (1936). The remainder of the differentiated blastoderm (the serosal area) is omitted in (*c*), (*d*) and (*e*). ab, first abdominal segment; an, antenna; lb, labium; mb, mandible; mx, maxilla; t$^{1-3}$, thoracic segments.

then become, what are the differences between the cells of these rudiments and how do they arise? To say, for example, that the stomodaeum develops from ectoderm, begs the question of what is ectoderm, except a synonym for outer layer. What we really want to know is how the cells of the stomodaeal presumptive area acquire and express their fate in normal development before, during and after the blastoderm stage of development. The terms outer layer and inner layer can usefully be retained as descriptive generalizations for pterygote embryos after gastrulation, but only if shorn of their germ layer implications.

VII. EXTRA-EMBRYONIC MEMBRANES

In addition to the embryonic presumptive areas which aggregate during differentiation of the blastoderm to form the embryonic primordium, there is also an area of presumptive *extra-embryonic ectoderm* covering the remainder of the yolk mass (Fig. 8a). In Hemimetabola, as aggregation of the cells of the embryonic primordium proceeds, the extra-embryonic ectoderm becomes attenuated and spread over a larger area of the surface of the yolk mass (Fig. 8b). In species in which a precocious differentiation of the blastoderm takes place as soon as the cleavage energids arrive at the surface of the yolk mass, especially in Isoptera and Cheleutoptera, the extra-embryonic ectoderm is the last part of the blastoderm to be formed.

Specialization of part of the blastoderm as a temporary, attenuated, extra-embryonic ectoderm is typical of arthropod embryos with dense yolk and superficial cleavage, being found in arachnids and many Crustacea, as well as in the Onychophora, myriapods and apterygotes. In pterygote embryos, however, for reasons which yet escape functional explanation, the development of the extra-embryonic ectoderm shows an added specialization. The simplest expression of this additional step is found in orders whose germ band remains at the surface of the yolk mass as it grows (Dictyoptera, Cheleutoptera, Embioptera and Dermaptera) and is similarly observed in the Ephemeroptera, Orthoptera and Plecoptera before the germ band becomes immersed in the yolk. The margin of the embryonic primordium is composed of cells which, although aggregated and columnar, are not part of the presumptive embryonic ectoderm. As soon as the embryonic primordium enters into elongation and gastrulation, this marginal tissue folds ventrally over the embryonic ectoderm, carrying the margin of the attenuated extra-embryonic ectoderm with it (Figs 9a, b). The first sign of folding is usually seen around the posterior margin of the embryonic primordium. Paired anterior folds then arise at the margins of the head lobes, and folding spreads along the lateral edges of the germ band. The folds are called *amniotic folds*. They extend rapidly towards the ventral midline, where they merge to form a

double layer of extra-embryonic ectoderm external to the ventral surface of
the germ band. Formation and fusion of the amniotic folds in this way has
been described for the Dictyoptera by Wheeler (1889*a*, 1893), Heymons
(1895), Hagan (1917) and Görg (1959); for the Cheleutoptera by Leuzinger
et al. (1926) and Thomas (1936); for the Embioptera by Kershaw (1914) and
Stefani (1961); for the Dermaptera by Heymons (1895) and Bhatnagar and
Singh (1965); for the Orthoptera by Wheeler (1893), Heymons (1895),

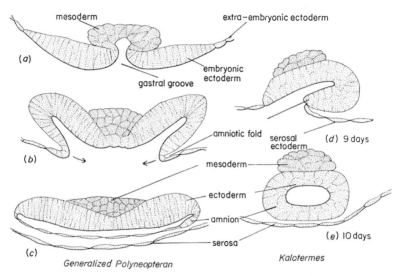

FIG. 9. (*a*)–(*c*) Diagrammatic representation of typical embryonic membrane formation in Polyneoptera, as seen in transverse sections; (*d*) and (*e*) Stages in formation of the embryonic membranes of *Kalotermes flavicollis* (Isoptera), in diagrammatic sagittal section with the anterior end on
the left, after Striebel (1960). Figures 7*f* and 7*g* illustrate preceding stages of the same embryonic
primordium.

Roonwal (1936), Krause (1938*b*), Kanellis (1952), Mahr (1960) and Rakshpal
(1962); and for the Plecoptera by Miller (1939, 1940).

The outer wall of the amniotic folds is an extension of the attenuated
extra-embryonic ectoderm covering the remainder of the surface of the yolk
mass. As the folds merge, the attenuated epithelium becomes a complete,
external, cellular membrane, covering both the yolk mass and the germ band.
This membrane is now called the *serosa* (Fig. 9*c*). The inner walls of the
amniotic folds merge to form an internal cellular membrane, continuous
with the margin of the embryonic ectoderm and covering only the ventral
surface of the germ band (Fig. 9*c*). This membrane is the *amnion*. The
amnion encloses a fluid-filled space, the *amniotic cavity*, between itself and
the ventral surface of the germ band. The distribution of presumptive

amniotic tissue at the margin of the embryonic primordium is indicated in Fig. 8b.

During later development, as will be described below, the amnion participates in a process of *provisional dorsal closure* of the embryo, before the definitive, dorsal body wall is formed. Various speculations have been offered on the functional significance of the amnion as a membrane enclosing an amniotic cavity around the external surface of the pterygote germ band and separating this surface, with its numerous developing protuberances, from the inner surface of the tough egg membranes. Generally, some sort of mechanical advantage, such as space to grow and a fluid cushion separating the embryo from the egg shell, has been imputed to this arrangement. Since, however, the embryos of myriapods, apterygotes and arachnids and the later stages of pterygote embryonic development have no need of this fluid cushion, it seems likely that the pterygote amnion and amniotic cavity have a more subtle role which has yet to be elucidated.

Amnion formation at the margin of the small, disc-shaped embryonic primordium of the Isoptera proceeds in a modified way (Figs 8d, 9d, e). The presumptive amnion occupies the margin of only the posterior half of the disc. Folding is precocious and rapid (Striebel, 1960) and is accompanied by numerous cell divisions. The amnion folds forward until it reaches the anterior edge of the embryonic primordium, taking the serosal edge with it in the usual way. The edge of the amnion separates from the serosal ectoderm, which merges to form a continuous serosa. The amnion, meanwhile, unites with the anterior margin of the embryonic primordium. A stage is thus reached at which a small sphere of cells lies between the serosa and the yolk mass (Fig. 21a), the external half of the sphere being the amnion, the internal half, the embryonic primordium, and the central cavity, the amniotic cavity.

As elongation and segmentation of the germ band proceed, the amnion becomes highly attenuated (Figs 10a–c). In the Orthoptera and Plecoptera, the amnion is carried with the germ band as the latter is immersed in the yolk mass. Other orders that develop an immersed germ band show some delay in the closure of the amniotic cavity and completion of the amnion and serosa (Odonata: Seidel, 1929; Johannsen and Butt, 1941; the paraneopteran orders: Shinji, 1919; Seidel, 1924; Mellanby, 1936; Schölzel, 1937; Böhmel and Jancke, 1942; Butt, 1949; Gerwel, 1950; Goss, 1952; Piotrowski, 1953; Sander, 1959; Behrendt, 1963). In these orders, when the growing germ band turns into the yolk, the posterior and lateral margins fold over to enclose the beginnings of an amniotic cavity, but the cavity remains open to the exterior at the point of inturning (Fig. 16d). The extra-embryonic ectoderm which will give rise to the serosa remains entirely at the surface of the yolk mass. With continued growth of the germ band forwards and upwards into the yolk, the amniotic fold becomes attenuated as a thin cellular membrane

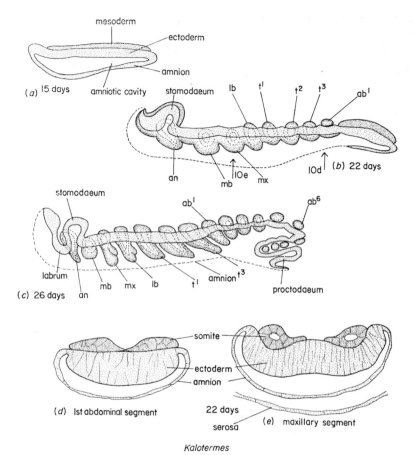

Kalotermes

FIG. 10. (*a*)–(*c*) Stages in elongation and segmentation of the germ band of *Kalotermes flavicollis* (Isoptera), shown as diagrammatic reconstructions based on sagittal sections, after Striebel (1960). (*d*) and (*e*) Diagrammatic transverse sections through the first abdominal and the maxillary segment of the germ band of *K. flavicollis* at the stage illustrated in Fig. 10*b*, after Striebel (1960). ab^1–ab^{10}, abdominal segments; an, antenna; lb, labial segment; mb, mandibular segment; mx, maxillary segment; t^1–t^3, thoracic segment.

separating the ventral surface of the germ band from the yolk in which it is immersed. A delayed formation of anterior amniotic folds finally takes place around the margins of the head lobes and the superficial opening of the amniotic cavity is closed off. In the Odonata (Fig. 6*i*), the amnion and serosa retain contact at the point of closure (Seidel, 1929), but complete separation is usually attained (Figs 7*b*, *c*, 16*e*).

The role of the amnion is even more enigmatic in embryos with immersed germ bands than in those with superficial germ bands. No mechanical advantage can be postulated, yet the amnion always persists, as it does in analagous circumstances in the Lepidoptera (*vide* Chapter 4). Whatever the functional significance of the amnion, it is independent of the topographical relationship between the embryo and the yolk mass.

The subsequent development of the extra-embryonic membranes will be taken up in conjunction with the later development and movements of the embryo itself. The serosa sometimes secretes an external cuticle beneath the vitelline membrane soon after amnio-serosal separation has taken place (Kershaw, 1914; Slifer, 1937; Miller, 1940; Ibrahim, 1957; Striebel, 1960; Cobben, 1968).

VIII. SOMITES AND GANGLIA

A. Somite Formation

External delineation of the segments and formation of the limb buds in the hemimetabolan germ band are outward manifestations of a deeper segregation and elaboration of segmental units within the embryonic ectoderm and mesoderm. In palaeopteran and polyneopteran embryos, metameric segmentation is expressed first in the mesoderm (Roonwal, 1936, 1937; Miller, 1939; Johannsen and Butt, 1941; Bergerard, 1958; Striebel, 1960), but in the Paraneoptera, the ectoderm tends to take the lead and mesodermal segmentation is to some extent suppressed (Mellanby, 1937; Butt, 1949; Goss, 1952). Associated with the growth of the germ band through the activity of a posterior growth zone, the mesoderm of the head and thorax leads that of the abdomen in development. For the present, however, we may confine our attention to the stages leading to the formation of the paired, hollow *somites* (Fig. 10).

As the germ band grows longer, the cells of the inner layer become concentrated as paired lateral bands and thin out along the ventral midline (Fig. 10*d*). At the same time, the ectoderm begins to broaden and turn dorsally at its lateral margins. The bilaterally thickened inner layer now separates into segmental blocks. In all orders of Hemimetabola except the Isoptera, the blocks are exclusively mesodermal. The segmental blocks of the Isoptera are comprised of thickened mesoderm laterally and thinner, segmental midgut rudiments along the ventral midline (Striebel, 1960).

The thickened lateral parts of the segmental blocks now develop as paired, hollow somites (Fig. 10*e*). Usually, as in the Isoptera and Orthoptera (Roonwal, 1937; Striebel, 1960), the gnathal and thoracic somites develop more or less simultaneously (Figs 10*b*, *c*), followed by those in front of the mandibular segment (see below), then those along the abdomen. In Cheleutoptera, however, somite formation, like subsequent external delineation of the segments, proceeds from a thoracic focus (Bergerard, 1958; Fournier, 1967). Two modes of somite formation are exhibited among the Hemimetabola. The simplest, seen in all the somites of the Cheleutoptera and

Paraneoptera (Leuzinger *et al.*, 1926; Thomas, 1936; Mellanby, 1937; Schölzel, 1937; Böhmel and Jancke, 1942; Goss, 1952), in the abdominal somites of *Locusta* and *Kalotermes* (Roonwal, 1937; Striebel, 1960) and perhaps in all the somites of *Gryllotalpa* and *Acheta* (Graber, 1888a, b, c, 1890, 1891; Heymons, 1895) is by *internal splitting* of the paired mesodermal blocks. The second, unique to pterygote embryos and presumably secondary, is by a *median folding* of the lateral parts of the blocks to enclose a pair of *coelomic cavities*. This mode of somite formation is found in the Odonata (Johannsen and Butt, 1941), Dictyoptera (Wheeler, 1889a; Faussek, 1911; Görg, 1959) and Mallophaga (Schölzel, 1937) and is also described with especial clarity for the gnathal and thoracic segments of *Locusta migratoria*, *Tachycines asynamorus* and *Kalotermes flavicollis* by Roonwal (1937), Ibrahim (1957) and Striebel (1960) respectively. Between each pair of somites, the median mesoderm persists as a thin layer in the midline, sometimes bilaterally separated (Roonwal, 1937; Striebel, 1960). Exceptionally, in Isoptera, the median cells are midgut cells.

In orders in which the paired hollow somites are conspicuously retained, the labial, thoracic, and first abdominal somites are large (Fig. 10c). The mandibular, maxillary and second to tenth pairs of abdominal somites are relatively small. Behind the tenth pair of abdominal somites, a small mass of mesoderm persists in association with the proctodaeum. A pair of temporary cavities is developed in this mesoderm in *Blatella* (Wheeler, 1889a; Cholodkowsky, 1891; Heymons, 1895), *Periplaneta* (Heymons, 1895) and *Locusta* (Roonwal, 1937).

In front of the mandibular somites, the mesoderm continues forward on either side of the stomodaeum, beneath the ectoderm of the head lobes, and meets anteriorly beneath the labral ectoderm (Roonwal, 1937; Jhingran, 1947; Striebel, 1960). Just behind the level of the stomodaeum a pair of large antennal somites (Figs 10b, c) is formed simultaneously with, and in the same manner as, the gnathal somites (Leuzinger *et al.*, 1926; Roonwal, 1937; Striebel, 1960; Scholl, 1965). In front of the stomodaeum, some of the mesoderm cells usually aggregate as a second, smaller pair of masses, the preantennal or labral pair. These become hollow by splitting in the Odonata (Ando, 1962), Plecoptera (Miller, 1940), Cheleutoptera (Leuzinger *et al.*, 1926; Scholl, 1969), Orthoptera (Roonwal, 1937; Jhingran, 1947), Homoptera (Sander, 1956) and Heteroptera (Mellanby, 1937), but remain solid in the Isoptera (Striebel, 1960) and Dermaptera (Heymons, 1895). The claim by Leuzinger *et al.* (1926) that a second pair of preantennal somites is also developed in *Carausius* has never been substantiated by other workers and is generally regarded as doubtful (Manton, 1928, 1949, 1960; Eastham, 1930; Tiegs, 1940, 1947; Tiegs and Manton, 1958; Matsuda, 1965; Scholl, 1965, 1969).

In the mesoderm linking the antennal and mandibular somites, an intermediary pair of thickenings develops, usually after segmentation of the germ band has been completed (Dictyoptera: Wheeler, 1889a; Isoptera: Striebel, 1960; Cheleutoptera: Leuzinger et al., 1926; Scholl, 1965, 1969; Orthoptera: Wheeler, 1893; Roonwal, 1937; Jhingran, 1947; and Dermaptera: Heymons, 1895). These thickenings are interpreted as the vestiges of a pair of premandibular somites. It is generally agreed that a basic six pairs of somites is formed in the developing pterygote head, though their significance as indicators of the segmental composition of the head is still in dispute (e.g. Butt, 1960; Manton, 1960; Matsuda, 1965; Scholl, 1965, 1969; Gouin, 1968; see Section XIII).

B. Early Development of the Brain and Ventral Nerve Cord

During the early stages of somite formation in the mesoderm, the unsegmented embryonic ectoderm develops a longitudinal thickening on either side of the ventral midline, producing paired *neural ridges* bordering a midventral *neural groove*. The neural ridges result from the onset of proliferative activity of *neuroblasts* differentiated in the ventral ectoderm (Fig. 7e). The neuroblasts comprise 3–5 rows of enlarged ectoderm cells on each side of the midline (Wheeler, 1893; Heymons, 1895; Shinji, 1919; Seidel, 1924; Baden, 1936; Thomas, 1936; Mellanby, 1937; Roonwal, 1937; Miller, 1939; Johannsen and Butt, 1941; Goss, 1952, 1953; Ibrahim, 1957; Görg, 1959; Striebel, 1960). Through teloblastic budding, the neuroblasts proliferate radial rows of small cells inwards as ganglion cells (Figs 14a, b). The neuroblasts sink slightly inwards as they bud, leaving other ectoderm cells (*dermatoblasts*) at the ventral surface as future epidermal cells (Fig. 14c). Neuroblast differentiation and budding along the length of the germ band precedes external delineation of the segments. Between the neural ridges a *median strand* of tall ectoderm cells forms the floor of the neural groove. Occasional neuroblasts differentiate as a single row along the median strand. As the number of cells proliferated by the neuroblasts increases, the radial rows tend to merge. At the same time, neuroblast activity falls off intersegmentally so that the ridges become paired segmental swellings and the ganglion cells begin to segregate into paired, segmental *ganglia*.

In front of the mandibular segment, the neuroblast rows diverge on either side of the stomodaeum and are much broader over the anterior parts of the head lobes. Malzacher (1968) and Scholl (1969) have recently made detailed studies of brain development in *Carausius* and *Periplaneta*. Proliferation by the neuroblasts follows the usual course, but the resulting cell masses are set apart laterally on either side of the stomodaeum as paired premandibular or tritocerebral ganglia behind the stomodaeum, paired antennal or deutocerebral ganglia on either side of the stomodaeum and large, paired protocerebral ganglia in front of the stomodaeum (Fig. 15b). The further development of the brain and the light thus shed on the composition of the pterygote head will be taken up in subsequent Sections (X, D and XIII).

IX. RUPTURE OF THE EMBRYONIC MEMBRANES: KATATREPSIS

Following the completion of elongation and segment formation, the hemi-metabolan germ band undergoes further growth of its component parts, including elongation of the limbs, upgrowth of the lateral walls of the ecto-derm and preliminary organogeny, while retaining the position attained by the end of elongation (Figs 6b, j, 7c). This period ends sharply (Fig. 12) with the fusion and rupture of the extra-embryonic membranes immediately external to the head of the embryo. The head, and then the remainder of the embryo, is exposed as the extra-embryonic membranes roll back over the yolk mass. The serosa becomes concentrated into a cup of tall cells, the *dorsal organ*, on the anterodorsal surface of the yolk mass and the amnion replaces the serosa as a provisional epithelium, the *provisional dorsal closure*, covering the yolk mass dorsal to the germ band.

In the Dictyoptera, in which the germ band remains on the ventral surface of the yolk mass throughout elongation and segmentation, little or no move-ment of the segmented germ band takes place as the extra-embryonic mem-branes rupture and roll back (Bruce, 1887; Wheeler, 1889a; Heymons, 1895; Hagan, 1917; Görg, 1959). All other hemimetabolan embryos reach this stage with the segmented germ band facing the dorsal surface and posterior pole of the egg rather than the ventral surface and anterior pole. Several orders display the additional complication of total immersion of the germ band in the yolk as a result of anatrepsis. Rupture of the embryonic mem-branes in these species is always followed by an active migratory movement which restores the embryo to a more normal orientation within the egg space. Wheeler (1893), who gave the first detailed discussion of embryonic move-ments in the Hemimetabola, called this movement *katatrepsis*, a term that has subsequently come into general use.

Katatrepsis is essentially the same in all orders of hemimetabolous insects except certain Plecoptera, where the movement is modified in relation to the unusual shape of the space enclosed by the hemispherical egg membranes. Following fusion and rupture of the amnion and serosa, the segmented germ band begins to move over the posterior pole of the yolk mass and forwards along the ventral surface until its posterior end has reached the posterior pole of the egg. At the same time, the amnion rolls back over the yolk surface and the serosa contracts into a dorsal organ. Usually (Figs 6b, 12d, e, j and k, 13a, b) the movement is a straight migration over the posterior pole from the dorsal to the ventral surface (Ephemeroptera: Heymons, 1896a, b; Illies,

1968; Isoptera: Striebel, 1960; Dermaptera: Heymons, 1895; Cheleutoptera: Strindberg, 1914; Leuzinger *et al.*, 1926; Moscona, 1950; Koch, 1964;
Fournier, 1967; Bedford, 1970; Orthoptera: Ayers, 1884; Wheeler, 1893;
Heymons, 1895; Nelsen, 1931, 1934; Slifer, 1932*a*; Else, 1934; Roonwal,
1937; Krause, 1939; Jannone, 1939; Steele, 1941; Jhingran, 1947; Salt, 1949;
Bodenheimer and Shulov, 1951; Matthée, 1951; Brookes, 1952; Kanellis,
1952; Ibrahim, 1957; Shulov and Pener, 1959, 1963; Mahr, 1960; Riegert,
1961; Rakshpal, 1962; Van Horn, 1966; Chapman and Whitham, 1968;
Embioptera: Kershaw, 1914; Dermaptera: Heymons, 1895; and the paraneopteran orders: Shinji, 1919; Seidel, 1924; Mellanby, 1937; Schölzel,
1937; Böhmel and Jancke, 1942; Butt, 1949; Gerwel, 1950; Goss, 1952,
1953; Sander, 1956; Bournier, 1960; Polivanova, 1960, 1961). Some
Odonata (Seidel, 1929), many Heteroptera (Cobben, 1968) and the homopteran *Euscelis plebejus* (Sander, 1959), express the same movement with a
spiral twist (Figs 12*f, g*, 13*d*). The head of the embryo returns to the anterior
pole of the egg but the embryo twists as it reverses itself so as to remain facing
the original dorsal surface of the egg. This modification is associated with an
elongate, narrow egg-space whose dorsal boundary is convex, and brings the
embryo into the position of most economical fit for its long, bulky limbs.
Plecopteran embryos exhibit the same spiral twist in a more exaggerated form
(Miller, 1939; Khoo, 1968). In *Pteronarcys*, the embryo moves into a position
around the periphery of the hemispherical egg space, lying coiled on its right
side with the ventral surface facing outwards.

The relative rapidity of the katatreptic movement in relation to the general
rate of development is well shown by the fact that in the isopteran *Kalotermes
flavicollis*, with a developmental period of 54 days, the movement is completed in eight hours (Striebel, 1960). In *Locusta migratoria*, blastokinesis is
completed in 17–20 hours (Roonwal, 1937), and in *Acheta domesticus*, in
about twelve hours (Brookes, 1952; Mahr, 1960; Rakshpal, 1962). Slifer
(1932*a*) and Roonwal (1937) showed that vigorous caudo-cephalic waves of
peristaltic contraction of the germ band accompany katatrepsis in Orthoptera. Slifer (1932*a*) also found unicellular, spindle-shaped, unstriated muscle
fibres at the sites of contraction in *Melanoplus differentialis*. Striated muscle
does not develop for a further nine days. According to Le Berre (1952, 1953),
Mahr (1960) and Cobben (1968), contractions of the serosa play an important
part in blastokinesis in *Locusta migratoria*, *Acheta domesticus* and the Heteroptera. In general, the causal role of contractile activity in hemimetabolan
katatrepsis seems not in doubt, though the precise details of the process are
still unresolved.

Several hemimetabolan embryos undergo further accommodatory movements within the egg space during later development. The Isoptera and the
orthopteran *Melanoplus differentialis*, for example, display a final rotation

through 180° on the long axis which brings the ventral surface of the embryo finally beneath the concave dorsal surface of the egg-space and fits the dorsal surface of the embryo into the convex ventral surface of the egg-space (Slifer, 1932*a*, *b*; Striebel, 1960; see also Figs 21*f*, *g* and *h*). Time-lapse photomicrographic studies by Striebel have shown that this movement, which proceeds more slowly than the blastokinetic movement, involves contractions of the yolk-mass.

Katatrepsis in the Hemimetabola thus brings the embryo into a position within the egg-space in which further growth and change of shape can be accommodated most economically (Fig. 11). The crucial question raised by

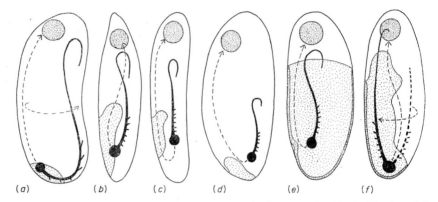

(*a*)   (*b*)   (*c*)   (*d*)   (*e*)   (*f*)

FIG. 11. A summary of growth, anatrepsis and katatrepsis of the germ band in the Hemimetabola, modified after Weber (1954) and Striebel (1960). (*a*) *Kalotermes* (Isoptera); (*b*) *Platycnemis* (Odonata); (*c*) *Acheta* (Orthoptera); (*d*) *Tachycines* (Orthoptera); (*e*) *Pediculus* (Anoplura); (*f*) *Notonecta* (Heteroptera). All diagrams are drawn with the ventral surface on the left.

this phenomenon is why so many hemimetabolan orders display a mode of formation and elongation of the germ band which necessitates an active restorative movement, when such a movement is not a necessary part of the development of the Onychophora, myriapods, apterygotes and Dictyoptera. The absence of katatrepsis in the Holometabola further shows that pterygote development can proceed satisfactorily in the direct manner. As discussed in the next chapter, the Lepidoptera display a remarkable series of embryonic movements, but they are specialized movements associated with features peculiar to the order and have no affinity with anatrepsis and katatrepsis (blastokinesis) in the Hemimetabola. Perhaps, however, when the causal processes of hemimetabolan embryonic development are analysed more deeply, both anatrepsis and katatrepsis will prove to have sound functional explanations in terms of the progress of embryonic development towards its end point as a functional nymph in the orders in which these phenomena occur.

X. FURTHER DEVELOPMENT OF THE EMBRYONIC ECTODERM

A. Dorsal Closure: Fate of the Extra-embryonic Membranes

Throughout areas of the surface of the embryo occupied by the developing ganglia, the ganglion tissue and the intervening median strand separate into the interior, leaving dermatoblasts at the surface (Fig. 14). The dermatoblasts give rise to epidermal cells. Lateral to the ganglionic areas, the columnar embryonic ectoderm begins to spread upwards, after membrane rupture and katatrepsis have occurred, to replace the amnion cells (provisional dorsal closure) at the surface (Figs 12a–c, g, h and k; 13b, c; 14e). The upward spread of the ectoderm effects definitive dorsal closure (Odonata: Johannsen and Butt, 1941; Dictyoptera: Hagan, 1917; Roonwal, 1937; Isoptera: Striebel, 1960; Plecoptera: Miller, 1939; Cheleutoptera: Roonwal, 1937; Orthoptera: Wheeler, 1893; Roonwal, 1937; Embioptera: Kershaw, 1914; paraneopterans: Mellanby, 1937; Schölzel, 1937; Böhmel and Jancke, 1942; Butt, 1949; Goss, 1952, 1953; Sander, 1959; Behrendt, 1963). As dorsal closure proceeds, the serosal vestige or dorsal organ is resorbed into the yolk, followed by the shrinking amnion.

Functional differentiation of the epidermis and secretion of the first nymphal cuticle takes place only after dorsal closure is complete. In some orders, notably the Orthoptera and Cheleutoptera, an embryonic cuticle is formed and shed before the definitive first nymphal cuticle is secreted (Jones, 1956; Bedford, 1970).

B. Appendage Formation

As pointed out above, the antennal, gnathal and thoracic limb buds first develop as ectodermal outpouchings at a time when the abdominal segments are still being formed. Following fusion and rupture of the embryonic membranes and the extension of the segmented germ band along the ventral surface of the yolk (dorsal in *Platycnemis* and *Euscelis*), the antennae grow longer, trailing back ventrally beneath the embryo (Figs 12 and 13). The labrum also increases in size and, if previously formed as paired lobes, merges into a unitary structure. The mouthparts and thoracic limbs lengthen and the maxillary and labial limbs become bifid, heralding the development of palps. Growth of the limb buds, like dorsal spread of the ectoderm, is due to generalized ectodermal proliferation as a single epithelial layer (Fig. 14). Heymons (1899), Muir and Kershaw (1911, 1912), Shinji (1919), Fernando (1933), Mellanby (1937), Schölzel (1937), Newcomer (1948) and Young (1953) have shown that the specialized mouthparts of heteropterans, homopterans and anoplurans develop as modifications of the three basic pairs of pterygote gnathal appendages.

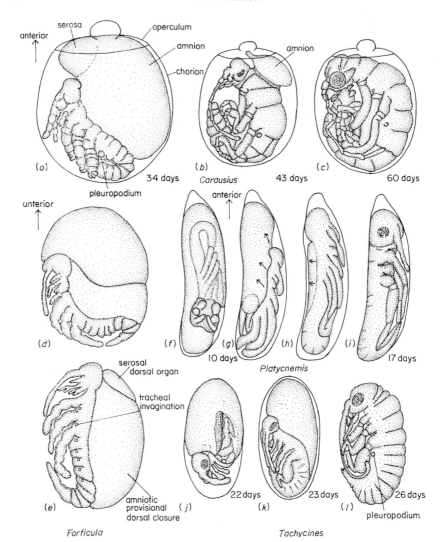

Forficula   *Tachycines*

Fig. 12. (*a*)–(*c*) Stages in dorsal closure of the embryo of *Carausius morosus* (Cheleutoptera), in left lateral view, after Fournier (1967). Stage (*a*) results from katatrepsis in this species. Before katatrepsis, the segmented germ band (Fig. 6*h*) lies on the postero-dorsal face of the yolk mass. Stages (*b*) and (*c*) are drawn on a smaller scale than stage (*a*); (*d*) and (*e*) Stages of katatrepsis in *Forficula auricularia* (Dermaptera), in left lateral view, after Heymons (1895). Stage (*d*) follows the segmented germ band stage illustrated in Fig. 6*b*; (*f*)–(*i*) Katatrepsis and dorsal closure in *Platycnemis pennipes* (Odonata), after Seidel (1929). Stage (*f*) follows completion of the segmented germ band stage shown in Fig. 6*i*. The left lateral view is maintained in all diagrams but the embryo executes katatrepsis with a spiral twist and reverses its position within the egg membrane; (*j*)–(*l*) Katatrepsis and dorsal closure in *Tachycines asynomorus* (Orthoptera), in left lateral view, after Ibrahim (1957). Stage (*j*) follows the segmented germ band stage illustrated in Fig. 6*j*.

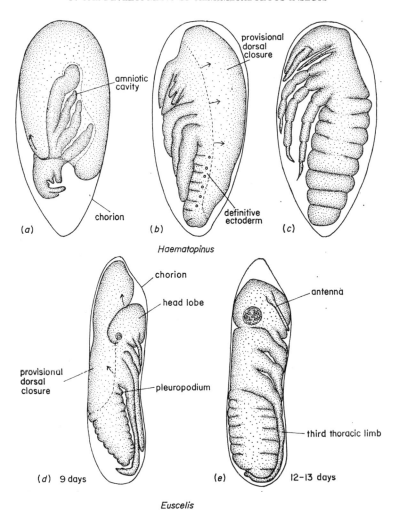

Haematopinus

Euscelis

FIG. 13. (a)–(c) Katatrepsis and dorsal closure in *Haematopinus eurysternus* (Anoplura) in left lateral view, after Schölzel (1937). Stage (a) follows the segmented germ band stage illustrated in Fig. 7b; (d) and (e) Dorsal closure in *Euscelis plebejus* (Homoptera), in right lateral view, after Sander (1959). Katatrepsis intervenes between stage (d) and the earlier stage illustrated in Fig. 7c.

Before membrane rupture takes place in the Palaeoptera and Polyneoptera, eleven pairs of *abdominal limb buds* are developed (Figs 6b, h), the first and last pairs being formed before the intervening pairs (Ephemeroptera: Heymons, 1896a, b; Odonata: Heymons, 1896a, b; Dictyoptera: Wheeler, 1889a; Heymons, 1895; Hagan, 1917; Görg, 1959; Isoptera: Striebel, 1960; Plecoptera: Miller, 1939; Cheleutoptera: Leuzinger *et al.*, 1926; Fournier, 1967; Orthoptera: Wheeler, 1893; Nelsen, 1931, 1934; Slifer, 1932b; Else,

1934; Roonwal, 1937; Steele, 1941; Jhingran, 1947; Salt, 1949; Bodenheimer and Shulov, 1951; Matthée, 1951; Brookes, 1952; Shulov and Pener, 1959, 1963; Riegert, 1961; Rakshpal, 1962; Van Horn, 1966; Dermaptera: Heymons, 1895; Bhatnagar and Singh, 1965). Among the Paraneoptera, the first and last pairs only are developed in homopteran and heteropteran embryos (Wheeler, 1889*b*, *c*, 1890; Heymons, 1899; Seidel, 1924; Hussey, 1926; Mellanby, 1937; Butt, 1949; Sander, 1959) while the Psocoptera, Mallophaga and Anoplura lack abdominal limbs (Schölzel, 1937; Goss, 1952, 1953).

The further development of the abdominal limbs is variable. The last pair form the cerci (Figs 6*b*, *j*). The first pair remain small and are resorbed soon after blastokinesis in the Ephemeroptera, Odonata, Isoptera, Plecoptera, Embioptera and Dermaptera (Heymons, 1895, 1896*a*, *b*; Kershaw, 1914; Miller, 1939; Striebel, 1960; Bhatnagar and Singh, 1965) but develop in the Dictyoptera, Cheleutoptera, Orthoptera, Homoptera and Heteroptera as *pleuropodia* (Figs 12*a*, *l*, 13*d*). The pleuropodia of the Dictyoptera, Cheleutoptera and Orthoptera are glandular swellings (Graber, 1888*a*, *b*, *c*, 1890; Heymons, 1895; Hagan, 1917; Hussey, 1926; Slifer, 1932*b*, 1937; Roonwal, 1937; Salt, 1949; Brookes, 1952; Görg, 1959; Shulov and Pener, 1959; Mahr, 1960; Rakshpal, 1962; Bedford, 1970) and are cast off before or during hatching. Those of Homoptera and Heteroptera are less conspicuous, but are also of glandular appearance. In many species they are cast off before hatching (Wheeler, 1889*b*, *c*, 1890; Heymons, 1899) but in the heteropteran genera *Naucoris*, *Belastoma*, *Ranatra* and *Rhodnius* (Wheeler, 1890; Heymons, 1899; Hussey, 1926; Mellanby, 1937), the pleuropodia become invaginated into the body and are then resorbed. Pleuropodial function during embryonic development is still not entirely clear, though Slifer (1937), Jones (1956) and Ibrahim (1957) have given evidence that in the Orthoptera the pleuropodia secrete a hatching enzyme which digests the serosal cuticle, and Polivanova (1965) has implicated the pleuropodia of certain Heteroptera in embryonic excretion.

The second to seventh (and sometimes eighth) pairs of abdominal limb rudiments remain vestigial and are resorbed during or shortly after blastokinesis (e.g. Figs 12*a*, *d* and *e*). The eighth to tenth abdominal limbs contribute variously to the formation of the external genitalia (e.g. Wheeler, 1893; Nelsen, 1931; Else, 1934; Roonwal, 1937; Jhingran, 1947; Van Horn, 1966).

In the ectoderm immediately ventrolateral to the developing tritocerebral ganglia, a pair of ectodermal thickenings is formed just in front of the mandibles (Viallanes, 1891; Mellanby, 1937; Roonwal, 1937). These are the vestigial *premandibular limb buds*, which soon merge back into the general epithelium as dorsal closure of the mouthpart region is completed. The *hypopharynx* develops as a median protuberance in the floor of the buccal cavity in front of the labium (Heymons, 1895, 1899; Leuzinger *et al.*, 1926; Roonwal, 1937; Young, 1953), and is generally regarded as a product of the sternal regions of some or all of the premandibular and gnathal segments (Matsuda, 1965; Wada, 1966*a*; Scholl, 1969).

C. Ectodermal Invaginations

While the abdominal limb buds are forming, a series of localized ecto-dermal invaginations appear. Those on the trunk give rise to the thoracic and abdominal apodemes, the tracheal system and the genital openings (Fig. 14) while those on the head develop into cephalic apodemes and glands (Fig. 15).

The largest ectodermal ingrowths on the head are the salivary glands, which are generally stated to invaginate near the bases of the labial limbs. Only Roonwal (1937) gives them a maxillary origin. The labial invaginations grow back beneath the stomodaeum into the thorax and differentiate as salivary glands and ducts. With fusion of the labial limb buds, the salivary gland openings come together in the ventral midline as a common opening onto the hypopharynx. The remaining ectodermal invaginations on the head give rise to the cephalic apodemes and the corpora allata. A general indica-tion of the sites of origin of these structures is given in Fig. 15*a*. The anterior tentorial arms originate in the ventrolateral ectoderm between the antennal and mandibular segments (Heymons, 1895; Riley, 1904; Strindberg, 1913; Mellanby, 1937; Roonwal, 1937; Sander, 1959; Striebel, 1960; Ando, 1962; Matsuda, 1965; Wada, 1966*a*; Scholl, 1969; Vignau-Rogueda, 1969). The mandibular apodemes arise close to the bases of the mandibles. The posterior tentorial arms originate in the ventrolateral ectoderm between the mandibu-lar and labial segments (Heymons, 1895; Roonwal, 1937; Young, 1953; Matsuda, 1965; Wada, 1966*a*; Scholl, 1969; Vignau-Rogueda, 1969). The origin of the corpora allata is closely associated with the posterior tentorial arms. Heymons (1895, 1897) was the first to show that the corpora allata of the Hemimetabola arise as a pair of lateral ectodermal invaginations, origi-nating in *Forficula* at the bases of the maxillae. In *Carausius* and *Locusta*, their origin is slightly more anterior, as ectodermal invaginations of the mandibular-maxillary intersegment (Leuzinger *et al.*, 1926; Roonwal, 1937). The invaginations become cut off as hollow vesicles which move dorsally and come to rest on the stomodaeum. Here they become invested with a thin sheath of antennal splanchnic mesoderm.

In the trunk, the tracheal invaginations constitute a lateral pair on each segment from the second thoracic to the eighth abdominal (Heymons, 1895; Mellanby, 1937; Roonwal, 1937; Schölzel, 1937; Goss, 1952; Görg, 1959; Striebel, 1960). The opening of each invagination becomes a spiracle. The invagination bifurcates and the branches join longitudinally and send further anastomosing branches through the embryo. Oenocytes arise as segmental groups of ectoderm cells associated with the tracheal invaginations (Roonwal, 1936). In *Forficula*, similar groups of oenocytes are also formed in the ninth, tenth and eleventh abdominal segments (Heymons, 1895). The genital openings form in the ventral midline as a vagina on the seventh or eighth abdominal segment in females and an ejaculatory duct on the ninth or tenth abdominal segment in males (Wheeler, 1893; Roonwal, 1937; Cavallin, 1968).

D. The Nervous System

Little further need be said of the development of the ventral nerve cord, which proceeds in the same general manner through the Hemimetabola (Korotneff, 1885; Cholodkowsky, 1891; Wheeler, 1893; Heymons, 1895; Strindberg, 1913; Shinji, 1919; Seidel, 1924; Baden, 1936; Mellanby, 1937; Roonwal, 1937; Schölzel, 1937; Böhmel and Jancke, 1942; Butt, 1949; Goss, 1952; Görg, 1959; Striebel, 1960). As the ganglionic masses move into the interior of the embryo (Fig. 14), they become more compact and begin to form neuropile as aggregates of axon outgrowths from their cells. At first the neuropile is localized in each ganglion, but with further axon development it becomes linked longitudinally between successive segments by longitudinal connectives, then transversely across each pair of ganglia by transverse commissures. Three pairs of gnathal ganglia, three thoracic pairs and ten abdominal pairs are always developed. An eleventh pair of abdominal ganglia has been identified in Ephemeroptera, Odonata, Dictyoptera and Orthoptera (Graber, 1890; Heymons, 1895, 1896a; Roonwal, 1937) but is usually lost. In later development, the ganglia of the gnathal segments fuse to form a composite sub-oesophageal ganglion. The eighth to tenth (eleventh) abdominal ganglia fuse. Further fusion may also occur, depending on the order of insects, especially in the short-bodied paraneopterans.

The fate of the median strand in later development is still controversial. The intrasegmental regions of the median strand are incorporated into the ganglia (Baden, 1937; Johannsen and Butt, 1941). The intersegmental regions were thought by Wheeler (1893) to give rise to the neurilemma of the ventral nerve cord, but this has since been shown to originate from peripheral ganglion cells (Heymons, 1895; Strindberg, 1913; Baden, 1936; Roonwal, 1937; Görg, 1959; Ashhurst, 1965) and the fate of the intersegmental regions of the median strand remains unknown.

The development of the antennal (deutocerebral) and premandibular (tritocerebral) ganglia follows the same course as the ventral ganglia, except that the deutocerebral ganglia move forwards in front of the mouth and do not develop a transverse commissure. The tritocerebral commissure remains postoral. Anteriorly, the neuroblasts on either side of the labrum give rise to

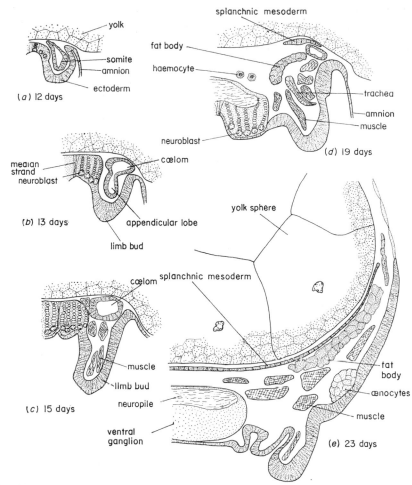

Fig. 14. Diagrammatic transverse sections showing stages in the development of the prothoracic segment of *Tachycines asynomorus* (Orthoptera) at (*a*) 12 days; (*b*) 13 days; (*c*) 15 days; (*d*) 19 days; (*e*) 23 days, after Ibrahim (1957). All diagrams are drawn to the same scale. (*a*), (*b*) and (*c*) illustrate development during the immersed, segmenting germ band stage; (*d*) is at the segmented germ band stage, three days before katatrepsis (compare Fig. 6*j*); (*e*) is at the stage just after katatrepsis, when dorsal closure is beginning (compare Fig. 12*k*).

the paired lobes of the proctocerebrum (Fig. 15*b*), connected by the supra-oesophageal commissure. There has been considerable controversy over the existence of preantennal segmental ganglia, as distinct from protocerebral ganglia, in pterygote embryos (Matsuda, 1965). In recent detailed studies, Malzacher (1968) and Scholl (1969) have provided strong evidence that a pair of preantennal ganglia can be distinguished in the developing brain of *Carausius* and *Periplaneta*.

The lateral optic ganglia of the proctocerebrum are generally recognized to develop somewhat separately, as proliferations of the anterolateral ectoderm of the head lobes, without the intervention of neuroblasts (Viallanes, 1891; Cholodkowsky, 1891; Wheeler, 1893; Heymons, 1895; Baden, 1936; Roonwal, 1937; Ando, 1962; Malzacher, 1968). The optic ganglia are cut off into the interior by delamination, leaving at the surface a layer of ectoderm

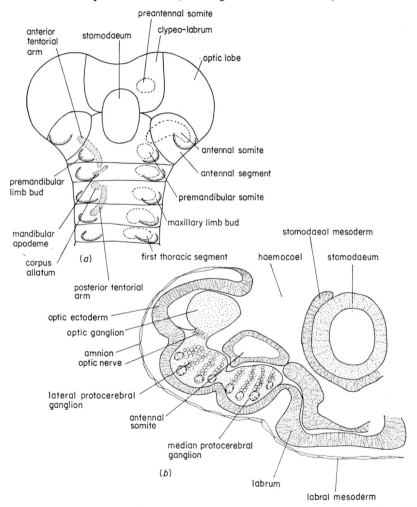

Fig. 15. (*a*) Diagrammatic representation of the cephalic region of the segmenting germ band of a polyneopteran, seen in ventral view, modified after a diagram of Wada (1966*b*). Ectodermal components and attendant limb buds are outlined. The corresponding somites are shown, on the right only. The sites of origin of cephalic ectodermal invaginations are indicated, on the left only; (*b*) Diagrammatic frontal section through the head of *Locusta migratoria* (Orthoptera) at the segmented germ band stage, after Roonwal (1937).

which gives rise to the eye discs (Fig. 15*b*). The separation may be complete (Viallanes, 1891; Wheeler, 1893; Roonwal, 1937) or only partial, retaining connections which develop directly as the optic nerves (Heymons, 1895; Strindberg, 1913). The development of the compound eyes from the eye discs has been described by Kühn (1926), Ludtke (1940), Butt (1949) and Ando (1957).

<h3 style="text-align:center">XI. FURTHER DEVELOPMENT OF THE GUT</h3>

A. The Stomodaeum and the Stomatogastric Nervous System

The general course of development of the stomodaeum is the same throughout the Hemimetabola. The stomodaeum (Fig. 16*b*) grows inwards and backwards during elongation of the germ band, forming a simple epithelial tube (Odonata: Seidel, 1929; Johannsen and Butt, 1941; Dictyoptera: Wheeler, 1893; Heymons, 1895; Hagan, 1917; Görg, 1959; Isoptera: Striebel, 1960; Plecoptera: Miller, 1939; Cheleutoptera: Leuzinger *et al.*, 1926; Thomas, 1936; Orthoptera: Heymons, 1895; Roonwal, 1937; Kanellis, 1952; Ibrahim, 1957; Mahr, 1960; Dermaptera: Heymons, 1895; Psocoptera: Goss, 1953; Anoplura: Schölzel, 1937; Homoptera: Böhmel and Jancke, 1942; Sander, 1956; Heteroptera: Seidel, 1924; Mellanby, 1937; Butt, 1949). The distal end of the tube becomes reflexed on itself, forming the core of the proventriculus, while the remainder of the stomodaeal wall differentiates as the epithelium of the oesophagus.

Before histodifferentiation of the stomodaeal epithelium takes place, three median outgrowths arise along the mid-dorsal line of the stomodaeum, either as thickenings or as evaginations (Wheeler, 1893; Heymons, 1895; Leuzinger *et al.*, 1926; Mellanby, 1937; Roonwal, 1937; Striebel, 1960; Scholl, 1969). They give rise to the frontal, occipitopharyngeal and ventricular ganglia of the stomatogastric nervous system.

B. The Proctodaeum and Malpighian Tubules

The development of the proctodaeum begins slightly later than that of the stomodaeum, but proceeds initially in the same way (Fig. 16*c*), by ingrowth as a simple epithelial tube (Heymons, 1895; Seidel, 1924, 1929; Thomas, 1936; Mellanby, 1937; Roonwal, 1937; Johannsen and Butt, 1941; Böhmel and Jancke, 1942; Kanellis, 1952; Görg, 1959; Mahr, 1960; Striebel, 1960). The tube becomes convoluted as it grows, and the wall develops directly as the lining epithelium of the hindgut. The distal end of the proctodaeum becomes pouched out as the rudiments of the Malpighian tubules, which grow as blind-ending tubes coiling in the haemocoele (Wheeler, 1889*a*; Thomas, 1936; Mellanby, 1937; Roonwal, 1937; Miller, 1939; Henson, 1944, 1946; Butt, 1949; Goss, 1952, 1953; Striebel, 1960; Srivastava and Bahadur, 1961; Savage, 1962; Bahadur, 1968).

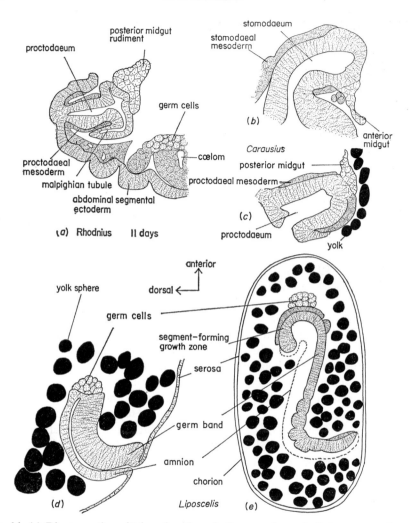

FIG. 16. (*a*) Diagrammatic sagittal section through the posterior end of the segmented germ band of *Rhodnius prolixus* (Heteroptera), after Mellanby (1937); (*b*) and (*c*) Diagrammatic sagittal sections through the early stomodaeum and proctodaeum of *Carausius morosus* (Cheleutoptera), after Thomas (1936); (*d*) and (*e*) Diagrammatic sagittal sections showing early and late stages of growth of the segmenting germ band of *Liposcelis divergens* (Psocoptera), after Goss (1953).

C. The Midgut

The anterior and posterior midgut rudiments are carried inwards at the ends of the stomodaeum and proctodaeum (Figs 16*a*–*c*; except in Isoptera, see below) but do not begin to proliferate until just before or just after kata-trepsis. When proliferation begins, the midgut rudiments extend between the developing nerve cord and the surface of the yolk-mass, usually as paired ventrolateral strands which meet in the middle region of the embryo (Wheeler, 1889a; Heymons, 1895; Rabito, 1898; Nusbaum and Fulinski, 1906, 1909; Hirschler, 1912; Strindberg, 1915; Seidel, 1924; Ries, 1931; Nelsen, 1934; Thomas, 1936; Mellanby, 1937; Roonwal, 1936, 1937; Schölzel, 1937; Böhmel and Jancke, 1942; Butt, 1949; Goss, 1952; Görg, 1959; Stefani, 1961). As soon as two continuous strands have been established, the strands begin to spread, first ventrally, then dorsally, over the surface of the shrinking yolk mass. The resulting midgut is an elongate, ovoid sac, filled with yolk, joining the stomodaeum to the proctodaeum. From this sac, the definitive midgut epithelium develops. The development of the midgut in Isoptera proceeds in the same way, except that the midgut strands are formed by the linking up of the paired series of segmental midgut rudiments formed by the midventral cells of the inner layer (Striebel, 1960).

D. Resorption of the Yolk Mass

As described by Roonwal (1937) in *Locusta*, the embryonic midgut cells send temporary processes into the yolk, presumably with a digestive function. The vitellophages formed earlier in development often migrate to the surface of the yolk during midgut formation, to establish a *temporary yolk-sac* epithelium beneath the definitive midgut epithelium (Ayers, 1884; Korotneff, 1885; Graber, 1890, 1891; Heymons, 1895; Leuzinger *et al.*, 1926; Roonwal, 1937; Miller, 1939; Striebel, 1960; Stefani, 1961). Earlier, during elongation of the germ band, the yolk-mass in many species becomes temporarily cellularized into nucleated *yolk spheres* (=yolk cleavage) (e.g. Figs 7b, 14e; Heymons, 1895; Thomas, 1936; Roonwal, 1937; Schölzel, 1937; Krause, 1938b, 1939; Miller, 1939; Kanellis, 1952; Piotrowski, 1953; Sander, 1959; Mahr, 1960), but the spheres fuse together again into a single mass before the midgut epithelium spreads around the yolk.

Although a number of early workers claimed that the vitellophages play a part in the formation of the definitive midgut epithelium (see Johannsen and Butt, 1941), the only case for which this claim can still be regarded with any degree of certainty is that of the Odonata (Tschuproff, 1903; Johannsen and Butt, 1941). Here, the temporary yolk sac cells formed by the vitellophages may persist as the middle part of the midgut epithelium. In other orders, the vitellophages are digested.

XII. FURTHER DEVELOPMENT OF THE MESODERM AND GONADS

A. The Labial and Trunk Somites

The further development of the mesoderm is remarkably uniform throughout the Hemimetabola. From the labial to the tenth abdominal segment each segmental unit follows essentially the same pattern of development after the somites have been formed (Fig. 14). The median mesoderm, occupying the floor of the epineural sinus, gives rise to haemocytes (Heymons, 1895; Leuzinger et al., 1926; Mellanby, 1937; Roonwal, 1937; Görg, 1959; Wigglesworth, 1959). In the Isoptera, in which the median cells of the inner layer are midgut cells, the haemocytes probably arise from mesoderm cells adjacent to the midgut rudiments (Striebel, 1960). The somites themselves undergo a tripartite outpouching as anterior, posterior and ventrolateral pouches, the latter bulging into the attendant limb bud (Dictyoptera: Cholodkowsky, 1890a, b; Heymons, 1895; Görg, 1959; Isoptera: Striebel, 1960; Plecoptera: Miller, 1939; Cheleutoptera: Leuzinger et al., 1926; Orthoptera: Graber, 1890; Heymons, 1895; Roonwal, 1937; Ibrahim, 1957; Dermaptera: Heymons, 1895). The ventrolateral pouch develops directly as the intrinsic musculature of the limb. The ventral somatic walls of the anterior and posterior pouches break up to form extrinsic limb muscles, ventral longitudinal muscles and masses of fat body cells. The dorsal somatic walls develop as dorsal longitudinal muscles and further masses of fat body cells. The splanchnic walls of the anterior and posterior pouches separate off and become applied to the outer surface of the developing midgut epithelium, where they give rise to the musculature of the midgut, contribute to the fat body and also participate in formation of the gonads. As the somites break up into their component tissues, the haemocoele incorporates the coelomic cavities of the somites.

Along the line of dorsal junction of the splanchnic and somatic mesoderm of each somite from the labial to the eighth abdominal, a row of cells enlarges as cardioblasts (Fig. 14e; Korotneff, 1883, 1885; Wheeler, 1889a, 1893; Heymons, 1895; Faussek, 1911; Mellanby, 1937; Butt, 1949; Görg, 1959; Striebel, 1960). As the mesoderm grows dorsally around the developing gut during dorsal closure, the cardioblasts move towards the dorsal midline. Eventually, the cells come together to enclose a tubular haemocoelic space and form the walls of the heart. Adjacent somatic mesodermal cells give rise to the alary muscles, pericardial septum and pericardial cells (Heymons, 1895; Leuzinger et al., 1926; Roonwal, 1937).

Behind the tenth pair of abdominal somites, the residual mesoderm associated with the proctodaeum spreads as a splanchnic sheath around the proctodaeal epithelium. No instance of an eleventh pair of abdominal somites has ever been recorded for Hemimetabola, although the occasional occurrence of an eleventh pair of abdominal ganglia and the recognition of the cerci as the eleventh pair of abdominal limbs suggest that the residual mesoderm is in part mesoderm of an eleventh abdominal segment. It is possible that the temporary pair of cavities developed in the proctodaeal mesoderm of Blattella, Periplaneta and Locusta (Wheeler, 1889a; Cholodkowsky, 1891; Heymons, 1895; Roonwal, 1937) are the coelomic cavities of this segment.

B. The Gonads and Gonoducts

The development of the gonads within the abdominal splanchnic meso-derm varies according to the stage in development at which the primordial germ cells become visible. The Orthoptera represent one extreme. The prim-ordial germ cells first become recognizable in the splanchnic walls of the abdominal somites. In *Xiphidium ensiferum*, the germ cells appear in the first six pairs of abdominal somites (Wheeler, 1893). In *Locusta migratoria*, they have a more extended distribution at first, being present in the second to tenth pairs of abdominal somites, but later persist only in the third to sixth pairs of somites (Roonwal, 1937). The segmental groups of germ cells pro-liferate and merge to form two continuous strands, each covered by a thin splanchnic epithelium. From these strands, the gonads arise. The Dermap-tera, Psocoptera and Homoptera display the opposite extreme in their germ cell formation (Heymons, 1895; Gerwel, 1950; Goss, 1953). In these orders the germ cells become visibly differentiated during blastoderm formation, as they do in many Holometabola. Their subsequent development has been traced in detail by Goss (1953) in *Liposcelis divergens* (Figs 16d, e). When aggregation of the cells of the embryonic primordium takes place in the differentiated blastoderm, the mass of germ cells lies internal to the posterior end of the primordium. During elongation of the immersed germ band, the germ cells are carried through the yolk to the anterior end of the egg. At the same time the mass of germ cells becomes invested by mesoderm cells. When caudal flexure of the abdomen takes place, the germ cells become associated with the 3rd 4th abdominal segments and come to lie between the developing nerve cord and the midgut strands. The mass of germ cells now separates into right and left halves, which give rise directly to the gonads.

The Dictyoptera, Cheleutoptera (Fig. 17), Embioptera and Heteroptera display an intermediate condition (Heymons, 1895; Seidel, 1924; Leuzinger *et al.*, 1926; Mellanby, 1936, 1937; Stefani, 1961; Cavallin, 1968). The primordial germ cells become segregated during early gastrulation, but sub-sequently migrate to the splanchnic walls of the anterior abdominal somites and continue their development in the same manner as in the Orthoptera. A segmental grouping of primordial germ cells in the walls of the somites is probably more primitive than the direct development of compact gonads, since it takes place in annelids (Anderson, 1966a, b, 1969b), onychophorans (Manton, 1949), myriapods (Tiegs, 1940, 1947) and apterygotes (Jura, 1972).

The gonoducts of the Hemimetabola arise from abdominal somite meso-derm, except for the short, unpaired vagina and ejaculatory duct, which are formed as ectodermal invaginations. Typically, as in the Dictyoptera (Hey-mons, 1891, 1895), Isoptera (Strindberg, 1913), Cheleutoptera (Leuzinger *et al.*, 1926; Cavallin, 1968), Orthoptera (Wheeler, 1893; Roonwal, 1937; Jhingran, 1947), Dermaptera (Heymons, 1895) and Heteroptera (Seidel,

1924), some of the abdominal somites give rise to paired coelomoducts, of which one or more posterior pairs enlarge and persist as gonoducts while the remainder disappear. Cavallin (1968, 1969) has recently made a careful study

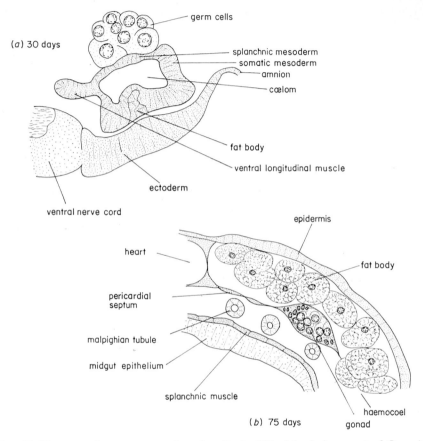

FIG. 17. Diagrammatic transverse sections through the fifth abdominal segment of *Carausius morosus* (Cheleutoptera), after Cavallin (1968). (*a*) At 30 days, just before katatrepsis; (*b*) At 75 days, shortly after hatching.

of this process in the phasmids *Carausius morosus* and *Clitumnus extradentatus*, and finds that the 7th and 8th abdominal somites contribute to the female gonoducts, the 9th and 10th to the male gonoducts.

C. The Cephalic Mesoderm

The small mandibular and maxillary somites have a specialized development, giving rise only to the extrinsic and intrinsic limb musculature of their respective segments (Roonwal, 1937; Jhingran, 1947; Scholl, 1969). The vestigial premandibular somites have an even more aberrant fate. There seems little doubt that they give rise to the sub-oesophageal body (Dictyoptera: Heymons, 1895; Görg, 1959; Isoptera, Strindberg, 1913; Plecoptera: Miller, 1939; Cheleutoptera: Leuzinger *et al.*, 1926; Scholl, 1969; Orthoptera: Wheeler, 1893; Kessel, 1961; Mallophaga: Strindberg, 1915; Heteroptera: Heymons, 1899; and also Lepidoptera: Eastham, 1930; Anderson and Wood, 1968). An origin from mandibular somites has been attributed to the sub-oesophageal body of Orthoptera by Roonwal (1937) and Jhingran (1947), but confirmation of this interpretation seems to be required. The bilateral rudiments of the sub-oesophageal body come together beneath the oesophagus and differentiate precociously as a group of gland cells before katatrepsis begins (Heymons, 1895; Strindberg, 1915; Leuzinger *et al.*, 1926; Roonwal, 1937; Kessel, 1961; Anderson and Wood, 1968). The function of the gland in the embryo is still obscure. Usually the sub-oesophageal body degenerates before hatching takes place, but in the Blattidae it persists into the nymphal stages and in the Isoptera it is retained in the adult. A recent careful investigation of the premandibular somites of *Carausius* by Scholl (1969) has shown that in addition to the sub-oesophageal body, these somites give rise to certain of the muscles associated with the stomodaeum.

The antennal somites follow a more typical course of development (Heymons, 1895; Strindberg, 1913; Leuzinger *et al.*, 1936; Roonwal, 1937; Jhingran, 1947). The somites undergo tripartite outpouching and the appendicular pouches then give rise to the musculature of the antennae. The somatic wall of the anterior and posterior pouches develops as fat body, while the median walls come together in the midline above the stomodaeum to form the walls of the anterior aorta. The median mesoderm between the antennal somites develops as musculature of the stomodaeum, while the preantennal somites and their associated median mesoderm develop as the labral and other musculature at the front of the head (Scholl, 1969).

XIII. THE COMPOSITION OF THE HEAD IN HEMIMETABOLA

The segmental composition of the pterygote head has recently been discussed by Matsuda (1965), Ullman (1967), Gouin (1968), Malzacher (1968) and Scholl (1969). The origin and development of the components of the hemimetabolan head is outlined again in various parts of the above account. There is no doubt, as pointed out by Manton (1960), Matsuda (1965) and others, that all but the anterior part of the head is formed through the cephalized development of five segments, the antennal, premandibular and three gnathal segments, all of which originate postorally. The antennal and, to some extent, the premandibular segment migrate forwards in front of the mouth as development proceeds. The composition of the preantennal part of the head remains less certain (Gouin, 1968). Matsuda argued that there is no evidence for the presence of any segmental components in the ectodermal development of this region, all of which can be attributed to an enlarged acron, and that the preantennal somites are themselves insufficient as criteria of a segment. If the preantennal somites are vestiges of a preantennal segment, he wrote, then the ectoderm of this segment must have been wholly suppressed. Scholl (1965, 1969) and Malzacher (1968), however, maintain that a distinct pair of preantennal ganglia can be recognized in *Carausius* and *Periplaneta*, and on the basis of this evidence it becomes more probable that the pterygote head incorporates a preantennal segment as well as the five distinct segments behind its large acron. The preantennal segment, however, makes little contribution to the structure of the head of modern Hemimetabola. Furthermore, the phylogenetic importance once attached to the comparative segmental composition of the arthropod head has now been outmoded by recent evidence (e.g. Manton, 1964, 1970; Anderson, 1966*a*, *b*, 1969) that neither the Crustacea nor the Arachnida have played any part in the evolutionary history of the onychophoran-myriapod-hexapod assemblage of arthropods. The question of the presence or absence of a vestigial preantennal segment in the pterygote head thus becomes less significant.

XIV. COMPARATIVE EMBRYOLOGY AND THE PHYLOGENETIC RELATIONSHIPS OF THE HEMIMETABOLA

At the present time, the embryonic development of the Hemimetabola is insufficiently known to provide much evidence on the phylogenetic relationships between the orders. We are still exceptionally ignorant, for example, of the development of the Ephemeroptera and still unable to see any embryological features which support the sub-grouping of the blattopteroid, orthopteroid and dermapteroid orders within the Polyneoptera. The embryonic development of the Polyneoptera can be regarded at the present time as no more than variations on a theme. The Paraneoptera share a specialized pattern of embryonic development, obviously derived from that of primitive pterygotes, but not allied directly with any one order. At the same time, the accumulated evidence summarized above makes it possible to discern a basic developmental pattern for all pterygotes, on which a reappraisal of their relationships with the apterygotes, myriapods and onychophorans might be based.

The most rewarding comparisons of the embryonic development of related groups are attained through consideration of the formation and fates of the presumptive areas of the blastula or blastoderm (Fig. 18). The presumptive areas of the onychophoran blastoderm and their pattern of subsequent development were summarized by Anderson (1966*b*). The general similarity between the onychophoran fate map (Fig. 18*a*) and that of Hemimetabola (Fig. 8*a*) is obvious, but there are two striking differences. The posterior midgut component of the Onychophora, which augments the midgut after the yolk mass has been enclosed by cells of the anterior midgut component, is absent in pterygotes and the presumptive midgut is confined to two rudiments, one behind the stomodaeum and one in front of the proctodaeum. This difference could result from a bipolar restriction of the onychophoran anterior midgut and loss of the posterior midgut component, associated with

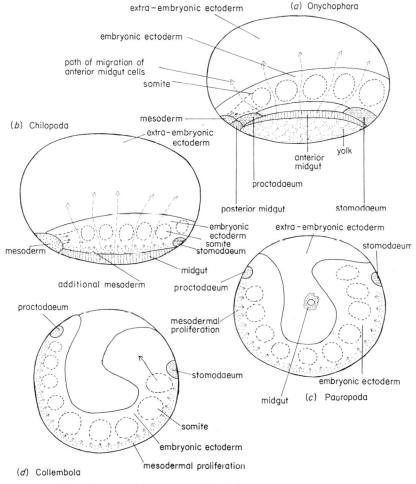

FIG. 18. The presumptive areas of the blastoderm and the formation of mesodermal somites in the embryos of (*a*) Onychophora, after Anderson (1966*b*); (*b*) Chilopoda, after Heymons (1901); (*c*) Pauropoda, after Tiegs (1947); (*d*) Collembola, after Jura (1972); diagrammatically illustrated in right lateral view.

a precocious segregation of vitellophages during cleavage and blastoderm formation in pterygotes, and is thus acceptable as a functional specialization. The second difference, however, is more fundamental. The presumptive mesoderm in Onychophora comprises a small area of blastoderm cells behind the proctodaeum and posterior midgut components, while the presumptive mesoderm of pterygotes lies along the ventral midline between the bipolar midgut rudiments, in an entirely new position.

In examining whether this difference can be resolved in terms of a functionally feasible sequence of intermediate steps, we can seek evidence from the comparative formation and fates of presumptive areas in the myriapods and apterygotes. As pointed out by Jura (1972), the early stages of the development of apterygote embryos are still poorly known and the available facts bearing on the present question are few and doubtful. Among the myriapods, the embryology of the Pauropoda and Symphyla has been analysed in detail by Tiegs (1940, 1947), but that of the Chilopods (Heymons, 1901) and Diplopoda (Dohle, 1964) is less well understood. It is a remarkable fact, however, that even this fragmentary information provides a positive answer to the question at hand. In the Chilopoda (Heymons, 1901) the mesoderm originates mainly from a small posterior presumptive area as in Onychophora, but is supplemented along the length of each mesodermal band by cells migrating in from the overlying surface layer, which then becomes the ectoderm of the germ band (Fig. 18b). This condition is intermediate to one shared by the Pauropoda, Diplopoda and Symphyla, in which the posterior area is absent and the mesodermal bands are formed by direct bilateral immigration of mesoderm cells along the length of the germ band (Fig. 18c). As far as is known, the Collembola also exhibit the latter condition (Fig. 18d). A functional transition from scattered bilateral immigration along the length of the germ band to a more precise separation of bilateral ectoderm from mid-ventral mesoderm as presumptive areas of the blastoderm is not difficult to envisage. This level of precision has evolved in the Thysanura and Pterygota (Fig. 8a). The major difference between the fate maps of the Onychophora and Pterygota is thus not as fundamental as it seems and there is nothing in the embryology of the two groups that denies the possibility of a common ancestry. Much more information is required on the embryology of myriapods and apterygotes, however, before this type of evidence can be brought fully to bear on the phylogenetic relationships of the onychophorans, myriapods and hexapods.

XV. NORMAL TABLES OF HEMIMETABOLAN DEVELOPMENT

In order to display the development of hemimetabolan embryos as a continuous sequence of change and elaboration, summaries of the development of selected species are presented in Tables III, IV and V. The examples selected, *Carausius morosus*, *Kalotermes flavicollis* and *Tachycines asynamorus* have been chosen primarily because they have been studied in detail, but also because they represent particular types of hemimetabolan development. *C. morosus*, as has been discussed above, retains a relatively generalized type of embryo with a superficial germ band. *K. flavicollis* is also generalized in most respects, but displays an extreme shortening of the embryonic primordium. Both of these species have a strikingly slow rate of embryonic development. *T. asynamorus*, in contrast, develops at a somewhat faster rate and is a typical example of an immersed germ band embryo. Illustrations of the development of two related species, the cheleutopteran *Didymuria violescens* (Figs 19 and 20) and the isopteran *Nasutitermes exitiosus* (Figs 21 and 22), are also included for comparative purposes.

TABLE III. The Embryonic Development of *Carausius morosus* (Cheleutoptera) at 22°C: Modified after Fournier (1967)

0–4 days:	Intralecithal cleavage is followed by a first emergence of cleavage energids at the posterior pole of the yolk mass, gradually extending anteriorly as heterochronous divisions ensue. Compare Fig. 19*b*.
5 days:	Concentration of numerous energids to form the paired bilateral rudiments of the embryonic primordium takes place at the posterior pole of the yolk mass. Compare Fig. 19*c* and *d*.
6–8 days:	Further concentration leads to the establishment of a short, heart-shaped embryonic primordium (compare Fig. 19*e*). Immigration of inner layer cells begins in the midline.
8–10 days:	Inner layer formation continues (Fig. 7*d*).
11–12 days:	Preliminary delineation of the major part of the embryonic primordium as head lobes precedes the onset of elongation (Fig. 6*d*; compare Fig. 19*e*).
13–14 days:	The segment-forming growth zone becomes active and the embryonic primordium begins to grow. The head lobes become more sharply delineated. The stomodaeal rudiment invaginates. The amniotic folds arise and merge, forming the amnion and serosa. Compare Figs 19*f* and 20*a*.
15–18 days:	As elongation continues, the three thoracic segments become delineated and develop rudimentary limb buds, followed by the gnathal segments and antennal rudiments (Figs 6*e, f*; compare Figs 19*g*, 20*b* and *c*). Coelomic sacs are now present in the thorax.
19–21 days:	With further elongation of the segmenting germ band, the head lobes, labrum and antennal rudiments enlarge; the gnathal segments develop limb rudiments and coelomic sacs; the first four abdominal segments are delineated and the first two of them develop limb rudiments (Fig. 6*g*; compare Fig. 20*d*). At this stage the segmenting germ band begins a 180° rotation at the posterior pole of the egg, turning in an anticlockwise direction.
22–24 days:	Continued elongation is accommodated by caudal flexure. The fifth to seventh abdominal segments are delineated, accompanied by the formation of coelomic sacs and limb buds. The germ band thickens anteriorly and the cephalic and thoracic limbs increase in length (Fig. 6*h*).

TABLE III—(continued)

25–27 days: Segmentation of the germ band is completed, the last three abdominal segments (8, 9 and 10) being flexed forward. Ten pairs of abdominal coelomic sacs are formed. The first pair of abdominal limbs enlarges as pleuropodia. Compare Figs 19*h* and 20*f*.

28–29 days: While the antennae, mouthparts and thoracic limbs continue to elongate and acquire incipient jointing, the abdominal limbs other than the pleuropodia are resorbed. The tracheal rudiments invaginate.

30 days: Fusion and rupture of the embryonic membranes takes place and katatrepsis begins.

31–35 days: The germ band migrates forwards along the ventral surface of the yolk mass until the posterior, flexed end of the germ band lies at the posterior pole. At the same time, the head and thorax continue to enlarge and differentiate, and ommatidial pigmentation begins. The abdominal segments undergo dorsal closure (Fig. 12*a*). Compare Figs 19*i, j* and 20*g*.

36–45 days: The embryo enlarges and spreads dorsally around the yolk mass, almost completing dorsal closure (Fig. 12*b*; compare Figs 19*j*, 20*h*). The thoracic limbs become S-shaped as they grow longer. The mouthparts turn forwards. Pigmentation of the eyes is almost completed. Towards the end of this period, the heart begins to beat.

46–50 days: Dorsal closure is completed, cuticular secretion takes place and the embryo becomes highly differentiated (Fig. 12*c*; compare Fig. 19*k*).

61–85 days: Resorption of pleuropodia, digestion of the remaining yolk, completion of histodifferentiation and cuticular pigmentation, and the onset of muscular movements lead to hatching at 85 days.

TABLE IV. The Embryonic Development of *Kalotermes flavicollis* (Isoptera) at 26°C: Modified after Striebel (1960).

0–24 hours: Completion of maturation and fertilization are followed by division of the zygote nucleus into two cleavage energids. The zygote of *Zootermopsis nevadensis*, which is similar to but smaller than that of *K. flavicollis* (Table II), is illustrated in Fig. 1*a*.

24–36 hours: The second and third cleavage divisions take place. Six energids lie in the posterior half of the egg, two in the anterior half (Fig. 2*a*).

36–48 hours: The fourth to sixth cleavage divisions occur (Fig. 2*b*). 64 energids are scattered uniformly near the surface of the yolk mass.

48–72 hours: The seventh cleavage division is followed by migration of 116 energids to the surface of the yolk mass, accumulating more densely at the postero-ventral surface than elsewhere (Fig. 2*c*). 12 energids remain within the yolk mass. Mitotic divisions become heterochronous and the superficial energids increase in number more rapidly posteroventrally than elsewhere on the surface (Fig. 2*d*).

4–6 days: The posteroventral energids merge to form a syncytial disc, the embryonic primordium, at the surface of the yolk mass. Over the remainder of the surface, the individual energids are still separated from one another.

7 days: The embryonic primordium becomes cellularized and begins to release vitellophages into the yolk mass. The size of the embryonic primordium relative to the yolk mass at this stage is illustrated for *Zootermopsis nevadensis* by Fig. 4*c*.

TABLE IV—(continued)

8 days: The inner layer is formed, as a result of immigration of cells in the midline of the embryonic primordium (Fig. 7*f*). Vitellophages continue to be released into the yolk mass from the periphery of the inner layer. The extra-embryonic energids at the surface of the yolk mass merge to form an attenuated extra-embryonic ectoderm.

9 days: The posterior margin of the embryonic rudiment folds forward as the amnion (Fig. 7*g*). The extra-embryonic ectoderm is carried with it (Fig. 9*d*). At the completion of this process, the amnion forms the external wall and the embryonic rudiment the internal wall, of a sphere of cells lying between the yolk mass and the serosa at the posterior end of the egg (Fig. 9*e*; compare Fig. 21*a*).

10–15 days: The sphere of cells gradually flattens and begins to extend along the postero-dorsal surface of the yolk mass. The two-layered internal wall remains thick and shows numerous cell divisions. The amnion soon becomes attenuated (Fig. 10*a*; compare Figs 21*b*, *c* and 22*a*).

16–17 days: As growth in length continues, the germ band begins to segment. The pre-antennal region and the antennal, mandibular and maxillary segments become delineated, and the stomodaeum begins to invaginate. An equivalent stage of *Zootermopsis nevadensis* is illustrated in Fig. 4*e*.

21 days: The segmenting germ band now extends from the posterior pole along two thirds of the dorsal surface of the yolk mass. Growth is concentrated mainly in the posterior, segment-forming growth zone. Segments are delineated as far back as the third thoracic segment. An equivalent stage of *Zootermopsis nevadensis* is illustrated in Fig. 4*f*. Compare Fig. 21*d*.

22 days: The first abdominal segment is delineated (Figs 10*b*, *d*). Coelomic cavities are present in the antennal, gnathal and thoracic somites (Fig. 10*b*). Neuroblasts have differentiated in the pre-antennal and antennal ectoderm.

23–25 days: Growth in length of the segmenting germ band is completed, abdominal segments 2–10 become delineated and the posterior end of the abdomen flexed forwards as a tail fold (Fig. 10*c*). Cephalic and thoracic limb buds become well developed, and the first six pairs of abdominal limb buds are formed. Each segment from the antennal to the tenth abdominal contains a pair of hollow somites. Equivalent stages of *Zootermopsis nevadensis* are illustrated in Figs 4*g* and 6*a*. Compare Figs 21*e*, 22*b* and *c*.

26–30 days: The segmented germ band retains its position while undergoing preliminary organogenesis. Limb buds develop on the last four abdominal segments. The cephalic and thoracic limbs grow longer. Tracheal invaginations develop in the lateral ectoderm. Internally, neuropile, somatic and splanchnic myoblasts, fat body cells, haemocytes and midgut strands become differentiated.

31 days: The embryonic membranes fuse and rupture and the embryo undergoes katatrepsis. The germ band migrates head first over the posterior pole and forwards along the ventral surface of the yolk mass. The serosa contracts to form an anterodorsal dorsal organ and the amnion spreads upwards over the yolk mass as a provisional dorsal closure. Compare Figs 21*f* and *g*.

34 days: The embryo rotates through 180° on its long axis, bringing the ventral surface of the germ band beneath the concave, originally dorsal surface of the egg membranes (compare Fig. 21*h*). Malpighian tubules grow out from the distal end of the proctodaeum and cardioblasts differentiate at the dorsolateral edges of the splanchnic mesoderm strands.

TABLE IV—(*continued*)

38–40 days: The dorsal organ and provisional dorsal closure are resorbed into the yolk as the lateral walls of the germ band spread upwards, effecting definitive dorsal closure. The midgut strands spread to enclose the remaining yolk within a tubular midgut. Compare Figs 22*e* and *f*.

41–42 days: The heart forms and begins to contract. The brain and sub-oesophageal ganglion attain their definitive form. The somatic musculature gains cross striations and the hypodermis begins to secrete the cuticle.

43–53 days: The remaining yolk is resorbed and organogenesis and histodifferentiation are completed. Compare Fig. 21*i*.

54 days: Hatching occurs.

TABLE V. The Embryonic Development of *Tachycines asynomorus* (Orthoptera) at 26°C: Modified after Krause (1938*a*, *b*, 1939) and Ibrahim (1957)

0–3 days: Intralecithal cleavage is followed by the emergence of cleavage energids at the surface of the yolk mass and formation of a uniform blastoderm.

4–6 days: Bilateral concentration of blastoderm cells towards the posteroventral midline gives rise to a small, heart-shaped embryonic primordium.

6–7 days: Amniotic folds arise and merge, forming the amnion and completing the serosa.

7–9 days: The embryonic rudiment increases in length, due to activity of the posterior, segment-forming growth zone, and at the same time, turns into the yolk mass and migrates forward beneath the dorsal surface of the serosa (anatrepsis, resulting in immersion of the segmenting germ band in the yolk). The gnathal, thoracic and first abdominal segments are delineated, and the stomodaeum invaginates.

10–14 days: Activity of the growth zone continues until ten abdominal segments are formed. The posterior end of the abdomen flexes forwards as a tail fold. The head lobes enlarge, the antennae and labrum develop. The gnathal and thoracic limb buds become conspicuous (Figs 14*a* and *b*) and ten pairs of limb buds arise on the abdominal segments. At the posterior end of the abdomen, the proctodaeum invaginates and cercal rudiments begin to grow.

15–21 days: Remaining immersed, the germ band shortens slightly, then begins to thicken. The antennae, gnathal and thoracic limbs and cerci grow longer and show preliminary jointing. The first abdominal limbs develop into pleuropodia, while the remainder are resorbed. The bases of the antennae move forward in front of the mouth and the eyes begin to develop pigmentation (Fig. 6*j*). Figures 14*c* and *d* indicate the degree of internal differentiation taking place during this period.

22 days: The amnion and serosa fuse, rupture and roll back and the germ band undergoes katatrepsis (Figs 12*j* and *k*).

23–25 days: Dorsal closure takes place (Figs 12*l* and 14*e*).

26–37 days: The cuticle is secreted and yolk resorption and final histodifferentiation follow. The first muscular contractions are seen on the 29th day. Secretion of enzymes by the pleuropodia also begins on the same day. Hatching takes place at 37 days.

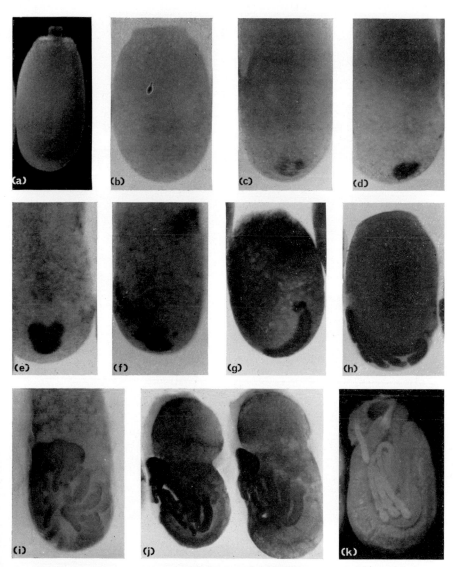

FIG. 19. Development of *Didymuria violescens* (Cheleutoptera), reproduced with permission from original material prepared by G. O. Bedford. (*a*) Egg; (*b*) Differentiating blastoderm; (*c*)–(*d*) Formation of the embryonic primordium; (*e*)–(*h*) Elongation and segmentation of the germ band; (*i*) Katatrepsis; (*j*) Stages in dorsal closure; (*k*) Shortly before hatching.

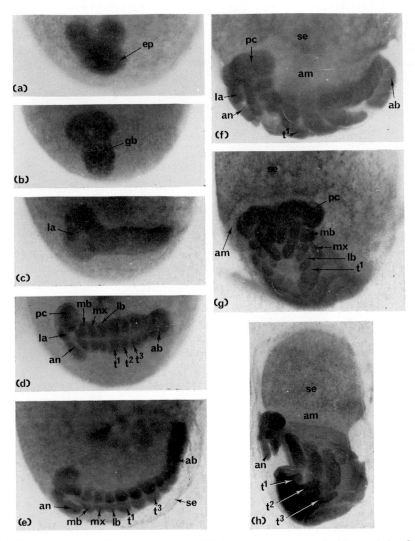

FIG. 20. Development of *Didymuria violescens* (Cheleutoptera), reproduced with permission from original material prepared by G. O. Bedford. (*a*) Embryonic primordium at the onset of elongation; (*b*)–(*e*) Stages in growth and segmentation of the germ band; (*f*)–(*g*) Katatrepsis; (*h*) Early dorsal closure. *ab*, abdomen; *am*, amnion; *amc*, amniotic cavity; *an*, antenna; *br*, brain; *do*, dorsal organ; *ep*, embryonic primordium; *gb*, germ band; *la*, labrum; *lb*, labium; *mb*, mandible; *mx*, maxilla; *pc*, protocerebrum; *pr*, proctodaeum; *se*, serosa; t^1–t^3, thoracic limbs.

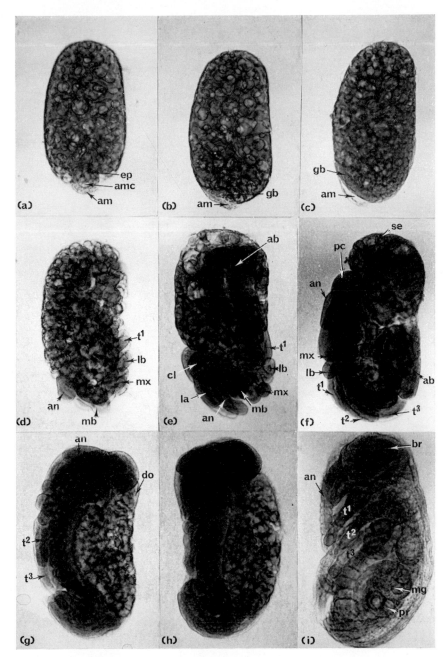

Fig. 21. Development of *Nasutitermes exitiosus* (Isoptera). The material on which these illustrations are based was supplied to the author by Dr F. Gay. (*a*) Embryonic primordium after amnion formation; (*b*)–(*c*) Early growth of the germ band; (*d*)–(*e*) Completion of growth and segmentation of the germ band; (*f*) Katatrepsis; (*g*) End of katatrepsis, before 180° rotation; (*h*) After 180° rotation of the germ band on the yolk mass; (*i*) Shortly before hatching. *ab*, abdomen; *am*, amnion; *amc*, amniotic cavity; *an*, antenna; *br*, brain; *do*, dorsal organ; *ep*, embryonic primordium; *gb*, germ band; *la*, labrum; *lb*, labium; *mb*, mandible; *mx*, maxilla; *pc*, protocerebrum; *pr*, procto-daeum; *se*, serosa; t^1–t^3, thoracic limbs; *mg*, midgut; *cl*, cephalic limb.

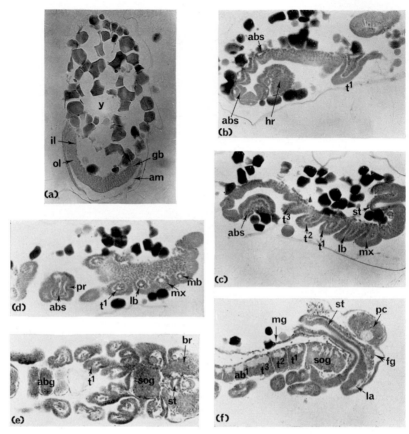

FIG. 22. Development of *Nasutitermes exitiosus* (Isoptera). Histological sections prepared from material supplied to the author by Dr F. Gay. (*a*) Sagittal section through early, growing germ band; (*b*) Parasagittal and (*c*) Sagittal sections through the segmented germ band; (*d*) Frontal section through the segmented germ band; (*e*) and (*f*) Frontal and sagittal sections through the embryo shortly before hatching. *ab¹*, first abdominal segment; *abg*, abdominal ganglion; *abs*, abdominal somite; *am*, amnion; *fg*, frontal ganglion; *gb*, germ band; *il*, inner layer; *la*, labrum; *lb*, labium; *mb*, mandibular segment; *mg*, midgut strand; *mx*, maxillary segment; *ol*, outer layer; *pc*, protocerebrum; *pr*, proctodaeum; *sog*, sub-oesophageal ganglion; *st*, stomodaeum; *t¹–t³*, thoracic segments; *br*, brain; *y*, yolk; *hr*, hindgut rudiment.

REFERENCES

Anderson, D. T. (1966*a*). *Acta Zool., Stockh.*, **47**, 1–42.

Anderson, D. T. (1966*b*). *Proc. Linn. Soc. N.S.W.*, **91**, 10–43.

Anderson, D. T. (1969*a*). *Phil. Trans. R. Soc.* **B 256**, 183–235.

Anderson, D. T. (1969*b*). *The Embryology of Aquatic Oligochaetes.* In *Aquatic Oligochaeta of the World* (R. O. Brinkhurst and B. G. Jamieson, eds.), pp. 73–103. Oliver and Boyd, Edinburgh.

Anderson, D. T. and Wood, E. C. (1968). *Aust. J. Zool.*, **16**, 763–793.

Ando, H. (1957). *Sci. Rep. Tokyo Kyoiku Daig.*, **B8**, 174–216.
Ando, H. (1962). *The Comparative Embryology of Odonata With Special Reference to a Relict Dragonfly* Epiophlebia superstes *Selys*. Japanese Society for the Promotion of Science, Tokyo.
Ando, H. and Kawana, T. (1956). *Kontyû, Tokyo*, **24**, 224–233.
Ashhurst, D. E. (1965). *Q . J. microsc. Sci.*, **106**, 61–73.
Ayers, H. (1884). *Mem. Boston Soc. nat. Hist.*, **3**, 225–281.
Baden, V. (1936). *J. Morph.*, **60**, 156–190.
Baden, V. (1937). *J. Morph.*, **63**, 219–223.
Bahadur, J. (1968). *Beitr. Ent.*, **18**, 239–247.
Beament, J. W. L. (1946a). *Q . J. microsc. Sci.*, **87**, 393–439.
Beament, J. W. L. (1946b). *Proc. R. Soc.* **B133**, 407–418.
Beament, J. W. L. (1947). *J. exp. Biol.*, **23**, 213–233.
Beament, J. W. L. (1948). *Bull. ent. Res.*, **39**, 359–383.
Beament, J. W. L. (1949). *Bull. ent. Res.*, **39**, 467–488.
Beams, H. W. and Kessel, R. G. (1968). *J. cell Biol.*, **39**, 10a.
Bedford, G. O. (1970). *Aust. J. Zool.*, **18**, 155–169.
Behrendt, K. (1963). *Zool. Jb. Physiol.*, **70**, 309–398.
Bergerard, J. (1958). *Bull. biol. Fr. Belg.*, **92**, 87–182.
Bhatnagar, R. D. S. and Singh, J. P. (1965). *Res. Bull. Panjab Univ. Sci.*, **16**, 19–30.
Bodenheimer, F. S. and Shulov, A. (1951). *Bull. Res. Coun. Israel*, **1**, 59–75.
Böhmel, W. and Jancke, O. (1942). *Z. angew. Ent.*, **29**, 636–658.
Bournier, A. (1960). *C. r. hebd. Séanc. Acad. Sci. (Paris)*, **250**, 1347–1348.
Brookes, H. M. (1952). *Trans. R. Soc. S. Aust.*, **75**, 150–159.
Bruce, A. T. (1887). *Observations on the Embryology of Insects and Arachnids*. John Hopkins University, Baltimore.
Butt, F. H. (1949). *Mem. Cornell Univ. agric. Exp. Stn*, **283**, 1–43.
Butt, F. H. (1960). *Biol. Rev.*, **35**, 43–91.
Cavallin, M. (1968). Thesis, University of Bordeaux.
Cavallin, M. (1969). *C. r. hebd. Séanc. Acad. Sci. (Paris)*, **268**, 2189–2192.
Chapman, R. F. and Whitham, F. (1968). *Proc. R. ent. Soc. Lond.*, **43A**, 161–169.
Cholodkowsky, N. (1890a). *Zool. Anz.*, **13**, 137–138.
Cholodkowsky, N. (1890b). *Biol. Zbl.*, **10**, 425.
Cholodkowsky, N. (1891). *Zool. Anz.*, **14**, 115–116.
Cobben, R. H. (1968). *Evolutionary trends in Heteroptera*. Part I. Eggs, architecture of the shell, gross embryology and eclosion. Centre for Agricultural Publishing and Documentation, Wageningen.
Counce, S. J. (1972). *Developmental Systems: Insects* (S. J. Counce and C. H. Waddington, eds), Vol. 2, p. 1. Academic Press, London and New York.
Dohle, W. (1964). *Zool. Jb. Anat. Ont.*, **81**, 241–310.
Eastham, L. E. S. (1930). *Phil. Trans. R. Soc.*, **B219**, 1–50.
Else, F. L. (1934). *J. Morph.*, **55**, 577–610.
Faussek, V. (1911). *Z. wiss. Zool.*, **98**, 529–625.
Fernando, W. (1933). *Q . J. microsc. Sci.*, **76**, 231–241.
Fournier, B. (1966). Thesis, University of Bordeaux.
Fournier, B. (1967). *Act. Soc. linn. Bordeaux*, **104A**, 1–30.
Gerwel, C. (1950). *Pr. Kom. biol., Poznan*, **12**(10), 1–33.
Giardina, A. (1897). *Monitore Zool. Ital.*, **8**, 275–280.
Görg, I. (1959). *Dt. ent. Z.*, **6**, 390–450.
Goss, R. J. (1952). *J. Morph.*, **91**, 135–167.

Goss, R. J. (1953). *J. Morph.*, **92**, 157–191.

Gouin, F. L. (1968). *Fortschr. Zool.*, **19**, 194–282.

Graber, V. (1878). *Arch. mikrosk. Anat. EntwMech.*, **15**, 630–640.

Graber, V. (1888*a*). *Morph. Jb.*, **13**, 586–613.

Graber, V. (1888*b*). *Denkschr. Akad. Wiss. Wien*, **55**, 109–162.

Graber, V. (1888*c*). *Morph. Jb.*, **14**, 345–368.

Graber, V. (1890). *Denkschr. Akad. Wiss. Wien*, **57**, 621–734.

Graber, V. (1891). *Denkschr. Akad. Wiss. Wien*, **58**, 803–866.

Hagan, H. R. (1917). *J. Morph.*, **30**, 223–243.

Hammerschmidt, J. (1910). *Z. wiss. Zool.*, **95**, 221–242.

Henson, H. (1944). *Proc. R. ent. Soc. Lond.*, **19A**, 73–91.

Henson, H. (1946). *Proc. R. ent. Soc. Lond.*, **21A**, 29–39.

Heymons, R. (1891). *Z. wiss. Zool.*, **53**, 434–536.

Heymons, R. (1895). *Die Embryonalentwickelung von Dermapteren und Orthopteren unter besonderer Berucksichtigung der Keimblatterbildung.* Gustav Fischer, Jena.

Heymons, R. (1896*a*). *Dt. Akad. Wiss. Abb.*, **1896**, 1–66.

Heymons, R. (1896*b*). *Sber. Ges. naturf. Freunde Berl.*, **1896**, 82–96.

Heymons, R. (1897). *Sber. preuss. Akad. Wiss.*, **1897**, 363–373.

Heymons, R. (1899). *Nova Acta Acad. Caesar. Leop. Carol.*, **74**, 351–456.

Heymons, R. (1901). *Zoologica, Stuttg.*, **13**, 1–224.

Heymons, R. (1912). *Zool. Jb. Suppl.*, **15**, 141–184.

Hirschler, J. (1912). *Z. wiss. Zool.*, **100**, 393–446.

Hussey, P. B. (1926). *Entomologica am.*, **7**, 1–80.

Ibrahim, M. M. (1957). *Zool. Jb. Anat. Ont.*, **76**, 541–594.

Illies, J. (1968). In *Handbuch der Zoologie*, 4 (2) 2/5 (M. Bieier, ed.), pp. 1–63. Gruyter, Berlin.

Jannone, G. (1939). *Boll. R. Lab. Ent. agr. Portici.*, **4**, 1–443.

Jhingran, V. G. (1947). *Rec. Indian Mus.*, **45**, 181–200.

Johannsen, O. A. and Butt, F. H. (1941). *Embryology of Insects and Myriapods.* McGraw-Hill, New York.

Jones, B. M. (1956). *J. exp. Biol.*, **33**, 685–696.

Jura, C. Z. (1959). *Zoologica Pol.*, **9**, 17–34.

Jura, C. Z. (1972). In *Developmental Systems: Insects* (S. J. Counce and C. H. Waddington, eds), Vol. 1, p. 49. Academic Press, London and New York.

Kanellis, A. (1952). *Wilhelm Roux Arch. EntwMech. Org.*, **145**, 417–461.

Kershaw, J. C. (1914). *J. R. microsc. Soc.*, **1914**, 24–27.

Kessel, R. G. (1961). *J. Morph.*, **109**, 289–322.

Khoo, S. G. (1968). *Proc. R. ent. Soc. Lond.*, **43A**, 141–146.

Koch, P. (1964). *Wilhelm Roux Arch. EntwMech. Org.*, **155**, 549–593.

Korotneff, A. (1883). *Zool. Anz.*, **6**, 687–690.

Korotneff, A. (1885). *Z. wiss. Zool.*, **41**, 507–604.

Krause, G. (1938*a*). *Z. Morph. Ökol. Tiere*, **34**, 1–78.

Krause, G. (1938*b*). *Z. Morph. Ökol. Tiere*, **34**, 499–564.

Krause, G. (1939). *Biol. Zbl.*, **59**, 495–536.

Krause, G. and Sander, K. (1962). *Adv. Morphog.*, **2**, 259–303.

Kühn, O. (1926). *Z. Morph. Ökol. Tiere*, **5**, 489–558.

Le Berre, J. R. (1952). *C. r. hebd. Séanc. Acad. Sci. (Paris)*, **234**, 1487–1489.

Le Berre, J. R. (1953). *Bull. biol. Fr. Belg.*, **87**, 227–273.

Leuzinger, H. *et al.* (1926). *Zur Kenntnis der Anatomie und Entwicklungsgeschichte der Stabheuschrecke Carausius morosus.* Gustav Fischer, Jena.

Louvet, J. P. (1964). *Bull. Soc. zool. Fr.*, **89**, 688–701.
Ludtke, H. (1940). *Z. Morph. Ökol. Tiere*, **37**, 1–37.
McFarlane, J. E. (1965). *Can. J. Zool.*, **43**, 911–913.
Mahowald, A. P. (1972). In *Developmental Systems: Insects* (S. J. Counce and C. H. Waddington, eds), Vol. 1, p. 1. Academic Press, London and New York.
Mahr, E. (1957). *Naturwissenschaften*, **44**, 226–227.
Mahr, E. (1960). *Z. Morph. Ökol. Tiere*, **49**, 263–311.
Malzacher, P. (1968). *Z. Morph. Ökol. Tiere*, **62**, 103–161.
Manton, S. M. (1928). *Phil. Trans. R. Soc.*, **B216**, 363–463.
Manton, S. M. (1949). *Phil. Trans. R. Soc.*, **B233**, 483–580.
Manton, S. M. (1960). *Biol. Rev.*, **35**, 265–282.
Manton, S. M. (1964). *Phil. Trans. R. Soc.*, **B247**, 1–183.
Manton, S. M. (1970). In *Chemical Zoology* (M. Florkin, ed.), **5**, 1–34.
Matsuda, R. (1965). *Mem. Am. Inst. Ent.*, **4**, 1–334.
Matthée, J. J. (1951). *Sci. Bull. Dep. Agric. For. Un. S. Afr.*, **316**, 1–83.
Mellanby, H. (1936). *Q. Jl. microsc. Sci.*, **78**, 71–90.
Mellanby, H. (1937). *Q. Jl. microsc. Sci.*, **79**, 1–42.
Miller, A. (1939). *J. Morph.*, **64**, 555–609.
Miller, A. (1940). *Ann. ent. Soc. Am.*, **33**, 437–447.
Moscona, A. (1950). *Experientia*, **6**, 425–426.
Muir, F. and Kershaw, J. C. (1911). *Psyche, Camb.*, **18**, 75–79.
Muir, F. and Kershaw, J. C. (1912). *Psyche, Camb.*, **19**, 77–89.
Nelsen, O. E. (1931). *J. Morph.*, **51**, 467–526.
Nelsen, O. E. (1934). *J. Morph.*, **55**, 545–574.
Newcomer, W. S. (1948). *J. Morph.*, **82**, 365–411.
Nusbaum, J. and Fulinski, B. (1906). *Zool. Anz.*, **30**, 362–381.
Nusbaum, J. and Fulinski, B. (1909). *Z. wiss. Zool.*, **93**, 306–348.
Piotrowski, F. (1953). *Acta parasit. pol.*, **1**, 61–84.
Polivanova, E. N. (1960). *Dokl. Akad. Nauk. SSSR.*, **135**, 880–882.
Polivanova, E. N. (1961). *Zool. Zh.*, **40**, 512–522.
Polivanova, E. N. (1965). *Zh. obshch. Biol.*, **26**, 700–710.
Rabito, L. (1898). *Naturalista sicil.*, **2**, 181–183.
Rakshpal, R. (1962). *Proc. R. ent. Soc. Lond.*, **37A**, 1–12.
Rempel, J. G. and Church, N. S. (1969). *Can. J. Zool.*, **47**, 1157–1171.
Riegert, R. W. (1961). *Can. J. Zool.*, **39**, 491–494.
Ries, E. (1931). *Z. Morph. Ökol. Tiere*, **20**, 233–376.
Riley, W. A. (1904). *Am. Nat.*, **38**, 777–810.
Roonwal, M. L. (1936). *Phil. Trans. R. Soc.*, **B226**, 391–421.
Roonwal, M. L. (1937). *Phil. Trans. R. Soc.*, **B227**, 175–244.
Salt, R. W. (1949). *Can. J. Res.*, **D27**, 233–235.
Salzen, E. A. (1960). *J. Embryol. exp. Morph.*, **8**, 139–162.
Sander, K. (1956). *Aligarh Musl. Univ. Publs. (Indian Insect Types)*, **4**, 1–61.
Sander, K. (1959). *Wilhelm Roux Arch. EntwMech. Org.*, **151**, 430–497.
Sauer, H. W. (1966). *Z. Morph. Ökol. Tiere*, **56**, 143–251.
Savage, A. A. (1962). *Q. Jl. microsc. Sci.*, **103**, 417–438.
Scholl, G. (1965). *Zool. Anz. Suppl.*, **28**, 580–596.
Scholl, G. (1969). *Z. Morph. Ökol. Tiere*, **65**, 1–142.
Schölzel, G. (1937). *Z. ParasitKde.*, **9**, 730–770.
Seidel, F. (1924). *Z. Morph. Ökol. Tiere*, **1**, 429–506.
Seidel, F. (1929). *Wilhelm Roux Arch. EntwMech. Org.*, **119**, 322–440.

Seidel, F. (1935). *Wilhelm Roux Arch. EntwMech. Org.*, **132**, 671–751.
Shinji, G. (1919). *J. Morph.*, **33**, 73–167.
Shulov, A. and Pener, M. P. (1959). *Locusta*, **6**, 73–88.
Shulov, A. and Pener, D. (1963). *Anti-Locust Bull.*, **41**, 1–59.
Slifer, E. H. (1932*a*). *Biol. Zbl.*, **52**, 223–229.
Slifer, E. H. (1932*b*). *J. Morph.*, **53**, 1–22.
Slifer, E. H. (1937). *Q . Jl. microsc. Sci.*, **79**, 493–506.
Slifer, E. H. (1938*a*). *Q . Jl. microsc. Sci.*, **80**, 437–457.
Slifer, E. H. (1938*b*). *J. Morph.*, **63**, 181–205.
Slifer, E. H. (1946). *J. exp. Zool.*, **102**, 333–356.
Slifer, E. H. (1949*a*). *J. exp. Zool.*, **110**, 183–204.
Slifer, E. H. (1949*b*). *Ann. ent. Soc. Am.*, **42**, 134–140.
Slifer, E. H. (1950). *J. Morph.*, **87**, 239–274.
Slifer, E. H. (1958). *J. exp. Zool.*, **138**, 259–282.
Srivastava, U. S. and Bahadur, I. (1961). *Q . Jl. microsc. Sci.*, **102**, 347–360.
Steele, H. V. (1941). *Trans. R. Soc. S. Aust.*, **65**, 329–332.
Stefani, R. (1961). *Caryologia*, **12**, 1–70.
Striebel, H. (1960). *Acta trop.*, **17**, 193–260.
Strindberg, H. (1913). *Z. wiss. Zool.*, **106**, 1–227.
Strindberg, H. (1914). *Zool. Anz.*, **45**, 7–14.
Strindberg, H. (1915). *Zool. Anz.*, **45**, 624–631.
Thomas, A. J. (1936). *Q . Jl. microsc. Sci.*, **78**, 487–512.
Tiegs, O. W. (1940). *Q . Jl. microsc. Sci.*, **82**, 1–225.
Tiegs, O. W. (1947). *Q . Jl. microsc. Sci.*, **88**, 165–267 and 275–336.
Tiegs, O. W. and Manton, S. M. (1958). *Biol. Rev.*, **33**, 255–337.
Tschuproff, H. (1903). *Zool. Anz.*, **27**, 29–34.
Ullman, S. L. (1967). *Phil. Trans. R. Soc.*, **B252**, 1–25.
van Horn, S. N. (1966). *J. Morph.*, **120**, 83–114.
Viallanes, H. (1891). *Annls Sci. nat. 7th ser. Zool.*, **11**, 282–328.
Vignau-Rogueda, J. (1969). *C. r. hebd. Séanc. Acad. Sci. (Paris)*, **268**, 352–355.
Wada, S. (1966*a*). *Zool. Jb. Anat. Ont.*, **83**, 235–326.
Wada, S. (1966*b*). *Naturwissenschaften*, **53**, 414.
Weber, H. (1954). *Grundrisse der Insektenkunde*. Fischer, Stuttgart.
Wheeler, W. M. (1889*a*). *J. Morph.*, **3**, 201–386.
Wheeler, W. M. (1889*b*). *Zool. Anz.*, **12**, 500–504.
Wheeler, W. M. (1889*c*). *Am. Nat.*, **23**, 644–645.
Wheeler, W. M. (1890). *Am. Nat.*, **24**, 187.
Wheeler, W. M. (1893). *J. Morph.*, **8**, 1–160.
Wigglesworth, V. B. (1959). *A. Rev. Ent.*, **4**, 1–16.
Wigglesworth, V. B. and Beament, J. W. L. (1950). *Q . Jl. microsc. Sci.*, **91**, 429–452.
Wigglesworth, V. B. and Beament, J. W. L. (1960). *J. Insect Physiol.*, **4**, 184–189.
Young, J. H. (1953). *Microentomology*, **18**, 85–133.

APPENDIX

Since the manuscript of this chapter was completed, a number of publications have come to hand to which brief reference can be made. Bohle (1969), Stringer (1969) and Melnikov (1970) have confirmed the results of earlier workers on the development of the germ band in the Ephemeroptera, Cheleutoptera and Isoptera. Mori (1969, 1970) has described the development of the embryo of the heteropteran *Gerris paludum insularis* Motchulsky, paying particular attention to the formation of the midgut. His general results are in accord with the principles of heteropteran development outlined in this chapter, but his proposition that a major part of the midgut epithelium arises from vitellophages is not adequately supported by the evidence presented in these papers. Springer (1967) and Springer and Rutschky (1969) have commented more effectively on the fate of the median strand in the homopteran *Oncopeltus*, several Heteroptera and other Hemimetabola and Holometabola. They find that the intrasegmental regions of the median strand are incorporated into the ganglia, as previously thought, where they develop as glial elements in the midline of the ganglionic neuropile. The intersegmental regions also migrate into the adjacent ganglionic regions, but subsequently degenerate without producing any definitive structures. The same workers have confirmed that the neurilemma of the ventral nerve cord originates from peripheral ganglion cells. Finally, in the context of general annelid and arthropod embryology, a more extended discussion of the embryological evidence bearing on the phylogenetic relationships of the onychophorans, myriapods and hexapods is given by Anderson (1972).

REFERENCES

Anderson, D. T. (1972). *Embryology and Phylogeny in Annelids and Arthropods*. Pergamon, Oxford, (in press).
Bohle, H. W. (1969). *Zool. Jb. Anat. Ont.*, 86, 493–575.
Melnikov, O. A. (1970). *Zool. Zh.*, 49, 838–854.
Mori, H. (1969). *Jap. J. Zool.*, 16, 53–67.
Mori, H. (1970). *Jap. J. Zool.*, 16, 89–98.
Springer, C. A. (1967). *J. Morph.*, 122, 1–18.
Springer, C. A. and Rutschsky, C. W. (1969). *J. Morph.*, 129, 375–400.
Stringer, I. A. N. (1969). *Tane*, 15, 141–152.

4 | The Development of Holometabolous Insects

D. T. ANDERSON

School of Biological Sciences, University of Sydney, Australia

I. INTRODUCTION

The eggs of hemimetabolous insects, (cf. Chapter 3), pose a number of technical problems for the descriptive embryologist. Holometabolous insects are in many ways more suitable for embryological investigation. The Holometabola are generally more prolific and more amenable to laboratory culture than the Hemimetabola. The eggs of most holometabolans develop relatively rapidly (Table I) and have smaller dimensions (Table II), less yolk and less

TABLE I. Duration of Development in Holometabola

Order	Species	Time	Source
Coleoptera	*Popilius disjunctus*	16 days	Krause and Ryan (1953)
	Tenebrio molitor	6½ days	Ullman (1967)
	Bruchidius obtectus	9 days	Jung (1966*a*)
	Calandra oryzae	4 days	Tiegs and Murray (1938)
	Bruchus quadrimaculatus	4 days	Brauer (1949)
Megaloptera	*Sialis lutaria*	8–12 days	Du Bois (1938)
Neuroptera	*Chrysopa perla*	9 days	Tichomirowa (1890, 1892)
Lepidoptera	*Epiphyas postvittana*	7 days	Reed and Day (1966)
	Diacrisia virginica	5½ days	Johannsen (1929)
	Anagasta kühniella	4½ days	Sehl (1931)
Diptera	*Simulium pinctipes*	5–6 days	Gambrell (1933)
	Smittia parthenogenetica	3½ days	Kalthoff and Sander (1968)
	Dacus tryoni	42–48 hours	Anderson (1962)
	Culex fatigans	36 hours	Davis (1967)
	Drosophila melanogaster	22 hours	Ede and Counce (1956)
	Lucilia sericata	20–24 hours	Davis (1967)
Siphonaptera	*Ctenocephalides felis*	6 days	Kessel (1939)
Hymenoptera	*Aglaostigma occipitosa*	12 days	Ando and Okada (1958)
	Pontania capreae	8–10 days	Ivanova-Kasas (1959)
	Pteronidea ribesii	3½ days	Shafiq (1954)
	Apis mellifera	70–72 hours	DuPraw (1967)

TABLE II. Representative Egg Dimensions in Holometabolous Insects

Order	Species	Length × Width in mm	Source
Coleoptera	*Popilius disjunctus*	3·00 × 2·40	Krause and Ryan (1953)
	Dermestes frischi	1·74 × 0·50	Küthe (1966)
	Euryope terminalis	1·70 × 0·90	Paterson (1931)
	Mylabris pustulatus	1·38 × 0·48	Deobahkta (1957)
	Tenebrio molitor	1·37 × 0·62	Ullman (1964)
	Dermestes maculatus	1·00 × 0·20	Ede and Rogers (1964)
	Bruchidius obtectus	0·70 × 0·25	Jung (1966a)
	Calandra oryzae	0·60 × 0·27	Tiegs and Murray (1938)
Megaloptera	*Sialis lutaria*	0·65 × 0·25	Du Bois (1938)
Neuroptera	*Chrysopa perla*	1·00 × 0·50	Bock (1939)
Mecoptera	*Panorpa pryeri*	1·10 × 0·70	Ando (1960)
Lepidoptera	*Antheraea pernyi*	3·50 × 3·00	Saito (1934)
	Bombyx mori	1·20 × 0·80	Grandori (1932)
	Epiphyas postvittana	1·00 × 0·80	Reed and Day (1966)
	Chilo suppresalis	1·00 × 0·60	Okada (1960)
	Diacrisia virginica	0·75 spherical	Johannsen (1929)
	Heliothis zeae	0·60 spherical	Presser and Rutchsky (1957)
	Anagasta kühniella	0·55 × 0·28	Sehl (1931)
Diptera	*Lucilia sericata*	1·05 × 0·22	Davis (1967)
	Dacus tryoni	1·05 × 0·18	Anderson (1962)
	Drosophila melanogaster	0·42 × 0·15	Sonnenblick (1950)
	Culex fatigans	0·55 × 0·10	Davis (1967)
	Simulium pinctipes	0·36 × 0·20	Gambrell (1933)
	Sciara coprophila	0·25 × 0·15	Du Bois (1932)
Siphonaptera	*Histrichopsylla dippiei*	1·90 × 0·90	Kessel (1939)
	Notopsyllus fasciatus	0·80 × 0·40	Kessel (1939)
	Ctenocephalides felis	0·50 × 0·30	Kessel (1939)
Hymenoptera	*Chalicodoma muraria*	3·75 × 0·85	Carrière and Bürger (1897)
	Ammophila campestris	2·50 × 0·75	Baerends and Baerends-von Roon (1950)
	Apis mellifera	1·70 × 0·35	Müller (1957), DuPraw (1967)
	Aglaostigma occipitosa	1·70 × 0·60	Ando and Okada (1958)
	Mesoleius tenthredinis	0·80 × 0·30	Bronskill (1964)
	Habrobracon juglandis	0·55 × 0·16	Amy (1961)
	Pontania capreae	0·49 × 0·16	Ivanova-Kasas (1959)
	Eurytoma aciculata	0·34 × 0·13	Ivanova-Kasas (1958)

formidable external membranes than their hemimetabolous counterparts. Consequently, good histological preparations of all stages can usually be obtained with relative ease. In spite of these advantages, however, the Holometabola were still a frustrating challenge to the insect embryologists of the nineteenth century, who found difficulty, not only with histological manipulations of their specimens, but also because the embryos of many Holometabola manifest extremes of specialization which the early workers were unable to interpret. Among the large body of nineteenth century students of holometabolan embryology, only Graber (1889), Heider (1889) and Wheeler (1889) can be said to have succeeded in interpreting their results in a way which retains a reasonable degree of validity today. In fact, it was not until fundamental advances had been made in hemimetabolous embryology by Wheeler (1893) and Heymons (1895), as discussed in the preceding chapter, that the comparative description of holometabolous development began to assume the outlines of its modern form. Even then, the pace of progress was slow, and the foundations of the subject were laid only as a result of the cumulative efforts of several workers during the twenty years preceding the First World War (Carrière and Bürger, 1897; Lecaillon, 1897a, b, c, 1898; Escherich, 1900a, b, 1901a, b, 1902; Noack, 1901; Toyama, 1902; Hirschler, 1909; Hegner, 1909, 1910, 1911, 1912, 1914, 1915; Korschelt, 1912; Strindberg, 1913, 1914, 1915a, b, 1917; Blunck, 1914; Nelson, 1915).

Following this period, as was also the case in hemimetabolan embryology, a fuller investigation and description of holometabolous embryos was achieved only in the 1930's, associated with the rise of experimental embryology and an increasing contemporary knowledge of hemimetabolous development. The Coleoptera (Paterson, 1931, 1932, 1936; Smreczyński, 1932, 1934, 1938; Inkmann, 1933; Mansour, 1934; Butt, 1936; Ewest, 1937; Wray, 1937; Tiegs and Murray, 1938), the Lepidoptera (Eastham, 1927, 1930; Johannsen, 1929; Sehl, 1931; Saito, 1934, 1937; Mueller, 1938), the Diptera (Hardenburg, 1929; Du Bois, 1932; Gambrell, 1933; Butt, 1934; Lassman, 1936; Poulson, 1937) and the Hymenoptera (Henschen, 1928; Schnetter, 1934; Speicher, 1936) formed the focus of this renewed attention, but during the same period the first modern accounts were also published of embryonic development in the Megaloptera (Du Bois, 1936, 1938), the Neuroptera (Bock, 1939) and the Siphonaptera (Kessel, 1939). Many of the controversies of classical holometabolan embryology were resolved by these studies, the main factual and theoretical conclusions of this period being reviewed by Johannsen and Butt (1941). Several aspects, however, such as the segmental composition of the head, the relationship between the vitellophages and midgut development, and the development of germ cells and gonads, still lacked a unified interpretation.

During the last twenty years, holometabolan embryology has seen its most fruitful period of investigation. Although the several lesser orders of Holometabola have fallen once more into neglect (e.g. the Trichoptera remain almost unknown embryologically [Patten, 1884; Hirschler, 1905], the Mecoptera only by a single paper [Ando, 1960], the Megaloptera, Neuroptera and Siphonaptera only by the work of the 1930's), the larger orders have been subjected to numerous searching studies. The embryos of several Coleoptera, for example, have been described by Brauer (1949), Krause and Ryan (1953), Haget (1953, 1955, 1957), Jura (1957), Surowiak (1958), Dobrowski (1959), Such and Haget (1962), Such (1963), Jung (1966a, b), Zakhvatkin (1967a, b, 1968) and Rempel and Church (1969), and with especial clarity in the important work of Ullman (1964, 1967) on *Tenebrio molitor*. Studies on the Lepidoptera have flowered for the Tortricidae, in association with their significance as pests and a fortuitous ease of observation of their flattened eggs (Stairs, 1960; Bassand, 1965; Guénnelon, 1966; Reed and Day, 1966, Anderson and Wood, 1968). Other useful contributions to lepidopteran embryology have been made by Presser and Rutchsky (1957), Okada (1960) and Krause and Krause (1964). The Diptera have received a major share of the recent attention of insect embryologists, stemming from the fundamental work of Sonnenblick (1950) and Poulson (1950) on *Drosophila melanogaster* and continued in the work of Ede and Counce (1956), Anderson (1962, 1963a, b, 1966), Schoeller (1964), Riemann (1965), Craig (1967, 1969), Davis (1967), Davis *et al.* (1968), Kalthoff and Sander (1968), Mahowald (1968), West *et al.* (1968), Garcia-Bellido and Merriam (1969), Wolf (1969) and others on a variety of Nematocera and Cyclorrhapha. Finally, a new understanding of the embryonic development of the non-parasitic Hymenoptera has been gained through the work of Baerends and Baerends-von Roon (1950), Shafiq (1954), Ando and Okada (1958), Ivanova-Kasas (1959), Ochiai (1960), Farooqui (1963) and DuPraw (1967), while the development of a number of species of parasitic Hymenoptera has been elucidated by Ivanova-Kasas (1954, 1958, 1960, 1972), Bronskill (1959, 1964), Amy (1961) and Meng (1968). The time is now appropriate to synthesize from this extensive series of studies a new picture of the theme and variations of holometabolan development.

II. EGGS

A. The Zygote

With few exceptions, mainly among the Coleoptera and Lepidoptera, the eggs of holometabolous insects have dimensions of about one millimetre or less (Table I) and develop to hatching in only a few days (Table II). Klausnitzer (1969), for example, has listed the egg dimensions of twenty-four species of coccinellid beetles. Among these species, most have eggs about a millimetre long, but the largest egg listed, that of *Anatis ocella*, is 1·94 mm long by 0·87 mm broad. The smallest, that of *Stethorus punctillum*, is 0·39 mm long by 0·21 mm broad. A standard egg form, reminiscent of the eggs of Hemimetabola, is expressed among the more generalized holometabolan orders (Coleoptera: Hirschler, 1909; Paterson, 1931; Inkmann, 1933; Butt,

1936; Tiegs and Murray, 1938; Mulnard, 1947; Deobahkta, 1952, 1957; Ullman, 1964; Ede, 1964; Rempel and Church, 1965; Jung, 1966*a*; Küthe, 1966; Zakhvatkin, 1967*a*, *b*; Megaloptera: Strindberg, 1915*a*; Du Bois, 1936, 1938; Neuroptera: Tichomirowa, 1890, 1892; Bock, 1939; Mecoptera: Ando, 1960; Trichoptera: Patten, 1884) and also in the Siphonaptera (Kessel, 1939). The egg is usually ovoid (Fig. 1), with some distinction of the anterior and posterior poles, and has a convex ventral surface and a flattened to concave dorsal surface. A chorion and vitelline membrane lie externally, defining

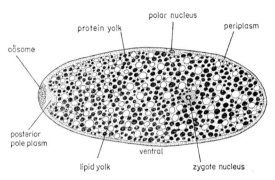

FIG. 1. Diagrammatic sagittal section through the zygote of *Bruchidius obtectus* (Coleoptera), after Jung (1966*a*).

the egg-space. (For details concerning origin and structure of these membranes, see Mahowald, 1972.)

The egg is only moderately yolky, with a conspicuous cytoplasmic reticulum enmeshing the yolk. Peripherally the reticulum merges, except in Megaloptera, with a yolk-free periplasm. A periplasm emerges at the surface of the megalopteran egg during early cleavage (Du Bois, 1938). The periplasm in Coleoptera is usually thickened posteriorly as a pole plasm containing a mass of basophilic granular material, the oösome (Hegner, 1909, 1911, 1914; Paterson, 1931; Butt, 1936; Deobahkta, 1957; Jung, 1966*a*). The oösome is more conspicuous (Fig. 2) in the specialized eggs of Diptera (see Anderson, 1966; Davis, 1967; Mahowald, 1968, 1972; Wolf, 1969) and Hymenoptera (Hegner, 1909, 1914; Nelson, 1915; Henschen, 1928; Ivanova-Kasas, 1958; Meng, 1968). The zygote nucleus, surrounded by a halo of yolk-free cytoplasm, is usually centrally placed, but may be more anterior or more posterior (e.g. Ullman, 1964).

Variations in egg form are evident in the Lepidoptera, Diptera and Hymenoptera. The majority of lepidopteran eggs are ovoid or spherical and stand upright, attached to a leaf or other vegetation by the posterior pole (Toyama, 1902; Eastham, 1927, 1930; Johannsen, 1929; Sehl, 1931; Grandori, 1932; Lautenschlager, 1932; Saito, 1934, 1937; Mueller, 1938;

Gross and Howland, 1941; Christensen, 1943a, b; Rempel, 1951; Presser and Rutchsky, 1957; Krause and Krause, 1964). In several families, however, (e.g. the Tortricidae) a flattened, dome-shaped egg has evolved in which the outline remains ovoid but the ventral surface is flattened and applied to the substratum, while the dorsal surface is convex (Huie, 1918; Wiesmann, 1935; Gaumont, 1951; Christensen, 1953; Okada, 1960; Bassand, 1965; Guénnelon, 1966; Reed and Day, 1966; Anderson and Wood, 1968). The egg-space within which development proceeds is considerably restricted in eggs of this

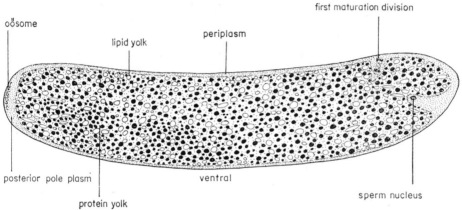

FIG. 2. Diagrammatic sagittal section through the egg of *Dacus tryoni* (Diptera) during maturation and fertilization, after Anderson (1962).

type and the development of the embryo displays a number of peculiarities, analogous to those of some plecopteran eggs.

Elongation of the anteroposterior axis is the characteristic feature of dipteran and hymenopteran eggs. The more primitive member of these orders, among the Nematocera (Kahle, 1908; Du Bois, 1932; Gambrell, 1933; Butt, 1934; Kraczkiewicz, 1935; Reitberger, 1940; Geyer-Duzynska, 1959; Yajima, 1960; Craig, 1967; Kalthoff and Sander, 1968; Wolf, 1969) and Symphyta (Shafiq, 1954; Ando and Okada, 1958; Ivanova-Kasas, 1959) respectively, usually retain an elongate ovoid egg, though in the Culicidae a more cylindrical shape is already evident (Ivanova-Kasas, 1949; Telford, 1957; Rosay, 1959; Christophers, 1960; Idris, 1960; Davis, 1967). The Cyclorrhapha (Pauli, 1927; Auten, 1934; Sonnenblick, 1950; Formigoni, 1954; Anderson, 1962; Riemann, 1965; Davis, 1967; Davis et al., 1968; West et al., 1968) and the majority of Apocrita (Carrière and Bürger, 1897; Nelson, 1915; Schnetter, 1934; Baerends and Baerends-von Roon, 1950; Müller, 1957; Ivanova-Kasas, 1958; Bronskill, 1959, 1964; Ochiai, 1960; Reinhardt, 1960; Amy, 1961; DuPraw, 1967) emphasize an elongate, cylindrical egg form (e.g. Fig. 2) in which the diameter is much less than the length (Table II). Development proceeds rapidly (Table I) and hatching is precocious, with little of the adult organization represented in the morphologically simple larva.

The majority of holometabolan eggs develop at the expense of nutrients already in the egg at oviposition and show little or no change in the volume of the egg-space due to fluid uptake during development. In a number of families, the eggs develop in a nutrient environment which may result from parasitizing oviposition or from viviparity. In the former, development may be little modified, e.g. in ichneumonid and some braconid Hymenoptera (Bronskill, 1959, 1964), or may proceed from a small, yolkless egg which takes up nutrients and grows as it develops, e.g. other Hymenoptera, Strepsiptera (see Ivanova-Kasas, 1972). Viviparity, summarized by Hagan (1951), is similar. The egg may be yolky, with an unmodified embryonic development, e.g. in glossinid and hippoboscid Diptera, or may be more or less devoid of yolk, taking up nutrients and growing as it develops, e.g. in cecidomyid Diptera (Ivanova-Kasas, 1965). In the present account, the developmental peculiarities of secondarily yolkless eggs in the Holometabola are not discussed.

B. Maturation and Fertilization

As in the Hemimetabola, the holometabolan oocyte is typically in the metaphase of the first maturation division when released from the ovariole during oviposition. The maturation divisions continue after insemination has begun (Fig. 2), yielding three polar nuclei grouped together in the periplasm, usually in an anterodorsal location. The female pronucleus migrates into the interior of the egg, surrounded by a small island of cytoplasm, and fuses with a male pronucleus (e.g. Sonnenblick, 1950). Polyspermy is usual in the Holometabola (Huettner, 1924, 1927; Sonnenblick, 1950; Davis, 1967) and the excess sperm degenerate after fusion of the pronuclei has taken place. Occasional examples of monospermy have been reported among the higher Diptera (Anderson, 1962; Hildreth and Luchesi, 1963).

III. CLEAVAGE AND BLASTODERM FORMATION

A. Early Cleavage

Cleavage in the Holometabola, as in the Hemimetabola, proceeds in most instances (but *cf.* Counce, 1972) through a succession of synchronous mitotic divisions of the zygote nucleus and its daughter nuclei, accompanied by the accretion of islands of cytoplasm around the nuclei and by the spread of the resulting cleavage energids through the yolk mass. The cytoplasm of the cleavage energids originates as aggregated cytoplasm of the cytoplasmic reticulum of the egg. An especially obvious feature of holometabolan eggs with relatively little yolk, such as those of the cyclorrhaphous Diptera, is that the cleavage energids retain continuity with the cytoplasmic reticulum during the early cleavage divisions and are thus linked both with each other and with the periplasm at the surface of the yolk mass. This syncytial condition appears to be characteristic of all holometabolan eggs during early cleavage.

Examples of early holometabolan cleavage are illustrated in Figs 3a and b and Fig. 4a for the coleopteran *Bruchidius obtectus* and the dipteran *Dacus*

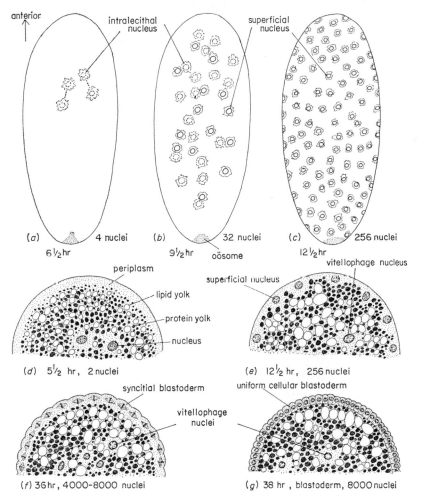

FIG. 3. Stages in cleavage and blastoderm formation in *Bruchidius obtectus* (Coleoptera), after Jung (1966a). (a)–(c) The distribution of cleavage energids after the second, fifth and eighth synchronous cleavage mitoses. (d) Transverse section after the first cleavage division; (e) Transverse section after the eighth cleavage division (compare Fig. 3c); (f) Transverse section during the thirteenth synchronous cleavage, leading to formation of the syncitial blastoderm; (g) Transverse section through the uniform cellular blastoderm.

tryoni respectively. These illustrations are typical for Holometabola in that nuclear division and spread can be seen to be both uniform and synchronous. In most species, as in Fig. 4*a*, the mitotic spindles of each synchronous division are randomly orientated, but a number of cases have been described in which the cleavage energids occupy a surface concentric with the surface of the yolk mass, and progressively approach the periplasm as the number of energids increases, e.g. the coleopteran *Calomela parilis* (Fig. 29*b*; Anderson,

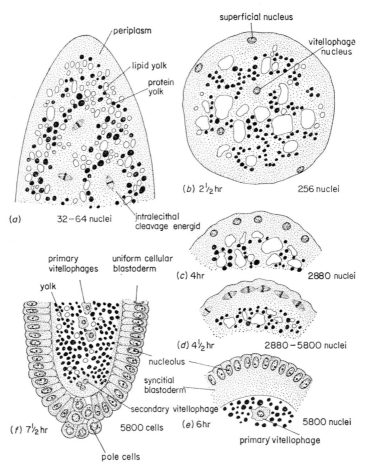

FIG. 4. Stages in cleavage and blastoderm formation in *Dacus tryoni* (Diptera), after Anderson (1962). (*a*) Frontal section through the anterior end during the sixth synchronous cleavage division; (*b*) Transverse section after the eighth synchronous cleavage division. (*c*) Transverse section after the twelfth synchronous cleavage division; (*d*) Transverse section during the thirteenth synchronous cleavage division; (*e*) Transverse section through the syncytial blastoderm; (*f*) Frontal section through the posterior end of the uniform cellular blastoderm.

unpublished), the hymenopteran *Apis mellifera* (DuPraw, 1967) and the dipteran *Lucilia sericata* (Davis, 1967).

The mode of early cleavage summarized above has been described for a wide variety of holometabolous species by numerous workers (Coleoptera: Heider, 1889; Wheeler, 1889; Lecaillon, 1898; Saling, 1907; Hirschler, 1909; Hegner, 1914; Paterson, 1931, 1936; Inkmann, 1933; Smreczyński, 1934; Butt, 1936; Wray, 1937; Mulnard, 1947; Deobahkta, 1952; Luginbill, 1953; Ede, 1964; Ullman, 1964; Rempel and Church, 1965; Jung, 1966*a, b*; Küthe, 1966; Megaloptera: Strindberg, 1915*a*; Du Bois, 1938; Neuroptera: Bock, 1939; Mecoptera: Ando, 1960; Lepidoptera: Huie, 1918; Eastham, 1927; Johannsen, 1929; Sehl, 1931; Lautenschlager, 1932; Mueller, 1938; Gross and Howland, 1941; Christensen, 1943*a*; Rempel, 1951; Presser and Rutchsky, 1957; Stairs, 1960; Okada, 1960; Bassand, 1965; Guénnelon, 1966; Diptera: Riemann, 1965; Anderson, 1966 (who lists earlier references); Davis, 1967; Davis *et al.*, 1968; West *et al.*, 1968; Wolf, 1969; Siphonaptera: Kessel, 1939; Hymenoptera: Carrière and Bürger, 1897; Nelson, 1915; Schnetter, 1934; Speicher, 1936; Baerends and Baerends-von Roon, 1950; Müller, 1957; Ivanova-Kasas, 1958, 1959; Ochiai, 1960; Reinhardt, 1960; Amy, 1961; Bronskill, 1964; DuPraw, 1967; Meng, 1968). The rate at which the synchronous divisions proceed within the yolk mass, and the number of energids that are present when the periplasm of the egg becomes populated by nuclei, are listed for a number of representative species in Table III. It can be seen from this table that the rate of synchronous cleavage in the Holometabola always exceeds the fastest known rates for the Hemimetabola

TABLE III. Cleavage Sequences in Holometabola

Order	Species	Rate of Mitosis	Invasion of the Periplasm	Total No. of Mitoses	Source
Coleoptera	*Dermestes frischi*	1 per $\frac{1}{2}$ hr	$256–512n$	11	Küthe (1966)
	Bruchidius obtectus	1 per 1 hr	$256n$	13	Jung (1966*a*)
Megaloptera	*Sialis lutaria*	—	$128n$	9	Du Bois (1938)
Neuroptera	*Chrysopa perla*	—	—	10	Bock (1939)
Mecoptera	*Panorpa pryeri*	1 per 1 hr	$1024n$	—	Ando (1960)
Lepidoptera	*Anagasta kühniella*	1 per 1 hr (approx.)	$512n$	11	Sehl (1931)
	Chilo suppressalis	1 per $\frac{1}{2}$ hr (approx.)	$512n$	11	Okada (1960)
Diptera	*Culex fatigans*	1 per $\frac{1}{4}$ hr	$128n$	12	Davis (1967)
	Dacus tryoni	1 per $\frac{1}{4}$ hr	$128n$	13	Anderson (1962)
	Drosophila melanogaster	1 per 10 mins	$512n$	12	Sonnenblick (1950)
	Lucilia sericata	1 per 10 mins	$512n$	13	Davis (1967)
	Cochliomyia hominivorax	1 per 5 mins	$256n$	12	Riemann (1965)
Siphonaptera	*Ctenocephalides felis*	—	$128n$	10	Kessel (1939)
Hymenoptera	*Habrobracon juglandis*	1 per $\frac{1}{4}$ hr	$1024n$	13	Amy (1961)
	Apis mellifera	1 per $\frac{1}{2}$ hr	$1024n$	12	{ Schnetter (1934) { DuPraw (1967)

(compare Chapter 3). Furthermore, among the Hymenoptera and especially among the Diptera, the rate of cleavage is markedly accelerated as compared with that of the more generalized holometabolans. The mitotic rate observed in the cleavage of cyclorrhaphan eggs is among the fastest known for animal mitosis. Table III also indicates that the number of synchronous mitoses that precedes the arrival of cleavage energids at the periplasm of the egg varies from species to species, even within orders. For example, seven synchronous mitoses precede the nuclear invasion of the periplasm in *Sialis lutaria* (Megaloptera) and *Dacus tryoni* (Diptera), whereas nine synchronous mitoses is the corresponding figure for *Drosophila melanogaster* (Diptera), and ten for *Apis mellifera* (Hymenoptera). Comparison with Table I indicates that this figure bears no direct relationship to the shape and dimensions of the yolk mass in which cleavage is proceeding. Each species follows its own sequence of cleavage and must be treated individually.

B. The Blastoderm

As in the paraneopteran eggs described in the previous chapter, the cleavage energids that migrate to the surface of the yolk mass of a holometabolan egg merge with the periplasm, so that the periplasm becomes irregularly thickened and at the same time populated by nuclei (Figs 3c, e, 4b). This process has been described in varying degrees of detail by the workers listed above, as a continuation of their descriptions of early cleavage. Table III lists the number of nuclei present in the yolk mass in different species when invasion of the periplasm takes place. As will be further discussed below, however, some of the cleavage energids may not participate in invasion of the periplasm. A small number of them usually remain within the yolk mass as primary vitellophages.

In most species of Holometabola, the cleavage energids first populate the periplasm uniformly throughout the surface of the yolk mass (e.g. Fig. 3c). In other species, a uniform distribution is attained gradually, following a localized first emergence, which may take place at the equator of the egg, at the posterior pole or at both poles simultaneously. A uniform distribution of nuclei throughout the periplasm is always developed, however, before the nuclei enter into further mitoses. This is the first stage in formation of the *syncytial blastoderm*. Further mitotic divisions of the peripheral nuclei now ensue. In most species, these divisions are synchronous (Figs 3f, 4c, d), though an antero-posterior gradient of mitotic division at this stage has been described for the nuclei of several cyclorrhaphous Diptera (Agrell, 1963; Counce, 1972). The mitotic spindles are orientated tangential to the surface and the number of peripheral nuclei doubles at each division. At the same time, cytoplasm from the interior of the yolk mass also flows into the peripheral layer, so that the forming syncytial blastoderm thickens as its nuclear population increases (Fig. 3f). The thickening is especially marked in the Diptera, to which we will return below.

The number of mitotic divisions that intervenes between invasion of the periplasm by cleavage energids and completion of the syncytial blastoderm varies from egg to egg, depending among other things on the number of energids that first populates the periplasm (Table III). In the coleopteran *Bruchidius obtectus*, for example, there are five mitotic cycles during this period, in the hymenopteran *Apis mellifera*, only two, out of a total of thirteen synchronous divisions of the nuclei in the former species and twelve in the latter. In other words, the cleavage energids of *Apis* undergo more mitotic cycles within the yolk mass than those of *Bruchidius*. Once more we are able to discern no general rules about this process, and every species must be treated individually. Table III shows, however, that the total number of mitotic cycles, both within the yolk mass and at the surface during formation of the syncytial blastoderm, varies among species from nine to thirteen, so that the subsequent number of blastoderm cells is of the order of 500–8000 in Holometabola.

When the nuclear divisions in the forming syncytial blastoderm are completed, the nuclei are packed in close array within the surface layer of cytoplasm, which itself is of uniform thickness. In the majority of species, the thickness of the syncytial blastoderm is about twice the diameter of the nuclei. Diptera, however, as can be seen in Figs 4d and e, develop a syncytial blastoderm of much greater thickness. The cytoplasm from the interior of the yolk mass continues to accumulate beneath the nucleated peripheral layer as the tangential synchronous mitoses proceed. A thick inner layer of cytoplasm is thus built up, which eventually becomes as thick as the nucleated peripheral layer. In the muscid and calliphorid Cyclorrhapha, the inner layer of the syncytial blastoderm contains numerous yolk granules, especially ventrally (Davis, 1967).

When the mitotic divisions of the peripheral nuclei cease, the nuclei change in shape from rounded to ovoid (Fig. 4e) and develop nucleoli. The syncytial blastoderm now transforms into a *uniform cellular blastoderm*. Cell membranes penetrate inwards from the surface of the syncytial blastoderm, isolating each nucleus in a radial cylinder of cytoplasm projecting from the yolk mass. Then, as has been investigated in detail by Mahowald (1962) and Wolf (1969), the membranes pinch in concentrically beneath each cylinder, separating it from the yolk mass as an individual cell, and at the same time forming a continuous plasma membrane at the surface of the yolk mass beneath the resulting uniform cellular blastoderm (Figs 3g, 4f). The uniform cellular blastoderm is cuboidal in most holometabolans (Coleoptera: Hirschler, 1909; Hegner, 1914; Mansour, 1927; Paterson, 1931, 1936; Smreczyński, 1934; Wray, 1937; Tiegs and Murray, 1938; Mulnard, 1947;

Weglarska, 1950, 1955; Luginbill, 1953; Ede, 1964; Ullman, 1964; Jung, 1966a; Küthe, 1966; Megaloptera: Strindberg, 1915a; Du Bois, 1938; Neuroptera: Tichomirowa, 1890, 1892; Bock, 1939; Trichoptera: Patten, 1884; Lepidoptera: Huie, 1918; Eastham, 1927; Lautenschlager, 1932; Mueller, 1938; Gross and Howland, 1941; Christensen, 1943a; Rempel, 1951; Presser and Rutchsky, 1957; Stairs, 1960; Okada, 1960; Bassand, 1965; Guénnelon, 1966; Anderson and Wood, 1968; Siphonaptera: Kessel, 1939). The Hymenoptera have been generally said to have a columnar blastoderm (Carrière and Bürger, 1897; Nelson, 1915; Schnetter, 1934; Baerends and Baerends-von Roon, 1950; Shafiq, 1954; Müller, 1957; Ivanova-Kasas, 1958, 1959; Bronskill, 1959, 1964; Ochiai, 1960; Reinhardt, 1960; Amy, 1961), as is indicated in Fig. 15a, but recent studies by DuPraw (1967) on *Apis* have revealed that a cuboidal blastoderm is first established and that the cells become columnar by a specialized process during differentiation of the uniform blastoderm to form the embryonic primordium. Further details of this process will be given in Section IV below. It seems, therefore, that the Hymenoptera should also be included among those holometabolans which develop a cuboidal cellular blastoderm. Only the Diptera remain as an exception to this, with their direct formation of a columnar blastoderm (Fig. 4f) by cellularization of a deep syncytial blastoderm (Riemann, 1965; Anderson, 1966; Davis, 1967; Davis et al., 1968; West et al., 1968; Wolf, 1969).

In the apocritan Hymenoptera and cyclorrhaphous Diptera, and also in the coleopteran *Dermestes maculatus* (Ede, 1964), the innermost part of the syncytial blastoderm is not incorporated into the blastoderm cells, but is left as an anucleate cytoplasmic layer at the periphery of the yolk mass (e.g. Fig. 4f). The fate of this layer will be taken up below.

C. Vitellophages

In most Holometabola, when the cleavage energids migrate to the surface of the yolk mass and initiate the formation of the syncytial blastoderm, a number of energids remain within the yolk mass as primary vitellophages (Figs 3e–g, 4b–f). The number varies, depending among other things on the number of cleavage divisions that take place before the energids invade the periplasm. A typical figure, given for *Dacus tryoni* by Anderson (1962), is about 30 energids, but there may be more than this, up to two or three hundred in some eggs. The formation of primary vitellophages in this way has been described for species of all orders except the Trichoptera, which have yet to be investigated on this point (Coleoptera: Wheeler, 1889; Hegner, 1914; Paterson, 1931, 1936; Butt, 1936; Tiegs and Murray, 1938; Mulnard, 1947; Ullman, 1964; Rempel and Church, 1965; Jung, 1966a; Megaloptera: Strindberg, 1915a; Du Bois, 1938; Neuroptera: Tichomirowa, 1890, 1892; Mecoptera: Ando, 1960; Lepidoptera: Anderson and Wood, 1968; Diptera:

Idris, 1960; Anderson, 1962, 1966; Davis, 1967; West *et al.*, 1968; Siphonaptera: Kessel, 1939; Hymenoptera: Carrière and Bürger, 1897; Nelson, 1915; Schnetter, 1934; Müller, 1957; Ivanova-Kasas, 1958, 1959; Amy, 1961; Bronskill, 1964). The primary vitellophages remain linked by the cytoplasmic reticulum enmeshing the yolk bodies. Further mitotic divisions of the primary vitellophages usually take place as formation of the syncytial blastoderm proceeds. For example, the primary vitellophages of *Dacus tryoni* increase in number to about 300 during this period. Synchrony of division persists among the vitellophage nuclei, but is no longer maintained with the blastoderm nuclei. The resulting primary vitellophages persist within the yolk mass during later development (e.g. Fig. 25*a*) and can be reasonably presumed to play a part in the digestion of yolk, although the details of their functional operation have yet to be investigated.

The primary vitellophages of many species of Holometabola are augmented by secondary vitellophages (Fig. 4*f*), which invade the yolk mass from either the syncytial blastoderm or the uniform cellular blastoderm (Coleoptera: Mansour, 1927; Butt, 1936; Ullman, 1964; Rempel and Church, 1969; Neuroptera: Bock, 1939; some Diptera: Anderson, 1962; Davis, 1967; West *et al.*, 1968; Siphonaptera: Kessel, 1939; Hymenoptera: Nelson, 1915; Müller, 1957). In other species, these are the first vitellophages to enter the yolk mass, after all cleavage energids have migrated to the surface of the yolk mass and entered the periplasm. The absence of primary vitellophages seems to be a feature of several Lepidoptera (Toyama, 1902; Huie, 1918; Eastham, 1927; Sehl, 1931), although each of these cases may require further investigation. It is also a well established feature of nematocerous Diptera (Kahle, 1908; Hasper, 1911; Du Bois, 1932; Butt, 1934; Davis, 1967; Counce, personal communication). The re-entry of secondary vitellophages into the yolk mass usually takes place from all parts of the blastoderm, although in several Diptera, this process is confined to immigration from one or both poles (Hasper, 1911; Anderson, 1962; Mahowald, 1962; Davis, 1967; West *et al.*, 1968).

A few Cyclorrhapha and Hymenoptera also develop tertiary vitellophages as cells budded from their proliferating anterior and posterior midgut rudiments into the yolk mass during later embryonic development (Lassman, 1936; Müller, 1957; Anderson, 1962; Davis, 1967). The terminological distinction between vitellophages in the Holometabola is based on the timing and mode of origin of the cells, but it is possible that functional differences between the three types will emerge as vitellophage function becomes more clearly understood. Müller (1957), who is the only worker to have examined this possibility, described histological differences between the primary, secondary and tertiary vitellophages of *Apis* which may indicate functional differences between them (see also Counce, 1972).

D. Pole Cells

The primordial germ cells of the Holometabola are almost always recognizable as a distinct group of cells by the time the embryonic primordium has been established and has begun to elongate as a germ band. The cells are

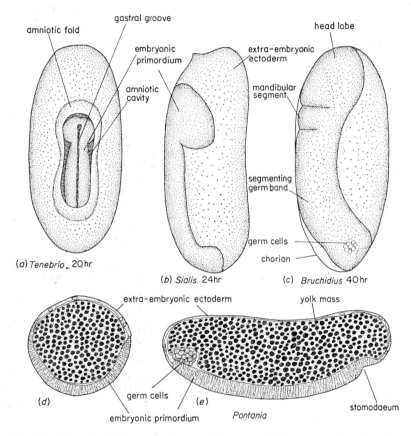

FIG. 5. (*a*) *Tenebrio molitor* (Coleoptera), in ventral view, at the 20-hour stage, when the embryonic primordium becomes a germ band, after Ullman (1964); (*b*) *Sialis lutaria* (Megaloptera) in lateral view at the differentiated blastoderm stage, after Du Bois (1938); (*c*) *Bruchidius obtectus* (Coleoptera) in ventrolateral view at the onset of segmentation of the germ band, after Jung (1966*a*); (*d*) and (*e*) Diagrammatic transverse and sagittal sections of the differentiated blastoderm of *Pontania capreae* (Hymenoptera, Symphyta) at the stage when concentration of the embryonic primordium is complete, after Ivanova-Kasas (1959).

distinctively spherical, with relatively larger nuclei than the general cells of the embryonic primordium, and are grouped together beneath the posterior end of the primordium (e.g. Fig. 5*e*). In tenebrionid coleopterans, the primordial germ cells cannot be identified in this position until gastrulation has begun (Hodson, 1934; Ullman, 1964), and it is generally thought that they originate as cells at the posterior end of the forming inner layer. In some other coleopterans, the posteroventral group of primordial germ cells is seen to lie beneath the posterior end of the forming embryonic primordium soon after the completion of the uniform cellular blastoderm (some chrysomelids, Paterson, 1931, 1936; *Phyllobius*: Smreczyński, 1934; *Calandra oryzae*: Tiegs and Murray, 1938; *C. callosa*: Wray, 1937; *Brachyrhinus lingustici*: Butt, 1936). The exact origin of the primordial germ cells of these species has not been established. A similar first visible differentiation of primordial germ cells is observed in the Megaloptera (Du Bois, 1938), Lepidoptera (Huie, 1918; Sehl, 1931; Lautenschlager, 1932; Presser and Rutchsky, 1957; Anderson and Wood, 1968), and symphytan Hymenoptera (Ivanova-Kasas, 1959), as shown in Figs 5e and 17f. The development of the primordial germ cells in the Neuroptera, Mecoptera and Trichoptera has not yet been described.

In other coleopterans, the primordial germ cells are segregated more precociously, during formation of the syncytial blastoderm, as a group of rounded cells separated off at the posterior pole of the yolk mass (*Bruchidius obtectus*, Mulnard, 1947; Jung, 1966a, b; other chrysomelids, Hegner, 1909, 1914; *Calandra granaria*, Inkmann, 1933). When segregated early in this way, the primordial germ cells are usually referred to as pole cells. A precocious segregation of pole cells during cleavage or blastoderm formation is also characteristic of the Diptera (for references see Anderson, 1966 and Davis, 1967; Mahowald, 1968; West et al., 1968; Wolf, 1969), the Siphonaptera (Kessel, 1939) and the parasitic apocritan Hymenoptera (Henschen, 1928; Ivanova-Kasas, 1958; Bronskill, 1959, 1964; Amy, 1961; Meng, 1968). Eggs in which pole cells are later formed usually contain an oösome (Figs 1, 2), the material of which becomes distributed among pole cells. Initially, a small number of cells is cut off at the posterior pole (e.g. one in cecidomyids and chironomids, four in *Dacus tryoni*). The cells then undergo further divisions, but do not maintain mitotic synchrony with the nuclei of the forming blastoderm. The pole cells remain few in number in the Nematocera (Anderson, 1966; Davis, 1967; Wolf, 1969) but vary between 20 and 80 in other species. When numerous, as in the Cyclorrhapha, some of the pole cells may develop as components other than primordial germ cells. For example, in *Drosophila melanogaster*, the pole cells are believed to contribute to the formation of the secondary vitellophages and the midgut epithelium (Poulson, 1950; Poulson and Waterhouse, 1960; Hathaway and Selman, 1961; Mahowald, 1962; Counce, 1963, 1972). In *Dacus tryoni*, some of the pole cells develop as part of the epithelium of the hindgut. The re-entry of the pole cells into the interior of the embryo and the further development of the gonads is discussed below in Sections VI and XII.

IV. THE DIFFERENTIATED BLASTODERM

As soon as the uniform cellular blastoderm is completed, changes ensue which lead to the formation of a dense embryonic primordium and an attenuated extra-embryonic ectoderm as components of the differentiated blastoderm. With the exception of certain specializations in the apocritan Hymenoptera, the culicid and cyclorrhaphan Diptera and the Lepidoptera, which will shortly be described, the basis of formation of the differentiated blastoderm is essentially the same in the Holometabola as it is in the Hemimetabola (*vide* Chapter 3). The presumptive cells of the embryonic primordium, initially making up a broad ventral to ventrolateral area of the uniform cellular blastoderm, become concentrated into a smaller area as a result of cellular aggregation and also increase in number through cell divisions. The embryonic primordium thus comes to consist of a monolayer of columnar cells, in the form of a broad ventral band, usually expanded anteriorly as a pair of rounded head lobes (Figs 5a, b, d and e, 12a). The remainder of the uniform cellular blastoderm simultaneously becomes more attenuated, revealing itself as the extra-embryonic ectoderm. Differentiation of the blastoderm in this way has been described in the Coleoptera (Hegner, 1909; Hirschler, 1909; Blunck, 1914; Mansour, 1927; Paterson, 1931, 1936; Inkmann, 1933; Smreczyński, 1934; Butt, 1936; Wray, 1937; Tiegs and Murray, 1938; Mulnard, 1947; Krause and Ryan, 1953; Luginbill, 1953; Jura, 1957; Ede, 1964; Ullman, 1964; Jung, 1966a, b; Küthe, 1966; Zakvhatkin, 1967a, b, 1968; Rempel and Church, 1969), the Megaloptera (Strindberg, 1915a; Du Bois, 1936, 1938), the Neuroptera (Bock, 1939), the Mecoptera (Ando, 1960), the Trichoptera (Patten, 1884), the Siphonaptera (Kessel, 1939), the Symphyta (Shafiq, 1954; Ando and Okada, 1958; Ivanova-Kasas, 1959) and most Nematocera (Du Bois, 1932; Gambrell, 1933; Butt, 1934; Craig, 1967; Kalthoff and Sander, 1968; Wolf, 1969).

The form of the embryonic primordium relative to the egg as a whole resembles that of the presumptive embryonic primordium revealed experimentally in the uniform cellular blastoderm of the odonatan *Platycnemis pennipes* by Seidel (1929, 1935) (compare Figs 5a and 16a with Fig. 8a of Chapter 3). The holometabolan embryonic primordium, then, is formed in a manner which largely eliminates the processes of aggregation of the thinly spread presumptive embryonic rudiments, followed by massive growth in length and breadth of the germ band, typical of the Hemimetabola. At a deeper level of analysis, the evidence for which is discussed in later paragraphs, the embryonic presumptive areas of the blastoderm are more advanced in development at the uniform cellular blastoderm stage than those of the Hemimetabola and can continue their development more directly and rapidly. This change is a consequence of the changed proportions of cytoplasm and yolk in the holometabolan egg, which permit a deeply cuboidal blastoderm to be formed directly. Each embryonic presumptive area is thus deep as well as broad when first formed and can proceed into further development after relatively little additional concentration and proliferation.

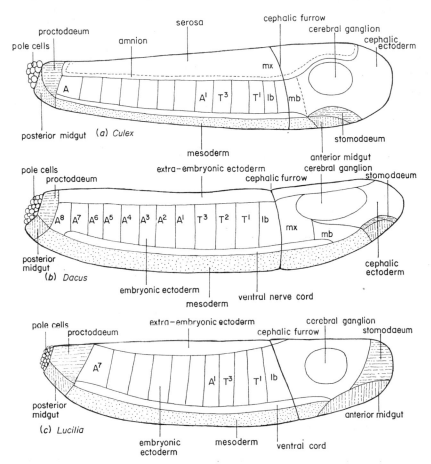

Fig. 6. Presumptive areas of the blastoderm in Diptera, seen in right lateral view. (*a*) *Culex fatigans*, after Davis (1967); (*b*) *Dacus tryoni*, after Anderson (1962); (*c*) *Lucilia sericata*, after Davis (1967). A^1–A^8, abdominal segmental ectoderm; lb, labial ectoderm; mb, mandibular ectoderm; mx, maxillary ectoderm; T^1–T^3, thoracic segmental ectoderm.

The culicid and cyclorrhaphan Diptera display this condition in a more advanced form. As Figs 6*a*–*c* show, the embryonic presumptive areas make up a large proportion of the uniform cellular blastoderm in these insects, and only the dorsal part of the blastoderm is presumptive extra-embryonic ecto-derm. Furthermore, the latter is relatively less in area in the Cyclorrhapha than in the Nematocera, and is especially reduced in the calliphorids and muscids. The uniform cellular blastoderm is columnar throughout (see Section III, B), having incorporated a thick inner layer of cytoplasm added to the syncytial blastoderm from the interior of the yolk mass. Differentiation of the embryonic primordium as a result of aggregation and cell division is thus eliminated in these embryos, since the embryonic primordium is already formed in the uniform cellular blastoderm. Development proceeds directly from this stage into gastrulation, and the attenuation of the extra-embryonic ectoderm is a corollary of gastrulation rather than of differentiation of the blastoderm.

An interesting intermediate level of specialization has recently come to light as a result of new investigations by DuPraw (1967) on the formation and differentiation of the blastoderm of *Apis*, a representative apocritous hymenopteran. Most workers on this group have described the formation of a columnar cellular blastoderm, generally similar to that of the higher Diptera (Carrière and Bürger, 1897; Nelson, 1915; Schnetter, 1934; Baerends and Baerends-von Roon, 1950; Müller, 1957; Ivanova-Kasas, 1958; Bronskill, 1959, 1964; Ochiai, 1960; Reinhardt, 1960; Amy, 1961). When differentiation of the blastoderm takes place, the embryonic primordium is established with little further aggregation of the cells, and occupies a large part of the surface of the yolk mass (e.g. Figs 11*a*, *b*). The extra-embryonic ectoderm becomes attenuated in the usual way, but is confined to the dorsal surface of the yolk mass. The evidence provided by DuPraw (1967), however, indicates a more complex sequence of events. In *Apis*, the uniform cellular blastoderm is cuboidal, as in most Holometabola. The presumptive cells of the embryonic primordium now enter into numerous cell divisions and become more closely packed. At the same time, an inner layer of cytoplasm gathers beneath the dividing cells, from within the yolk mass. This layer of cytoplasm becomes thickest ventrally and thins out laterally until it terminates at the margins of the presumptive extra-embryonic ectoderm. The cells of the forming embryonic primordium now unite with the inner layer of cytoplasm, and a portion of this cytoplasm is finally cut off as an extension of each cell. Thus the embryonic primordium comes to consist of numerous, densely packed, columnar cells, but in the attainment of this differentiated condition, there is no reduction in area of the embryonic presumptive rudiments that make up the primordium. The latter still occupies the entire anteroposterior length of the ventral surface of the yolk mass and extends up the sides of the yolk mass, almost to the dorsal surface. It is possible that other Apocrita attain a differentiated blastoderm in the same way. The higher Diptera, as we have seen, exhibit a convergent formation of an inner layer of cytoplasm which becomes incorporated into the cells of the embryonic primordium, but manifest this process more precociously, during formation of the syncytial blastoderm. Associatedly, as has already been mentioned, differentiation of the blastoderm prior to the onset of gastrulation is eliminated in these insects.

Specialization during formation of the embryonic primordium in the Lepidoptera takes another course. After the uniform cellular blastoderm has been formed, the embryonic cells become aggregated and the extra-embryonic cells become attenuated in the usual way, but the resulting embryonic primordium is unusually broad (Figs 7a, b). It extends transversely across

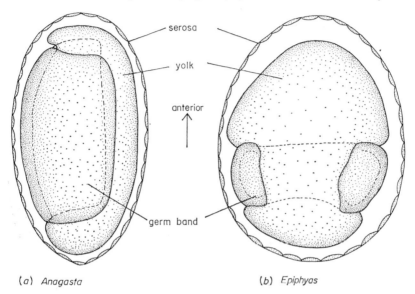

(a) Anagasta   (b) Epiphyas

FIG. 7. (a) Left lateral view of the germ band of *Anagasta kühniella* (Lepidoptera), after Sehl (1931). The serosa is complete, but formation of the amnion and elongation and segmentation of the germ band have not yet begun. (b) The corresponding stage of *Epiphyas postvittana* (Lepidoptera), in dorsal view, after Anderson and Wood (1968).

the ventral face of the yolk mass, either at or just behind the equator of the egg. The anterior and posterior margins of the embryonic primordium are straight and parallel, the lateral margins rounded, and there are no distinct head lobes at this stage (Anderson and Wood, 1968, who give earlier references). The further development of the embryonic primordium of the Lepidoptera reveals that this modified shape is associated with subsequent immersion of the germ band in the yolk mass as development continues.

V. ELONGATION AND SEGMENTATION OF THE GERM BAND

A. Basic Elongation and Segmentation

In spite of the relatively greater length of the embryonic primordium in the Holometabola than in the Hemimetabola, those holometabolan orders which retain the basic type of pterygote embryonic primordium, with enlarged head lobes and a long post-antennal region (e.g. Figs 5a, b) also retain a subsequent mode of growth (Figs 8–10) similar to that of blattid Dictyoptera, gryllotalpid Orthoptera and Dermaptera. The head lobes give rise to the postoral antennal segment and the preantennal region in front of it. The major part of the post-antennal length of the embryonic primordium gives rise directly to the gnathal and thoracic segments of the segmenting germ band, with little in-

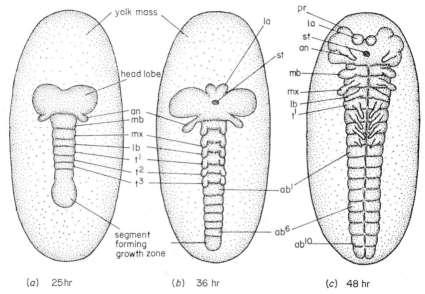

(a)   25 hr   (b)   36 hr   (c)   48 hr

FIG. 8. Elongation and segmentation of the germ band of *Tenebrio molitor* (Coleoptera), in ventral view, after Ullman (1964). (a) At 25 hours, the gnathal and thoracic segments are delineated and the segment-forming growth zone has become active; (b) At 36 hours, limb buds have formed on the head and thorax, and six abdominal segments are delineated; (c) By 48 hours the germ band is fully segmented. ab^1–ab^{10}, abdominal segments; an, antenna; lb, labial segment; mb, mandibular segment; mx, maxillary segment; pr, protocerebral lobe; st, stomodaeum; t^1–t^3, thoracic segments; la, labrum.

crease in length and breadth during elongation and segmentation. Posteriorly, just in front of the posterior end, a growth zone proliferates the rudiments of ten abdominal segments. Except in the elongate eggs of some Coleoptera, e.g. *Leptinotarsa, Dytiscus, Tenebrio* (Fig. 8), the segmenting germ band extends over the posterior pole and forwards along the dorsal surface of the yolk mass, sometimes almost as far as the level of the head lobes (Figs 9, 10). This pattern of elongation and segmentation of the germ band has been described for the Coleoptera by Hegner (1909), Hirschler (1909), Blunck (1914), Mansour (1927), Paterson (1932, 1936), Inkmann (1933), Smreczyński (1934), Butt (1936), Wray (1937), Tiegs and Murray (1938), Mulnard (1947),

Krause and Ryan (1953), Luginbill (1953), Jura (1957), Ede (1964), Ullman (1964), Miya (1965), Jung (1966a, b), Küthe (1966) and Zakhvatkin (1967a, b, 1968), for the Neuroptera by Bock (1939), for the Mecoptera by Krause and Sander (1962), and for the Trichoptera by Patten (1884). Unlike the Hemimetabola, these holometabolans do not develop a caudal flexure during elongation of the germ band.

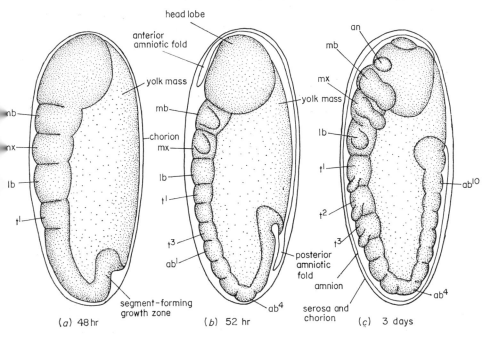

FIG. 9. Elongation and segmentation of the germ band of *Bruchidius obtectus* (Coleoptera), in left lateral view, after Jung (1966a). (a) At 48 hours, the gnathal and thoracic segments are delineated and the segment-forming growth zone is extending the segmenting germ band along the dorsal surface of the yolk mass (compare Fig. 5c); (b) At 52 hours, limb buds are beginning to form; (c) by 3 days, the germ band is fully segmented. ab^1–ab^{10}, abdominal segments; an, antenna; lb, labial segment; mb, mandibular segment; mx, maxillary segment; t^1–t^3, thoracic segments.

Accompanying elongation, the segments become delineated externally in anteroposterior succession, followed by an anteroposterior sequence of formation of the antennae, transitory premandibular limb vestiges, mouthparts and thoracic limbs. Only rarely does segment delineation and limb bud formation proceed from a thoracic focus as it does in some hemimetabolans [e.g. *Dermestes*, Küthe (1966)]. As in the Hemimetabola, no abdominal limb buds are formed until elongation and segmentation of the germ band are completed.

The posterior margin of the antennal segment is delineated at the level of the posterior border of the head lobes, as in the Hemimetabola. The antennae also arise in the usual way, at the posterolateral corners of the head lobes, behind the invaginating stomodaeum. The stomodaeum invaginates at an early stage of elongation and segmentation of the germ band, forming a pit in the midline between the head lobes. Invagination of the proctodaeum behind the growth zone follows soon after. An eleventh abdominal segment almost never becomes externally obvious in holometabolous embryos, being recorded only by Carrière and Bürger (1897) for *Chalicodoma*.

B. Hymenoptera

The primitive Hymenoptera (Fig. 10*c*) retain the sequence of elongation and segment delineation described above (Shafiq, 1954; Ando and Okada, 1958; Ivanova-Kasas, 1959) but in the more direct development of the large

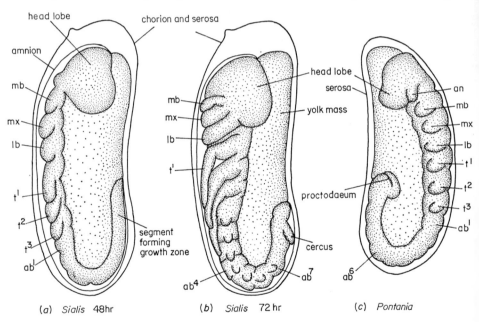

(a) *Sialis* 48hr   (b) *Sialis* 72 hr   (c) *Pontania*

Fig. 10. (*a*) The segmenting germ band of *Sialis lutaria* (Megaloptera), in left lateral view, after Du Bois (1938); (*b*) The segmented germ band of *S. lutaria*, in left lateral view, after Du Bois (1938); (*c*) The segmenting germ band of *Pontania capreae* (Hymenoptera, Symphyta), after Ivanova-Kasas (1959). ab¹–ab⁷, abdominal segments; lb, labial segment; mb, mandibular segment; mx, maxillary segment; t¹–t³, thoracic segments; an, antenna.

embryonic primordium of the Apocrita (Fig. 11), growth through the activity of a posterior growth zone is eliminated and the germ band extends at most only a little onto the dorsal surface of the yolk (Carrière and Bürger, 1897;

Nelson, 1915; Schnetter, 1934; Baerends and Baerends-von Roon, 1950; Ivanova-Kasas, 1958; Bronskill, 1959, 1964; Ochiai, 1960; Reinhardt, 1960; Amy, 1961; DuPraw, 1967). The anteroposterior sequence of segment delineation and limb bud formation is retained, but the anterior segment rudiments arise directly in the positions which in more primitive Holometabola

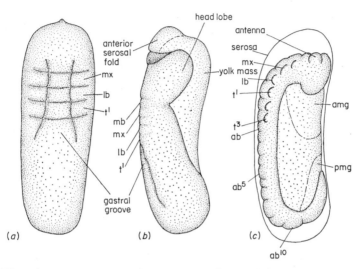

FIG. 11. Elongation and segmentation of the germ band of *Apis mellifera* (Hymenoptera, Apocrita), after Schnetter (1934). (*a*) Ventral view, early in gastrulation; (*b*) Lateral view, towards the end of gastrulation; (*c*) Lateral view, after completion of elongation and segmentation. ab¹–ab¹⁰, abdominal segments; lb, labial segment; mb, mandibular segment; mx, maxillary segment; t¹–t³, thoracic segments; amg, anterior midgut; pmg, posterior midgut.

are attained as a result of a shortening of the germ band after elongation (see below). The antennal segment is delineated directly in the pre-oral position, with the antennae anterodorsal, and the gnathal segments are already grouped around the mouth when first delineated.

C. Diptera

A convergent evolutionary trend is displayed in the Diptera, but with several unique specializations (Ede and Counce, 1956; Anderson, 1962, 1963a, 1964a; Schoeller, 1964; Craig, 1967; Davis, 1967; Davis et al., 1968; Wolf, 1969). In most Nematocera, a posterior growth zone is still the source from which the last few abdominal segments arise (Du Bois, 1932; Gambrell, 1933; Craig, 1967, 1969; Kalthoff and Sander, 1968), but as growth proceeds, the germ band extends rapidly along the dorsal surface of the yolk mass (Figs 12a, b). External segment delineation does not begin until this extension has been completed. Wolf (1969) has shown by means of time lapse photo-micrography that the major site of extension is the thoracic and anterior abdominal region of the germ band. Almost no extension takes place anterior to this level. Culicid and cyclorrhaphan embryos, like those of Apocrita, have the rudiments of all segments already established in the embryonic primor-dium (Fig. 6) and lack a posterior growth zone, but the germ band still undergoes a massive extension of the thoraco-abdominal region before any of its segments become delineated externally (Figs 12c–e). The description given by Kessel (1939) suggests that a similar mode of development occurs in the Siphonaptera. Elongation is due to a change in the shape and arrange-ment of the cells of the embryonic ectoderm (Ede and Counce, 1956; Anderson, 1962, 1966; Davis, 1967). These become both more cuboidal, in-creasing the area of surface covered, and more crowded towards the ventral midline, with associated increase in the length of the germ band. Simul-taneously, a deep ring fold, the cephalic furrow, forms in the blastoderm at the level of the mouthpart segments (Fig. 12d). It has been postulated (Sonnenblick, 1950; Anderson, 1962, 1966) that the cephalic furrow forms an anchor point for elongation, which takes place mainly behind the furrow. The posterior end of the germ band moves along the dorsal surface almost as far as the furrow, which disappears as elongation is completed (Fig. 12e). Several temporary smaller furrows also develop during the rapid elongation of the germ band and are eliminated as elongation is completed.

The external delineation of the segments in the Diptera and Siphonaptera will be discussed in connection with shortening of the germ band, in a later section. The functional advantages of the rapid elongation of the thoraco-abdominal portion of the dipteran germ band are not yet clear, though it seems possible for Cyclorrhapha (see below) that they rest with the mech-anics of a series of precocious gastrulation movements.

D. Lepidoptera

Elongation and segmentation of the aberrant embryonic primordium of the Lepidoptera is specialized in other ways (Fig. 13). The basic sequence of events is similar to that of the Coleoptera, but complications arise from a new relationship between the germ band and the yolk and also from the variety of forms of the egg-space in Lepidoptera. Following the first phase of concentration of cells which established the embryonic primordium, the edges of the primordium curl upwards, producing a small bowl of columnar cells cupping into the yolk mass (Figs 17f, g). A small amount of yolk is cut off within the cavity of the bowl. The cells now begin to become more cuboidal and the resulting increase in surface area is accommodated by elongation of the bowl and expansion of its anterior end as a pair of deeply cupped head lobes (Figs 13a, b). At this stage, the germ band attains the form established directly in the embryonic primordium of the more primitive Holometabola, with paired head lobes and a long postantennal region. It is upturned along the margins, however, rather than flat, is partially or wholly immersed in the yolk mass and has partially enclosed a portion of the yolk. In upright ovoid or spherical eggs (Eastham, 1927; Johannsen, 1929; Sehl, 1931; Lautenschlager, 1932; Grandori, 1932; Saito, 1934, 1937; Mueller, 1938; Gross and Howland, 1941; Christensen, 1943*a*; Rempel, 1951; Presser

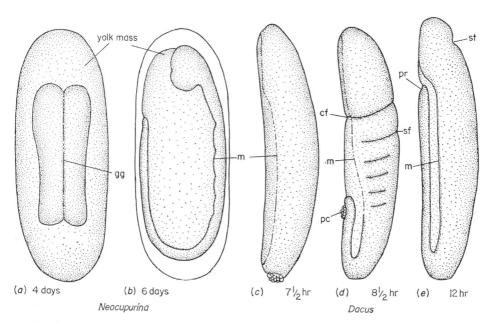

(*a*) 4 days   (*b*) 6 days   (*c*)   7½ hr   (*d*)   8½ hr   (*e*)   12 hr

      Neocupurina   *Dacus*

Fig. 12. (*a*) and (*b*) Stages in elongation of the germ band of *Neocupurina chiltoni* (Diptera, Nematocera), after Craig (1967). (*a*) 4 days, ventral view, (*b*) 6 days, right lateral view. (*c*)–(*e*) Stages in elongation of the germ band of *Dacus tryoni* (Diptera, Cyclorrhapha), in right lateral view, after Anderson (1962). (*c*) 7½ hours; (*d*) 8½ hours; (*e*) 12 hours. cf, cephalic furrow; gg, gastral groove, m, margin between germ band and extra-embryonic ectoderm; pc, pole cells; pr, proctodaeum; sf, secondary furrows; st, stomodaeum.

and Rutchsky, 1957; Krause and Krause, 1964), the germ band becomes dorsoventrally curved as it undergoes this preliminary change of shape, so that the head lobes and caudal end dip into the yolk and face the poles of the egg-space. In flattened, dome-shaped eggs (Huie, 1918; Christensen, 1953; Stairs, 1960; Okada, 1960; Bassand, 1965; Guénnelon, 1966; Anderson and Wood, 1968; Mrkva, 1968) the dorsoventral curvature is accommodated by a rotation of the germ band onto its side (Fig. 13*b*), beautifully displayed in the time-lapse cinephotomicrographic record prepared by Reed and Day (1966) of the embryonic development of *Epiphyas postvittana*. The head lobes and caudal end still face the poles of the egg space, but the ventral surface of the germ band now faces the periphery of the egg.

The further elongation of the lepidopteran germ band proceeds mainly through the activity of a typical posterior growth zone from which are added the rudiments of the ten abdominal segments. At the same time, segment delineation takes place in antero-posterior sequence and the cephalic and thoracic limb buds form in the usual way (Figs 13c, d). The further growth and development of the segment rudiments sets in rapidly as the activity of the growth zone proceeds and the embryo becomes longer relative to the egg space than it does in any other holometabolan. Associated with this, the germ band coils as it grows. In upright eggs, the coiling is usually in a plane spiral in the dorso-ventral plane of the egg, the head turning back to face the dorsal surface of the egg space, the abdomen coiling forwards behind the head. In flattened eggs, the coiling is augmented by twisting of the head downwards and the thorax upwards within the narrow egg space (Fig. 13d).

E. Stomodaeum, Proctodaeum and Labrum

In spite of the specializations in the mode of elongation and segmentation of the germ band in apocritan Hymenoptera, Siphonaptera, Diptera and Lepidoptera, the formation of the stomodaeum and proctodaeum still proceed in a simple basic manner throughout the Holometabola. The stomodaeum invaginates midventrally between the head lobes as soon as elongation of the germ band begins. Formation of the proctodaeum is more delayed, except in Diptera, but then proceeds by typical invagination at the posterior end of the germ band. During the completion of elongation, the proctodaeum is carried forwards along the dorsal midline or, in Lepidoptera, more deeply into the yolk.

The labrum pouches out simultaneously with the antennal rudiments, either as a single lobe (some Coleoptera: Butt, 1936; Diptera: Anderson, 1966; Craig, 1967; Davis, 1967; also Megaloptera, Neuroptera, Mecoptera and Trichoptera), or as paired lobes (Figs 8c, 13d; other Coleoptera: Blunck, 1914; Williams, 1916; Paterson, 1932, 1936; Tiegs and Murray, 1938; Haget, 1955; Ullman, 1964; Lepidoptera: Toyama, 1902; Johannsen, 1929; Eastham, 1930; Okada, 1960; Anderson and Wood, 1968; Siphonaptera: Kessel, 1939) in front of the mouth. The Hymenoptera display either single or paired labral lobes (Nelson, 1915; Schnetter, 1934; Shafiq, 1954; Ando and Okada, 1958; Bronskill, 1959, 1964; Ryan, 1963; Farooqui, 1963; DuPraw, 1967). As pointed out in Chapter 3 the origin of the labrum as a bilobed structure is now generally regarded as a secondary condition (Matsuda, 1965). The paired lobes always fuse together during later development.

VI. GASTRULATION

A. Gastrulation Movements

In consequence of the relatively large size of the embryonic primordium in holometabolous embryos, gastrulation movements are much better understood in the Holometabola than in the Hemimetabola. The movement of cells into the interior begins as the embryonic primordium enters into elongation and segmentation as a germ band, and the gastrulation movements are completed before elongation has proceeded far. Gastrulation takes place

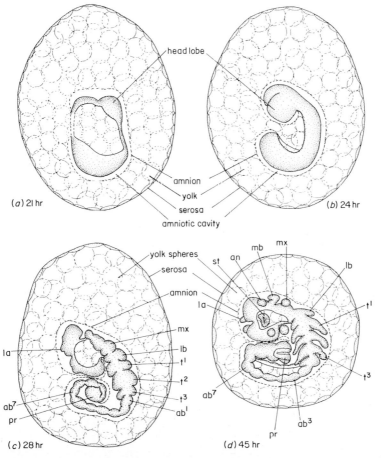

FIG. 13. Stages in elongation and segmentation of the germ band of *Epiphyas postvittana* (Lepidoptera), in dorsal view, after Anderson and Wood (1968). (*a*) 21 hours; (*b*) 24 hours; (*c*) 28 hours; (*d*) 45 hours. ab^1–ab^{10}, abdominal segments; an, antenna; la, labrum; lb, labium; mb, mandible; mx, maxilla; pr, proctodaeum; st, stomodaeum; t^1–t^3, thoracic segments.

in the same general manner in most orders of Holometabola, and has been described by numerous workers (Coleoptera: Heider, 1889; Wheeler, 1889; Lecaillon, 1898; Deegener, 1900; Hirschler, 1909; Mansour, 1927; Paterson, 1931, 1936; Inkmann, 1933; Smreczyński, 1934; Butt, 1936; Wray, 1937; Tiegs and Murray, 1938; Mulnard, 1947; Luginbill, 1953; Deobahkta, 1957; Jura, 1957; Ede, 1964; Ullman, 1964; Jung, 1966a; Küthe, 1966; Megaloptera: Strindberg, 1915a; Neuroptera: Bock, 1939; Trichoptera: Patten, 1884; Lepidoptera: Toyama, 1902; Eastham, 1927; Presser and Rutchsky, 1957; Okada, 1960; Krause and Krause, 1964; Vaidya, 1967; Anderson and Wood, 1968; Symphyta: Ivanova-Kasas, 1959). The basic pattern of cell movements is essentially the same as that of the Hemimetabola described in the preceding chapter. The cells along the ventral midline of the embryonic primordium first undergo cellular elongation (Fig. 14a), and then migrate into the interior as a wedge shaped strip of cells (Figs 14b, c). As they move inwards, the immigrating cells leave a temporary longitudinal furrow, the gastral groove, at the surface of the germ band (Fig. 5a). In some species of Coleoptera, the gastral groove is of sufficient depth and clarity to be called an invagination (Fig. 29; Deobahkta, 1957; Ullman, 1964). At the anterior end of the germ band, the immigrating strip of midventral cells is broadened into an anterior cell mass between the head lobes (Fig. 17g). At the posterior end is a similar but smaller posterior cell mass.

As the midventral cells of the germ band migrate into the interior, they are overgrown from each side by the more lateral, superficial cells of the germ band. These cells come together in the ventral midline, eliminating the gastral groove (Figs 14d, e). The cells which lie beneath the surface spread out to form an inner layer, broadest beneath the head lobes. The cells which remain at the surface form the outer layer.

After the inner layer has been formed, the cells which had covered the anterior cell mass midventrally during closure of the gastral groove invaginate to form the stomodaeum. The cells at the centre of the anterior cell mass are carried inwards at the tip of the stomodaeal invagination and give rise to the anterior midgut rudiment. Similarly, at the posterior end of the germ band, the superficial cells in the ventral midline behind the growth zone invaginate to form the proctodaeum, and carry the central part of the posterior cell mass inwards as the posterior midgut rudiment. The anterior and posterior midgut rudiments usually become histologically distinct only after the stomodaeum and proctodaeum have invaginated (e.g. Eastham, 1930; Ullman, 1964; Anderson and Wood, 1968), although a few cases have been described in which these rudiments can be identified at the beginning of gastrulation (e.g. Hirschler, 1909). The remainder of the inner layer develops as mesoderm. The remainder of the outer layer of the germ band develops as embryonic ectoderm.

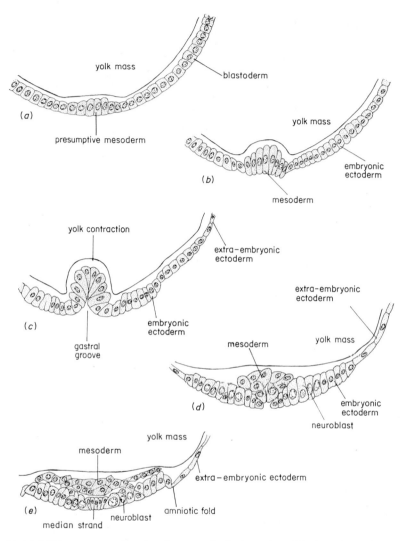

FIG. 14. (a)–(e) Transverse sections showing stages in the formation of the inner layer of *Chrysopa perla* (Neuroptera), after Bock (1939).

Modifications of the basic pattern of holometabolan gastrulation are displayed by the more specialized embryonic primordia of the apocritan Hymenoptera, the Diptera and the Siphonoptera. In these orders, a much broader band of midventral cells enters the interior than in the generalized embryos described above. The ventral cells of the Hymenoptera (Figs 15a, b) begin to sink in as a broad plate, which separates marginally from the cells

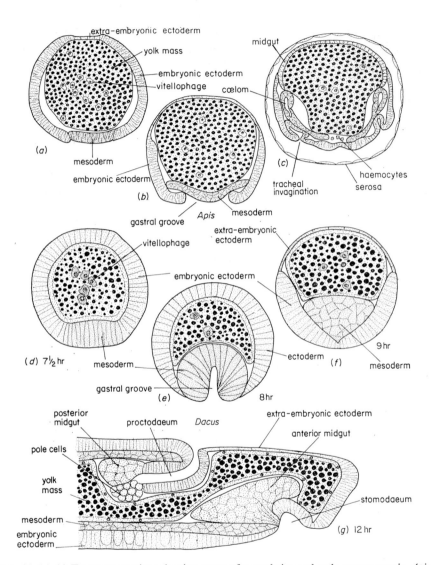

FIG. 15. (a)–(c) Transverse sections showing stages of gastrulation and early organogeny in *Apis mellifera* (Hymenoptera, Apocrita), after Schnetter (1934); (d)–(f) Transverse sections showing invagination of the mesoderm during gastrulation in *Dacus tryoni* (Diptera), after Anderson (1962); (g) Diagrammatic sagittal section through the anterior half of the gastrula of *D. tryoni*, after Anderson (1962).

on either side of it. The lateral cells then spread rapidly towards the ventral midline, covering the broad inner layer and closing the broad but shallow gastral groove (Grassi, 1886; Carrière and Bürger, 1897; Nelson, 1915; Strindberg, 1915b; Schnetter, 1934; Baerends and Baerends-von Roon, 1950; Ivanova-Kasas, 1958; Reinhardt, 1960; Amy, 1961; DuPraw, 1967). Within the forming inner layer, the terminal anterior and posterior midgut rudiments can be distinguished from the intervening mesoderm as soon as gastrulation begins.

Gastrulation in the Diptera, in contrast, involves the formation of a deep gastral groove, as a result of invagination of a broad midventral plate of cells (Figs 15d, e) followed by rapid midventral closure of the gastral groove by apposition of the bilateral embryonic ectoderm (Fig. 15f). In the Nematocera, the inner layer spreads rapidly beneath the outer layer, but the anterior and posterior midgut rudiments cannot be distinguished from the mesoderm until the stomodaeum and proctodaeum have formed (Kahle, 1908; Du Bois, 1932; Gambrell, 1933; Ivanova-Kasas, 1949; De Coursey and Webster, 1953; Telford, 1957; Christophers, 1960; Idris, 1960; Oelhafen, 1961; Davis, 1967). The Cyclorrhapha are more specialized. Here, the invaginate mode of entry is displayed only by the gastrulating mesoderm (Noack, 1901; Hardenburg, 1929; Lassman, 1936; Fish, 1947, 1949; Poulson, 1950; Sonnenblick, 1950; Ede and Counce, 1956; Breuning, 1957; Anderson, 1962; Schoeller, 1964; Davis, 1967). The large anterior and posterior midgut rudiments can be identified, as soon as gastrulation begins, in the form of two subterminal groups of cells which become internal by cellular elongation and immigration, followed by further inward passage at the tips of the invaginating stomodaeum and proctodaeum (Fig. 15g). The stomodaeum itself arises from an arc of cells around the anterior face of the anterior midgut rudiment. As the anterior midgut rudiment sinks into the interior, the stomodaeal arc closes to form a ring and then invaginates. The proctodaeum arises by invagination of a posterior plate of cells lying above and behind the posterior midgut rudiment.

The same topographical relationships between the rudiments of the stomodaeum, anterior midgut, mesoderm, posterior midgut and proctodaeum are observed in the embryonic primordium of the Siphonaptera. In the latter order (Kessel, 1939), the midgut rudiments sink in and become overgrown before mesodermal entry begins. The mesodermal cells of siphonapterans also become internal mainly as a result of overgrowth, as in the Hymenoptera, but the posterior part of the mesoderm enters the interior through a deep invagination reminiscent of that of Diptera.

A little more can be said of gastrulation in the Cyclorrhapha, since the precision with which it can be followed and the manner in which gastrulation is interlocked with the specialized elongation of the germ band (Section V, C) reveal something of the mechanics of the process (Poulson, 1950; Sonnenblick, 1950; Counce and Selman, 1955; Counce, 1956; Ede, 1956a, b, c; Ede and Counce, 1956; Hathaway and Selman, 1961; Anderson, 1962, 1966; Nitschmann, 1962; Schoeller, 1964; Davis, 1967) and may be pertinent to gastrulation in all Holometabola.

The first gastrulation movement, as described above, is an invagination of the mesoderm (Figs 15e, f). At the same time, the embryonic ectoderm begins to move towards the ventral midline and the dorsal part of the blastoderm attenuates as extra-embryonic ectoderm. Simultaneously, the cephalic furrow forms (Fig. 16c). The embryonic ectoderm cells continue to crowd towards the ventral midline after the gastral groove has closed. In front of the cephalic furrow, the anterior midgut cells move inwards, followed by the stomodaeum. Ventral crowding of the ectoderm in front of the cephalic furrow can be presumed to set up stresses which assist the inward movement of the anterior gut rudiments. Behind the cephalic furrow, ventral crowding of the ectoderm is more intense and the ectoderm elongates over the posterior pole and along the dorsal surface of the yolk mass, displacing the attenuated extra-embryonic ectoderm as it goes. The mesoderm lying internal to the ectoderm keeps pace with this elongation by a combination of cell rearrangement and proliferation. As ectodermal elongation begins, the posterior midgut cells start to move inwards, closely followed by the invaginating proctodaeum. There is good evidence that forces set up due to elongation of the ectoderm through ventral crowding play an important role in pushing the posterior midgut rudiments into the interior. The temporary cephalic furrow may act functionally as a ring girder against which this system of forces operates. The furrow disappears as soon as elongation and gastrulation are complete.

It is likely, then, that the specialized, rapid elongation of the germ band in cyclorrhaphan embryos is an aspect of a specialized process of gastrulation in which ventral crowding of the ectoderm plays a major mechanical role. Since ventral crowding of the ectoderm is manifested in the gastrulation of all Holometabola, and to a lesser extent in all Hemimetabola, it may be a crucial factor in the mechanics of gastrulation in pterygotes, though the details must vary considerably among species.

B. Presumptive Areas of the Blastoderm

In Section VI, B of Chapter 3, the point was made that the uniform cellular blastoderm of a hemimetabolan embryo, such as that of *Platycnemis pennipes*, can be zoned topographically into a precise pattern of presumptive areas of the major rudiments of the embryo (Fig. 8a of Chapter 3). Furthermore, this fate map, with various modifications, characterizes all Hemimetabola. By retracing the events of holometabolan gastrulation, a similar fate map can be drawn for the embryonic primordium, and hence for the uniform cellular blastoderm, of various holometabolan embryos. This process is most accurately performed for the Diptera and apocritan Hymenoptera, in which the major rudiments of the embryo become distinct from one another as soon as gastrulation begins, and each rudiment is large and

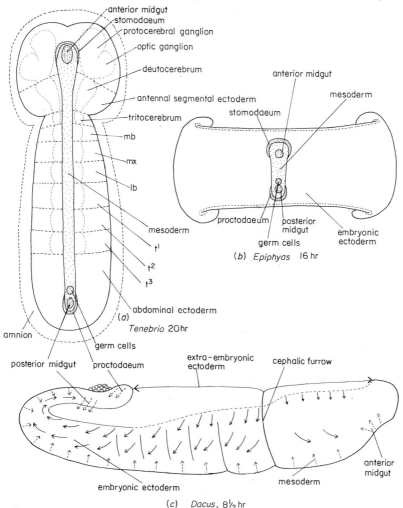

FIG. 16. (a) Presumptive areas of the embryonic primordium of *Tenebrio molitor* (Coleoptera) in ventral view, before the onset of gastrulation, based on data of Ullman (1964, 1967); (b) Presumptive areas of the embryonic primordium of *Epiphyas postvittana* (Lepidoptera), in ventral view, based on data of Anderson and Wood (1968); (c) The probable pattern of gastrulation forces in *Dacus tryoni* (Diptera), after Anderson (1966). lb, labial ectoderm; mb, mandibular ectoderm; mx, maxillary ectoderm; t¹–t³, thoracic segmental ectoderm.

conspicuous. Fate maps of the uniform cellular blastoderm of three species of Diptera, based on the work of Anderson (1962, 1966) and Davis (1967) are shown in Fig. 6. Similar maps have been demonstrated for *Drosophila melanogaster* by Poulson (1950), Hathaway and Selman (1961) and Garcia-Bellido and Merriam (1969) and for the hymenopteran *Apis mellifera* by DuPraw (1967). A comparison of the pattern of presumptive areas of the blastoderm in these species with that of *Platycnemis* as a representative primitive hemimetabolan, reveals that the same basic pattern of presumptive areas is retained throughout the pterygotes.

Presumptive mesoderm occupies the ventral midline, with presumptive anterior and posterior midgut at its ends. Presumptive stomodaeum lies in front of the presumptive anterior midgut. Presumptive proctodaeum lies behind the presumptive posterior midgut. The cells bordering the mid-ventral areas form paired lateral bands of presumptive embryonic ectoderm, segmentally zoned. The remainder of the surface of the yolk mass is occupied by presumptive extra-embryonic ectoderm.

The presumptive areas of the uniform cellular blastoderm of the Diptera and Hymenoptera are simply larger in area and consist of deeper, more columnar cells than those of *Platycnemis*, with an attendant reduction in area of the presumptive extraembryonic ectoderm. Consequently, each area proceeds more directly and rapidly into subsequent development. In the more generalized holometabolans, where the embryonic primordium becomes established in the differentiated blastoderm as a result of cellular aggregation, the pattern of presumptive areas is most easily deduced in the differentiated blastoderm rather than in the uniform cellular blastoderm. Although the midgut cells do not become histologically distinct until a later stage, the mode of origin of these cells allows them to be assigned to tentative sources in the embryonic primordium, yielding a fate map as constructed in Fig. 16*a* from the data of Ullman (1964, 1967) for *Tenebrio molitor*. This example can be regarded as a characteristic pattern for all generalized holometabolan embryos. Brauer (1949) has provided experimental evidence which suggests that the same zonation is present, more broadly spread, in the uniform cellular blastoderm before differentiation of the embryonic primordium takes place, as it is in *Platycnemis*. The basic holometabolan fate map thus differs from the basic hemimetabolan fate map only in that the cells of each area are cuboidal rather than flattened when they are first formed as components of the uniform cellular blastoderm. In the Diptera and apocritan Hymenoptera, as we have seen, the same cells are columnar rather than cuboidal. With each step in this sequence, the cellular aggregation which establishes the embryonic primordium as a monolayer of columnar cells in the differentiated blastoderm becomes less important, and the embryonic primordium occupies a relatively greater area of the surface of the yolk mass, has larger component presumptive areas and enters more directly into subsequent development. A consideration of presumptive areas of the blastoderm thus underscores the common theme of embryonic development in all pterygotes and reveals that the basic difference between hemimetabolous embryos and holometabolous embryos lies in the thickness of the uniform cellular blastoderm.

A comparison of fate maps can also be used to reveal the basic mode of specialization of the germ band of the Lepidoptera. As already described, the Lepidoptera display a unique cupping of the embryonic primordium accompanied by immersion into the yolk mass. After the embryonic primordium has reached the head-lobe stage (Fig. 13b), gastrulation then proceeds in the basic manner of Holometabola. When the events of cupulation and gastrulation are extrapolated back onto the broad embryonic primordium established before cupulation takes place, a fate map can be constructed as in Fig. 16b. Comparison with Fig. 16a shows that the disposition of the presumptive areas is the same, but that the presumptive embryonic ectoderm is relatively much broader at this stage in the Lepidoptera than in the basic type of embryonic primordium shown in Fig. 16a. This broadened presumptive ectoderm cups into the yolk mass as differentiation of the embryonic primordium continues, setting in train the unique series of events through which the lepidopteran germ band becomes immersed.

C. Pole Cell Movements During Gastrulation

In the majority of Holometabola, the primordial germ cells move into the interior of the embryo by an independent migratory movement prior to the onset of gastrulation. As a result, they become grouped beneath the germ band in the ventral midline, usually near the posterior end (Fig. 5e). The inward migration of the germ cells may be direct, or may involve traversing the blastoderm in species in which the germ cells are cut off precociously as pole cells and lie outside the blastoderm, as in some Nematocera.

A modified entry of pole cells into the interior is seen in some culicids (Idris, 1960; Davis, 1967) and in the Cyclorrhapha (Poulson, 1950; Anderson, 1962, 1966; Davis, 1967). The pole cells are intimately associated with the presumptive posterior midgut and adjacent presumptive proctodaeal areas of the blastoderm (Fig. 6). As elongation of the germ band begins and the presumptive midgut immigrates into the interior, followed by the presumptive proctodaeum, the pole cells sink into the proctodaeal invagination (Figs 12c–e, 15g, 16c). It seems likely that this movement is passive.

The primordial germ cells now move from the proctodaeal invagination out into the adjacent mesoderm as two bilateral groups, by an active migration equivalent to that which carries the germ cells of other species into the interior at an earlier stage of development. All the pole cells are primordial germ cells in culicids and some Cyclorrhapha (Davis, 1967), but in certain species, as mentioned in Section III, D, a number of pole cells remain associated with the posterior gut rudiments and develop as part of the wall of the midgut (*Drosophila melanogaster*, Poulson, 1950; Mahowald, 1962) or hindgut (*Dacus tryoni*, Anderson, 1962). In view of the fact that the determination of blastodermal presumptive areas occur very early in the Cyclorrhapha and that the pole cells develop in close proximity to the posterior gut areas, some overlap between presumptive area determination and pole cell formation is not surprising (Anderson, 1966).

VII. EXTRA-EMBRYONIC MEMBRANES

In the majority of Holometabola, excluding only the apocritan Hymenoptera, cyclorrhaphous Diptera and Lepidoptera, the embryo develops embryonic membranes in the same manner as in the Hemimetabola, (Coleoptera: Heider, 1889; Wheeler, 1889; Hirschler, 1909; Blunck, 1914; Paterson, 1931, 1936; Inkmann, 1933; Butt, 1936; Wray, 1937; Tiegs and Murray, 1938; Mulnard, 1947; Luginbill, 1953; Weglarska, 1955; Krzysztofowicz, 1960; Ede, 1964; Ullman, 1964; Jung, 1966*a*; Küthe, 1966; Zakhvatkin, 1967*a*, *b*; Megaloptera: Strindberg, 1915*a*; Du Bois, 1938; Neuroptera: Bock, 1939; Trichoptera: Patten, 1884; nematocerous Diptera: Anderson, 1966; Davis, 1967; Craig, 1967; Siphonaptera: Kessel, 1939; symphytan Hymenoptera: Shafiq, 1954; Ivanova-Kasas, 1959). The periphery of the embryonic primordium is presumptive amnion (Fig. 16*a*), while the extra-embryonic ectoderm is presumptive serosa. Coincident with the onset of elongation of the germ band, the presumptive amnion folds ventrally, first at the posterior end, then around the head lobes and finally along the lateral margins (Figs 5*a*, 9*b*, 17*a*). The folds attenuate and grow together in the midline, fusing antero-ventrally to complete the formation of the amnion and serosa (Figs 9*c*, 10*a*, *b*, 17*b*, *c*). Yolk invades the amnio-serosal space only in the Lepidoptera and certain Coleoptera. As the germ band continues to elongate, the amnion is stretched and becomes highly attenuated.

The formation of the embryonic membranes in the Lepidoptera (Figs 17*e*–*g*) proceeds in a modified way, associated with immersion of the germ band into the yolk (Anderson and Wood, 1968). During completion of the embryonic primordium, the edges of the latter separate from the extra-embryonic ectoderm and begin to curl up into the yolk mass. At the same time, the extra-embryonic ectoderm spreads beneath the ventral surface of the embryonic primordium and merges to form the serosa. The edges of the embryonic primordium then become reflexed downwards, first laterally, then along the anterior and posterior edges, and spread to form the amnion. As the embryonic primordium cups into the yolk, the amnio-serosal space is

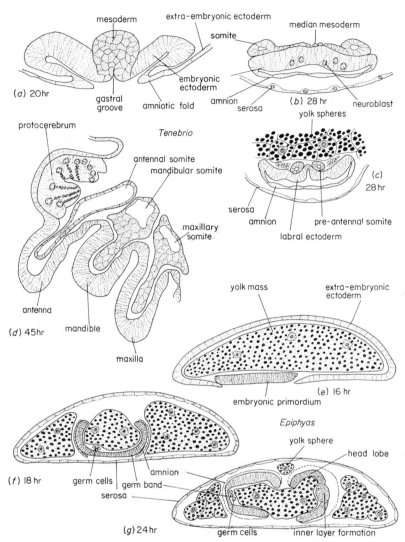

FIG. 17. (a) Transverse section through the 20-hour germ band of *Tenebrio molitor* (Coleoptera) during formation of the inner layer and embryonic membranes (compare Fig. 5a). (b) Transverse section through a thoracic segment of the 28-hour segmenting germ band and embryonic membranes of *T. molitor* (compare Fig. 8a); (c) Transverse section through the labral region of the 28-hour segmenting germ band of *T. molitor*; (d) Parasagittal section through the antennal and gnathal segments of the 45-hour segmented germ band of *T. molitor* (compare Fig. 8c). (a)–(d) are modified after Ullman (1964). (e) Sagittal section through the 16-hour differentiated blastoderm of *Epiphyas postvittana* (Lepidoptera) at the stage when the embryonic primordium first separates from the serosal rudiment (compare Figs. 7b and 16b); (f) Sagittal section through the 18-hour stage of *E. postvittana*, showing cupulation of the germ band and formation of the amnion; (g) Sagittal section through the 24-hour stage of *E. postvittana* (compare Fig. 13b). (e), (f) and (g) are modified after Anderson and Wood (1968).

invaded by yolk and the primordium becomes fully immersed. The basic modification in Lepidoptera is a precocious separation of the presumptive amnion from the presumptive serosa, preliminary to immersion of the germ band through cupulation. It is obvious that the evolution of an immersed embryo in Lepidoptera has proceeded independently of the analogous process in various hemimetabolan orders.

In the apocritan Hymenoptera and cyclorrhaphous Diptera, associated with the formation of a large embryonic primordium comprising most of the blastoderm, the embryonic membranes are variously reduced. Most Apocrita (Figs 11b, c, 15b, c) develop a complete serosa, through separation of the margins of the dorsal extra-embryonic ectoderm from the germ band and ventral spread over the surface of the germ band (Carrière and Bürger, 1897; Nelson, 1915; Baerends and Baerends-von Roon, 1950; Ivanova-Kasas, 1958; Bronskill, 1959, 1964; Ochiai, 1960; DuPraw, 1967). Usually there is no trace of an amnion, but in a few species, some of the cells at the margin of the germ band spread temporarily across the exposed dorsal surface of the yolk, beneath the serosa, as an amniotic vestige (Nelson, 1915; Baerends and Baerends-von Roon, 1950). In the Cyclorrhapha, even the formation of a serosa is eliminated, the extra-embryonic ectoderm simply persisting as a temporary dorsal epithelium until definitive dorsal closure takes place (Figs 12e, 15g, 25a, b; Anderson, 1966; Davis, 1967). Reduction of the embryonic membranes and loss of the amniotic cavity is presumably related functionally to the evolution of a disproportionately large, rapidly developing germ band, but since we have no clear picture of the functional role of an intact amnion, it is not yet possible to assess the functional implications of the evolutionary loss of this membrane.

VIII. SOMITES AND GANGLIA

A. Somite Formation

Commensurate with their relatively unmodified embryonic primordia and gastrulation processes, the embryos of many Holometabola (Coleoptera, Megaloptera, Neuroptera, Mecoptera, Trichoptera, Lepidoptera) exhibit a sequence of somite formation similar to that of the palaeopteran and polyneopteran Hemimetabola. Ullman (1964) has recently studied somite formation in detail in the primitive beetle *Tenebrio molitor*. The formation of somites is preceded by the usual bilateral aggregation of mesoderm cells along the sides of the germ band (Fig. 17b) At the same time, the growth zone is active posteriorly, adding the ectoderm and mesoderm of successive abdominal segments (Figs 8a, b). Median mesoderm persists along the ventral midline between the bilateral thickenings. The latter now segregate in anteroposterior sequence into paired blocks, which transform into hollow somites by internal splitting. The somites comprise a small preantennal

(Figs 17*c*, 18*c*, *e*), large antennal (Fig. 18*d*), small premandibular, mandibular and maxillary (Fig. 17*d*), large labial and three large thoracic pairs, followed by ten small abdominal pairs (Fig. 18*b*). Behind these lies a mass of

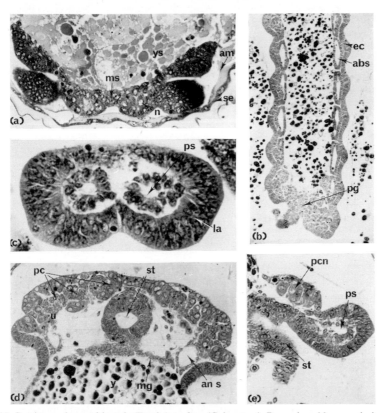

FIG. 18. Somites and neuroblasts in *Tenebrio molitor* (Coleoptera). Reproduced by permission from Ullman (1964, 1967). (*a*) Transverse section through the mandibular segment of a 43-hour embryo; (*b*) Frontal section through the abdomen of a 44-hour embryo; (*c*) Transverse section through the labrum of a 45-hour embryo; (*d*) Frontal section through the head lobes of a 45-hour embryo; (*e*) Sagittal section through the labrum and stomodaeum of a 45-hour embryo. Shortly after the stages represented by the above sections, the embryo attains the stage of development illustrated in Fig. 8*c*. abs, abdominal somite; am, amnion; ans, antennal somite; ec, segmental ectoderm; la, labral ectoderm; mg, midgut strand; ms, median strand; n, neuroblast; pc, protocerebral lobes; pcn, protocerebral neuroblast; pg, primordial germ cells; ps, preantennal somite; se, serosa; st, stomodaeum; y, yolk; ys, yolk sphere.

residual mesoderm associated with the proctodaeum. There is no trace of an eleventh pair of abdominal somites in this or any other holometabolan embryo. Anteriorly, around the stomodaeum, most of the mesoderm is not taken up into the pregnathal somites.

The formation of coelomic cavities by internal splitting is usual in the

Holometabola (Coleoptera: Hirschler, 1909; Paterson, 1932; Butt, 1936; Mansour, 1927; Tiegs and Murray, 1938; Luginbill, 1953; Deobahkta, 1957; Jura, 1957; Ullman, 1964; Rempel and Church, 1969; Neuroptera: Bock, 1939; Lepidoptera: Eastham, 1927; Siphonaptera: Kessel, 1939). The folding process observed during somite formation in many Hemimetabola has only a scattered occurrence in the Holometabola (Coleoptera: Wray, 1937; Megaloptera: Strindberg, 1915a; Lepidoptera: Johannsen, 1929; Presser and Rutchsky, 1957) and is confined even then to the labial and thoracic somites. Somite formation, however, is not usually as marked in other holometabolan embryos as it is in *Tenebrio*. Even among the Coleoptera, the cephalic mesodermal segmentation is often partially suppressed (Wheeler, 1889; Lecaillon, 1897a, b, 1898; Hirschler, 1909; Paterson, 1932, 1936; Smreczyński, 1932; Wray, 1937; Tiegs and Murray, 1938; Deobahkta, 1957; Such and Haget, 1962). The preantennal somites are usually absent, the premandibular somites always lack coelomic cavities and may be absent, the mandibular somites usually lack coelomic cavities, the maxillary somites develop coelomic cavities only in *Corynodes pusis* (Paterson, 1936) and *Calandra callosa* (Wray, 1937), while in *Donacia crassipes*, *Silpha obscura*, *Calandra oryzae* and *Leptinotarsa decemlineata*, somite formation in the mandibular and maxillary segments is wholly suppressed (Hirschler, 1909; Smreczyński, 1932; Tiegs and Murray, 1938; Such and Haget, 1962). The Megaloptera, Neuroptera and Lepidoptera, as far as is known, retain the full sequence of somites, but in the Lepidoptera the somites are small, much of the lateral mesoderm is not incorporated into them and the pregnathal somites have no coelomic cavities (Eastham, 1930). The Siphonaptera lack preantennal and premandibular somites (Kessel, 1939), while in the Diptera and Hymenoptera, all cephalic somite formation is suppressed.

The development of the mesoderm in the last two orders is also specialized in other ways. The Nematocera and some Cyclorrhapha develop paired trunk somites, but lack coelomic cavities within them. Other Cyclorrhapha, e.g. *Dacus*, *Lucilia*, omit somite formation entirely (Figs 25b, c) and show direct development of the mesoderm into functional components (Anderson, 1962, 1966; Davis, 1967). Some apocritan Hymenoptera, e.g. *Habrobracon*, also follow this course (Amy, 1961), but in most Hymenoptera the paired bilateral aggregations of mesoderm hollow out as longitudinal coelomic tubes (Fig. 15c), without transverse subdivisions, before proceeding into organogenesis (Carrière and Bürger, 1897; Nelson, 1915; Schnetter, 1934; Ivanova-Kasas, 1958, 1959; Bronskill, 1958, 1964).

B. Early Development of the Brain and Ventral Nerve Cord

The initial development of the nervous system in the Holometabola also proceeds as in the Hemimetabola. Recent studies by Ullman (1967) on

Tenebrio molitor and Rempel and Church (1969) on *Lytta viridana* have fully confirmed the findings of earlier workers (Coleoptera: Wheeler, 1889; Hirschler, 1909; Paterson, 1932, 1936; Butt, 1936; Wray, 1937; Tiegs and Murray, 1938; Mulnard, 1947; Deobahkta, 1957; Ede, 1964; Jung, 1966*a*; Megaloptera: Strindberg, 1915*a*; Neuroptera: Bock, 1939; Trichoptera: Patten, 1884; Lepidoptera: Johannsen, 1929; Eastham, 1930; Sehl, 1931; Grandori, 1932; Mueller, 1938; Rempel, 1951; Presser and Rutchsky, 1957; Okada, 1960; Bassand, 1965; Anderson and Wood, 1968; Siphonaptera: Kessel, 1939; Diptera: Gambrell, 1933; Butt, 1934; Schaeffer, 1938; Poulson, 1950; Anderson, 1962; Davis, 1967; Hymenoptera: Carrière and Bürger, 1897; Nelson, 1915; Shafiq, 1954; Ivanova-Kasas, 1958, 1959; Bronskill, 1959, 1964; Amy, 1961) that three to five rows of neuroblasts differentiate in the ectoderm on each side of the ventral midline behind the stomodaeum (Figs 14*d*, *e*, 17*b*, 18*a*, 24*a*), diverging into broader areas over the head lobes, and bud off radial rows of ganglion cells into the interior. The radial rows merge into a pair of longitudinal bands (Figs 24*b*, *c*, 25*b*), with concomitant formation of neural ridges on either side of the ventral midline, before beginning to segregate into paired segmental ganglia. A median strand is formed by the cells of the floor of the neural groove in the usual way (Fig. 18*a*).

IX. SHORTENING AND ITS CONSEQUENCES FOR DORSAL CLOSURE

When the germ band is fully elongated and segmented in the Coleoptera, (Figs 8*c*, 9*c*), Megaloptera (Fig. 10*a*), Neuroptera, Mecoptera and Trichoptera, it retains its position with the head and thorax ventral and the abdomen usually extended over the posterior pole and along the dorsal surface of the yolk mass, during a further period of broadening and preliminary organogeny. At a critical point of growth in many Coleoptera, including *Dytiscus marginalis*, *Hydrophilus piceus*, *Dermestes frischi*, *Tenebrio molitor*, *Bruchidius obtectus* and *Donacia crassipes* (Heider, 1889; Hirschler, 1909; Blunck, 1914; Paterson, 1932; Deobahkta, 1957; Ullman, 1964; Jung, 1966*a*; Küthe, 1966), and in the other orders listed above (Patten, 1884; Strindberg, 1915*a*; Du Bois, 1938; Bock, 1939), the amnion and serosa fuse beneath the anterior part of the germ band, then rupture and withdraw in the same manner as in the Hemimetabola. The embryo is exposed, the serosa contracts to form a dorsal organ and the amnion forms a provisional dorsal closure over the dorsal surface of the yolk mass. At the same time, the segmented germ band undergoes a rapid contraction in length (Fig. 19*a*). As a result, the posterior end usually returns to the posterior pole of the yolk mass and the segmented germ band broadens, extending up the sides of the yolk mass and effecting partial, definitive dorsal closure. The rapidity with which shortening takes

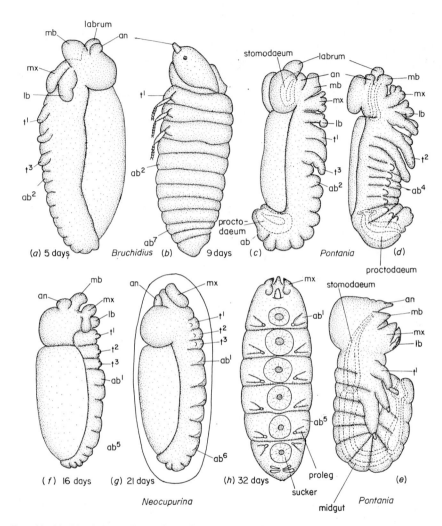

F$_{IG}$. 19. (*a*) The 5-day embryo of *Bruchidius obtectus* (Coleoptera) in left lateral view, following shortening of the germ band, after Jung (1966*a*); (*b*) The embryo of *B. obtectus* at the hatching stage; (*c*)–(*e*) Stages in dorsal closure of *Pontania capreae* (Hymenoptera, Symphyta) in right lateral view, after Ivanova-Kasas (1959); (*f*) The 16-day shortened germ band of *Neocupurina chiltoni* (Diptera, Nematocera) in right lateral view, after Craig (1967); (*g*) The 21-day embryo of *N. chiltoni* in right lateral view; (*h*) *N. chiltoni* at the hatching stage, ventral view. ab^1 –ab^{10}, abdominal segments; an, antenna; lb, labial segment; mb, mandibular segment; mx, maxillary t^1–t^3, thoracic segments.

place indicates that contractile activity is involved. The process can be interpreted as a modification of the manner in which the germ band becomes exposed in the Dictyoptera and Dermaptera, the contraction being essential to straightening the elongated, usually flexed, embryos.

The same shortening and partial dorsal closure occurs in other coleopteran genera (*Chrysomela, Clytra, Leptinotarsa, Euryope, Corynodes, Calandra, Phyllobius*: Wheeler, 1889; Paterson, 1931, 1936; Smreczyński, 1934; Wray, 1937; Tiegs and Murray, 1938), but is associated with a modified behaviour of the embryonic membranes. The serosa remains intact and the amnion spreads upwards as paired folds across the dorsal surface of the yolk mass. The folds come together and the amnion then separates into two parts, a provisional dorsal closure on the surface of the yolk mass and a complete amniotic membrane beneath the serosa. The amnion and serosa then remain intact until hatching. The same mode of shortening and dorsal closure, leaving the shortened, almost tubular embryo within an intact amnion and serosa, is also displayed in Lepidoptera (Fig. 21*a*), although here the space between the amnion and serosa contains most of the yolk (Toyama, 1902; Johannsen, 1929; Eastham, 1930; Sehl, 1931; Grandori, 1932; Saito, 1937; Mueller, 1938; Rempel, 1951; Presser and Rutchsky, 1957; Okada, 1960; Stairs, 1960; Bassand, 1965; Guénnelon, 1966). Shortening has recently been studied in detail in the tortricid moth *Epiphyas postvittana* by Reed and Day (1966) and Anderson and Wood (1968), using a combination of time lapse cinephotomicrography and histological techniques. The process is completed in a few hours and the time-lapse record reveals that it is brought about by a series of strong, slow contractions of the entire germ band.

Other holometabolan orders exhibit other specializations. In the Siphonaptera, as shortening proceeds, the serosa ruptures and withdraws to the dorsal surface, but the amnion remains intact. As the serosa contracts to form a dorsal organ and is drawn into the yolk, the amnion spreads above it to form a complete amniotic membrane. The amnion then also ruptures ventrally and contracts onto the dorsal surface, forming a provisional dorsal closure (Kessel, 1939). The nematocerous Diptera show an opposite trend (Davis, 1967). The amnion and serosa may fuse in the usual way before rupturing and retracting, or the amnion alone may rupture and withdraw, leaving the serosa intact until hatching. The symphytan Hymenoptera also retain an intact serosa while the amnion ruptures precociously and is resorbed (Shafiq, 1954; Ivanova-Kasas, 1959). The majority of Apocrita retain an intact serosa until hatching (Figs 21*a*, *b*), but effect a direct dorsal closure without the intervention of an amnion (Carrière and Bürger, 1897; Nelson, 1915; Schnetter, 1934; Baerends and Baerends-von Roon, 1950; Bronskill, 1959, 1964; DuPraw, 1967). Finally, in the Cyclorrhapha, the vestigial extra-embryonic ectoderm persists as a provisional dorsal closure during shortening

(Figs 21*d–f*; Poulson, 1950; Anderson, 1962; Davis, 1967; Davis *et al.*, 1968). Thus the dorsal surface of the yolk mass at the termination of shortening of the germ band may be covered by a typical amniotic provisional dorsal closure with an anterodorsal, serosal dorsal organ or by a part of the amnion only, a persistent serosa only, or a vestigial extra-embryonic ectoderm.

As pointed out above, in the specialized embryos of Diptera, external delineation of the segments is also a corollary of shortening, following precocious rapid elongation of the germ band during gastrulation (Figs 12*b*, *e*, 19*f*, 21*d–g*). In spite of this, the Nematocera retain the typical anteroposterior sequence of segment delineation, post-oral antennal buds, transitory premandibular segment and even, in the Blepharoceridae (Fig. 19), transitory thoracic limbs (Gambrell, 1933; Ivanova-Kasas, 1949; Idris, 1960; Davis, 1967; Craig, 1967, 1969; Kalthoff and Sander, 1968; Wolf, 1969). In *Simulium venustum*, the premandibular limb buds persist and develop as the larval cephalic fans. In the Cyclorrhapha, however, (Anderson, 1962, 1963*a*, 1964*a*; Schoeller, 1964; Davis, 1967) the head lobes are delineated directly in their preoral position, the mouth-part segments are already crowded forward behind the mouth when first delineated, and there is no trace of a premandibular segment. The thoraco-abdominal segments retain the antero-posterior sequence of delineation, but lack external limb buds. Involution of the head (see below) begins during the final phase of abdominal segment delineation.

X. FURTHER DEVELOPMENT OF THE EMBRYONIC ECTODERM

A. The Epidermis and Limb Buds

In the majority of Holometabola, the embryonic ectoderm completes its development in the same manner as in the Hemimetabola. Major modifications of ectodermal development are observed only in embryos which develop as apodous larvae (some Coleoptera and Hymenoptera, all Siphonaptera and Diptera).

As the developing neural tissue moves into the interior, before and during shortening of the germ band, dermatoblasts are left at the surface in the usual way (Figs 24*c*, *d*) and give rise to epidermis ventrally behind the mouth and laterally on the head lobes (Bock, 1939; Ullman, 1967). The lateral ectoderm spreads dorsally (Fig. 19), effecting definitive dorsal closure. The cells forming the provisional dorsal closure are simultaneously resorbed into the yolk. During and after dorsal closure, the cephalic ectoderm crowds forward (e.g. Figs 19*c–e*, 21*a*), bringing the mouthparts into close association around and behind the mouth and carrying the antennae and their associated deutocerebral ganglia forwards and upwards into a preoral position. In cyclorrhaphous embryos, the forward migration of the cephalic ectoderm is exaggerated into a process of involution of the head (Figs 21*f–i*; Ludwig, 1949;

Poulson, 1950; Bull, 1956; Ede and Counce, 1956; Tsai, 1961; Anderson, 1962, 1963a, 1966; Menees, 1962; Schoeller, 1964; Davis, 1967), in which the head ectoderm gives rise to the lining of the larval cephlopharynx.

Typically, the ventrolateral ectoderm of the antennal, gnathal and thoracic segments pouches out as appendage buds (Fig. 24b) outside the corresponding somites as elongation of the abdomen proceeds. No vestiges of pre-antennal limbs have been reported for the Holometabola. The outpouching of the abdominal ectoderm as limb buds, in contrast, is delayed until shortening has commenced. In most orders, ten pairs of abdominal limb buds are

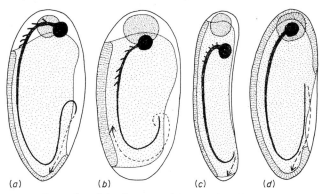

(a)   (b)   (c)   (d)

FIG. 20. A summary of growth and development of the germ band in the Holometabola, modified after Weber (1954). (a) *Chrysopa* (Neuroptera); (b) *Anagasta* (Lepidoptera); (c) *Apis* (Hymenoptera); (d) *Drosophila* (Diptera). All diagrams are drawn with the ventral surface on the left. The dotted area is the embryonic primordium.

formed. The first pair becomes enlarged in some Coleoptera and Lepidoptera as pleuropodia (Blunck, 1914; Eastham, 1930) but is resorbed before hatching. The remaining pairs are quickly resorbed except where they persist as prolegs, e.g. on segments three to six and ten in the Lepidoptera (Eastham, 1930; Friedmann, 1934; Anderson and Wood, 1968) and on segments two to seven and ten in the Symphyta (Ivanova-Kasas, 1959). The Siphonaptera, Diptera and apocritan Hymenoptera retain no trace of abdominal limbs (Nelson, 1915; Schnetter, 1934; Kessel, 1939; Baerends and Baerends-von Roon, 1950; Ivanova-Kasas, 1958; Bronskill, 1959; Anderson, 1962; Davis, 1967).

Generally the labrum and the cephalic and thoracic limbs grow longer after the embryo has shortened, before entering into functional differentiation (e.g. Figs 19c–e). Associated with the development of apody, however, they may shorten during later development (e.g. *Brachyrhinus*, Butt, 1936; *Calandra*, Tiegs and Murray, 1938) or be reduced to mere epidermal thickenings (e.g. the thoracic limbs of apocritan Hymenoptera (Figs 21b, c) and blepharocerid Diptera (Figs 19f, g; Carrière and Bürger, 1897; Nelson,

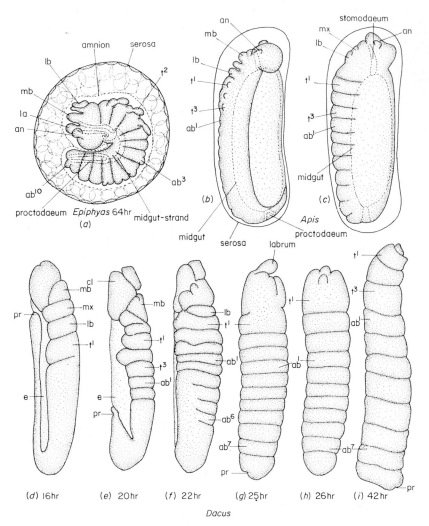

FIG. 21. (*a*) The embryo of *Epiphyas postvittana* (Lepidoptera) at 64 hours, following shortening and dorsal closure, after Anderson and Wood (1968). The egg is viewed from the dorsal surface. The embryo lies on its left side within the amniotic cavity (compare Fig. 13); (*b*) and (*c*) Stages in dorsal closure of *Apis mellifera* (Hymenoptera, Apocrita), in left lateral view, after Schnetter (1934), (compare Fig. 11); (*d*)–(*i*) Shortening and segmentation of the germ band, dorsal closure, involution of the head and further development to hatching in *Dacus tryoni* (Diptera), in right lateral view, after Anderson (1963a). (*d*) 16 hours; (*e*) 20 hours; (*f*) 22 hours; (*g*) 25 hours; (*h*) 26 hours; (*i*) 42 hours. ab^1–ab^{10}, abdominal segments; an, antenna; cl, cephalic lobe; e, extra-embryonic ectoderm; la, labrum; lb, labial segment; mb, mandibular segment; mx, maxillary segment; pr, proctodaeum; t^1–t^3, thoracic segments.

1915; Schnetter, 1934; Baerends and Baerends-von Roon, 1950; Bronskill, 1959, 1964; Ochiai, 1960; Amy, 1961; Craig, 1967) or, in the extreme case, may never develop beyond the stage of epidermal thickenings (e.g. the thoracic limb rudiments of Cyclorrhapha, Anderson, 1963a).

B. Ectodermal Invaginations

Before and during shortening of the segmental germ band, ectodermal invaginations develop in the usual way on the head and trunk. The tentorium is developed, as in Hemimetabola, from an anterior pair of invaginations just behind the antennae and a posterior pair just behind the maxillae (Coleoptera: Heider, 1889; Strindberg, 1913, 1917; Paterson, 1932, 1936; Smreczyński, 1932; Wray, 1937; Tiegs and Murray, 1938; Deobahkta, 1957; Ullman, 1967; Megaloptera: Strindberg, 1915a; Lepidoptera: Eastham, 1930; Presser and Rutchsky, 1957; Okada, 1960; Siphonaptera: Kessel, 1939; Diptera: Schoeller, 1964; Hymenoptera: Carrière and Bürger, 1897; Nelson, 1915; Baerends and Baerends-von Roon, 1950; Ivanova-Kasas, 1959; Amy, 1961). Between the anterior and posterior pairs of tentorial invaginations, a pair of invaginations at the bases of the mandibles gives rise to the mandibular apodemes. There may also be invaginations forming mandibular glands (Eastham, 1930; Wray, 1937) or maxillary glands (Smreczyński, 1932; Tiegs and Murray, 1938) and all holometabolous embryos develop a pair of labial ectodermal invaginations which form the salivary glands or silk glands (Coleoptera: Tiegs and Murray, 1938; Ullman, 1967; Trichoptera: Patten, 1884; Lepidoptera: Eastham, 1930; Anderson and Wood, 1968; Siphonaptera: Kessel, 1939; Diptera: Sonnenblick, 1941, 1950; Poulson, 1950; Anderson, 1962, 1966; Schoeller, 1964; Davis, 1967; Hymenoptera: Carrière and Bürger, 1897; Nelson, 1915; Pflugfelder, 1934; Baerends and Baerends-von Roon, 1950; Ivanova-Kasas, 1959; Ochiai, 1960; Amy, 1961; Bronskill, 1964).

The corpora allata arise from the cephalic ectoderm as in the Hemimetabola. Their origin has been traced to invaginations of the ventro-lateral ectoderm of the mandibular-maxillary intersegment in several Coleoptera (Smreczyński, 1932; Paterson, 1936) and Hymenoptera (Carrière and Bürger, 1897; Janet, 1899; Strindberg, 1913; Nelson, 1915), while in the Lepidoptera, the corpora allata are said to arise from cells associated with the mandibular apodemes (Eastham, 1930). After becoming internal, the cells move upwards and forwards to become attached to the median walls of the antennal somites, which subsequently gives rise to the anterior aorta. An origin of the corpora allata from the ectoderm of the head has also been demonstrated for the Diptera (Poulson, 1945, 1950; Oelhafen, 1961; Tsai, 1961).

Invaginations of the ectoderm of the trunk, laterally on the second thoracic to eighth abdominal segments, give rise during shortening of the germ band to the rudiments of the tracheal system (Fig. 24d; Coleoptera: Hirschler, 1909; Paterson, 1932, 1936; Butt, 1936; Wray, 1937; Tiegs and Murray, 1938; Mulnard, 1947; Luginbill, 1953; Deobahkta, 1957; Ullman, 1967; Megaloptera: Strindberg, 1915a; Neuroptera: Bock, 1939; Trichoptera: Patten, 1884; Lepidoptera: Eastham, 1930; Presser and Rutchsky, 1957; Okada, 1960; Anderson and Wood, 1968; Diptera: Poulson, 1950; Anderson, 1962, 1966; Davis, 1967; Siphonaptera: Kessel, 1939; Hymenoptera: Carrière and Bürger, 1897; Nelson, 1915; Schnetter, 1934; Baerends and Baerends-von Roon, 1950; Shafiq, 1954; Bronskill, 1959; Ivanova-Kasas, 1959; Ochiai, 1960; Amy, 1961). The tracheal system develops in the usual way, but may exhibit closure of one or more of its initial spiracular openings. The metathoracic pair, for instance, becomes closed in Lepidoptera, while in Cyclorrhapha, all except the first and last pairs are closed off.

After the tracheal system has gained a cuticular lining, but before the embryo has escaped from the egg membranes, a gas is secreted within the tracheal lumen (Wigglesworth and Beament, 1950, 1960; Ede and Counce, 1956; Reed and Day, 1966; Anderson and Wood, 1968). Time lapse films of the development of *Epiphyas* show that gas secretion is followed by a sudden increase in the muscular activity of the embryo. Final differentiation of the organ systems awaits this phase of development, but the physiology and causal significances of gas secretion in insect embryos still require investigation. The development of oenocytes is associated with the tracheal invaginations, as it is in the Hemimetabola. Eight paired groups of ectoderm cells adjacent to the abdominal tracheal invaginations give rise to these cells (Hirschler, 1909; Strindberg, 1913; Nelson, 1915; Eastham, 1930; Paterson, 1932; Tiegs and Murray, 1938; Kessel, 1939; Davis, 1967; Ullman, 1967).

C. The Nervous System

The further development of the brain and ventral nerve cord (Fig. 22) in Holometabola warrant little discussion, since it proceeds in general in the same manner as in the Hemimetabola (Coleoptera: Hirschler, 1909; Paterson, 1932, 1936; Butt, 1936; Wray, 1937; Tiegs and Murray, 1938; Mulnard, 1947; Luginbill, 1953; Deobahkta, 1957; Ullman, 1967; Rempel and Church, 1969; Megaloptera: Strindberg, 1915a; Neuroptera: Bock, 1939; Lepidoptera: Eastham, 1930; Presser and Rutchsky, 1957; Okada, 1960; Anderson and Wood, 1968; Diptera: Poulson, 1950; Anderson, 1962, 1966; Davis, 1967; Siphonaptera: Kessel, 1939; Hymenoptera: Carrière and Bürger, 1897; Nelson, 1915; Baerends and Baerends-von Roon, 1950; Bronskill, 1959, 1964; Ochiai, 1960; Amy, 1961). Primitively, as in *Tenebrio* (Figs 22e, 23), the protocerebral ganglia become bilobed, while the optic ganglia develop as separate ectodermal invaginations. The antennal deutocerebral ganglia and the premandibular tritocerebral ganglia become preoral in the usual way and the tritocerebral commissure remains postoral. The only features of note are those associated with larval specialization, such as the lack of subdivision of the cerebral ganglia in Lepidoptera and Diptera and the extreme condensation of the nervous system in the later embryos of the Cyclorrhapha (Fig. 32*e*; Poulson, 1950; Anderson, 1962; Alléaume, 1965; Davis, 1967) and some Coleoptera.

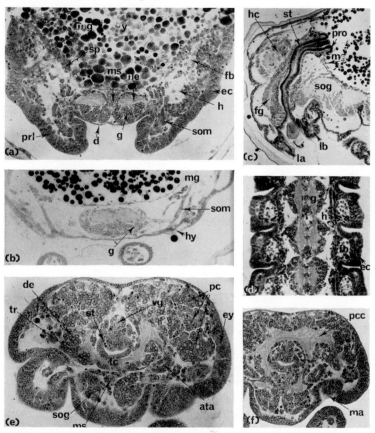

FIG. 22. Development of the nervous system in *Tenebrio molitor* (Coleoptera). Reproduced by permission from Ullman (1967). (*a*) Transverse section through the prothoracic segment of a 64-hour embryo (compare Fig. 23*d*); (*b*) Transverse section through an abdominal ganglion of a 94-hour embryo; (*c*) Sagittal section through the anterior end of a 5-day embryo, nearing eclosion; (*d*) Frontal section through the abdominal ganglia of a 64-hour embryo; (*e*) and (*f*) Successive transverse sections through the mandibular-maxillary intersegment of a 64-hour embryo. ata, anterior tentorial arm; d, dermatoblasts; de, deutocerebrum; ec, ectoderm; ey, optic ectoderm; fb, fat body; fg, frontal ganglion; g, ganglion; h, haemocoel; hy, hypodermis; la, labrum; lb, labium; ma, mandibular apodeme; mg, midgut strand; ms, median strand; ne, neuropile; pc, protocerebral ganglia; pcc, protocerebral commissure; prl, prothoracic limb; pro, proventriculus; sog, suboesophageal ganglion; som, somatic musculature; sp, splanchnic mesoderm strand; st, stomodaeum; tc, tritocerebral commissure; tr, tritocerebrum; vg, ventricular ganglion; y, yolk.

The contribution of the median strand to the development of the nervous system in the Holometabola is still controversial. It is generally agreed that the intrasegmental regions of the median strand, as in the Hemimetabola, contribute to the ganglia (Nelson, 1915; Ullman, 1967), but the fate of the intersegmental portions is said to be variable. According to Tiegs and Murray (1938) and Ullman (1967), the intersegmental parts of the median strand of Coleoptera contribute to the ganglia and to the neurilemma. Poulson (1950), on the other hand, found that they contribute only to the neurilemma in

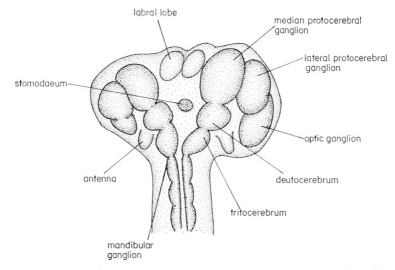

labral lobe

median protocerebral ganglion

lateral protocerebral ganglion

stomodaeum

optic ganglion

antenna

deutocerebrum

tritocerebrum

mandibular ganglion

Fɪɢ. 23. Diagrammatic reconstruction of the brain of *Tenebrio molitor* (Coleoptera) in ventral view at the 48-hour, segmented germ band stage (compare Fig. 8*c*). After Ullman (1967).

Drosophila. He also found, as did Tiegs and Murray (1938) and Ullman (1967), that the intrasegmental portions add cells to the neurilemma. Conversely, according to Strindberg (1913), Eastham (1930), Paterson (1935) and Mazur (1960), the neurilemma develops exclusively from peripheral ganglion cells. Differences in the interpretation of the fate of the median strand cells and the origin of the neurilemma in the Holometabola probably rest more with problems of the resolution of events than with actual differences between species.

XI. FURTHER DEVELOPMENT OF THE GUT

A. The Stomodaeum and Stomatogastric Nervous System

The stomodaeum in the Holometabola, as in the Hemimetabola, grows inwards as a simple epithelial tube, penetrating as far as the thorax. The walls of the tube give rise in the usual way to the lining epithelium of the foregut and the core of the proventriculus (Fig. 22c; Coleoptera: Heider, 1889; Wheeler, 1889; Hirschler, 1909; Paterson, 1932, 1936; Smreczyński, 1932; Inkmann, 1933; Butt, 1936; Wray, 1937; Tiegs and Murray, 1938; Mulnard, 1947; Luginbill, 1953; Deobahkta, 1957; Jura, 1957; Mazur, 1960; Ede, 1964; Ullman, 1967; Rempel and Church, 1969; Megaloptera: Strindberg, 1915a; Du Bois, 1938; Neuroptera: Bock, 1939; Trichoptera: Patten, 1884; Lepidoptera: Srivastava, 1967; Anderson and Wood, 1968, giving earlier references; Diptera: Du Bois, 1932; Gambrell, 1933; Poulson, 1950; Christophers, 1960; Anderson, 1962, 1966; Davis, 1967; Siphonaptera: Kessel, 1939; Hymenoptera: Carrière and Bürger, 1897; Nelson, 1915; Schnetter, 1934; Baerends and Baerends-von Roon, 1950; Shafiq, 1954; Ivanova-Kasas, 1958, 1959; Bronskill, 1959, 1964; Ochiai, 1960; Amy, 1961). Three median evaginations of the dorsal wall of the stomodaeum give rise to the frontal, hypocerebral and ventricular ganglia of the stomatogastric nervous system (Fig. 22c).

B. The Proctodaeum and Malpighian Tubules

The proctodaeum, as described by the same workers, also grows inwards as an epithelial tube and develops into the lining epithelium of the hind gut. At the distal end of the proctodaeum, blind outpouchings of the wall grow out into the haemocoele as Malpighian tubules (Figs 25a, b).

C. The Midgut

The midgut rudiments, anterior and posterior, are carried inwards at the distal ends of the stomodaeum and proctodaeum respectively, apposed to the ends of the shrinking yolk mass. In the majority of Holometabola, each midgut rudiment proliferates a pair of strands which grow ventrolaterally along the surface of the yolk mass and meet to form two continuous midgut strands (Figs 18d, 22a, 24d, 25a, b). With continued proliferation, the midgut cells now spread over the surface of the yolk mass, covering it first ventrally, then dorsally, to enclose the yolk within an ovoid epithelial sac. During further digestion of the yolk mass, the wall of the sac gives rise to the lining epithelium of the midgut (Fig. 25c). This mode of development has been described in some Coleoptera (Mansour, 1927; Smreczyński, 1932; Schienert, 1933; Butt, 1936; Wray, 1937; Tiegs and Murray, 1938; Luginbill, 1953; Deobahkta, 1957; Ullman, 1964; Rempel and Church, 1969) and in the Megaloptera (Strindberg, 1915a; Du Bois, 1938), Neuroptera (Bock, 1939), Trichoptera (Strindberg, 1915a), Diptera (Noack, 1901; Du Bois, 1932; Gambrell, 1933; Butt, 1934; Lassman, 1936; Ivanova-Kasas, 1949; Poulson, 1950; Formigoni, 1954; Christophers, 1960; Anderson, 1962, 1966;

Davis, 1967) and Siphonaptera (Kessel, 1939). In some chrysomelid beetles, the median cells of the inner layer, which normally develops as mesoderm and gives rise to haemocytes (see below), are said to contribute to the midgut (Hirschler, 1909; Paterson, 1932, 1936; Jura, 1957), but the evidence for this is far from convincing. In the chrysomelid *Calomela parilis*, the midgut

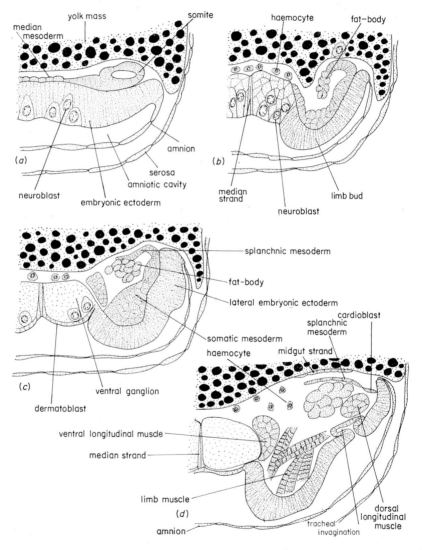

Fig. 24. Diagrammatic transverse sections through the metathoracic segment of *Chrysopa perla* Neuroptera) at stages from the first delineation of the segment (*a*), through (*b*) and (*c*), to the fully segmented germ band just before the onset of shortening (*d*). After Bock (1939).

develops from typical anterior and posterior midgut rudiments (Anderson and Creasey, unpublished).

The further development of the bipolar midgut rudiments proceeds in a modified way in both the Hymenoptera and the Lepidoptera. In the Hymenoptera (Figs 11c, 19b, c), rather than growing ventrally beneath the yolk

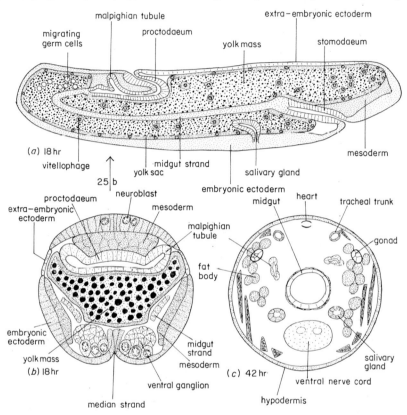

FIG. 25. (a) Diagrammatic reconstruction of the embryo of *Dacus tryoni* (Diptera) at 18 hours, during shortening of the germ band (compare Figs 15g, 21d, e); (b) Diagrammatic transverse section through the same stage at the level indicated on Fig. 25a; (c) Diagrammatic transverse section through the fifth abdominal segment of *D. tryoni* at the hatching stage. After Anderson (1962).

mass, the midgut rudiments grow first along the dorsal surface of the yolk mass, then spread ventrally (Carrière and Bürger, 1897; Nelson, 1915; Schnetter, 1934; Baerends and Baerends-von Roon, 1950; Shafiq, 1954; Ivanova-Kasas, 1959; Bronskill, 1959, 1964; Ochiai, 1960; Amy, 1961; DuPraw, 1967). It can be presumed that this modification is functionally associated with the vestigiality of the amnion of Hymenoptera, which leaves the dorsal surface of the yolk mass temporarily devoid of an epithelium after the serosa has formed. The modifications exhibited in the development of the midgut in Lepidoptera, on the other hand, are functionally associated with the unique mechanism of blastokinesis in this order (see below). Anderson and Wood (1968) have summarized the evidence that the midgut strands of the Lepidoptera are formed in the usual way, ventrolateral to the enclosed yolk in the immersed germ band (Figs 26*a*, *b*), but spread to form a tubular sac surrounding the enclosed yolk only after blastokinesis.

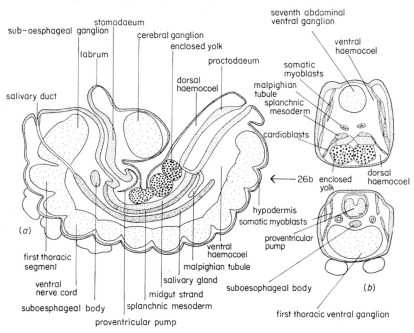

FIG. 26. (*a*) Diagrammatic sagittal section through the 72-hour embryo of *Epiphyas postvittann* (Lepidoptera), just before the onset of blastokinesis; (*b*) Frontal section through the same embryo at the level indicated on Fig. 26*a*. Due to the curvature of the embryo, the first thoracic and seventh abdominal segments are cut more or less transversely. After Anderson and Wood (1968).

D. Resorption of the Yolk Mass

There is no sound evidence that the vitellophages contribute to the midgut epithelium in any holometabolan. Usually the vitellophages are digested with the yolk (e.g. Nelson, 1915; Kessel, 1939; Anderson, 1962, 1966; Davis, 1967). Some holometabolan orders exhibit a temporary cellularization of the yolk mass into nucleated yolk spheres. This process of yolk cleavage, as it is usually called, has been described in some Coleoptera (Wheeler, 1889; Lecaillon, 1898; Strindberg, 1913; Paterson, 1931; Butt, 1936; Ullman, 1964, 1967), the Megaloptera (Du Bois, 1938), the Lepidoptera (Huie, 1918; Eastham, 1927; Johannsen, 1929; Sehl, 1931; Grandori, 1932; Saito, 1934;

Gross and Howland, 1941; Christensen, 1943*a*; Rempel, 1951; Krause and Krause, 1964; Bassand, 1965; Guénnelon, 1966; Reed and Day, 1966; Anderson and Wood, 1968; Mrkva, 1968), and the symphytan Hymenoptera (Ivanova-Kasas, 1959). Fusion of the yolk spheres takes place before the residue of the yolk is finally enclosed within the midgut epithelium. In some species of Diptera (Poulson, 1950; Anderson, 1962; Davis, 1967) and Hymenoptera (Bronskill, 1964), the vitellophages move to the surface of the yolk mass to form a temporary epithelium around which the definitive midgut epithelium is laid down.

XII. FURTHER DEVELOPMENT OF THE MESODERM AND GONADS

A. The Labial and Trunk Somites

In general terms, the further development of the mesoderm in the Holometabola follows the course described for the Hemimetabola in Chapter 3, although the detailed outcome is often highly specialized, especially in the arrangement of the larval musculature, and the origin of haemocytes is often diffuse in those embryos which omit the hollow somite stage of mesodermal development.

In orders in which hollow somites are developed, as was demonstrated by Bock (1939) and has recently been confirmed in detail by Ullman (1964) for *Tenebrio*, mesodermal development retains the full hemimetabolan pattern (Figs 22, 24; Coleoptera: Hirschler, 1909; Paterson, 1932, 1936; Wray, 1937; Tiegs and Murray, 1938; Deobahkta, 1957; Ullman, 1964; Neuroptera: Bock, 1939; Lepidoptera: Eastham, 1930; Presser and Rutchsky, 1957; Okada, 1960; Anderson and Wood, 1968; Siphonaptera: Kessel, 1939). The median mesoderm between the somites from the labial to the tenth abdominal segment proliferates as haemocytes (Hirschler, 1909; Nelson, 1915; Eastham, 1930; Smreczyński, 1932; Butt, 1936; Bock, 1939; Wigglesworth, 1959; Amy, 1961). The splanchnic walls of the somites separate off and become applied to the midgut strands as splanchnic mesoderm strands, whose major product is the musculature of the midgut (Fig. 22*a*). The somatic walls break up into somatic musculature and fat body. Cardioblasts differentiate at the dorsal junction of the somatic and splanchnic walls, are carried upwards during dorsal closure and give rise to the heart (Heider, 1889; Wheeler, 1889; Hirschler, 1909; Strindberg, 1913; Nelson, 1915; Paterson, 1932; Tiegs and Murray, 1938; Bock, 1939; Kessel, 1939; Amy, 1961). Adjacent somatic mesoderm cells form the alary muscles and pericardial septum. The proctodaeal musculature develops from a sheath of mesoderm formed around the proctodaeum by the residual mesoderm behind the tenth abdominal segment.

When somite formation is reduced or eliminated, as in the Hymenoptera and Diptera, the mesoderm still follows the same course of later development and gives rise to the same components (Figs 25*b*, *c*). Splanchnic strands usually separate off before the somatic mesoderm begins to differentiate into segmental musculature and fat body (Diptera: Du Bois, 1932; Gambrell, 1933; Poulson, 1950; Christophers, 1960; Anderson, 1962, 1966; Davis, 1967; Hymenoptera: Carrière and Bürger, 1897; Nelson, 1915; Schnetter, 1934; Baerends and Baerends-von Roon, 1950; Bronskill, 1959, 1964; Ivanova-Kasas, 1959).

Lepidopteran embryos, which otherwise retain the basic pattern of meso-derm development, combine delayed tubulation of the midgut with delayed formation of the heart. The cardioblasts (Fig. 26*b*) extend from the dorsolateral ectoderm to the splanchnic mesoderm strands as paired sheets of cells which separate the ventral epineural haemocoele from a small dorsal space occupied by yolk and walled by the amniotic provisional dorsal closure (Johannsen, 1929; Eastham, 1930; Sehl, 1931; Saito, 1937; Presser and Rutchsky, 1957; Anderson and Wood, 1968). The separation is effective over the entire distance between the stomodaeum and the proctodaeum, from the second thoracic to the seventh abdominal segment, and persists until blastokinesis is completed. Tubulation of the midgut, combined with definitive dorsal closure, then carries the cardioblasts into their mid-dorsal, heart-forming position. The delayed shift of the cardioblasts consequent on delayed tubula-tion of the gut is a second essential factor in the mechanism of lepidopteran blastokinesis, as will shortly be explained.

B. The Gonads and Gonoducts

The development of the gonads in the Holometabola is always completed in a relatively direct manner, reminiscent of that of the Paraneoptera. The primordial germ cells, once internal, subdivide into two groups which migrate either through or around the yolk (Fig. 25*a*) to enter the splanchnic mesoderm of the fifth and sixth abdominal segments. Here, each group of germ cells is enclosed in a mesodermal sheath, forming a pair of compact gonads (Carrière and Bürger, 1897; Hegner, 1909, 1914; Hirschler, 1909; Nelson, 1915; Henschen, 1928; Lautenschlager, 1932; Paterson, 1932, 1936; Inkmann, 1933; Hodson, 1934; Wray, 1937; Tiegs and Murray, 1938; Kessel, 1939; Baerends and Baerends-von Roon, 1950; Presser and Rutch-sky, 1957; Ivanova-Kasas, 1958, 1959; Amy, 1961; Bronskill, 1964; Anderson, 1966; Davis, 1967; Rempel and Church, 1969). The development of the genital ducts in the Holometabola takes place during post-embryonic development and is not included in the present account.

C. The Cephalic Mesoderm

The small mandibular and maxillary somites of the Holometabola give rise only to the limb musculature of their segments. The premandibular somites, also small, have usually been found to develop into the suboesophageal body (Coleoptera: Wray, 1937; Tiegs and Murray, 1938; Ullman, 1964; Megaloptera: Strindberg, 1915a; Lepidoptera: Eastham, 1930; Anderson and Wood, 1968), although Rempel and Church (1969) have ascribed an ectodermal origin to this structure in *Lytta viridana* (Coleoptera).

The antennal somites are larger. Their somatic walls give rise to the antennal musculature and to some additional fat body cells, while their splanchnic walls come together above the stomodaeum to form the anterior aorta in the same manner as in the Hemimetabola (Coleoptera: Smreczyński, 1932; Ullman, 1964; Lepidoptera: Eastham, 1930). The pre-antennal somites, when present, are usually said to contribute to the labral musculature, but according to Ullman (1964) they also give rise in *Tenebrio* to part of the stomodaeal musculature. In general, the stomodaeal musculature arises from the mesoderm between the antennal somites. This mesoderm forms a sheath around the stomodaeum as the latter grows into the interior. The terminal part of the stomodaeal mesodermal sheath in the Lepidoptera develops into a small sac, the proventricular pump (Figs 26a, b), which plays an essential role in blastokinesis before reverting to its normal differentiation as proventricular muscle (Toyama, 1902; Strindberg, 1915c; Johannsen, 1929; Eastham, 1930; Sehl, 1931; Grandori, 1932; Henson, 1932; Drummond, 1936; Saito, 1937; Mueller, 1938; Rempel, 1951; Presser and Rutchsky, 1957; Anderson and Wood, 1968).

XIII. LEPIDOPTERAN BLASTOKINESIS

The Lepidoptera are the only holometabolans whose embryos undergo marked changes in position and orientation within the egg space as development proceeds. Most other holometabolans, as has been described above, retain a constant position within the egg space both before and after rupture of the embryonic membranes. A few species with elongated, narrow eggs exhibit a 180° revolution of the embryo on the long axis during or after dorsal closure (some Nematocera: Gambrell, 1933; Craig, 1967; Kalthoff and Sander, 1968; some Hymenoptera: DuPraw, 1967).

The lepidopteran embryonic movements are usually referred to as blastokinesis, though they differ fundamentally from the blastokinesis of the Hemimetabola. The recent work of Reed and Day (1966) and Anderson and Wood (1968) has gone far towards explaining the mechanism of blastokinesis in the Lepidoptera. We have seen above that the embryonic primordium of Lepidoptera becomes immersed in the yolk mass, where it undergoes elongation, followed by shortening and provisional dorsal closure with accompanying preliminary organogeny, until the embryo lies free within the amniotic cavity, surrounded by a yolk-filled amnioserosal space (Figs 13, 21a). At this stage the embryo is short and tubular, with a convex ventral surface (Fig. 26a). The stomodaeum is large, with a terminal, mesodermal, proventricular pump opening into a dorsal haemocoelic space, enclosed by the provisional dorsal body wall and partially filled with yolk. Below the yolk, short midgut strands flanked by cardioblast sheets separate the dorsal space from a large ventral haemocoele (Fig. 26b). Around the proctodaeum, the dorsal space and ventral haemocoele are in communication.

Now, by a suctorial action of the stomodaeum, fluid is rhythmically transferred from the amniotic cavity to the proventricular pump, then forced by contraction of the pump along the narrow dorsal channel above the midgut-cardioblast membrane. Each pulse of fluid expands the posterior end of the embryo before flowing on into the capacious ventral haemocoele. The dilations of the posterior end produce a flexure, first ventrally, then forwards along the ventral surface, until the embryo has both doubled its length and reversed its curvature within the amniotic cavity (Figs 27a–c). The major source of fluid for this process is the amnioserosal space, in which the remaining yolk becomes densely packed as the fluid is transferred into the embryo.

As reversal proceeds, the somatic musculature differentiates to a striated condition. Muscular twitching begins when the caudal end is pressed hard against the head (Fig. 27b) and a series of rapid contractions pulls the tail into the space in the centre of the embryonic coil. With this final flexure, a further increase in length of the embryo becomes possible as the last of the fluid from the amnioserosal space is imbibed (Fig. 27c). Tubulation of the gut and formation of the heart now proceed.

Blastokinesis in *Epiphyas* takes about thirty hours in a total developmental period of seven days. The same change of position has been noted, without elucidation of its mechanism, in many other Lepidoptera (Johannsen, 1929; Eastham, 1930; Sehl, 1931; Wiesmann, 1935; Saito, 1937; Mueller, 1938; Rempel, 1951; Christensen, 1953; Presser and Rutchsky, 1957; Okada, 1960; Stairs, 1960; Bassand, 1965; Guénnelon, 1966; Mrkva, 1968) and is illustrated for *Anagasta mediterranea* (=*Ephestia kühniella*) in Figs 27d–f. A quiescent period now follows, during which organogeny proceeds to a preliminary functional condition and secretion of the cuticle begins. This period ends with the secretion of gas into the tracheal system (Christensen, 1953; Okada, 1960; Reed and Day, 1966), followed by the onset of complex muscular activity. The head and mouthparts become especially active and the embryo breaks through the amnion and begins to consume the solid residue of the yolk (Johannsen, 1929; Sehl, 1931; Rempel, 1951; Christensen, 1953; Okada, 1960; Stairs, 1960; Bassand, 1965; Guénnelon, 1966; Reed and Day, 1966; Anderson and Wood, 1968). The yolk, amnion and serosa are quickly ingested, accompanied by a further increase in volume which expands the embryo into the entire egg space. Functional organogeny is completed as the yolk is digested before hatching. Why the Lepidoptera should have evolved this astonishing series of embryonic modifications, which are not represented in a preliminary way in any other order of Holometabola, remains a mystery.

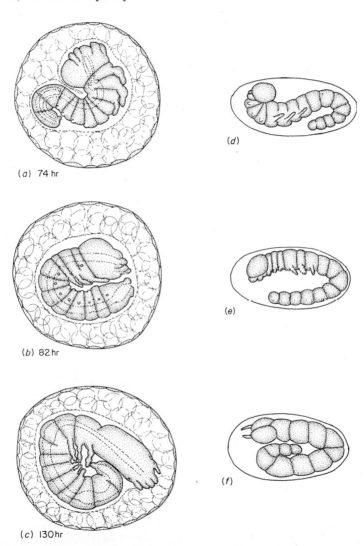

FIG. 27. (*a*) and (*b*) Stages in blastokinesis of the embryo of *Epiphyas postvittana* (Lepidoptera); (*c*) The same embryo after blastokinesis, during the ingestion of the remaining yolk; after Anderson and Wood (1968). The egg is viewed from the dorsal surface; (*d*)–(*f*) Corresponding stages of the embryo of *Anagasta kühniella* (Lepidoptera), after Sehl (1931).

XIV. THE COMPOSITION OF THE HEAD IN HOLOMETABOLA

As in the case of the hemimetabolan head, the existence of three gnathal, a premandibular and an antennal segment as components of the head in Holometabola is not in doubt (Matsuda, 1965; Gouin, 1968) and has been amply confirmed by Ullman (1964, 1967) and Rempel and Church (1969). The preantennal region presents the usual difficulties of interpretation. A pair of preantennal somites is sometimes retained in the Coleoptera (Ullman, 1964; Rempel and Church, 1969) and Lepidoptera (Eastham, 1930), but no trace of associated preantennal ganglia or limb vestiges can be discerned. As in the Hemimetabola, therefore, we have very little evidence for the existence of a preantennal segment between the large acron and the definitive antennal segment in Holometabola. Matsuda (1965) rejected the possibility that preantennal somites alone imply such a segment. Ullman (1967), on the other hand, finds this evidence acceptable. In fact, the Holometabola do nothing to further the argument either way and can only be interpreted in the same manner as the Hemimetabola

XV. THE ORIGINS OF THE ADULT ORGANIZATION IN DIPTERA

Temporal polymorphism in the post-embryonic development of the Holometabola manifests varying degrees of expression, from a slight sequential change in the Megaloptera and Neuroptera to an extreme of metamorphosis in the cyclorrhaphous Diptera. In all holometabolan orders except the Diptera, the development of the adult organization begins in the larvae, so that the changes leading to metamorphosis lie outside the scope of the present chapter. The Cyclorrhapha, however, exhibit a fundamental segregation of larval and adult structural rudiments during the development of the embryo. The details of this structural duality were analysed by Anderson (1963*a*, *b*, 1964*a*, *b*, 1966) in the Queensland fruit fly, *Dacus tryoni*.

During organogenesis in the embryo of *D. tryoni*, a number of groups of cells remain embryonic and undergo their first proliferation as adult rudiments. In the ectoderm, these groups comprise:

(a) A pair of cephalic discs, formed as small pockets evaginated at the posterolateral corners of the frontal sac, the dorsal part of the cephalopharynx.

(b) Three pairs of thoracic discs, formed ventrolaterally in the three thoracic segments. The prothoracic discs remain superficial, but the meso- and metathoracic discs each proliferate a stalk into the interior and the ends of the stalks enlarge and hollow out as paired wing and haltere discs.

(c) A median genital disc, invaginated in the ventral midline at the anterior lip of the anus.

Internally, imaginal rudiments are segregated in the wall of the gut of the embryo as:

(a) A foregut ring, formed in the proventriculus by the terminal cells of the stomodaeum.

(b) A hindgut ring, formed by the proctodaeal cells just behind the roots of the Malpighian tubules.

(c) Imaginal midgut cells, scattered throughout the midgut at the base of the larval epithelium and formed from embryonic midgut cells.

Each salivary gland also develops an imaginal salivary gland ring, formed by cells of the epithelium of the gland at the junction with the duct.

During larval development, a number of additional imaginal rudiments become detectable. These comprise:

(a) A pair of ectodermal labial discs, formed in the floor of the anterior end of the cephalopharynx.

(b) Two pairs of ectodermal abdominal discs in each of the seven segments of the abdomen.

(c) A small group of tracheal cells in the wall of each of the segmental junctions between the longitudinal tracheal trunks and their segmented branches.

Each rudiment develops from cells which arrived at these locations during embryonic development and differs from the previously listed rudiments only in a later onset of visible differentiation.

The heart, Malpighian tubules and nervous system do not contain separate adult rudiments either in the embryo or larva. The heart and Malpighian tubules remain functional throughout metamorphosis. The nervous system is extensively remodelled, but does not undergo the breakdown and replacement at metamorphosis that the other organ systems display. The somatic musculature, splanchnic musculature and fat body of the adult are not represented in the embryo or larva as distinct rudiments.

During larval development, the cells of all larval structures except the nervous system enlarge and develop polytene nuclei. The cells of the adult rudiments proliferate, but do not differentiate to a functional condition. The thoracic limb rudiments invaginate into the interior. During metamorphosis, the polytene larval tissues, excepting only the heart and Malpighian tubules, disintegrate and are replaced by the corresponding adult tissues. Each major component of the larval ectodermal wall (head, mouthparts, three thoracic segments, seven abdominal segments and terminal abdominal region) is replaced by the imaginal discs that it previously encompassed. Similarly, each major component of the larval gut (foregut, midgut, hindgut and salivary glands) is replaced by the imaginal cells lying within it. New outer and inner walls are thus formed, between which the adult mesodermal organs are laid down as new constructions, probably formed by cells proliferated as descendants of the embryonic mesoderm.

The extreme metamorphosis of the Cyclorrhapha can thus be seen to rest on a basically simple modification of embryonic development (Fig. 28). When the germ band is formed, each presumptive area with the exception of the mesodermal and neural areas comprises cells of two types, those which will give rise to the adult product of the area and those which will form its larval equivalent. Garcia-Bellido and Merriam (1969) have independently arrived at the same conclusion from a different point of view, through an analysis of gynandromorphs of *Drosophila*, and further evidence is provided by Bryant and Schneiderman (1969). The adult ectodermal and gut components develop

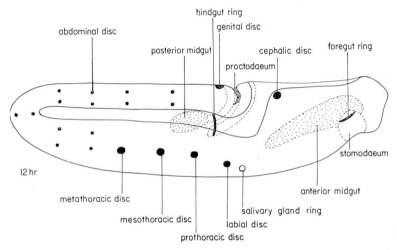

Fig. 28. The distribution of the imaginal hypodermal and gut rudiments in the gastrula of *Dacus tryoni* (Diptera), after Anderson (1966). Figures 12*e* and 15*g* show other aspects of the same embryo.

directly, but show modifications which give space for the temporary development of associated cells as corresponding larval parts. The latter evoke the development of a specialized larval mesodermal apparatus, subsequently replaced during metamorphosis by an adult mesodermal apparatus probably evoked from cells of the same blastodermal source, presumptive mesoderm.

A brief speculation can be made on the evolution of this system. Holometabolan metamorphosis originated, presumably, from hemimetabolan metamorphosis, itself based on the responses of growing tissues to a changing hormonal *milieu*. Wigglesworth has interpreted these responses as an interaction between genome and hormone system, in which each cell line manifests different expressions of gene-determined morphology according to the presence or absence of juvenile hormone. The Holometabola, it can be suggested, evolved through a change which segregated the larval and adult responses of the genome into separate cell lines. In most Holometabola the segregation is incomplete and takes place in the larva. Earlier segregation is advantageous in permitting greater larval specialization without destroying the capacity to develop into a normal adult insect. The extreme condition seen in the higher Diptera requires a shift of segregation into the prefunctional and prehormonal phase of development. Waddington's genetic assimilation provides an appropriate mechanism for such a shift. It is also of interest that ectodermal evocation of mesodermal differentiation, a known insectan feature, is a prerequisite for the evolution of this type of elaborate metamorphosis. If a reconstruction of the mesodermal organization was the first essential step in the causal sequence, rather than reconstruction of the ectodermal body wall and the gut wall, each individual muscle would have to contain its own adult rudiment and no major change in muscle pattern could take place.

XVI. HOLOMETABOLAN EMBRYOLOGY AND EVOLUTION

The comparative embryology of the Holometabola reveals almost nothing of the origin and phylogenetic history of this group of insects, other than a few general trends. It is obvious that holometabolan embryonic development, as expressed in the formation and fates of presumptive areas, is a modification of basic hemimetabolan embryonic development. It is also obvious that one fundamental innovation in the Holometabola has been a change in the ratio of cytoplasm to yolk in the egg, making possible the direct formation of larger presumptive areas and, consequently, a more direct and rapid development (see Section VI, B). Beyond this, the pattern of embryonic development has changed, in parallel in several orders, in the direction of further streamlining and simplification, associated with the reduction or elimination of ancestral irrelevancies such as somite formation, forward migration of the antennal segment and proliferation of abdominal segments from a growth zone, and with development to hatching as a structurally simplified, active larva. The Lepidoptera have evolved a unique new relationship with yolk, in consequence of which the larva is fully functional and highly active as soon as it hatches. The apocritan Hymenoptera and cyclorrhaphous Diptera have evolved the most rapid and direct sequences of embryonic development of all insects, hatching as simple vermiform larvae a day or two after oviposition. In the case of the Diptera, however, the apparent secondary simplicity of the embryo is deceptive. As discussed above, there has been a concomitant evolution of an elaborate process of segregation of larval and adult rudiments during embryonic development. Much remains to be learned of the extent to which this phenomenon is predicated in the embryos of other orders of Holometabola.

XVII. NORMAL TABLES OF HOLOMETABOLAN DEVELOPMENT

As in the previous chapter, the present account is terminated by three normal tables of development, accompanied by appropriate illustrations. The examples of holometabolan development summarized in these tables,

TABLE IV. The Embryonic Development of *Bruchidius obtectus* (Coleoptera) at 20°C: Modified after Jung (1966a)

0–6½ hours: Completion of maturation and fertilization is followed by the first two synchronous cleavage divisions (Figs 1, 3a and d). Compare Fig. 29a.

6½–12½ hours: The third to eighth synchronous cleavage divisions take place and the majority of the resulting 256 cleavage energids migrate outwards and merge with the periplasm (Figs 3b, c and e). Compare Fig. 29b.

12½–38 hours: The ninth to thirteenth synchronous nuclear divisions occur, followed by cellularization of the syncytial blastoderm (Figs 3f and g). The uniform blastoderm comprises about 8000 cells.

38–40 hours: The majority of the blastoderm cells concentrate into a long, broad embryonic primordium, accompanied and followed by formation of the inner layer (Fig. 5c). Compare Figs 29c–e.

40–48 hours: The segment-forming growth zone at the posterior end of the germ band becomes active, and the germ band begins to extend over the posterior pole of the yolk mass and forwards along the dorsal surface (compare Fig. 29g). The head lobes, gnathal segments and first thoracic segment are delineated (Fig. 9a).

2–3 days: As elongation and segment delineation continue, the embryonic membranes (amnion and serosa) are completed. The labrum, antennae, gnathal and thoracic limb rudiments develop (Figs 9b and c). Compare Figs 29e–g.

3–5 days: The germ band shortens, bringing the posterior end of the abdomen back to the posterior pole of the yolk mass, and spreads partially up the sides of the yolk mass (Fig. 19a). The amnion becomes applied to the remainder of the surface of the yolk mass. External to the embryo, the major part of the amnion persists as a second membrane beneath the serosa.

6–9 days: Dorsal closure is followed by secretion of the cuticle, completion of organogenesis and histodifferentiation, and resorption of the remaining yolk. When hatching takes place at 9 days (Fig. 19b), the amnion and serosa are left in the shell.

TABLE V. The Embryonic Development of *Epiphyas postvittana* (Lepidoptera) at 28°C: Modified after Reed and Day (1966) and Anderson and Wood (1968)

1–14 hours: Intralecithal cleavage leads to formation of the uniform cuboidal blastoderm of about 2000 cells (Fig. 30a).

14–16 hours: Over a broad, posteroventral area, the blastoderm cells concentrate to form the embryonic primordium, extending across the ventral face of the yolk mass and curving up onto the dorsal surface at each end (Figs 7b, 17e and 30b). The margin of the extra-embryonic blastoderm separates from the embryonic primordium and merges to complete the serosa.

TABLE V—(*continued*)

16–20 hours: The embryonic primordium becomes more compact and cup-shaped, enclosing part of the yolk mass (Fig. 30*c*). The margin of the cup-shaped primordium turns ventrally and spreads over the ventral face of the cup, forming the amnion (Fig. 17*f*). In the ventral midline of the primordium a small group of rounded cells separates into the interior as primordial germ cells.

20–24 hours: The embryonic primordium elongates, develops head lobes anteriorly and rotates onto its side (Figs 13*a*, *b*, 17*g*, 30*d* and *e*). The yolk mass becomes divided into yolk spheres. Formation of the inner layer begins.

24–28 hours: The segment-forming growth zone becomes active and the germ band increases in length and undergoes segment delineation and early limb bud formation (antennal, gnathal and thoracic). The germ band coils as it grows (Figs 13*c* and 30*f*). A small amount of yolk is enclosed along the length of the germ band. The remainder lies in the space between the amnion and serosa.

28–48 hours: Elongation and segmentation are completed, accompanied by formation of the stomodaeum and proctodaeum (Figs 13*d*, 30*g* and *h*). Midgut strands develop, and the segmental mesoderm undergoes preliminary differentiation as myoblasts and fat body cells.

48–64 hours: Shortening and dorsal closure occur (Figs 21*a*, 30*i* and *j*) as a result of a series of slow, generalized, muscular contractions of the germ band. The embryo now lies within the amniotic cavity.

64–72 hours: Muscular contractions become localized in a small mesodermal sac, the proventricular pump, at the distal end of the stomodaeum.

72–99 hours: Blastokinesis takes place. The proventricular pump transfers amniotic fluid, taken up by the stomodaeum, to the posterior end of the embryo. As the embryo increases in length, the posterior end pushes forward along the ventral surface until the curvature of the embryo is reversed (Figs 27*a*, *b*, 30*j–n*). Contractions of segmental muscles tuck the posterior end of the abdomen into the space enclosed by the curved body. During this period, the tracheal invaginations are formed, the midgut becomes tubular and the heart is established.

99–117 hours: The embryo becomes quiescent while further histodifferentiation takes place and the yolk enclosed in the midgut is resorbed. The cuticle is secreted.

117–124 hours: A sudden secretion of gas into the tracheal system (Fig. 30*o*) is followed by an increase in the rate of heart beat and in the general muscular activity of the head region and the gut.

124–140 hours: The head of the embryo thrusts through the amnion and begins to ingest the remaining yolk (Figs 27*c*, 30*p* and *q*). The yolk is packed into the midgut until none remains outside the embryo. The embryo enlarges until it occupies all of the space enclosed by the egg membranes.

140–160 hours: Muscular activity of the body wall and gut continue as the ingested yolk is digested. Histodifferentiation is completed, the cuticle becomes pigmented and sclerotized and the larva hatches by rupturing the enclosing chorion (Fig. 30*r*).

TABLE VI. The Embryonic Development of *Dacus tryoni* (Diptera) at 25°C: Modified from Anderson (1962, 1963a, 1964a)

0–½ hour: Completion of maturation and fertilization lead to formation of the zygote (Figs 2 and 31a).

½–1 hour: The first and second synchronous cleavage divisions occur (Fig. 31b).

1–2 hours: The third to sixth synchronous cleavage mitoses result in the formation of 64 energids, uniformly distributed through the yolk mass (Fig. 4a).

2–3 hours: The seventh synchronous cleavage is followed by uniform invasion of the periplasm by about 90 energids (Fig. 31c). The remainder persist within the yolk mass as primary vitellophages. The eighth to tenth synchronous cleavages now occur, yielding approximately 720 superficial nuclei and 300 primary vitellophages (Fig. 4b).

3–4 hours: The eleventh and twelfth synchronous mitoses of the superficial nuclei take place. At the posterior end, four pole cells are cut off and divide once, yielding eight cells.

4–5 hours: The last synchronous mitotic division of the superficial nuclei takes place (Fig. 4d) yielding approximately 5800 nuclei. The pole cells divide again, giving 16 cells.

5–6 hours: The syncytial blastoderm is established (Figs 4e and 31d) and the pole cells divide again, into 32 cells.

6–7½ hours: The blastoderm becomes cellular. The vitellophages aggregate along the midline of the yolk (Figs 4f, 31e, f and g).

7½–12 hours: Gastrulation takes place, accompanied by elongation of the germ band and attenuation of the extra-embryonic ectoderm (Figs 12c–e, 15d–g, 16c, 31h and 32a–e).

12–17 hours: External delineation of segments is initiated in anteroposterior succession (Fig. 21d).

17–24 hours: Continued delineation of trunk segments is accompanied by shortening of the germ band and associated partial dorsal closure (Figs 21e and f). The brain and ventral nerve cord become internal (Figs 32f and g) and involution of the head begins. During this period, the midgut strands are formed and the salivary glands and Malpighian tubules begin to develop (Figs 25a, b and 32h).

24–28 hours: Dorsal closure is completed, the midgut becomes tubular, involution of the head continues and histodifferentiation begins (Figs 21g and h). The thoracic, genital, foregut and salivary-gland imaginal rudiments become recognizable histologically.

28–32 hours: Involution of the head is completed, histodifferentiation continues, the midgut undergoes preliminary elongation and convolution and the central nervous system begins to condense. The cephalic imaginal discs and imaginal hindgut rudiment can be identified.

32–42 hours: Histodifferentiation is completed (Figs 21i and 25c), accompanied by secretion of the cuticle, resorption of the remaining yolk, condensation of the central nervous system and secretion of gas in the tracheal system. The larva hatches at 42 hours.

Bruchidius obtectus (Coleoptera), *Epiphyas postvittana* (Lepidoptera) and *Dacus tryoni* (Diptera) represent a basic and two widely divergent specialized types of holometabolan embryos. Other informative chronological summaries of holometabolan embryonic development can be found in the works of Poulson (1950) and Doane (1967) on *Drosophila melanogaster*, and DuPraw (1967) on the honey bee, *Apis mellifera*.

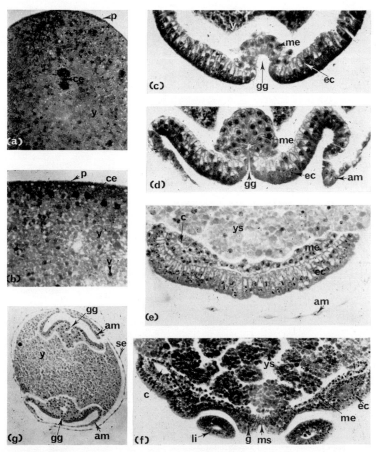

FIG. 29. Development of *Calomela parilis* (Coleoptera, Chrysomelidae). (*a*) A portion of the egg during the second cleavage division; (*b*) A portion of the egg after the eighth cleavage division; (*c*)–(*e*) Transverse sections of the germ band during formation of the inner layer and embryonic membranes; (*f*) Transverse section through the segmenting germ band; (*g*) Transverse section showing that the posterior end of the elongating germ band, as it extends along the dorsal surface of the yolk mass during gastrulation, becomes slightly immersed in the yolk mass. am, amnion; c, coelomic cavity; ce, cleavage energid; ec, segmental ectoderm; g, ganglion; gg, gastral groove; li, limb bud; me, mesoderm; ms, median strand; p, periplasm; v, vitellophage; y, yolk; ys, yolk sphere.

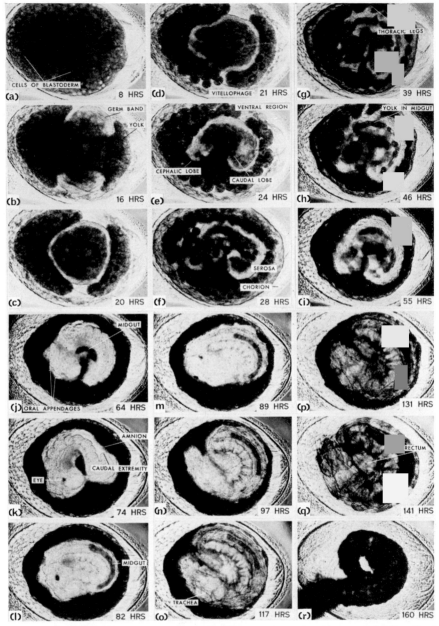

FIG. 30. Development of *Epiphyas postvittana* (Lepidoptera). Reproduced by permission from Reed and Day (1966). (*a*)–(*e*) Formation of the embryonic primordium; (*f*)–(*h*) Elongation and segmentation of the germ band; (*i*)–(*j*) Shortening and dorsal closure; (*k*)–(*n*) Blastokinesis; (*o*)–(*q*) Tracheal gas secretion, ingestion of residual yolk, completion or organogeny; (*r*) Hatching.

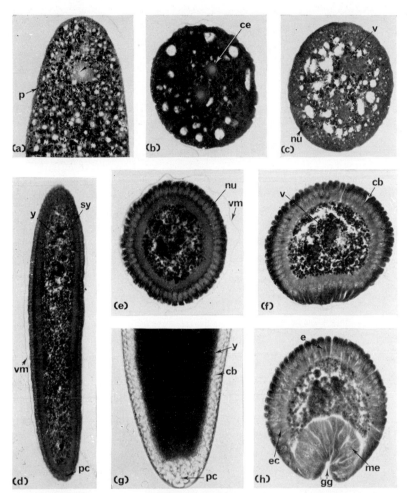

Fig. 31. Development of *Dacus tryoni* (Diptera). Reproduced from Anderson (1962). (*a*) Anterior end of the zygote, frontal section; (*b*) Transverse section through the egg after first cleavage; (*c*) Transverse section through the egg after seventh cleavage; (*d*) Frontal section through the syncytial blastoderm; (*e*) Transverse section during cellularization of the syncytial blastoderm; (*f*) Transverse section through the uniform cellular blastoderm at the onset of gastrulation; (*g*) The posterior end of a living embryo at the cellular blastoderm stage, showing the blastoderm and pole cells; (*h*) Transverse section during gastrulation. cb, cellular blastoderm; ce, cleavage energid; e, extra-embryonic ectoderm; ec, embryonic ectoderm; gg, gastral groove; me, mesoderm; nu, nucleus; p, periplasm; pc, pole cells; sy, syncytial blastoderm; v, vitellophage; vm, vitelline membrane; y, yolk; z, zygote nucleus.

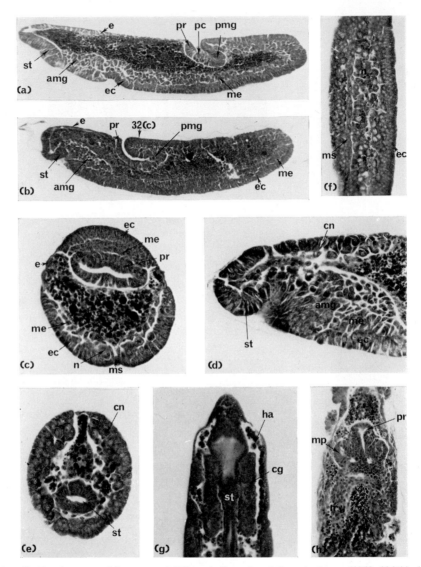

FIG. 32. Development of *Dacus tryoni* (Diptera). Reproduced from Anderson (1962, 1963b). (*a*) Sagittal section through a 9-hour embryo, during gastrulation and elongation of the germ band; (*b*) Sagittal section through a 12-hour embryo, after completion of gastrulation and elongation (compare Fig. 15*g*); (*c*) Transverse section through a 12-hour embryo, at the level indicated on Fig. 32*b*; (*d*) Sagittal section through the anterior end of a 12-hour embryo; (*e*) Transverse section through the anterior end of a 14-hour embryo; (*f*) Frontal section through the developing ventral nerve cord and median strand of a 14-hour embryo; (*g*) Frontal section through the anterior end of a 24-hour embryo; (*h*) Frontal section through an 18-hour embryo showing the development of Malpighian tubules and posterior midgut strands (compare Fig. 25*a*). amg, anterior midgut rudiment; cg, cerebral ganglion; cn, cerebral neuroblast; e, extra-embryonic ectoderm; ha, haemocyte; me, mesoderm; mg, midgut strand; mp, malpighian tubule; ms, median strand; n, neuroblast; pc, pole cells; pmg, posterior midgut; pr, proctodaeum; st, stomodaeum.

REFERENCES

Agrell, I. (1963). *Ark. Zool.*, **15**, 143–148.
Alléaume, N. (1965). *Proc. Soc. Sci. Phys. Nat. Bordeaux*, **1965**, 99–103.
Amy, R. J. (1961). *J. Morph.*, **109**, 199–218.
Anderson, D. T. (1962). *J. Embryol. exp. Morph.*, **10**, 248–292.
Anderson, D. T. (1963*a*). *J. Embryol. exp. Morph.*, **11**, 339–351.
Anderson, D. T. (1963*b*). *Aust. J. Zool.*, **11**, 202–218.
Anderson, D. T. (1964*a*). *J. Embryol. exp. Morph.*, **12**, 64–75.
Anderson, D. T. (1964*b*). *Aust. J. Zool.*, **12**, 1–8.
Anderson, D. T. (1966). *A. Rev. Ent.*, **11**, 23–64.
Anderson, D. T. and Wood, E. C. (1968). *Aust. J. Zool.*, **16**, 763–793.
Ando, H. (1960). *Sci. Rep. Tokyo Kyoiku Daig.*, **B9**, 141–143.
Ando, H. and Okada, M. (1958). *Acta hymenopt.*, **1**, 55–62.
Auten, M. (1934). *Ann. ent. Soc. Am.*, **27**, 481–506.
Baerends, G. P. and Baerends-von Roon, J. M. (1950). *Tijdschr. Ent.*, **92**, 53–112.
Bassand, D. (1965). *Revue suisse Zool.*, **72**, 431–542.
Blunck, H. (1914). *Z. wiss. Zool.*, **111**, 76–151.
Bock, E. (1939). *Z. Morph. Ökol. Tiere*, **35**, 615–702.
Brauer, A. (1949). *J. exp. Zool.*, **112**, 165–193.
Breuning, S. (1957). *Zool. Jb. Anat. Ont.*, **75**, 551–580.
Bronskill, J. F. (1959). *Can. J. Zool.*, **37**, 655–688.
Bronskill, J. F. (1964). *Can. J. Zool.*, **42**, 439–453.
Bryant, P. J. and Schneiderman, H. A. (1969). *Devl Biol.*, **20**, 263–290.
Bull, A. L. (1956). *J. exp. Zool.*, **132**, 467–500.
Butt, F. H. (1934). *Ann. ent. Soc. Am.*, **27**, 565–579.
Butt, F. H. (1936). *Ann. ent. Soc. Am.*, **29**, 1–13.
Carrière, J. and Bürger, O. (1897). *Nova. Acta. Acad. Caesar Leop. Carol.*, **69**, 255–420.
Christensen, P. J. H. (1943*a*). *Vidensk. Meddr. dansk. naturh. Foren.*, **106**, 1–223.
Christensen, P. J. H. (1943*b*). *Ent. Meddr.*, **23**, 204–223.
Christensen, P. J. H. (1953). *K. danske Vidensk. Selsk. Skr.*, **6**, no. 9, 1–46.
Christophers, Sir S. R. (1960). *Aedes aegypti L., The Yellow Fever Mosquito. Its Life History, Bionomics and Structure.* University Press, Cambridge.
Counce, S. J. (1956). *Z. indukt. Abstamm.-Vererblehre*, **84**, 38–70.
Counce, S. J. (1963). *J. Morph.*, **112**, 129–146.
Counce, S. J. (1972). *Developmental Systems: Insects* (S. J. Counce and C. H. Waddington, eds), Vol. 2, p. 1. Academic Press, London and New York.
Counce, S. J. and Selman, G. G. (1955). *J. Embryol. exp. Morph.*, **3**, 121–141.
Craig, D. A. (1967). *Trans. R. Soc. N.Z. Zool.*, **8**, 191–206.
Craig, D. A. (1969). *Can. J. Zool.*, **47**, 495–503.
Davis, C. W. (1967). *Aust. J. Zool.*, **15**, 547–579.
Davis, C. W., Krause, J. and Krause, G. (1968). *Wilhelm Roux Arch. EntwMech. Org.*, **161**, 209–240.
De Coursey, J. D. and Webster, A. P. (1953). *Ann. ent. Soc. Am.*, **45**, 625–632.
Deegener, P. (1900). *Z. wiss. Zool.*, **68**, 113–168.
Deobahkta, S. R. (1952). *Agra Univ. J. Res.*, **2**, 125–134.
Deobahkta, S. R. (1957). *Agra Univ. J. Res.*, **6**, 92–172.
Doane, W. W. (1967). In *Methods in Developmental Biology* (F. H. Wilt and N. K. Wessells, eds), pp. 219–244. Crowell, New York.
Dobrowski, Z. (1959). *Zesz. nauk. Uniw. jagiellonsk Zool.*, **4**, 5–29.
Drummond, M. (1936). *Q . Jl microsc. Sci.*, **79**, 533–542.

Du Bois, A. M. (1932). *J. Morph.*, **54**, 161–192.
Du Bois, A. M. (1936). *Revue suisse Zool.*, **43**, 519–523.
Du Bois, A. M. (1938). *Revue suisse Zool.*, **45**, 1–92.
DuPraw, E. J. (1967). In *Methods in Developmental Biology* (F. H. Wilt and N. K. Wessels, eds), pp. 183–217. Crowell, New York.
Eastham, L. E. S. (1927). *Q . Jl microsc. Sci.*, **71**, 353–394.
Eastham, L. E. S. (1930). *Phil. Trans. R. Soc.*, **B219**, 1–50.
Ede, D. A. (1956a). *Wilhelm Roux Arch. EntwMech. Org.*, **148**, 416–436.
Ede, D. A. (1956b). *Wilhelm Roux Arch. EntwMech. Org.*, **148**, 437–451.
Ede, D. A. (1956c). *Wilhelm Roux Arch. EntwMech. Org.*, **149**, 88–100.
Ede, D. A. (1964). *J. Embryol. exp. Morph.*, **12**, 551–562.
Ede, D. A. and Counce, S. J. (1956). *Wilhelm Roux Arch. EntwMech. Org.*, **148**, 259–266.
Ede, D. A. and Rogers, A. M. (1964). *J. Embryol exp. Morph.* **12**, 539–549.
Escherich, K. (1900a). *Verh. dt. zool. Ges.*, **10**, 130–134.
Escherich, K. (1900b). *Nova Acta Acad. Caesar Leop. Carol.*, **77**, 299–357.
Escherich, K. (1901a). *Allg. Z. Ent.*, **6**, 79.
Escherich, K. (1901b). *Biol. Zbl.*, **21**, 416–431.
Escherich, K. (1902). *Z. wiss. Zool.*, **71**, 525–549.
Ewest, A. (1937). *Wilhelm Roux Arch. EntwMech. Org.*, **135**, 689–752.
Farooqui, M. M. (1963). *Aligarh Musl. Univ. Publs.*, **6**, 1–68.
Fish, W. A. (1947). *Ann. ent. Soc. Am.*, **40**, 15–28.
Fish, W. A. (1949). *Ann. ent. Soc. Am.*, **42**, 121–133.
Formigoni, A. (1954). *Boll. zool. ag. Bachic.*, **20**, 111–154.
Friedmann, N. (1934). *Commentat. Biol.*, **4**(10), 1–29.
Gambrell, F. L. (1933). *Ann. ent. Soc. Am.*, **26**, 641–671.
Garcia–Bellido, A. and Merriam, J. R. (1969). *J. exp. Zool.*, **170**, 61–76.
Gaumont, R. (1951). *Annls. Épiphyt.*, **1**, 253–273.
Geyer-Duzynska, I. (1959). *J. exp. Zool.*, **141**, 391–449.
Gouin, F. L. (1968). *Fortschr. Zool.*, **19**, 194–282.
Graber, V. (1889). *Denkschr. Akad. Wiss. Wien.*, **56**, 257–314.
Grandori, R. (1932). *Boll. zool. ag. Bachic.*, **3**, 43–128.
Grassi, B. (1886). *Archo. ital. Biol.*, **7**, 242–273.
Gross, J. B. and Howland, R. B. (1941). *Ann. ent. Soc. Am.*, **33**, 56–66.
Guénnelon, G. (1966). *Annls. Épiphyt.*, **17**, 3–135.
Hagan, H. R. (1951). *Embryology of Viviparous Insects.* Ronald Press, New York.
Haget, A. (1953). *Bull. biol. Fr. Belg.*, **87**, 123–217.
Haget, A. (1955). *C. r. Séanc. Soc. Biol.*, **149**, 690–692.
Haget, A. (1957). *Bull. Soc. zool. Fr.*, **82**, 269–295.
Hardenburg, J. D. F. (1929). *Zool. Jb. Anat. Ont.*, **50**, 497–570.
Hasper, M. (1911). *Zool. Jb. Anat. Ont.*, **31**, 543–612.
Hathaway, D. S. and Selman, G. G. (1961). *J. Embryol. exp. Morph.*, **9**, 310–325.
Hegner, R. W. (1909). *J. Morph.*, **20**, 231–296.
Hegner, R. W. (1910). *Biol. Bull. mar. biol. Lab., Woods Hole.*, **19**, 18–30.
Hegner, R. W. (1911). *Biol. Bull. mar. biol. Lab., Woods Hole.*, **20**, 237–251.
Hegner, R. W. (1912). *Science, N.Y.*, **36**, 124–126.
Hegner, R. W. (1914). *J. Morph.*, **25**, 375–509.
Hegner, R. W. (1915). *J. Morph.*, **26**, 495–561.
Heider, K. (1889). *Die Embryonalentwicklung von Hydrophilus piceus L.* Gustav Fischer, Jena.
Henschen, W. (1928). *Z. Morph. Ökol. Tiere*, **13**, 144–179.

Henson, H. (1932). *Q . Jl microsc. Sci.*, **75**, 283–309.
Heymons, R. (1895). *Die Embryonalentwickelung von Dermapteren und Orthopteren unter Besonderer Berucksichtigung der Keimblatterbildung.* Gustav Fischer, Jena.
Hildreth, P. F. and Luchesi, J. C. (1963). *Devl Biol.*, **6**, 262–278.
Hirschler, J. (1905). *Bull. int. Acad. Sci. Lett. Cracovie*, **B1905**, 802–810.
Hirschler, J. (1909). *Z. wiss. Zool.*, **92**, 627–744.
Hodson, A. C. (1934). *Ann. ent. Soc. Am.*, **27**, 278–288.
Huettner, A. F. (1924). *J. Morph.*, **39**, 249–265.
Huettner, A. F. (1927). *Z. Zellforsch. mikrosk. Anat.*, **4**, 599–610.
Huie, L. H. (1918). *Proc. R. Soc. Edinb.*, **38**, 154–165.
Idris, B. E. M. (1960). *Z. Morph. Ökol. Tiere*, **49**, 387–429.
Inkmann, F. (1933). *Zool. Jb. Anat. Ont.*, **56**, 521–558.
Ivanova-Kasas, O. M. (1949). *Izv. Akad. Nauk. SSSR Ser. Biol.*, **2**, 140–170.
Ivanova-Kasas, O. M. (1954). *Trudy leningr. Obshch. Estest.*, **72**, 53–73.
Ivanova-Kasas, O. M. (1958). *Ent. Obozr.*, **37**, 1–18.
Ivanova-Kasas, O. M. (1959). *Zool. Jb. Anat. Ont.*, **77**, 193–228
Ivanova-Kasas, O. M. (1960). *Ent. Obozr.*, **39**, 284–295.
Ivanova-Kasas, O. M. (1964). *Vestn. leningr. gos. Univ.*, *Ser. Biol.*, **21**, 12–27.
Ivanova-Kasas, O. M. (1965). *Acta Biol.*, *Szeged*, **16**, 1–24.
Ivanova-Kasas, O. M. (1972). In *Developmental Systems : Insects.* (S. J. Conce and C. H. Waddington, eds), Vol. 1, p. 243. Academic Press, London and New York.
Janet, C. (1899). *Mem. Soc. zool. Fr.*, **12**, 295–335.
Johannsen, O. A. (1929). *J. Morph.*, **48**, 493–541.
Johannsen, O. A. and Butt, F. H. (1941). *Embryology of Insects and Myriapods.* McGraw–Hill, New York.
Jung, E. (1966a). *Z. Morph. Ökol. Tiere*, **56**, 444–480.
Jung, E. (1966b). *Wilhelm Roux Arch. EntwMech. Org.*, **157**, 320–392.
Jura, C. (1957). *Zoologica Pol.*, **8**, 177–199.
Kahle, W. (1908). *Zoologica Stuttg.*, **21**, 1–80.
Kalthoff, K. and Sander, K. (1968). *Wilhelm Roux Arch. EntwMech. Org.*, **161**, 129–146.
Kessel, E. L. (1939). *Smithson, misc. Collns.*, **98**, 1–78.
Klausnitzer, B. (1969). *Acta ent. Bohemoslov.*, **66**, 146–149.
Korschelt, E. (1912). *Zool. Jb. suppl.*, **152**, 499–532.
Kraczkiewicz, Z. (1935). *C. r. Séanc. Soc. Biol.*, **119**, 1201–1206.
Krause, J. B. and Ryan, M. T. (1953). *Ann. ent. Soc. Am.*, **46**, 1–20.
Krause, G. and Krause, J. (1964). *Wilhelm Roux Arch. EntwMech. Org.*, **155**, 451–510.
Krause, G. and Sander, K. (1962). *Adv. Morphogenesis*, **2**, 259–303.
Krzysztofowicz, A. (1960). *Zoologica Pol.*, **10**, 3–27.
Küthe, H. W. (1966). *Wilhelm Roux Arch. EntwMech. Org.*, **157**, 212–302.
Lassman, G. W. P. (1936). *Ann. ent. Soc. Am.*, **29**, 397–413.
Lautenschlager, F. (1932). *Zool. Jb. Anat. Ont.*, **56**, 121–162.
Lecaillon, A. (1897a). *C. r. hebd. Séanc. Acad. Sci., Paris*, **125**, 876–879.
Lecaillon, A. (1897b). *C. r. Séanc. Soc. Biol.*, **4**, 1014–1016.
Lecaillon, A. (1897c). *Archs Anat. Microsc.*, **1**, 205–224.
Lecaillon, A. (1898). *Archs Anat. Microsc.*, **2**, 118–176.
Ludwig, C. E. (1949). *Microentomology*, **14**, 75–111.
Luginbill, P., Jr. (1953). *Ann. ent. Soc. Am.*, **46**, 505–528.
Mahowald, A. P. (1962). *J. exp. Zool.*, **151**, 201–216.
Mahowald, A. P. (1968). *J. exp. Zool.*, **167**, 237–262.

Mahowald, A. P. (1972). In *Developmental Systems: Insects* (S. J. Counce and C. H. Waddington, eds), Vol. 1, p. 1. Academic Press, London and New York.

Mansour, K. (1927). *Q . Jl microsc. Sci.*, **71**, 313–352.

Mansour, K. (1934). *Bull. Fac. Sci. Egypt. Univ.*, **2**, 1–34.

Matsuda, R. (1965). *Mem. Am. Inst. Ent.*, **4**, 1–334.

Mazur, Z. T. (1960). *Zesz. nauk. Univ. jagiellonsk. Zool.*, **5**, 205–229.

Menees, J. E. (1962). *Ann. ent. Soc. Am.*, **55**, 607–616.

Meng, C. (1968). *Wilhelm Roux Arch. EntwMech. Org.*, **161**, 162–208.

Miya, K. (1965). *J. Fac. Agric. Iwate Univ.*, **7**, 155–166.

Mrkva, R. (1968). *Acta ent. Bohemoslov.*, **65**, 403–408.

Mueller, K. (1938). *Z. wiss. Zool.*, **151**, 192–242.

Müller, M. (1957). *Zool. Jb. Allg. Zool.*, **67**, 111–150.

Mulnard, J. (1947). *Archs Biol., Liège*, **58**, 289–314.

Nelson, J. A. (1915). *The Embryology of the Honey Bee*. University Press, Princeton.

Nitschmann, J. (1962). "Ooplasmic Reaction Systems in Insect Embryogenesis." In *Advances in Morphogenesis* (Krause, G. and Sander, K., eds), vol. **2**, pp. 259–303. Academic Press, New York and London.

Noack, W. (1901). *Z. wiss. Zool.*, **70**, 1–57.

Ochiai, S. (1960). *Bull. Fac. Agric. Tamagawa Univ.*, **1**, 13–45

Oelhafen, F. (1961). *Wilhelm Roux Arch. EntwMech. Org.*, **153**, 120–157.

Okada, M. (1960). *Sci. Rep. Tokyo Kyoiku Daig.*, **B9**, 243–296.

Paterson, N. F. (1931). *S. Afr. Jl Sci.*, **28**, 344–371.

Paterson, N. F. (1932). *S. Afr. Jl Sci.*, **29**, 414–448.

Paterson, N. F. (1936). *Q . Jl microsc. Sci.*, **78**, 91–132.

Patten, W. (1884). *Q . Jl microsc. Sci.*, **24**, 549–602.

Pauli, M. E. (1927). *Z. wiss. Zool.*, **129**, 483–540.

Pflugfelder, O. (1934). *Z. wiss. Zool.*, **145**, 261–282.

Poulson, D. F. (1937). *The Embryonic Development of Drosophila melanogaster*. Hermann et Cie, Paris.

Poulson, D. F. (1945). *Trans. Conn. Acad. Arts Sci.*, **36**, 449–459.

Poulson, D. F. (1950). In *The Biology of Drosophila* (M. Demerec, ed.), pp. 168–274. Wiley, New York.

Poulson, D. F. and Waterhouse, D. F. (1960). *Aust. J. biol. Sci.*, **13**, 540–567.

Presser, B. D. and Rutchsky, C. W. (1957). *Ann. ent. Soc. Am.*, **50**, 133–164.

Reed, E. M. and Day, M. R. (1966). *Aust. J. Zool.*, **14**, 253–263.

Reinhardt, E. (1960). *Zool. Jb. Anat. Ont.*, **78**, 167–234.

Reitberger, A. (1940). *Chromosoma*, **1**, 391–473.

Rempel, J. G. (1951). *Can. Ent.*, **83**, 1–19.

Rempel, J. G. and Church, N. S. (1965). *Can. J. Zool.*, **43**, 915–925.

Rempel, J. G. and Church, N. S. (1969). *Can. J. Zool.*, **47**, 1157–1171.

Riemann, J. G. (1965). *Biol. Bull. mar. biol. Lab. Woods Hole*, **129**, 329–339.

Rosay, B. (1959). *Ann. ent. Soc. Am.*, **52**, 481–484.

Ryan, R. B. (1963). *Ann. ent. Soc. Am.*, **56**, 639–648.

Saito, S. (1934). *J. Coll. Agric. Hokkaido imp. Univ.*, **33**, 249–266.

Saito, S. (1937). *J. Coll. Agric. Hokkaido imp. Univ.*, **40**, 35–109.

Saling, T. (1907). *Z. wiss. Zool.*, **86**, 238–303.

Schaeffer, P. E. (1938). *Ann. ent. Soc. Am.*, **31**, 92–111.

Schienert, W. (1933). *Z. Morph. Ökol. Tiere*, **27**, 76–127.

Schnetter, M. (1934). *Z. Morph. Ökol. Tiere*, **29**, 114–195.

Schoeller, J. (1964). *Archs Zool. éxp. gen.*, **103**, 1–216.

Sehl, A. (1931). Z. Morph. Ökol. Tiere, 20, 535–598.
Seidel, F. (1929). Wilhelm Roux Arch. EntwMech. Org., 119, 322–440.
Seidel, F. (1935). Wilhelm Roux Arch. EntwMech. Org., 132, 671–751.
Shafiq, S. Q. (1954). Q . Jl microsc. Sci., 95, 93–114.
Smreczyński, S. (1932). Zool. Jb. Anat. Ont., 55, 233–314.
Smreczyński, S. (1934). Bull. int. Acad. Sci. Lett. Cracovie, B2, 287–312.
Smreczyński, S. (1938). Zool. Jb. Anat. Ont., 59, 1–58.
Sonnenblick, B. P. (1941). Proc. natn. Acad. Sci. U.S.A., 27, 484–489.
Sonnenblick, B. P. (1950). In The Biology of Drosophila (M. Demerec ed.), pp. 62–167. Wiley, New York.
Speicher, B. R. (1936). J. Morph., 59, 401–521.
Srivastava, U. S. (1966). J. Zool., 150, 145–163.
Stairs, G. R. (1960). Can. Ent., 92, 147–154.
Strindberg, H. (1913). Z. wiss. Zool., 106, 1–227.
Strindberg, H. (1914). Z. wiss. Zool., 112, 1–47.
Strindberg, H. (1915a). Zool. Anz., 46, 167–185.
Strindberg, H. (1915b). Zool. Anz., 45, 248–260.
Strindberg, H. (1915c). Zool. Anz., 45, 557–597.
Strindberg, H. (1917). Zool. Anz., 49, 177–197.
Such, J. (1963). Soc. Sci. Phys. et Nat. Bordeaux, 1962–63, 63–65.
Such, J. and Haget, A. (1962). Soc. Sci. Phys. et Nat. Bordeaux, 1961–62, 97–100.
Surowiak, J. (1958). Zesz. nauk. Univ. jagiellonsk. Zool., 3–29.
Telford, A. D. (1957). Ann. ent. Soc. Am., 50, 537–543.
Tichomirowa, O. (1890). Biol. Zbl., 10, 423.
Tichomirowa, O. (1892). Int. Congr. Zool. Moscow, 2, 112–119.
Tiegs, O. W. and Murray, F. V. (1938). Q . Jl microsc. Sci., 80, 159–284.
Toyama, K. (1902). Bull. Coll. Agric. Tokyo imp. Univ., 5, 73–118.
Tsai, L. S. (1961). J. exp. Zool., 147, 183–201.
Ullman, S. L. (1964). Phil. Trans. R. Soc., B248, 245–277.
Ullman, S. L. (1967). Phil. Trans. R. Soc., B252, 1–25.
Vaidya, V. G. (1967). Nature, Lond., 216, 936–937.
Weber, H. (1954). Grundrisse der Insektenkunde. Fischer, Stuttgart.
Weglarska, B. (1950). Bull. int. Acad. pol. Sci. Lett., BII, 277–302.
Weglarska, B. (1955). Polskie Pismo ent., 25, 193–211.
West, J. A., Cantwell, G. E. and Shortino, T. J. (1968). Ann. ent. Soc. Am., 61, 13–17.
Wheeler, W. M. (1889). J. Morph., 3, 291–386.
Wheeler, W. M. (1893). J. Morph., 8, 1–160.
Wiesmann, I. (1935). Mitt. schweiz. ent. Ges., 16, 370–377.
Wigglesworth, V. B. (1959). A. Rev. Ent., 4, 1–16.
Wigglesworth, V. B. and Beament, J. W. L. (1950). Q . Jl microsc. Sci., 91, 429–452.
Wigglesworth, V. B. and Beament, J. W. L. (1960). J. Insect Physiol., 4, 184–189.
Williams, F. X. (1916). J. Morph., 28, 145–207.
Wolf, R. (1969). Wilhelm Roux Arch. EntwMech. Org., 162, 121–160.
Wray, D. L. (1937). Ann. ent. Soc. Am., 30, 361–409.
Yajima, H. (1960). J. Embryol. exp. Morph., 8, 198–215.
Zakhvatkin, Y. A. (1967a). Zool. Zh., 46, 88–97.
Zakhvatkin, Y. A. (1967b). Zool. Zh., 46, 1209–1218.
Zakhvatkin, Y. A. (1968). Zool. Zh., 47, 1333–1342.

APPENDIX

Recent studies on the development of holometabolous insects include several accounts bearing on the descriptive embryology of the Holometabola. For the Coleoptera, the dimensions of the egg of 24 species of coccinellid are listed by Klausnitzer (1969). The size range within the family is similar to that given in Table II above for the eggs of the Coleoptera as a whole. Brief descriptions of embryonic development are also given by Ressouches (1969) for the circulionid *Pissodes notatus F.* and by Stanley and Grundmann (1970) for *Tribolium confusum*. Both species follow the normal pattern of coleopteran embryonic development, but *P. notatus* is of interest as a species in which the thoracic limb buds develop normally on the segmented germ band and then undergo marked regression during and after dorsal closure. *T. confusum* is reported to be unusual among Coleoptera in the development of its midgut from a posterior rudiment only, the anterior midgut rudiment being absent.

Lal (1969) has given a brief, general account of the embryos of the chalcid hymenopteran *Tetrastichus pyrillae* Craw. Among the Diptera, Harber and Mutchmor (1970) have described typical early embryonic development in *Culiseta inornata*, while Hillman and Lesnik (1970) have studied cuticle formation in the embryo of *Drosophila melanogaster*. More significantly, the concept of the early determination of the adult rudiments in the embryo of *Drosophila* has been given further support in the work of Hadorn *et al.* (1969) and Schubiger *et al.* (1969), reviewed by Fristrom (1969). Riddiford (1970) has also reported experimental observations bearing on the same question in the embryo of the silkworm *Hyalophora cecropia*. By applying juvenile hormone to the developing egg, she found that early application during the formation of the embryo results in abnormalities in larval development, whilst later application, during larval differentiation within the egg, produces effects that first appear at metamorphosis.

REFERENCES

Fristrom, J. W. (1970). *A. Rev. Genet.*, **4**, 325–346.
Hadorn, E., Hürlimann, R., Mindek, G., Schubiger, G. and Staub, M. (1969). *Revue suisse Zool.*, **76**, 551–569.
Harber, P. A. and Mutchmor, J. A. (1970). *Ann. ent. Soc. Am.*, **63**, 1609–1614.
Hillman, R. and Lesnik, L. H. (1970). *J. Morph.*, **131**, 383–396.
Klausnitzer, B. (1969). *Acta ent. Bohemoslov.*, **66**, 146–149.
Lal, K. (1969). *Proc. Nat. Inst. Sci. India*, **B35**, 197–204.
Ressouches, A. P. (1969). *C. r. hebd. Séanc. Acad. Sci., Paris*, **269**, 191–194.
Riddiford, L. M. (1970). *Devl. Biol.*, **22**, 249–263.
Schubiger, G., Schubiger-Staub, J. and Hadorn, E. (1969). *Wilhelm Roux Arch. Entw Mech. Org.*, **163**, 33–39.
Stanley, M. S. M. and Grundmann, A. W. (1970). *Ann. ent. Soc. Am.*, **63**, 1248–1256.

5 | Polyembryony in Insects

O. M. IVANOVA-KASAS

Department of Embryology, Leningrad State University, U.S.S.R.

I. INTRODUCTION

Polyembryony in animals is a form of asexual reproduction whereby several embryos develop from a single egg. The phenomenon of one-egg twins in man and animals has long been known, but the term "polyembryony" (taken from botany, where it has a wider meaning), was first introduced by Marchal in 1898, when he discovered this phenomenon in parasitic Hymenoptera.

A *Hyponomeuta* caterpillar infected with *Ageniaspis* (*Eucyrtus*) *fuscicollis* Dalm. contains long curled tubes filled with numerous embryos of the parasite. Marchal (1898–1904) proved that all these embryos developed from a single egg. In 1903 Marchal also discovered polyembryony in the Hessian-fly parasite *Platygaster zosinae* Walk. (=*Polygnotus minutus* Lind.). Reports of polyembryonic development in many other parasitic Hymenoptera followed, about 30 polyembryonic species now being known in this order (see Table I). Later, polyembryony was also discovered in the order Strepsiptera (Noskiewicz and Poluszynski, 1935).

Marchal (1904*a*) distinguished three forms of polyembryony: (1) *experimental*; (2) *accidental*, or teratological (formation of twins and twin monstrosities presenting deviations from normal growth); and (3) *specific polyembryony*, this being the normal manner of development in some species. Experimentally obtained doubling of some parts of the body is not a rarity.

TABLE I. Polyembryonic Hymenoptera

Family	N	Parasite	Host	Author
Braconidae	1	*Macrocentrus gifuensis* Ashm.	*Pyrausta nubilalis* Hübn.	Parker, 1931
	2	*M. ancylivorus* Rohwer	*Grapholitha molesta* Busck.	Daniel, 1932
	3	*M. homonae*		Gadd, 1946; Berland, 1951
	4	*Amicroplus collaris* Spin.	*Euxoa segetum* Schiff.	Paillot, 1940
Encyrtidae	5	*Ageniaspis fuscicollis* (Dalm.)	*Hyponomeuta spp.*	Marchal, 1898, 1904; Martin, 1914
	6	*A. fuscicollis var. praysincola* Silv.	*Prays oleelus* F.	Silvestri, 1908
	7	*A. testaceipes* Ratz.	*Lithocolletis cramerella* F.	Marchal, 1904
	8	*A. atricollis* Dalm.	*Argyresthia pruniella* L.	Clausen, 1940
	9	*Copidosoma gelechiae* How.	*Gnorimoschema spp.*	Patterson, 1915, 1927
	10	*C. buyssoni* Mayr	*Coleophora stefannii* Joan.	Silvestri, 1910
	11	*C. tortricis* Wat.	*Trotrix loeflingiana* L.	Silvestri, 1924
	12	*Copidosoma sp.*	*Olethreutes variegana* Hübn.	Sarra, 1918
	13	*C. nanellae* Silv.	*Recurvaria nanella* Hübn.	Clausen, 1940
	14	*C. thompsoni* Mercet.	*Nothrix senticetella* Staud.	Parker and Thompson, 1928
	15	*C. boucheanum* Ratz.	*Gelechia pinguinella* Triets.	Parker and Thompson, 1928
	16	*C. koehleri* Blanch.	*Gnorimoschema operculella* Zeller	Doutt, 1947
	17	*Litomastix truncatellus* Dalm.	*Plusia gamma* L. and *Phytometra brassicae* Riley	Silvestri, 1907; Leiby, 1929
	18	*L. (Paracopidosomopsis) floridanus* Ashm.	*Phytometra brassicae* Riley	Patterson, 1917, 1927
	19	*L. kriechbaumery* Mayr	*Depressaria alpiginella* Frey	Ferriére, 1926
	20	*L. delattrei*		Berland, 1951
	21	*Encyrtus variicornis* Nees	*Anarsia lineatella* Zeller	Sarra, 1915
	22	*Berecyntus bakeri*	*Euxoa auxiliaris* Grote	Snow, 1925
Platygasteridae	23	*Platygaster zosinae* Walk. (*Polygnotus minutus* Lind.)	*Phytophaga destructor* Say	Marchal, 1904
	24	*P. felti* Fouts.	*Walshomyia texana* and *Rhopalomyia sabinae*	Patterson, 1921, 1927
	25	*P. vernalis* Myers	*Phytophaga destructor* Say	Leiby and Hill, 1923
	26	*P. variabilis* Fouts.	*Rhopalomyia carolina*	Leiby, 1926, 1929
	27	*Polygnotus (Platygaster) hiemalis* Forb.	*Phytophaga destructor* Say	Leiby and Hill, 1923
Dry-inidae	28	*Aphelopus theliae* Gahan	*Thelia bimaculata* Fabr.	Kornhauser, 1919

For example, longitudinal splitting of the germ band of the camel cricket, *Tachycines*, (Krause, 1962) can result in the production of distinct twins (Fig. 1). Such phenomena, however, are discussed in Counce (1972) concerning experimental embryology in insects.

Occasional, or *teratologic polyembryony*, is observed in almost all kinds of animals, from Hydrozoa to man. But no information on cases of development of two independent embryos in one egg of an insect are to be found in the literature (except the two already mentioned orders of Hymenoptera and Strepsiptera, where polyembryony became a normal phenomenon). Comparatively rare are double monstrosities in insects (duplication of the anterior or posterior ends, development of additional limbs etc.), which might be considered as development of semidetached twins. An exception to this rule is presented by *Carausius morosus* Br., *Menexenus semiarmatus* Westw. and

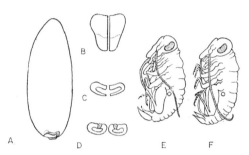

Fig. 1. Experimental polyembryony in *Tachycines* (after Krause, 1962). A, Lateral view of the egg showing the germ band and amniotic fold at posterior end; B and C, germ band cut, surface view and cross section; D, regulative changes in the halves of the germ band; E and F, two embryos ready to hatch.

some other phasmids which quite often form fused twins (Fig. 2A; Cappe de Baillon, 1927). In *Menexenus*, two separate germ bands are sometimes formed (Fig. 2C), but these soon perish, being unable to undergo normal blastokinesis (Cappe de Baillon, 1928). The physiological mechanism giving rise to such duplications is not yet clear, but the cause of their appearance raises no doubts. They develop from so-called *complex eggs* (oeufs composes) formed by the fusion of two or more oöcytes. Thus the monsters described by Cappe de Baillon, though being of great interest from a physiological point of view, have nothing to do with polyembryony as such. Such phenomena may be referred to as *pseudo-polyembryony*. Recently pseudo-polyembryony was detected in paedogenetic Diptera (Counce, 1968).

Another interesting peculiarity observed in *Carausius* has received the name of "*substitutive polyembryony*" (Vignau, 1967). In some cases an embryo well advanced in its development (with rudiments of limbs) perishes. It then sinks into the yolk and there degenerates. A new embryonic rudiment originates in its place and develops normally. The same is observed after experimental killing of an embryo. This proves that even at comparatively late stages of embryonic development, *Carausius* preserves cell elements (in the body of the embryo itself or in its embryonic membranes) at whose expense the embryo can regenerate. All this time the *Carausius* egg remains one complete whole.

This chapter will deal with specific polyembryony, polyembryony proper. As it is realized differently in Hymenoptera and Strepsiptera, it is most convenient to discuss these two orders separately.

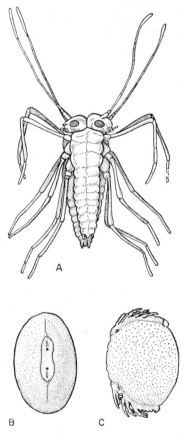

FIG. 2. Pseudopolyembryony in Phasmida (after Cappe de Baillon, 1927 and 1928). A, Januslike double monster of *Carausius morosus*; B, Composite egg of *Menexenus semiarmatus* with two micropyles indicating its double origin; C, Development of two embryos in the composite egg of *Menexenus*.

II. POLYEMBRYONY IN HYMENOPTERA

A. The General Features of Development of Parasitic Hymenoptera

As polyembryony has developed in Hymenoptera as a result of embryonic parasitism it is important to point out the influence of the latter on its development. This question is dealt with in the monograph by Ivanova-Kasas (1961).

The main advantage of the parasitic mode of life is the abundance of food. That is why the Hymenoptera which lay their eggs in the body or eggs of some other insect have adapted themselves to a very early nutrition at their host's expense. At the same time their eggs become poorer in yolk and smaller in size. The yolk syncytium formed by vitellophages, which has a trophic as well as morphogenetic significance in eggs rich in yolk, also undergoes gradual reduction. This leads to a change in morphogenetic mechanisms and superficial cleavage changes to total cleavage. In its pure form, total cleavage is described only in polyembryonic species, but in some monembryonic forms (as *Aphidius fabarum*) complete division of the egg into cells occurs very early too—by the eight blastomere stage.

Parasitic nutrition in Hymenoptera occurs in two different ways, and, accordingly, there are two different lines of evolution. In the first, nutrition at the expense of the host becomes possible only after the hatching of the larvae. This evolution tends to reduce the period of embryonic development and the larva hatches in a highly undeveloped state. Its embryonic development is simplified, and embryonic membranes are absent. We find a vivid example of this in *Prestwichia aquatica*, whose larva has no appendages at all, not even mouthparts. It has no nervous, respiratory, or circulatory systems, and the pharyngeal muscles represent the whole of the muscular system. The only well developed and functioning system is that of digestion (see Figs 88, 89 in Ivanova-Kasas, 1961).

In other endoparasitic forms the ability to acquire nutrition from their host's haemolymph appears at the embryonic stage. The serosa fulfils an important role in embryonic nutrition (the amnion being absent in most Hymenoptera). This is the cause of its extensive development, and the time of its formation shifts to much earlier stages. Simultaneously, changes occur in the mode of separation of embryonic and extra-embryonic parts. Development in such species is accompanied by considerable growth: *Dinocampus* embryos, for instance, increase more than 1000 times in volume. It is this second line of evolution that has led to the appearance of polyembryony. This problem will be discussed in more detail in a later section.

B. Some Examples of Polyembryonic Development

A classical example of polyembryonic development is presented by *Ageniaspis fuscicollis* (Fam. Encyrtidae). The development of this insect has been studied by Marchal (1898, 1904a), Silvestri (1906, 1908), Martin (1914), Ivanova-Kasas (1961) and Kościelska (1962, 1963). According to Martin (1914), late in the summer the female *Ageniaspis* deposits her eggs in the eggs of the moth *Hyponomeuta*. At that time the *Ageniaspis* eggs are 25 μ in length and are devoid of yolk or other nutrients. They are enclosed within a very thin, barely distinguishable chorion. Polar body nuclei lie in the anterior end of the egg, while the male and female pronuclei (or only the female one, when development proceeds without fertilization) lie near its caudal end (Fig. 3A). It is here that the oösome lies—a small body which is also present in the eggs of many monembryonic insects. Since, in subsequent development, the oösome usually enters the primordial germ cells, it is also

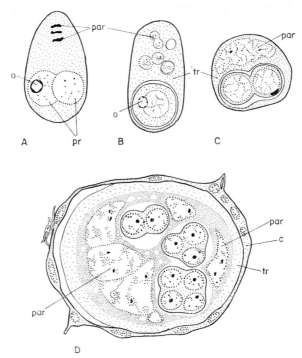

FIG. 3. Early development of *Ageniaspis fuscicollis* (after Martin, 1914). A, The egg during fertilization; B, development of the trophamnion; C, beginning of cleavage; D, beginning of polyembryonization; c, cyst; o, oösome; par, nuclei of polar bodies = paranuclei; pr, pronucleus; tr, trophamnion.

called the "germ cell determinant". There is no direct evidence, however, that it is the oösome that actually determines the germ line.

Pronuclei fuse to form the synkaryon, which, together with a small part of the surrounding oöplasm, then separates itself from the peripheral oöplasm, the polar body nuclei remaining in the latter. In this way an embryonal cell and its surrounding membrane—the trophamnion—are formed (Fig. 3B). The polar body nuclei swell and fuse to form one mass—the paranucleus—which later fragments amitotically and forms irregular paranuclear masses.

Cleavage in *Ageniaspis* is total, i.e., both the nucleus and the cytoplasm divide. The oösome soon disintegrates; at the four blastomere stage it is discernible no more. By the time eight to ten blastomeres have formed, they are surrounded by a cyst formed from host tissues. Numerous tracheae of host origin branch out in the cyst wall (Fig. 3D).

Late in September, caterpillars hatch from the eggs of *Hyponomeuta*, and the parasites inside them proceed with their development. In autumn and winter, growth and development of the *Ageniaspis* embryo proceeds slowly, its diameter reaching 50 μ in April. But in the spring it starts growing rapidly and forms a morula-shaped group of cells. As soon as the morula attains a 12 to 15-cell stage, it divides into two new groups and each group may become an independent embryo.

The paranucleus fragments irregularly and forms numerous nuclei, while the trophamnion forms partitions between the embryos, which may reach a total of 180.

The whole complex of embryos, along with the enveloping trophamnion, (the so-called "parasitic body" or "polygerm"), grows rapidly, first assuming a sausage form and then transforming into branching curling cords. By June the parasite body is 5 cm long (branching excluded) and 0·5–2 mm wide (Marchal, 1904), the total volume of the parasitic body exceeding more than 4 million times the original volume of the egg. At this time the fully developed larvae of *Ageniaspis* become visible in the parasitic body.

The process of separation of the embryonic material into independent embryos (polyembryonization) slows down in May. In some embryos the number of cells reaches 60–80 and development begins. Each embryo, a solid multilayered complex of cells, takes on a bean-like form. On the dorsal side, a deep furrow appears, while on the ventral convex side a median groove forms, and segmentation begins.

The central mass of cells gives rise to the midgut rudiment. The peripheral multilayered mass of cells is thicker on its ventral side, thinner on its lateral side, and is absent in the region of the dorsal concavity. Marchal considered the thickened ventral layer of cells to correspond to the embryonic rudiment of other insects. Its anterior and posterior ends curve dorsalward and almost touch one another, the dorsal concavity alone separating them. The mesoderm forms along the median groove. Embryonic development is completed in June.

Each young larva of *Ageniaspis* reaches 1 mm in length and consists of a head and 13 segments. Small mandibles are present as well as well-developed salivary glands and a tracheal system. At first the larvae feed on the trophamnion, then they emerge into the body cavity of the host and begin to devour its tissues.

We have already pointed out that the *Ageniaspis* parasite body increases greatly during its development. This enormous growth points to some extra-embryonic food supply. The trophamnion is supposed to play the part of a mediator in the process of metabolism between the parasite and its host. According to the investigations of Ivanova-Kasas (1961) and more especially those of Kościelska (1962, 1963), the trophamnion possesses the following properties:

1. The trophamnion is permeable to vital dyes (Neutral red, Methylene blue, Toluidin blue), and is consequently assumed to be permeable to many substances soluble in the haemolymph of the host.

2. The paranucleus disintegrates into numerous smaller fragments which show a positive Feulgen reaction. They are larger and are stained even more brightly than the embryonic nuclei, but they do not show any sign of degeneration. There is a strong supposition that the trophamnion nuclei are highly polyploid.

3. At early stages of development, the RNA content in the trophamnion and the embryo is negligible. Later on there is an increase and accumulation of RNA which is localized in the embryonic tissues and in the inner layer of the trophamnion. At the end of development the RNA content in the trophamnion falls again.

4. The trophamnion is almost entirely devoid of polysaccharides but it is very rich in fat inclusions (phospholipids) in the form of droplets which stain with Sudan black B after fixation by Elfman's method. The phospholipids apparently are the main source of energy for the developing embryos (Kościelska, 1962, 1963).

5. Mitochondria and elements of Golgi apparatus are found within the trophamnion which points to oxidation and synthesizing processes (Kościelska, 1963).

The data indicate that intense metabolism goes on in the trophamnion, that it is simply permeable for some substances, while it transforms others and passes them to the embryo in a changed form.

The trophamnion in *Ageniaspis fuscicollis* is covered with a thin one-layered membrane (Fig. 3D), formed from the host tissues and described as a cyst in many other parasitic Hymenoptera. The cyst in *Ageniaspis* starts forming very early (Martin, 1914). Soon after the deposition of *Ageniaspis* eggs into a *Hyponomeuta* embryo, fat body cells of the latter (obvious but only slightly differentiated elements) surround the trophamnion and soon form an epithelial-like layer, thus producing a cyst entirely separated from other tissues of the host. Polygerm cords lie loosely in the body cavity of the caterpillar hatched from the *Hyponomeuta* egg, the tracheal system being the only organ system of the host which is in constant contact with the parasite body. Fine tracheoles and sometimes even larger branches form a network around the polygerm loops, connecting them with one another and with the host organs, the tracheae being fixed on the polygerm surface by means of the cyst cells.

The above described early stages of cyst formation are similar to a defence reaction of the host organism against a foreign body or the presence of the invading parasite. The formation of such connective-tissue capsules, often leading to death of the parasite, has been known for a long time, a vast literature having been devoted to the problems of immunity in insects which will not be reviewed here. It is notable, however, that the cyst which forms around the germs of the polyembryonic Hymenoptera is not only harmless to the parasite, but is, as a matter of fact, necessary for its normal development. Martin (1914) noticed that *Ageniaspis* eggs which happen to be laid in the yolk of a *Hyponomeuta* egg die after reaching the two–three blastomere stage. He assumed this to show that "parasite eggs need the mediation of a

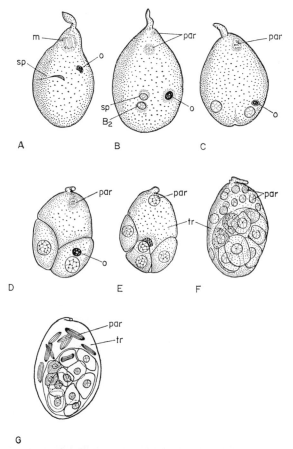

FIG. 4. Development of *Litomastix floridanus* (after Patterson, 1921). A and B, fertilization; C, beginning of cleavage; D, two-cell stage: E, F and G, the next stages. m, meiotic figure, o, oösome, par, nuclei of polar bodies = paranuclei; sp, sperm; tr, trophamnion.

host's embryonic cells for their nutriment, being unable to assimilate yolk themselves". The tracheal net covering the cyst certainly supplies the polygerm with oxygen. Glycogen found in the cyst cells gave Kościelska (1963) the basis for suggesting that later on it diffuses into the trophamnion and is utilized there.

In another Encyrtidae, *Litomastix* (=*Paracopidosomopsis*) *floridana* Ashm., a parasite of *Autographa brassicae* caterpillars, polyembryony develops in a similar way to that in *Ageniaspis*, though it differs markedly in certain details (Patterson, 1921).

The *Litomastix* oöcyte is pear-shaped and reaches 155 μ in length (Fig. 4A). At its narrow anterior part the oöcyte nucleus undergoes the maturation divisions, and the female pronucleus then migrates into the enlarged posterior part of the egg. In fertilized eggs, fusion of pronuclei takes place here too (Fig. 4B). Then cleavage starts, the egg dividing at once into three parts: two blastomeres, and one large "polar cell", which contains the polar body nuclei (Fig. 4D). The oösome becomes limited to one of the blastomeres. Cleavage is total. At the third cleavage, the oösome also divides and its derivatives are

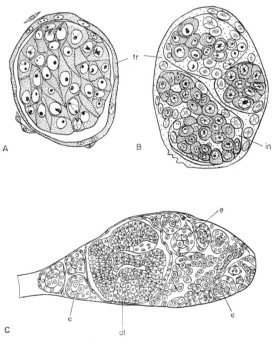

Fig. 5. Development of *Litomastix floridanus* (continued). A, the first appearance of spindle-cells; B, the division of the original embryo into second embryonic masses and the development of an inner embryonic envelope; C, the late parasitic body. al, asexual larva; e, normal embryo; in, inner envelope; tr, trophamnion.

shared by two blastomeres; cleavage of these blastomeres proceeds somewhat more slowly than that of the others, resulting in asynchrony of cleavage. After the 28-blastomere stage, the cells containing the oösome material are no longer discernible from the rest of the cells. (Fig. 5A).

Soon after cleavage begins, the "polar cell" coats the entire embryo and forms a "polar coating", which corresponds to the trophamnion in *Ageniaspis*, but, unlike the latter, the nuclei of this membrane divide mitotically. (Fig. 4G).

The first signs of polyembryony appear in *Litomastix* at the 220–225-blastomere stage, some blastomeres preserving their polygonal form, while others become spindle-shaped. (Fig. 5A). The latter cells divide the whole mass of blastomeres into several groups, forming membranes around each of them. These inner membranes soon become syncytial (Fig. 5B). In this way the "primary masses" of embryonic cells appear, each being surrounded by its own "inner" membrane and having a common external trophamnion. Then the primary masses start dividing by means of fission, forming secondary masses, this being achieved by the activity of the "inner" membranes. The trophamnion then invades the spaces between the secondary masses. These, in turn, divide into third order masses, this process going on for rather a long time. The final number of embryonic masses, each capable of giving rise to an embryo, may exceed 1000. At the end of embryonic development the whole polygerm disintegrates into fragments, each containing an embryo.

The trophamnion in *Litomastix* is not as conspicuous as in *Ageniaspis*, probably because it shares its functions with the "inner" membrane.

Among the Encyrtidae, polyembryony is also found in representatives of the genera of *Copidosoma* and *Berecyntus*.

Polyembryonic forms are also found in the family Platygasteridae. In *Platygaster hiemalis* Forbes, development may proceed in the monembryonic manner, but it often leads to twin formation. On indirect evidence, Leiby and Hill (1923) suggested that single embryos develop from unfertilized eggs while inseminated ones give rise to twins. The processes of trophamnion formation and concentration of the embryonic cells into groups giving rise to separate embryos are similar to those described for *Ageniaspis* (Fig. 6). But, unlike polyembryony in Encyrtidae, the number of embryos in Platygasteridae developing from one egg is never large.

Representatives of Platygasteridae give an opportunity of following the origin and development of polyembryony step by step. Along with typical monembryonic development (e.g. in *Synopeas rhanis* Walk., Marchal, 1906), occasional polyembryony (3% twins in *Allotropa burelli* Mues, Clancy, 1944) and facultative polyembryony (in *Platygaster hiemalis* Forbes) occur within the family.

A well established, though never very "productive", polyembryony has

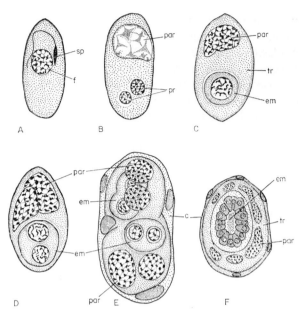

Fig. 6. Early development of *Platygaster hiemalis* (after Leiby and Hill, 1923; from Johannsen and Butt, 1941). A, the egg one hour after deposition; B, pronuclei about to fuse; C, the development of the trophamnion; D, the beginning of cleavage; E, twinning stage of parasitic body; F, developing embryo; c, cyst; em, embryo; f, female pronucleus; par, paranuclei; pr, pronuclei; sp, sperm; tr, trophamnion.

also been recorded in other Platygasteridae: two larvae from one egg in *Platygaster variabilis* Fouts, eight larvae in *Polygnotus* (=*Platygaster*) *vernalis* Myers (Leiby, 1929), 10–12 larvae in *Platygaster zosinae* Walk. (=*Polygnotus minutus* Lind., Marchal, 1903, 1904*b*), 11–18 larvae in *Platygaster felti* Fouts (Patterson, 1927). In the family Braconidae, polyembryony is found in representatives of the genera *Macrocentrus* and *Amicroplus* (Parker, 1931; Daniel, 1932; Gadd, 1946). Unfortunately, embryonic development in these forms is so insufficiently studied that no correlation is yet possible with that of Encyrtidae and Platygasteridae.

Finally, there are some scant data on polyembryony in *Aphelopus theliae* Gahan (suborder Aculeata, fam. Dryinidae), a parasite of the cicada *Thelia bimaculata* Fabr. (Kornhauser, 1919).

In *Aphelopus* and in polyembryonic forms of Braconidae, cleavage is total, and a trophic membrane is also present.

C. Specific Features of Development of Polyembryony in Hymenoptera

Development in polyembryonic Hymenoptera differs from that of typical insects not only by polyembryony as such, but in several other respects, namely:

1. The eggs are microscopically small and contain no yolk.

2. The chorion is very thin and permeable to various substances. It disappears very early and does not impede growth of the embryo.

3. Cleavage is total, no blastoderm or yolk syncytium being formed.

4. Early in development, a specialized membrane, the trophamnion, is formed which functions as a nutritive organ for the developing embryo.

5. The increase in mass during embryogenesis in all Hymenoptera is enormous. For example, a newly deposited egg of *Copidosoma gelechiae* How. is approximately 40–50 μ × 30–35 μ, but by the time of the first larvae hatch, the parasite body is 1370 μ long and 570 μ wide. In *Polygnotus* ($=Platygaster$) *vernalis* Myers the egg is 21 μ × 8 μ; within a month the parasite body becomes 800 μ × 400 μ (Leiby and Hill, 1924).

6. Many polyembryonic Hymenoptera, like *Ageniaspis*, are not only insensitive to the defence reaction of the host, but require close contact with the tissues of the latter: this has been observed in *Platygaster hiemalis* Forbes (Leiby and Hill, 1923), in *Litomastix truncatellus* Dalm. (Silvestri, 1937), and in *Copidosoma koehleri* Blanch. (Doutt, 1947). Eggs of *Litomastix floridana* Ashm. if deposited into an unfertilized host egg perish, because for their normal growth they need to be inside the tissues of a developing host embryo. (Patterson, 1921). According to Leiby (1922), the polygerm of *Copidosoma gelechiae* How. is enveloped in a cyst formed by the fat tissue of the host caterpillar, *Gnorimoschema gallaeosolidaginis* Riley, development being delayed if the cyst is not formed. Eggs of *Amicroplis collaris* Spin are usually deposited into the fat body of the *Euxoa segetum* caterpillar; if the egg happens to be laid into the body cavity, it soon becomes attached to some organ and is coated by amoebocytes of the host on the side next to the body cavity as if for phagocytosis, which, however, does not take place and the egg develops normally (Paillot, 1940).

Thus it becomes clear that polyembryonic Hymenoptera are conspicuous not only by their peculiar course of development, but also by their perfect adaptation to a parasitic mode of life. They have not only managed to resist the defence reaction of the host, but have distorted it and turned it to their own advantage. All these specific features of development of polyembryonic forms have certainly not appeared all at once; many of them are found in some monembryonic Hymenoptera, and thus create the possibility of polyembryony.

D. Asexual Larvae

Not all larvae produced by polyembryonic development are viable; not infrequently the reverse is observed, when unviable embryos and larvae, the so-called pseudogerms, pseudolarvae, abortive embryos, asexual larvae, teratoid larvae etc., are formed. Failure to develop normally results from a variety of causes. During division of the polygerm, some of the resulting masses may consist of too few embryonic cells (sometimes a mass may contain only a single cell) to develop normally. Some masses may be inadequately covered by the trophamnion or the host tissues, or they may lie so distant from the host fat body that they suffer from inadequate nourishment. This latter explanation has been suggested for the "abortive embryos" in *Copidosoma gelechiae* How. (Patterson, 1917, 1918; Leiby, 1922, 1929) and in *Platygaster hiemalis* Forbes (Leiby and Hill, 1923; Leiby, 1929).

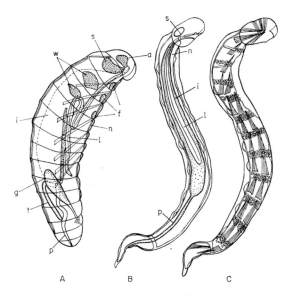

FIG. 7. Larvae of *Litomastix truncatellus* (after Silvestri, 1937). A, sexual larva; B, asexual larva showing the internal organs; C, the same seen superficially with the addition of the muscles. a, f and w, imaginal discs of the antennae, feet and wings; g, gonad; i and p, middle and posterior gut; l, labial gland; n, ganglionar chain; s, supra-oesophageal ganglion; t, malpighian tubes.

A more complicated phenomenon is presented by the "asexual larvae" discovered by Silvestri (1906), side by side with normal ones in *Litomastix truncatellus* Dalm. (Fig. 7). In multicellular early egg of *Litomastix*, two regions are discernible even before polyembryony appears: a posterior region consisting of small cells, and an anterior one consisting of both small and large cells. Silvestri called the caudal part, which gives rise to a single asexual larva, "massa monembryonale". The anterior region—"massa germinigena" —produces some asexual larvae and many normal ones. In one case, 1700 normal larvae and 200 "asexual" ones developed from one single egg of *Litomastix*. The "asexual" larvae hatch somewhat earlier than the normal ones and survive for some time (up to ten days), but then they invariably die.

"Asexual" larvae lack reproductive, respiratory, circulatory and excretory systems, but they are more muscular and active than normal larvae. The suggestion that these larvae belong not to *Litomastix*, but to some other insect, was rejected by Patterson (1918) on the basis of experimental evidence.

Similar asexual larvae have also been found in *Litomastix* (*Paracopidoso-mopsis*) *floridanus* Ashm. (Patterson, 1915), in *Copidosoma thompsoni* Mercet (Parker and Thompson, 1928; Leiby, 1929) and in C. *bucheanum* Ratz. (Leiby, 1929).

Attempts to elucidate the formation of "asexual" larvae have resulted in an abundant literature. Silvestri (1906) suggested that "asexual" larvae are produced when embryos happen to lack even the smallest particle of the "germ-cell-determinant". At the same time he compared dimorphism in *Litomastix* larvae with the polymorphism in social insects and attributed to "asexual" larvae the function of primary breakdown of the host tissues, thus making it easier for normal larvae to utilize the host tissues. This hypothesis encountered a number of objections from Patterson (1917, 1918, 1921) who observed development of "asexual" larvae in *Litomastix* (*Paracopidosomopsis*) *floridanus* Ashm. Patterson pointed out that he had not observed any regularity in the site of "asexual" larvae formation in the species he had studied. Nor are there sufficient grounds to believe that "asexual" larvae evidence "useful activity" by destroying the host's tissues. ". . . It is impossible to conceive of a mechanism", Patterson writes, "which could operate in such a manner as to parcel out exactly predestined germ cells to the several hundred embryos" (Patterson, 1921, page 22). But even if it could be assumed that such a mechanism does exist, and that "asexual" larvae appear owing to its imperfection, such problems as the lack of the excretory, respiratory and circulatory systems in these larvae remain unexplained; for it has been experimentally proved that the development of even secondary sex characters in insects does not depend on the presence of a sex rudiment. Patterson suggested that the oösome, inherited by polyembryonic Hymenoptera from their monembryonic ancestors, has lost its function of a sex determinant.

Patterson's own hypothesis was that during cleavage some blastomeres may form which lack the X-chromosome due to chance nondisjunction. ". . . A division might occur", he writes, "in which all the sex chromosomes, whether divided or not, pass to one pole of the spindle. In this event one of the daughter cells would contain no sex chromosome". ". . . I should be inclined to believe that the asexual larvae are sexless not because they have failed to inherit predestinated germ cells, but because of their failure to inherit X-chromosomes. If X-free blastomeres are formed during cleavage, such cells might become progenitors of sexless larvae" (Patterson, 1917, pp. 298 and 304). But Patterson provided no confirmatory cytological evidence.

In 1937 Silvestri returned to this problem once more. In his polemic with

Patterson he further developed his former ideas. To explain the absence of a number of somatic system organs in "asexual" larvae, he assumed that the "germ-cell-determinant" substance exerts some organizing influence on the development of these systems, and that somatic cells of insects lacking sex cells cannot produce normally developed organisms. Silvestri also referred to the fact that in many parasitic Hymenoptera, the primary larval stage differs considerably from the following stages, and advanced a new idea that "asexual" larvae reproduce atavistically such a stage, this having been present in their ancestors but lost in the process of their adaptation and specialization as internal parasites. This stage, now missing in normal development, persists in a latent form in the genotype and reveals itself only in the absence of sex cells. The lack of sex cells and of a number of other organs in "asexual" larvae prevents, however, their development to a normal insect and causes their early death. The purely speculative character of these elaborate deductions of Silvestri is clear.

The last to discuss this problem was Doutt (1947, 1952), who observed development of asexual larvae in *Copidosoma koehleri* Blanchard, a parasite of *Gnorimoschema operculata* Zeller caterpillars. He pointed out that there are 20 to 30 normal and only one or two "asexual" larvae in each infected caterpillar. Doutt had his doubts about the larvae in question being genuinely asexual, because they were only studied by means of very crude methods which would hardly permit the detection of a very small sex rudiment at this very early stage of development. That is why he chose the name of "teratoid" for such larvae and considered them to be simply monstrosities, as Parker and Thompson had earlier (1928). Doutt noticed that the "teratoid" larvae form only along with the development of inseminated eggs and proposed that the penetration of a spermatozoid into an egg has something to do with the appearance of such larvae. Still he did not give any clearly formulated hypothesis of his own on the problem of "asexual" larvae.

This short review shows that the nature and origin of "asexual", or "teratoid" larvae are still mysterious phenomena. If the causes of their development were simply some unfavourable conditions which happen to occur in some of the numerous embryos, the defects in these larvae would be expected to be far more varied in quantity as well as in quality. But "asexual" larvae, according to the data available, are of a quite definite morphological character in each of the species, which allows us to speak of a dimorphism of the larvae. Obviously there are some constant causes influencing larval growth and regularly inducing specific defects of development in a definite ratio in *Litomastix*, *Copidosoma* and other species. But as to the causes and mechanism of their action—all this still remains a mystery.

Finally, it is worth mentioning a paradoxical fact observed by Daniel (1932) when he was studying the development of *Macrocentrus ancylivorus*

Roh., a parasite of *Grapholita molesta* Busk. It is that the first hatched larva exerts an oppressive influence on the remaining embryos. As well as devouring the host tissues, it also devours all other embryos. Thus, in spite of an initial polyembryonic type of development, only one larva of *Macrocentrus* reaches maturity. To explain this, Daniel suggested that at some remote time, *Macrocentrus ancylivorus* had as its host a bigger insect, which allowed several larvae to grow to maturity; but then, due to some unknown cause, it was compelled to change to a smaller host, which proved unable to feed more than a single individual of *Macrocentrus*.

E. Hypotheses on the Origin of Polyembryony in Hymenoptera

Marchal (1904*a*) was the first to speculate on the origin of polyembryony. He considered abundance of food and its easy availability to be the first condition to bring about polyembryony. Excess food, however, is available to all parasites, and ease in its use, to many, but polyembryony is observed only as an exception. Marchal therefore sought the immediate cause of "polyembryonization" in external factors influencing the eggs of the species studied by him, similar to methods experimenters use for artificial division of blastomeres. *Platygaster zosinae* Walk., for instance, deposits its eggs into the intestine of late embryos of a Cecydomyid. When the Cecydomyid larva hatches and begins to feed, osmotic conditions in its intestine change drastically, which, Marchal speculated, brings about the separation of blastomeres by the mechanical shaking of the *Platygaster* germ during intestinal peristalsis. Similar (mainly osmotic) causes of dissociation of the germ, Marchal postulated to occur in *Ageniaspis fuscicollis* Dalm., which develops in the body cavity of a *Hyponomeuta* caterpillar: a strong dehydration of the caterpillar tissues takes place in winter, and in spring, when the caterpillar begins feeding energetically, osmotic conditions change sharply.

Silvestri, another author who studied a number of polyembryonic species (1937), considered hypernutrition, as a result of extremely favourable conditions of feeding, to be the immediate cause of the subdivision of the embryonic mass. After the chorion disappears and the trophamnion starts functioning in *Litomastix*, an intense proliferation of embryonic cells begins, and these behave as if they were in tissue culture: they try to disperse, press on the embryonal membrane from the inside, which, to counteract them, begins to form fissions and thus divides the whole mass of embryonic cells into separate groups. This ingenious explanation, however, leaves unanswered the question as to why such apparently favourable factors as the excess of food should disorganize the germ so effectively that it turns into something resembling tissue culture.

Most authors have regarded the problem of polyembryony in the light of results from experimental studies, and have sought to find its cause in some (usually unfavourable) external condition. Huxley and De Beer (1934) for example, suggested the following possible causes for twinning or polyembryony: complete separation of blastomeres; changes in polarity; retardation of placentation (armadillos); cooling of eggs before gastrulation (birds); death of some embryos and their putrefaction (oligochaetes). But, as Patterson (1927) justly pointed out, purely external causes could only evoke a sporadic polyembryony as an exceptional fact rather than the rule. Thus, it would be much more correct to look for an explanation of polyembryonic development from the point of view of the inner structure of the egg.

Proceeding along this line, Doutt (1947) tried to correlate polyembryony in Hymenoptera with the peculiarities of the nucleo-cytoplasmic ratio in the egg. He pointed out that, in polyembryonic forms, a considerable part of the oöcyte is spent to form the trophamnion, resulting in a disproportion and the loss of equilibrium between the chromatin and the cytoplasm, which may be the factor inducing polyembryony. When fertilization takes place, the nucleus of the sperm is added and the disproportion becomes still more accentuated. Consequently, the fertilized eggs are more "polyembryonic": Leiby and Hill (1923) drew attention to the fact that unfertilized eggs of Platygaster hiemalis Forbes develop monembryonically, while the fertilized ones form twins; Flanders (1942, 1946) noted that female broods of Copidosoma koehleri Blanch. (developing from fertilized eggs) are usually more numerous than the male ones (which develop from unfertilized eggs) etc. Yet, the facts mentioned here are not sufficient to prove this hypothesis. Moreover, it leaves unexplained the essentials of the interdependence supposed to exist between the quantitative predominance of nuclear substance and the division of the embryo into separate cell complexes capable of independent development.

Tokin (1959) suggested that polyembryony in Hymenoptera might have arisen owing to a sharp decline in integration of the embryo due to some unfavourable conditions induced by the host. But this idea is open to question since polyembryony is observed in the most specialized parasitic species (i.e. in the best-adapted to parasitism in general and to their selected hosts in particular). There is enough data in the literature pointing to the fact that monembryonic parasites, if they happen to get into the body of an unusual host, or are placed into that one by the experimenter, are often unable to resist the defence reaction of the host and perish, but do not produce any twins.

Nevertheless, the ideas suggested by the above authors are correct in that the precondition for polyembryony to arise must be some definite physiological state of the germ. This state need not be brought about only by some immediate external effects, but may also be the result of an evolution of the egg, of its structures and functions, the evolution being induced by some environmental factors in a wise ecological sense. Thus, while considering the origin of polyembryony, one should distinguish the morphological, physiological and ecological aspects of the problem.

All the above mentioned peculiarities of the development of the polyembryonic Hymenoptera are connected, directly or otherwise, with parasitism. Many of these peculiarities have already been observed in some monembryonic species. The eggs of *Aphidius fabarum* Marsh. (Aphidiidae), for instance, are 86 μ × 36 μ in size, and have no yolk. Their cleavage remains partial only up to the four-nucleus stage; in the next cleavage the cytoplasm divides too, resulting in eight cells. But these cells are not uniform from the very beginning: one of them, the biggest, is more basophilic and gives rise to the germ proper. The other seven cells, smaller and lighter in colour, give rise to the embryonic membrane which has a trophic function. Various representatives of Aphidiidae increase in volume 40 to 400 times during their development (Ivanova-Kasas, 1961).

Small-sized eggs, the presence of a trophic membrane, and a considerable embryonic growth are also characteristic of many monembryonic Platygasteridae [e.g. in *Platygaster* sp. from *Cecidomyia oenophila*, and in *Trichacis remulus* Walk. (Marchal, 1906)].

Diminution of eggs in parasitic Hymenoptera is the result of parasitism and is connected with the disappearance of the yolk, which has lost its functions, and with a decrease in size of adult insects. It is also probable that small-sized eggs facilitate oviposition, such eggs sliding more easily through the ovipositor down into an active and sometimes resisting host. Disappearance of the yolk results in a considerable simplification of the egg and involves a change in cleavage from a superficial to a total one; this, in turn, is an important prerequisite for polyembryony, for it facilitates the division of polyembryonal material into groups of cells which, in their turn, give rise to independent germs.

The trophamnion is of much interest in this connection, for it is a special organ providing for nutrition of the numerous embryos formed as a result of polyembryony. Many authors (Marchal, 1904; Martin, 1914; Roonwal, 1935; Silvestri, 1937) consider the trophamnion to be a product of fusion and hypertrophy of the polar bodies because it appears at the very beginning of development and is formed of a separated part of the oöplasm which contains these nuclei. This picture, however, leaves unexplained the question as to how such a peculiar structure could arise in the process of evolution.

The origin and true morphologic nature of the trophamnion can only be understood on the basis of a comparative embryological analysis (Ivanova-Kasas, 1954, 1961). Most insects have two embryonic membranes: the amnion and the serosa. Their functions are insufficiently studied as yet, but they presumably play a protective part and prevent the embryo, first of all, from drying up. It is also known that when an embryo develops in a liquid medium, it absorbs water through these membranes. In *Melanoplus differentialis* Tomas, permeability of the serosa for water changes in a regular manner during development, the changes regulating such important physiological states of the embryo as entering or leaving diapause (Slifer, 1938, 1946). And it is also certain that gas exchange is effected through the embryonal membranes.

In primitive Hymenoptera (saw-flies) the embryonic membranes are formed by the amniotic folds growing over the germ band. When the folds are fused, the amnion and serosa form, but the amnion is soon reduced. In the Aculeata and many monembryonic parasitic Hymenoptera only one membrane is present; it is formed by the extra-embryonic blastoderm separating from the germ band and then growing over it. Observations on the development of *Chalicodoma muraria* F. (Carriére and Bürger, 1897) and *Ammophila campestris* Jur. (Baerends and Baerends-van Roon, 1949), in which rudimentary amniotic folds form, indicate that single embryonic membrane in other Aculeata and parasitic Hymenoptera is the serosa.

In the conditions of parasitism, the serosal functions change. Drying up no longer threatens the embryo, but the serosa probably still acts as a protective membrane in preventing the embryo from coming into direct contact with the host's tissues in cases when the chorion is but slightly developed or when it disappears early in development. At the same time the exchange functions of the serosa increase greatly, for it transfuses to the embryo not only water, but nutritious substances as well.

The increase in the functional significance of the serosa results in shifting the time of formation of this embryonic organ to ever earlier stages of development, an excellent example of heterochronism. The following comparative-embryonic range illustrates it.

1. In the monembryonic parasites *Eurytoma aciculata* Ratz. and *Angitia vestigialis* Ratz., the serosa appears after the germ band is formed, the extra-embryonal blastoderm overgrowing the germ band and enveloping it (Ivanova-Kasas, 1958, 1960, 1961).

2. In *Platygaster instricator*, *Dinocampus terminatus* Nees and *Ephedrus plagiator* Nees, the serosa forms at the blastoderm stage by means of delamination (Kulagin, 1894; Ogloblin, 1924; Ivanova-Kasas, 1956, 1961).

3. In *Pesudaphycus* sp. the serosa is developed even before the blastoderm is formed, the first cleavage nuclei which enter the periplasm being used to form the serosa (Ioff, 1946).

4. Serosal formation may occur during cleavage at the expense of some blastomeres: at the 20-blastomere stage in *Platygaster zosinae* Walk. (Marchal, 1904a); at the eight-blastomere stage in *Aphidius fabarum* Marsh. (Ivanova-Kasas, 1956, 1961); at the four-nucleus stage of cleavage in *Syno-*

peas rhanis Walk., and at the two-nucleus stage of cleavage in *Inostemma piricola* Kieff; in this latter case, one nucleus becomes the nucleus of the embryonic cell, and the other that of the trophamnion (Marchal, 1906).

5. The serosa may also form prior to or at the time of first cleavage when some egg cytoplasm containing the polar body nuclei becomes detached from the rest of the egg and gives rise to a membrane containing nuclei. The relations formed in this manner are characteristic of polyembryonic Hymenoptera. This method of serosal formation (the membrane is given the special name "trophamnion" although in this instance "trophoserosa" would be more appropriate) is aberrant but it is similar in Encyrtidae and Platygasteridae and it may properly be understood only as the natural end result of the parallel evolution of embryonic membranes in these two families.

The transition from monembryonic to polyembryonic development has undoubtedly involved essential changes in the physiology of development. Gatenby (1918) was the first to consider the relationship between the evolution of polyembryony and the organization of the insect egg, in the light of what was then suggested by the pioneering experiments of Hegner (1911) on coleopteran eggs. In the ensuing five decades, the complex nature of the eggs of insects has been illuminated by numerous experimental studies (see reviews of Richards and Miller, 1937; Seidel, *et al.*, 1940; Krause, 1939, 1957; Pflugfelder, 1958; Counce, 1961, 1972). It is evident that the extent to which the developmental fates of various egg regions is determined, and the stage at which this determination becomes fixed, vary even between related species. However, even the extent to which development can be modified in those eggs which show the greatest developmental flexibility [e.g. Odonata and Orthoptera, including "substitutive polyembryony" in *Carausius* (Vignau, 1967) which can provide for the development of only one embryo at a time] is hardly consistent with the formation of many dozens and even hundreds of embryos from a single egg.

This obvious inconsistency led Krause (1939) to suggest, without confirmatory evidence, that what was observed in the parasitic Hymenoptera was not polyembryony, but early parthenogenetic development of the sex cells following early degeneration of the somatic blastomeres (*op. cit.*, p. 527). Thus he did not even consider the possibility that the developmental mechanism itself might be changed.

It should be borne in mind, that in the parasitic Hymenoptera, the numerous embryonic bodies are dispersed in disorder, with continuity between their main axes and the primary polarity of the egg being lost. Thus there appears to be no direct connection between the organization of the egg and the formative apparatus of the multiple embryos, the "egg system" developing anew in each individual. It is therefore unlikely that the formative apparatus is identical to that of the non-parasitic Hymenoptera.

An alternative hypothesis may therefore be advanced: the complex mechanisms of development in other insects are replaced in the parasitic Hymenoptera by a simpler mechanism. In most insects, the egg is large, with a rather extensive longitudinal axis, along which the influence of "Control Centres" (cf. Counce, 1961, 1972) are exerted, the yolk syncytium acting as the transferring medium. According to Seidel (1934) the action of the Differentiation Centre is dynamic, spreading from the centre in wave-like contractions of the yolk. The space formed between the contracting yolk and the chorion is filled by blastoderm cells which move in to produce a localized thickening which eventually gives rise to the embryo proper. By means of artificially induced contractions of the yolk, the time, place, size and form of the germ band may be changed. These ideas concerning the significance of the yolk system and morphogenesis have been confirmed and clarified in later investigations (cf. Counce, 1961, 1972). Concerning the Hymenoptera specifically, formation of the mesoderm and definitive endoderm in *Apis mellifera* L. appears to depend on the activity of the yolk system (Sauer-Löcher, 1954).

In parasitic Hymenoptera, however, the yolk system is gradually reduced, different stages of reduction being observed in various species (Ivanova-Kasas, 1961). In *Eurytoma aciculata* Ratz., for instance, the yolk system is well developed, but the number of yolk inclusions is relatively small. In *Angitia vestigialis* Ratz. although the yolk is absent, the yolk syncytium is still well formed, large vacuoles replacing the missing yolk. Here the yolk system has already lost its trophic function but probably retains its morphogenetic significance. The next stage of yolk system reduction may be observed in *Trichogramma evanescence* Westw., *Prestwichia aquatica* Lubb., *Ephedrus plagiator* Nees and in many other forms. The very small eggs of these insects have no yolk at all, but preserve superficial cleavage and a typical blastoderm, while the central part of the egg contains some uncleaved cytoplasm with degenerating nuclei—the last rudiment of the yolk system; its morphogenetic significance in these three species is very doubtful.

No sign of the yolk system remains in monembryonic species with total cleavage, or in polyembryonic species; the changes in the physiological mechanism are probably concurrent with its simplification. Unfortunately, experimental testing of this hypothesis is very difficult owing to the small size of the eggs of parasitic Hymenoptera and complications involved in their cultivation outside the organism.

In summary, we may conclude that parasitic conditions of development change the egg structure to such an extent that it would be reasonable to suppose that a considerable simplification of the formative apparatus occurs as well, the embryo cell material being therefore but slightly integrated at the early stages of development. This, in its turn, paves the way for the appearance of polyembryony. It is quite probable that specific polyembryony developed from accidental polyembryony induced by some external circumstances which had disturbed the normal course of development. But polyembryony could only have become hereditary and normal for a species because it proved very advantageous in parasitic conditions, the abundance of food supply being thus used most efficiently. Parasites generally show a wide range of various devices directed to increase their fecundity, this being expressed in an increase in the egg production, in the appearance of parthenogenetic generations, and in various forms of asexual reproduction, polyembryony being one of them.

It should further be noted that polyembryony is peculiar to the species best-adapted to parasitism. The polyembryonic Hymenoptera, for instance, usually have a narrow range of hosts, lay their eggs in quite definite parts of the host body, and successfully resist its defence reaction. Between the host and the parasite tissues the intimate trophic relations established are like those which only occur in the relations between the mother's and embryo's tissues in some viviparous animals.

And, finally, one cannot overlook the fact that polyembryony occurs in four different families of Hymenoptera: Braconidae, Encyrtidae, Platygasteridae and Drynidae, the first three belonging to the sub-order of Parasitica, and the fourth to Aculeata, each of them including typical monembryonic species along with the polyembryonic ones. This may be regarded as an indication of the independent origin of polyembryony in those four branches of Hymenoptera. Obviously, this is no chance occurrence and has developed as one of the main trends in the evolution of the parasitic Hymenoptera.

It is of interest to note that asexual reproduction—polyembryony being one of its forms—is rare in the arthropoda. Except for polyembryony in insects, asexual reproduction occurs only in the Rhizocephala where it has also developed against a background of parasitism (Dogiel, 1964).

III. POLYEMBRYONY IN STREPSIPTERA

If polyembryony in Hymenoptera appeared as an adaptation to parasitism, in Strepsiptera, it is associated with viviparity, which is not accidental. In viviparity and parasitism alike, some other organism (the mother or the host) acts as the medium for the developing embryo, supplying it with the nutrients and the oxygen it needs, and absorbing the products of its metabolism.

Among various forms of viviparity in insects (see Hagan, 1951) haemocoelic viviparity, in which the embryo develops in the mother's body cavity and not in the ovary, is most like parasitism. In paedogenetic Cecidomyidae, for example, the embryos behave as true parasites in that they completely utilize the mother's tissues for their development. Consequently, changes similar to those in parasitic Hymenoptera have taken place: their eggs become small, and lose their proteinaceous yolk and carbohydrates; the chorion is absent; and their development is characterized by a considerable increase in size and accumulation of reserve food substances (fat and glycogen) which are assimilated by means of the serosa and yolk syncytium (Ivanova-Kasas, 1965).

Analogous changes are observed in Strepsiptera, parasitism, as well as haemocoelic viviparity, being characteristic of this species. Strepsiptera females are neotenic: they do not attain maturity or the winged stage, but spend their lives as parasites of other insects and only protrude the foremost end of their bodies out of that of the host. Strepsiptera embryos develop at first in their mother's haemocoel, leaving it at the larval stage (triangulinid). Among Strepsiptera, polyembryony has been found, as yet, only in one species—*Halictoxenos simplicis* (Noskiewitcz and Poluszynski, 1935). The manner in which polyembryony reveals itself in *Halictoxenos* differs from that in Hymenoptera and is comprehensible only in the aspect of comparative embryology within the group.

In *Xenos bohlsi* Hoff. (Hoffman, 1914), the eggs still contain rather a large amount of the yolk. The blastoderm formed after intravitelline cleavage covers only a small part of the egg at its vegetative pole, making, as it were, a small hood there (Fig. 8A, B). Three or four nuclei (vitellophages) remain in the yolk. The edges of the blastodermic hood, as cells proliferate, do not spread over the rest of the egg, but curl up and join together to form a closed vesicle. The wall adjoining the yolk consists of large cells and forms the germ band, while its outer wall thins out and becomes an embryonic membrane, comparable to the amnion in other insects.

In species of the genus *Stylops* (Noskiewitcz and Poluzynski, 1928), eggs are covered by a double envelope of unknown origin, probably having some trophic significance. The eggs contain but little yolk, and cleavage is total (the cell boundaries appear at the four cell stage). A small central region of the egg containing some fat inclusions does not take part in the cleavage at first, but eventually it receives a nucleus and detaches itself in the form of a yolk cell (Fig. 8C, D). The number of nuclei increases to four and a rudimentary yolk syncytium is thus formed (a "yolk ball"). At the end of cleavage, the yolk ball is pushed to the periphery, while the periblastula becomes the coeloblastula, (Fig. 8E). Then that part of the blastula adjoining the yolk ball invaginates and forms the germ band while the remaining part thins out and becomes the amnion (Fig. 8F). The embryo thus acquires a structure similar to that of the *Xenos bohlsi* embryo, although it is attained in a different manner and is accompanied, in *Stylops*, by an inversion of polarity of the blastoderm cells.

Unfortunately, development of the polyembryonic species *Halictoxenos simplicis* has been described by Noskiewitcz and Poluszynski (1935) only in a somewhat fragmentary manner. It is clear, however, that cleavage results in the formation of a blastodermic vesicle containing a cytoplasmic mass corresponding to the yolk. Several nuclei penetrate into this mass and it disintegrates into separate cells. These "yolk cells" break through the blastoderm in one or more points and eventually cover it with a continuous syncytial layer (Figs 8G–I, 9A, B). In this way an embryonic membrane, which was called the "trophamnion", appears. This, however, is hardly an appropriate name for it: for this membrane, although functioning like a trophamnion, by origin, corresponds neither to the amnion in most insects, nor to the trophamnion in Hymenoptera.

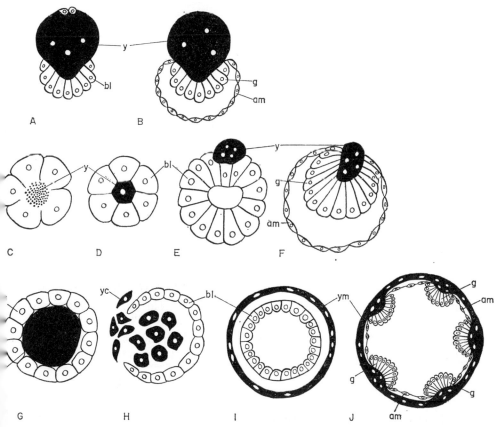

Fig. 8. Development of various *Strepsiptera* (a scheme composed after the data of Hoffmann, 1914, and Noskiewitz and Poluszynski, 1928 and 1935). A and B, *Xenos bohlsi;* C–F, *Stylops;* G–J, *Halictoxenos simplicis.* am, amnion; bl, blastoderm; g, germ disc; y, yolk; yc, yolk cells; ym, yolk membrane. Further details in text.

"Trophamnion" nuclei differentiate in two directions: the more peripheral ones are spindle-shaped and have nucleoli, these cells functioning as a trophamnion, while the deeper lying nuclei preserve the formative function of the yolk system. We have seen that in *Stylops* the germ band is formed at the spot where the blastoderm touches the yolk ball. In *Halictoxenos*, the inner yolk cells form several accumulations which induce, as it were, the formation of secondary germs, (Figs 8J, 9C), which increase in number up

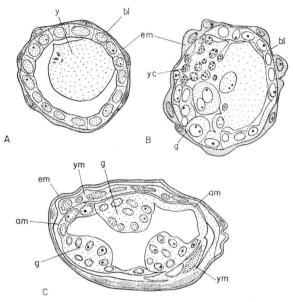

FIG. 9. Development of *Halictoxenos simplicis* (after Noskiewitz and Poluszynski, 1935). am, amnion; bl, blastoderm; em, embryonic envelope; g, germ disc; y, yolk; yc, yolk cells; ym, yolk membrane. Further details in text.

to 40–50, presumably owing to their division. Then the thin parts of the primary blastoderm epithelium and trophamnion fold up, form ingrowths between the germs, and isolate them from one another. The whole polygerm then disintegrates into many independent closed vesicles, each consisting of the embryonic rudiment with its amnion, and enveloped in the trophamnion.

IV. CONCLUSION

It is obvious that the "mechanism of polyembryony" in Strepsiptera differs greatly from that in Hymenoptera. In Hymenoptera only one of the usual two embryonic membranes is preserved—the serosa—this functioning as a trophamnion. The yolk system is completely reduced. The immediate causes of the division of the primary germ into secondary embryonic masses remain a mystery. In Strepsiptera, too, only one embryonic membrane remains—the amnion—which, however, does not take any essential part in the processes of development; the yolk system undergoes some reduction due to the loss of the yolk, but still retains its trophic functions by turning into the trophamnion; it also preserves morphogenetic significance as it is actually at its expense that numerous centres of the new germ formation arise.

Thus, in two different orders of insects—Hymenoptera and in Strepsiptera—similar biological conditions (parasitism and viviparity) have brought about one and the same phenomenon of polyembryony, attained, however by different evolutionary routes.

REFERENCES

Baerends, G. P. and Baerends-van Roon, J. M. (1949). *Tijdschr. Ent.*, **95**, 53–112.
Berland, L. (1951). *Traité de Zool.*, **10**, 820–843.
Cappe de Baillon, P. (1927). *Encycl. Ent.*, **8**, 1–292.
Cappe de Baillon, P. (1928). *Bull. biol. Fr. Belg.*, **62**, 378–387.
Carrière, J. and Bürger, O. (1898). *Nova Acta Acad. Caesar. Leop. Carol.*, **69**, 255–420.
Clancy, D. W. (1944). *J. agric. Res.*, **69**, 159–167.
Clausen, C. (1940). *Entomophagous Insects*. McGraw-Hill Book Company, New York.
Counce, S. J. (1961). *A. Rev. Ent.*, **6**, 295–312.
Counce, S. J. (1968). *Nature, Lond.*, **218**, 781–782.
Counce, S. J. (1972). *Developmental Systems: Insects* (S. J. Counce and C. H. Waddington, eds), Vol. 2, p. 1. Academic Press, London and New York.
Daniel, D. M. (1932). *Tech. Bull. N.Y. St. Agric. Exp. Sta.*, **187**, 1–101.
Dogiel, V. A. (1964). *General Parasitology*. Oliver and Boyd, Edinburgh–London.
Doutt, R. L. (1947). *Am. Nat.*, **81**, 435–453.
Doutt, R. L. (1952). *Can. Ent.*, **84**, 247–250.
Ferrière, Ch. (1926). *Revue suisse Zool.*, **33**, 585–596.
Flanders, S. E. (1942). *J. econ. Ent.*, **35**, 251–266.
Flanders, S. E. (1946). *Q . Rev. Biol.*, **21**, 135–143.
Gadd, C. H. (1946). *Ceylon Jl Sci.* (B) **23**, 72–79.
Gatenby, J. B. (1918). *Q . Jl Microsc. Sci.*, **63**, 175–196.
Hagan, H. R. (1951). *Embryology of the Viviparous Insects*. The Ronald Press Company, New York.
Hegner, R. W. (1911). *Biol. Bull.*, **20**, 237–251.
Hoffmann, R. W. (1914). *Ver. dt. Zool. Ges.*, **24**, 192–206.
Huxley, J. S. and De Beer, G. R. (1934). *The Elements of Experimental Embryology*. Cambridge University Press.
Ioff, N. A. (1948). *Dokl. Akad. Nauk USSR*, **60**, 1477–1480.
Ivanova-Kasas, O. M. (1954). *Trudy Vses. Ent. Obshch.*, **44**, 301–335.
Ivanova-Kasas, O. M. (1958). *Revue Ent. URSS*, **38**, 5–23.
Ivanova-Kasas, O. M. (1960). *Revue Ent. URSS*, **39**, 284–295.
Ivanova-Kasas, O. M. (1961). *Essays on the Comparative Embryology of Hymenoptera*. Leningrad Univ. Publ., in Russian.
Ivanova-Kasas, O. M. (1965). *Acta Biol. hung.*, **16**, 1–24.

Kornhauser, S. J. (1919). *J. Morph.*, **32**, 531–636.
Kościelska, M. K. (1962). *Studia Soc. Sci. torun.*, *Sect. E* (*Zool.*), **6**, 1–9.
Kościelska, M. K. (1963). *Zoologisa Pol.*, **13**, 255–276.
Krause, G. (1939). *Biol. Zbl.*, **59**, 495–536.
Krause, G. (1957). *Verh. dt. Zool. Ges.*, 396–424.
Krause, G. (1962). *Embryologia*, **6** (Suppl.), 355–386.
Kulagin, N. M. (1894). *Mitt. Ges. Liebh. von Naturwiss, Antrop., Ethnogr.*, **85**, 1–49.
Leiby, R. W. (1922). *J. Morph.*, **37**, 195–285.
Leiby, R. W. (1926). *Ann. Ent. Soc. Am.*, **19**, 290–299.
Leiby, R. W. (1929). *IV. Int. Congr. Ent.*, Vol. 2, 873–887.
Leiby, R. W. and Hill, C. C. (1923). *J. agric. Res.*, **25**, 337–350.
Leiby, R. W. and Hill, C. C. (1924). *J. agric. Res.*, **28**, 829–840.
Marchal, P. (1898a). *Ann. mag. Nat. Hist.*, **2**, 28–30.
Marchal, P. (1898b). *Nat. Sci. Skodaburg*, **12**, 316–318.
Marchal, P. (1898c). *C. r. Séanc. Biol.*, **5**, 238–240.
Marchal, P. (1898d). *Bull. Soc. Ent. Fr.*, **67**, 109–111.
Marchal, P. (1898e). *C. r. hebd. Séanc. Acad. Sci.*, *Paris*, **126D**, 662–664.
Marchal, P. (1903). *Bull. Soc. Ent. Fr.*, **72**, 90–93.
Marchal, P. (1904a). *Archs. zool. exp. gén.*, **2**, 257–335.
Marchal, P. (1904b). *C. r. Séanc. Soc. Biol.*, **56**, 468–470.
Marchal, P. (1906). *Archs. Zool. exp. gén.*, **4**, 485–640.
Martin, F. (1914). *Z. wiss. Zool.*, **110**, 419–479.
Noskiewicz, J. and Poluszynski, G. (1928). *Bull. Int. Acad. Sci. Leht. Cracovie Kl. Math Natur.*, **3**, 1093–1226.
Noskiewicz, J. and Poluszynski, G. (1935). *Zoologica Polo.*, **1**, 53–94.
Ogloblin, A. (1924). *Věstnik Krá. Čes. Společ. Nauk Tr.*, **2**, 1–27.
Paillot, A. (1940). *Annls. Épiphyt.*, **6**, 67–102.
Parker, H. L. (1931). *Tech. Bull. U.S. Dep. Agric.*, **230**, 1–62.
Parker, H. L. and Thompson, W. R. (1928). *Ann. Soc. Ent. Fr.*, **97**, 425–465.
Patterson, J. T. (1915). *Biol. Bull.*, **29**, 333–372.
Patterson, J. T. (1917). *Biol. Bull.*, **32**, 291–305.
Patterson, J. T. (1918). *Biol. Bull.*, **35**, 362–377.
Patterson, J. T. (1921). *J. Morph.*, **36**, 1–69.
Patterson, J. T. (1927). *Q. Rev. Biol.*, **2**, 399–426.
Pflugfelder, O. (1958). *Entwicklungsphysiologie der Insekten.* Leipzig. Akad. Verlags. Geest & Portig, K.-G.
Richards, A. G. and Miller, A. (1937). *Jl. N.Y. Ent. Soc.*, **15**, 1–60.
Roonwal, M. L. (1935). *Curr. Sci.*, **4**, 317–318.
Sarra, R. (1915). *Boll. Lab. Zool. gen. agr. R. Scuola Agric. Portici* **10**, 51–65.
Sarra, R. (1918). *Boll. Lab. Zool. gen. agr. R. Scuola Agric. Portici*, **12**, 175–187.
Sauer-Löcher, E. (1954). *Wilhelm Roux Arch. EntwMech. Org.*, **147**, 302–354.
Schnetter, M. (1936). *Ver. dt. Zool. Ges.*, **38**, 82–88.
Seidel, F. (1934). *Wilhelm Roux Arch. EntwMech. Org.*, **131**, 135–187.
Seidel, F., Bock, E. and Krause, G. (1940). *Naturwissenschaften*, **28**, 433–446.
Silvestri, F. (1906). *Atti. R. Accad naz Lincei. Rc.*, **15**, 650–657.
Silvestri, F. (1907). *Boll. Lab. Zool. gen. agr. R. Scuola Agric. Portici*, **1**, 17–64.
Silvestri, F. (1908). *Annali R. Scu. Sup. Agric. Portici*, **8**, 1–27.
Silvestri, F. (1910). *Monitore zool. ital.*, **21**, 296–298.
Silvestri, F. (1924). *Boll. Lab. Zool. gen. agr. R. Scuola Agric. Portici*, **17**, 41–107.
Silvestri, F. (1937). *Bull. Mus. comp. Zool. Harv.*, **81**, 469–496.

Slifer, E. H. (1938). *Q . Jl Microsc. Sci.*, **80**, 437–457.
Slifer, E. H. (1948). *J. exp. Zool.*, **102**, 333–356.
Snow, S. J. (1925). *J. econ. Ent.*, **18**, 602–609.
Tokin, B. P. (1959). *Regeneration and Somatic Embryogenesis.* Leningrad. (In Russian.)
    Leningrad Univ. Publ.
Vignau, J. (1967). *C. r. hebd. Séanc. Acad. Sci. Paris*, **265D**, 1404–1407.

AUTHOR INDEX

Numbers in italics refer to the pages on which the references appear in full

273

SUBJECT INDEX

Numbers in italics refer to the pages on which figures may be found.

INDEX OF SPECIES

299